Books by Daniel Gavron

THE END OF DAYS (novel)
WALKING THROUGH ISRAEL

Walking Through
ISRAEL

Daniel Gavron

Walking Through
ISRAEL

Illustrated with maps

BOSTON
Houghton Mifflin Company
1980

Library of Congress Cataloging in Publication Data

Gavron, Daniel.
　Walking through Israel.

1. Israel—Description and travel.
2. Gavron, Daniel.　3. Journalists—Israel—
Biography.　4. Israel—Social life and customs.
I. Title.
DS107.4.G34　　956.94′05　　80–16220
ISBN 0-395-27777-9

Printed in the United States of America

V 10 9 8 7 6 5 4 3 2 1

maps by Louise E. Jefferson

For Ang,
with me every mile of the way
these twenty-three years.

Acknowledgments

First, I would like to thank my friends — old and new — who offered help and hospitality along the way. I will not list them, since they are mentioned in the text, but special mention should be made of Ben Bardan and Mike Leaf, who accompanied me on sections of the walk.

The following assisted me in various ways: Alan Ben-Ami, Ishai Eldar, Jaime Greenblatt, David Krivine, Gil Krivine, Nehemia Myers, Rabbi Louis Rabinowitz, Neal Sandler, Haim Shapiro, and Shmuel Toledano (member of Israeli parliament).

I have decided not to list a bibliography, but mention must be made of the invaluable *Israel Tour Guide* of Avraham Lewensohn, and of the *Jerusalem Post* Archives and the Library of the Department of Antiquities, Rockefeller Museum, Jerusalem.

My thanks to my friend Arye Haskel, who read the manuscript and made some valuable suggestions, and to Charles Fenyvesi, who encouraged me to write the type of personalized journalism that led to this book. Some of the material in the present volume originally appeared (in a different form) in *The National Jewish Monthly* (Washington), which he edits.

My deep appreciation to Clancy Sigal and Margaret Walters, whose enthusiasm for the project prompted me to undertake it.

My gratitude to Israel Radio (Kol Yisrael), which

granted me leave; Robie Macauley, my editor, who urged, pushed, prodded, and cajoled the book into existence; and finally to my family, who put up with my absences, bad temper, and occasional despondency. Without their support, love, and understanding, this book could never have been undertaken, let alone completed.

Arise, walk through the land in the length of it
and in the breadth of it; for I will give it unto thee.

Genesis 13:17

Metulla (Walk Begins)
Kiryat Shmona
LEBANON
Safed
Haifa
LAKE KINNERET
(Sea of Galilee)
Nazareth
MEDITERRANEAN SEA
Zichron Yaacov
Alexander R.
JORDAN R.
Tel Aviv
Rehovot
Jerusalem
Ashkelon
DEAD SEA
Gaza
Beersheba
Arad
KINGDOM OF
JORDAN
Sde Boker
Mitzpe Ramon
ISRAEL
Paran Valley
(Walk Ends)
|||||||||| INTERNATIONAL BORDER
------ WALK
.... BUS
SINAI
(Journey Ends) Taba Elat

Introduction

FOR THE PAST eight years I have lived in Jerusalem, the capital of Israel, working as a reporter for the national radio. The overwhelming majority of Israelis live in Jerusalem, Haifa, and the big conurbation around Tel Aviv, where life is absorbing and stimulating, but also exhausting and enervating. Compared to Tel Aviv, Israel's capital is a mountain village, and life there is in many ways pleasant; but even in Jerusalem pressures can become unbearable.

Much of what is least admirable in Israeli society is to be found in the large towns. It is here that blocks of luxury apartments are going up, sometimes next to festering slums. Here the large, shiny cars (which even the Americans are beginning to find too extravagant) swish by, all too often driven with a boorish lack of consideration. Here it is that the buses are overcrowded and unpunctual, that civil servants are rude and incompetent, that empty offices mock the citizen vainly hoping for service. Here violence, once almost unknown in Israel, is on the increase; here crime, hard drugs, protection rackets, and intimidation have reared their heads.

Not that one should lose one's sense of proportion: it is still possible for a teen-age girl to walk unmolested through downtown Tel Aviv. Despite the terrorist bombs, I would rather stroll the nighttime streets of Jerusalem than those of London. But the days when the milkman would open your (unlocked) front door to put the milk in your icebox are long past.

Even today, however, there is another Israel: that of the farms and villages, border settlements and development towns. Not that these are without blemish — far from it — but here you can find real enterprise and achievement, pioneering and idealism. Although in terms of population it represents a small proportion of the country, I maintain that this other Israel is the real Israel.

Before coming to Jerusalem, I lived in Galilee, the coastal plain, and the Negev desert. I conceived the idea of renewing my acquaintance with that Israel, visiting old friends and, I hoped, making new ones. For a couple of months I would leave the hectic life of the newsroom, the political intrigues, the parliamentary maneuvering, the crime, and the social problems, and get out into the countryside again.

The question was how to travel. I abhor driving, loathe buses, and fear taxis. The trains in Israel do not reach most of the places I intended visiting. Cycling in our country is tantamount to suicide. I am ignorant of the ways of donkeys, horses, and camels. I decided to walk.

Once I had made the decision, it made more and more sense. I liked the idea of the slow pace. I would be independent of petrol engines and bus timetables, free to dally or to wander over open country. My route would be dictated by my personal inclinations, where it was not determined by the location of my friends.

All the events are described as they happened, but in certain cases I have avoided or altered names to obviate possible offense or embarrassment.

Part I
Galilee

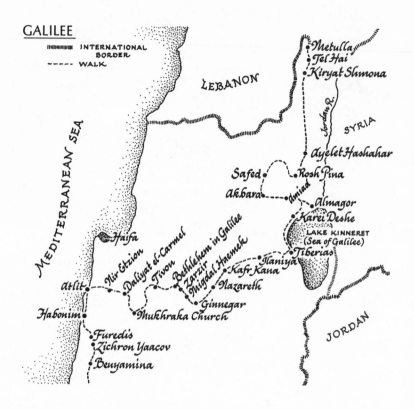

1

On the bus, leaving Jerusalem for the north, I found myself sitting next to an elderly man with a face the color and texture of fine old parchment. He was reading from a small card, which he subsequently handed to me, entitled, appropriately enough, "Prayer to be said when going on a journey." It appealed to God to "direct our steps in peace" and to "deliver us from any enemy, ambush, or hurt by the way." Reading, rather than praying, the ancient Hebrew text, I nevertheless saw it as a fitting start to my expedition.

"It has a particular relevance in Israel these days," remarked the old fellow.

"Yes, indeed," I agreed.

"Aha, a new immigrant!" he declared, spotting the British accent in my Hebrew, still clear after almost two decades.

"Certainly not," I protested. "I have been living in Israel for nearly eighteen years."

"New compared to me," he replied a trifle smugly. "My family has been in Jerusalem for sixteen generations."

I worked it out. More than four centuries, I reckoned. He was a dapper old boy in a smart, off-white linen suit, his straw hat bound with a black band. I was slightly overawed by him and did not feel inclined to contradict, even when he lauded the Jewish talent for making the desert bloom, while pointing to a field of corn that was manifestly being cultivated by Arabs.

I had decided to begin my walk in Metulla, the northernmost settlement in Galilee. The northern part of Galilee, only some six miles in width, is known as Etzba Hagalil, the Finger of Galilee. If northern Galilee is the finger, Metulla is the fingernail, a tiny, isolated village almost entirely surrounded by Lebanese territory.

It was founded in 1896 by men of the first *aliya,* the first wave of modern Jewish immigration to Palestine, which took place in the last two decades of the nineteenth century. During this period, there were repeated outbreaks of anti-Jewish violence in Russia and other parts of Eastern Europe. Far from preventing these pogroms, the authorities often encouraged them and in some cases initiated them.

The Jewish community reacted in a number of ways. Many Jews became active in the revolutionary movements and later played leading parts in the Bolshevik revolution. Enormous numbers left Russia: between 1880 and 1914, more than 2 million Jews migrated to Western Europe and America. A minority were prompted to revive Jewish national and cultural life, and these formed groups called Lovers of Zion. Like the majority, they were determined to leave Russia, but they decided to return to the Land of Israel, the ancient, Biblical homeland of the Jews, then a province of the Ottoman Empire. Their journey to Palestine was regarded as something more than mere immigration; they called it "aliya" (going up). They believed that they were elevating themselves in reviving the Jewish nation.

The Lovers of Zion established a number of villages in Palestine, such as Rishon Lezion, near modern Tel Aviv, and Rosh Pina, in Galilee. They were joined in their pioneering endeavors by young Jews from Jerusalem, the sons of the religious community there, which was supported by charity. Also aiming to establish a self-supporting Jewish community in Palestine, they founded Petah-Tikva. The

very names of these early villages give us a clue to the moti-
vations of their founders: Rishon Lezion means "the first in
Zion"; Rosh Pina is "the foundation stone"; and Petah-
Tikva, "the gateway of hope."

However, because of the swampy or stony nature of
much of the land, the villages foundered, and the villagers
faced poverty and near-starvation. They were rescued by
Baron Edmond de Rothschild of Paris. A member of the
rich banking family, he was deeply concerned about the
pogroms in Eastern Europe and also aware of the less brutal anti-Semitism in his own country.

Without "the Baron," as he came to be known, the early
Jewish villages in Palestine would probably not have survived, yet he was not popular among the pioneers.

As a businessman, he naturally expected to control his
ventures and to make his investments pay off, but the villagers fiercely resented the actions of the agents he sent out
to run the settlements, which in some instances extended
even to interference in the settlers' domestic arrangements.
They regarded the Baron as an unfeeling capitalist who did
not understand their national aspirations. In fact, there is
evidence to the contrary. In 1889 he told the settlers of Rishon Lezion:

> I did not come to your aid because of your poverty and suf-
> fering ... I did it because I saw in you the realizers of the
> renaissance of Israel and of that idea so dear to us all, the sa-
> cred goal of the return of Israel to its ancient homeland.

Metulla was founded on land the Baron bought from an
absentee landlord who resided in Sidon, Lebanon. A selected group of farmers, for whom there was no room in the
existing villages, was sent there to begin a new village. Almost at once, they had to fight off raids by local Druze, who
claimed that the land really belonged to them. More than

two decades were to pass before other Jewish settlements were established nearby. Its long isolation has made Metulla distinctive; other Israelis sometimes refer to the villagers as "half-Arabs."

*   *   *

The first sight of Metulla was disappointing. Dull, gray terrace houses, built since my first visit many years ago, straggled down the hillside. But then, as the bus climbed into the village, I found myself, this time as in the past, won over by its tatty charm. Modern hotels rubbed shoulders with rickety stone-and-wattle buildings dating back to the time of the Baron. I noted at least six hostelries of various standards, three restaurants, a couple of refreshment stalls, a garage, bank, and post office — but no shops. For even the most basic supplies, the villagers must travel to the town of Kiryat Shmona, six miles to the south.

I arrived on the day before the municipal elections, and every wall and blank space was plastered with election posters. Metulla is still a very small community. It has a population of some 600 and an electoral roll of just over 200, but there was enough political activity going on for a metropolis of thousands. Some half-dozen candidates were vying for the position of mayor: leaflets were being handed out, party functionaries hastened to and fro, vehicles plastered with manifestos dashed up and down the only street.

Apart from finding it a natural starting point for my journey, I had come to Metulla to see the "Good Fence,"* across which the Arabs of Lebanon come by the hundred to work, trade, and receive medical attention in Israel.

A border that people cross to visit and work may seem

---

* In vain did we pedantic journalists try to have it called the "Good-Will Fence," or the "Good-Neighbor Fence." How, after all, can a fence be "good"? But to no avail: the Good Fence it has remained.

normal enough, but not in Israel, which was hermetically sealed from its neighbors for three decades. The Good Fence, then, is a dramatic break with the past, and, like many of the best things in this country, it was unplanned.

A pregnant woman, wounded in the Lebanese civil war, came to an Israeli army border post. Responding to his normal instincts, a medical orderly bandaged her wounds, little imagining that he was inaugurating a new era. More wounded started coming to the border, and the Israel army made openings in the fence, which had been erected to prevent terrorist attacks. A temporary clinic was set up, and trucks began to bring in supplies of food and water to the Lebanese villagers, who had been cut off from their natural hinterland by the war. Within a few months, what had started as a hastily improvised plan to help a few dozen unfortunates had expanded into a full-scale institution. The Good Fence was born.

Today the welfare aspect is only a part of the story. A permanent clinic has been established, supplying free medical services to the Arab villagers (serious cases are sent to hospitals in Israel); agricultural instructors cross the border to help the Lebanese farmers; and the Good Fence has become a trading-post and checkpoint for the hundreds of Lebanese who commute daily to jobs in Israel.

The project has long since ceased to be a news story and has, indeed, become something of a local tourist attraction. The army spokesman in Jerusalem had told me that I would not even have to produce my journalist's card. Just go to Metulla, he said, and see it. However, when I descended from the bus, I found myself in a quandary, for the border in Metulla is north, east, and west. Which direction should I take? Two ancient villagers were sitting on a bench nearby conversing in Yiddish and, approaching them, I asked courteously, "Can you please tell me the way to the Good Fence?"

The two raised their heads, their gaze all hostility. They looked me up and down, taking in my faded jeans, rucksack, water bottle, and camera. Finally, one of them spoke. "Whoever needs to get there, gets there all right," he said with heavy significance. I had met the famous Metulla mentality face to face.

My next encounter was with an army officer. Apparently he felt satisfied that I was neither a spy nor a saboteur, for he set me on the road without delay.

Proceeding westward, I passed through the newer part of the village, a pleasant street lined with modern houses and well-tended gardens, and soon arrived at the end house on the right-hand side, famous in the media as "the last house in Israel." Its owner, Arik Yaacov (formerly Eric Jacobs of New York), teaches high school in nearby Kiryat Shmona and farms his apple orchards in his spare time. A stocky redhead, Arik was standing on a newly cast section of his roof. Although busy with the extension of his home, he invited me in for a cup of coffee.

Arik is a Metulla enthusiast. He laughed when I told him about the old men and defended their right to be unfriendly to strangers. Things had been tough for many years, he explained. "Oh, yes, I know that if a cow shat on your neighbor's plot in nineteen nineteen, it's a vendetta, but you have to get to know these people. Underneath it all, they're wonderful."

I did, of course, know something of the history, the struggles of the early pioneers to grow cereals and tobacco in the poor soil, their fights with the Druze raiders, the bitter cold they suffered in the winter. I also knew that the first settlers, like most of the first aliya, had exploited the local Arabs. One of the Baron's agents had written in 1905, "The Jew in Metulla is a supervisor, and for the most part a very bad supervisor."

It is easy enough to be critical, but I knew that much of the villagers' land was mountain rock; in 1912 they had suffered a typhus epidemic; in 1920 they had been forced to evacuate the village for almost a year; in 1948 they lost most of the good land they did possess. Following Israel's War of Independence against the Arabs in that year, the Lebanese border, like all the others, was sealed off. Metulla's farmland and its water source had been in the Ayun Valley, now on the wrong side of the border.

Arik told me that he and his wife got on well with everyone in the village. Once the locals realized that they had come to stay, they had been accepted wholeheartedly. It had been difficult, particularly during the intensified terrorist activity that followed the Yom Kippur War in 1973. Like most citizens of Israel, Arik had been in the army for much of 1973 and 1974; his wife, alone with their small children, had faced the *katyusha* rocket attacks on Metulla.

"It was only later that I understood quite how tough it had been," he confessed. "But even then, she never thought of leaving."

I thanked Arik for the coffee and walked out of the village through the apple orchards, finding myself in the company of Lebanese workers on their way home. In my inadequate Arabic, I struck up a conversation with Michael from the village of Kafr Killa, who told me that he was *mabsut* (happy). He came across the border at six o'clock each morning to work in the apple orchards. Now he was on his way home.

By the time I arrived at the complex of huts beside the fence, more and more Lebanese were streaming back to their villages. Elderly Arabs with the traditional *keffiya* headdresses, baggy trousers, and *galabiya* tunics walked beside young men in working clothes who could have passed for Israeli Jews. A party of young women, several of them wearing slacks and sleeveless blouses, licked ice creams and posed cheekily for my camera. Across the fence a line of cars waited to take them all home.

I looked in at the clinic, where an Israeli army doctor was

listening patiently to a couple who had brought their baby for treatment. A young soldier was translating from Arabic into Hebrew. The doctor examined the baby carefully before administering an injection.

"Ear infection," he told me, wiping his hands on a towel. After the parents left with the baby, he went on, "They were here this morning also. They're learning from us how to be *nudniks.*" (That's Yiddish for those who nag.) Tall and gangling, his nose and chin curving toward each other, a Mister Punch in tinted glasses, he introduced himself as Dr. Guttman. Then, catching sight of my souvenir postcard of the Good Fence, he left the clinic to buy one, saying that he might send it to Rumania. But when he returned with the card, he had decided not to, and he explained why. When he still had been living in Bucharest, Israeli friends had sent him a pound note, and he had been interrogated by the police and forced to deposit the pound in the bank to avoid being charged with currency speculation. He didn't know how the Rumanian authorities might react to a picture postcard of the Good Fence, but he did not want to take the risk of embarrassing his relatives.

In the clinic, he dealt courteously with the stream of patients. Complimenting him on his kindness and thoroughness, I told him a story current in Israel about a Metulla villager who was fed up with his local doctor. Dressing as an Arab, the villager went to the Good Fence and received top-notch medical care for the first time in years. Guttman smiled weakly and noted that in civilian life he too was a health-fund doctor.

"A good doctor is always good," he stated. "I don't behave differently here."

We returned to the village and sat on a wall in the street. Political activity had died down, but the whole community was out for its afternoon stroll. The army was much in evidence, soldiers walking in groups or entering a hotel to phone home. Old men ambled along, assisted by canes, mothers wheeled prams, children shot past on skateboards. A statuesque woman of indeterminate age, impressive teak-colored shoulders rising from her emerald dress, looked us up and down speculatively. The village whore? Surely not, I decided. Metulla would not have one.

On a month's stint of army service, Guttman was hungry for conversation and quizzed me about my work. What was my motivation? Fame, fortune, self-expression? He told me that he had written some chapters of a novel, which he kept in a drawer at home.

"I may go into competition with you one day" was his parting shot.

I sat and thought about the Good Fence, a splendid humanitarian gesture to an enemy country, nonetheless so for being so patently self-serving.

*   *   *

Until the Six Day War in 1967, Lebanon had been the quietest of Israel's borders. Soon after that war, the Palestinian refugees, who had been living in camps in Jordan, Syria, Lebanon, and Gaza since the Israel-Arab war of 1948, formed a new terrorist organization, El-Fatah, which started attacking Israeli targets. Initially, most of the attacks came from Jordan, but in 1971, after strong Israeli counterattacks, Jordan's King Hussein expelled the terrorists from his kingdom. Lebanon now became the main springboard for attacks against Israeli civilians.

Israeli retaliations had persuaded King Hussein to take drastic action, but in Lebanon there was no equivalent authority. Lebanon's population is roughly balanced between Muslims and Christians. The Muslims supported the terrorists; the Christians were less than enthusiastic about having their country dragged into conflict. The structure of Lebanese society thus made decisive action against the terrorists virtually impossible. Clashes between Palestinians and Christians developed, by 1975, into a full-scale civil war in Lebanon. Israel backed the Christians in the south, first covertly and then openly after the Syrian army invaded Lebanon in the guise of an inter-Arab peace-keeping force.

The terrorists continued to use Lebanon as a base for attacks, firing Russian-made katyusha rockets at Metulla and other northern settlements. Then, early in 1978, a group of terrorists came ashore some thirty-five miles north of Tel Aviv and hijacked a bus, which they drove southward. It was stopped by security forces just north of Israel's largest city, and there was a shoot-out. Thirty-seven Israeli civilians — men, women, and children — lost their lives.

This incident was followed by the largest-ever Israeli retaliation against the Palestinian bases in Lebanon. For three months, the Israel army occupied all of south Lebanon up to the Litani River. Eventually, Israel did withdraw, leaving a Christian-controlled security belt along the border. Beyond the belt and up to the Litani, a special United Nations force, UNIFIL, was stationed. At the time of my writing this book, the terrorists were back in the area controlled by UNIFIL and continued to launch attacks against Israel. Israel retaliations currently take the form of air and sea strikes. Israel says that it is taking care to strike only at bases and training camps. The Palestinians say that refugee camps are hit, with civilian casualties.

Despite the provocation that preceded it, many of us in Israel have ambivalent feelings about Operation Litani, as it was called, including the soldiers who carried it out, one of whom was my son.

One of the toughest moments in the life of an Israeli citizen occurs when his son goes into the army. And of course my son Etan — big, strong, good-looking, good-natured — had to be a hero and volunteer for a crack combat unit. His mother had suggested hopefully that he might like to join the special academic unit, where he could continue his studies. He just laughed. I took him to his mobilization station, bursting with things I wanted to say. I wanted to apologize for getting him into it, for our generation's failure to achieve peace. I wanted to tell him that we loved him and were proud of him and that he didn't have to prove anything to anybody, that all we wanted was for him to come home safely. But of course I didn't say any of that. I simply punched him on the shoulder and told him to take care.

I came back home, questioning for the first time my decision to come to Israel. I have served in two of our wars (though not, as it turned out, in combat); but it is quite different when someone else puts his life on the line as the result of a decision you have taken. Entirely different when that someone is your own son. My wife, Angela, and I had dreamed that Etan would never have to serve in the army, that by the time he grew up there would be peace — but it didn't work out that way.

During his first six months in the army, Etan underwent the incredibly tough basic training, coming home on leave like a zombie, exhausted to the far limit of his physical and mental endurance. Our athlete, who used to run three miles to school each day and three miles back just to keep fit, was incapable of remaining awake during supper. He sat at the table fast asleep, a spoonful of soup halfway to his lips.

If it was tough when he was mobilized, it was tougher still when we heard that he was in Lebanon. We were overwhelmingly relieved when he came back to us after a month, brown-faced and smiling, his army haircut slightly shaggy: the same Etan, saddened but not embittered by what he had experienced.

"We still don't know what it's like to be in a real war," he told us. "We didn't lose our friends or come under serious fire."

He and his friends had been shocked, though, by the intensity of the bombing and shelling; they had been trained for a braver, cleaner war. He was full of sympathy for the Lebanese refugees. He described the abandoned village hovels, but also the luxurious homes, left intact with beautiful furniture, pictures, and ornaments, color television and stereo sets. A number of soldiers were found guilty of looting and sentenced to jail terms, but Etan's unit had firmly rejected the idea of stealing. He admitted that he had thought of taking a cassette of Arabic music as a souvenir for his sister, but then he had decided no, nothing at all.*

*   *   *

The evening was becoming cool, so I went to search for accommodations, deciding at last on a shabby guest house with the pretentious name Manara Hotel. I found Leonid, the proprietor, in the backyard, playing with a couple of mongrel puppies. A solid, barrel-chested man in a singlet, he informed me that he was a new immigrant from the Soviet Union, married to a Metulla woman. His Hebrew was rudimentary, but he knew enough to say "Sixty pounds; cash in advance, please. No receipts."

He took me to my room, which contained a sink, table, and two iron beds. The paint was peeling and it was rather bare, but it looked clean, and I enjoyed a delicious hot shower in a bathroom off the yard.

I spent the evening with an old acquaintance, Yoram Hamizrachi, and his wife, Batami. Immensely stout, with dark hair and goatee, Yoram had left his job as a correspondent for German television to report for Israeli televi-

---

* Since the above was written, far more serious incidents of wrongdoing have come to light. There were a number of cases of the murder of civilians and prisoners, for which soldiers were sentenced in the military courts. The action of the Chief of Staff in reducing some of the sentences of soldiers convicted of these offenses merely served to increase public disquiet in Israel about the Litani Operation.

sion from the northern border during the terrorist raids of
the early 1970s. After the Good Fence was opened, his sense
of duty propelled him into the army, where his talent for
getting on with the Lebanese villagers was put to good use.
"Captain Yoram" (really a colonel) is well known all over
southern Lebanon. After a number of clashes between the
Christians and the UNIFIL forces in the region, a United
Nations spokesman accused Captain Yoram of stirring up
the local villagers, but he later withdrew his accusation
with a public apology. Despite his success, Yoram was
waiting impatiently for his release.

"I was a civilian too long," he explained. "I just can't
reaccustom myself to the way they do things in the army."

Their huge St. Bernard bitch lumbered across the room,
slobbered all over me, and lay down heavily on my feet. I
was a captive audience for Batami's description of their life
in Metulla. Her perception of the village was different from
that of Arik Yaacov. She had less patience for the eccentricity of the villagers. Most of them were not religious, she told
me, yet the only school in Metulla was religious. Her son
was forced to wear a skullcap at school, but he threw it
down when he came home. The final straw came when he
told her that a stomach upset was God's judgment on her
for failing to observe the Jewish religious dietary laws,
kashrut. Now her children attended the local kibbutz school.
But she had to pay tuition, and it was not cheap.

A number of Yoram's army colleagues stopped by during
the evening for a glass of whiskey. They discussed the recent acquittal of the leading mayoral candidate on a charge
of smuggling. Metulla was a traditional center of smuggling, they intimated, and many of the seemingly poor villagers were, in reality, wealthy smugglers. This dated from
the time that the border had been open before 1948; now
that it was open again, many people were up to their old
tricks.

Yoram showed me a short cut to my hotel through their backyard. Walking through a network of trenches and air-raid shelters, I was vividly reminded of Arik Yaacov's talk of the katyushas, and I realized that not all Metulla evenings were so peaceful. I felt a distinct admiration for the Hamizrachis and the Yaacovs, who deliberately placed themselves and their families on this sensitive border.

Looking into Leonid's kitchen for my key (the Manara doesn't boast anything as grand as a lobby), I found my host sitting peeling apples with his wife, Rachel, a sturdy, gray-haired veteran. I sat and peeled with Rachel while Leonid got up and stirred a saucepan of jam that he was making from the fruit.

"We always leave the last of the apples on the ground," she told me, "but he doesn't like to waste anything."

She had come to the country in 1925, a member of a group that was planning to establish a kibbutz near the coast. Her first husband had been a son of one of Metulla's founders. He had been abroad for a number of years, trying his luck in Canada and Australia, but he had decided to come home. They had become friendly on the boat, she recalled, and later he had come to visit her. Subsequently, she had left her group and come to live with him in Metulla.

The house in which we were sitting, she told me, had belonged to her husband's parents; it was the very first house built in Metulla. Life had been hard but satisfying in the early years. They would harvest the wheat by hand and take it by mule cart into Lebanon to have it milled. Gradually, things had improved, but in 1948 they were right back to square one; all their best land was on the other side of the border and they had no water. Those were the hardest years of all, she said. Many had left. They had stayed on and converted their house into a hotel. Other hotels were built, and Metulla had become a summer resort for Israelis fleeing from the muggy valleys and coastal plain. Agriculture had revived somewhat with the arrival of piped water in the mid-1950s, and the famous Metulla apples had appeared. Things were just looking up again when the terrorist attacks started, and the resort's popularity plummeted. Now, with the Good Fence, things were improving yet again, but who knew when the seesaw would tilt once more?

Her first husband had fallen off the roof while fixing a radio aerial. He had been a cripple for many years before he died, ten years before.

"I know that people looked askance at me when I married him." She nodded at Leonid. "But *baruch hashem* (praise the Lord), I haven't got anything missing!"

* * *

The following morning old Leonid gave me a fine breakfast of omelette, salad, sour milk, three kinds of cheese, and coffee. I finished up with a superb Metulla apple from his orchard. It was sharp and juicy.

Before I left, he asked me to take some photographs of him to send to his son in Russia. He had just heard from the boy after two years of silence. He dressed up in a smart shirt and tie, posing with his dog and his new Ford Escort. It was the first time that I had seen him in anything other than a singlet.

2

WALKING DOWN the hill out of the village, my first stop was the waterfall in the Israeli part of the Ayun Valley. When I first visited it, in 1954, the site had possessed a wild, undisciplined beauty; we had had to force our way through thick undergrowth to arrive at the spring. Since those days, the Nature Reserves Authority had been at work: paths had been laid out, steps cut in the cliffs, and wooden bridges thrown across the gorges. The society has done its job well, preserving much of the wild character of the site, but I could not suppress a pang of regret for the past. I think that beauty spots should be developed; it enables many more people to enjoy them. But I cannot get enthusiastic about the idea.

The name of the waterfall, Hatanur (the oven), is said to come from the smokelike spray thrown up by the water after its fifty-foot drop down the rust-colored cliffs of the natural chimney in which it is situated, but this morning there was no spray; the water was brown and murky.

There was no one else about at that time of the morning, and, as always in Galilee, the birds were singing loudly. I left my rucksack under a tree and climbed the steep, winding path cut in the cliff face toward the spring. I soon found myself out of breath, thigh and calf muscles twitching with the effort. The subtropical vegetation of the cleft below was in sharp contrast to the scrub of the Galilee hills above, still burned a yellowish brown by the summer sun, despite the first winter rains, which had already fallen.

Above the waterfall, not far from the spring, I discovered a charming little graveyard. The shrubs, the wildflowers, and the sound of rushing water created an environment in which, I reflected, I wouldn't mind being laid to rest myself one day.

Until such time should arrive, I determined to press on southward. On my right, gray basalt cliffs thrust up through the scrub; on my left, the hills rolled gently down to the Hula Basin, formerly a lake surrounded by swampland, now converted into fields and fishponds. The valley floor was a patchwork quilt of green, brown, and yellow fields, and water flashing in the sun. High up ahead to the right, beyond a smoking quarry that disfigured the scene, I could just make out the village of Manara; down below, the expanding town of Kiryat Shmona seemed to encroach on the farmland. Even on this winter day the sun burned, but then the road took me through a grove of eucalyptus, the shade refreshingly cool.

Walking up the tree-lined road toward Tel Hai, I reflected that in one hour's walk I had traversed two decades of history. The communes of Kefar Giladi, Hamra, and Tel Hai had been established in 1916, in the midst of the First World War. The dreamers-turned-colonists of the first aliya had been joined by the pioneer-revolutionaries of the second aliya, the second wave of Jewish immigration from Eastern Europe, which arrived during the first decade of the present century.

The men and women of the second aliya were to dominate Israel for a long time to come. Israel's first prime minister, David Ben-Gurion, and its second president, Itzhak Ben-Zvi, were both men of the second aliya, which added *kibbush haavoda* (the conquest of labor) to the ideal of a Jewish return to Zion. Disgusted by the colonies of the first aliya, with their Bedouin guards, Arab laborers, and Jewish overseers, they were determined to regenerate the Jewish people by converting them into a nation of landworkers. An early Socialist Zionist described the Jewish people as an "inverted pyramid," with the base in the air. The new pioneers wanted to create a large Jewish working class, which would form the base of a normal pyramid, standing the right way up. They also decided to defend their new villages themselves. They formed Hashomer (the Watchman), a self-defense organization, and Jewish guards replaced Arabs and Bedouin in the settlements.

In Israel today, the second aliya is often laughed at, but it is still a symbol of the courage, idealism, self-reliance, and backbreaking toil that founded the nation. In fact, the number of immigrants who arrived was only some 40,000, and many of them subsequently left. Ben-Gurion would often recall that of the ninety-odd people on the boat that brought him to Jaffa, only two others apart from himself remained in Palestine.

The second wave of immigration came, of course, after the foundation of the Zionist movement by Theodor Herzl. Herzl, an urbane Viennese journalist, had been shattered by the Dreyfus case in France in 1895, which he had covered in Paris. Alfred Dreyfus, a Jewish captain in the French army, was found guilty of treason and sent to Devil's Island. Although the verdict was later overturned and Dreyfus was released, the trial revealed the ugly fact that anti-Semitism pervaded all levels of French society.

Herzl wrote a pamphlet, *The Jewish State*, in which he argued that the Jews must return en masse to their ancient homeland, and two years later, in 1898, he convened the first World Zionist Congress at Basel in Switzerland. The response was overwhelming, particularly in Eastern Europe. Somehow Herzl had struck a chord that the Lovers of Zion had only touched. Writing in his diary after the congress, he averred:

At Basel I founded the Jewish state. If I said this out loud today, I would be answered by universal laughter. Perhaps in five years and certainly in fifty everyone will know it.

It was a ridiculous declaration — unjustified, unrealistic, and vain. The remarkable thing about it is that it came true: fifty years later, on May 15, 1948, the State of Israel was proclaimed.

Herzl and Baron de Rothschild did not hit it off. Herzl despised what he thought was the Baron's small-minded approach; the Baron considered Herzl an arrogant visionary. But if the practical Baron scorned Herzl's utopian dreaming, he found himself ambivalent toward the men of the second aliya. Although he deplored their revolutionary ideas, he admired their dedication and independence. The settlers were no less ambivalent in their attitude to the Baron. They rebelled against his paternalism but came to respect his integrity and practical assistance.

After Herzl's death, and the transfer of leadership of the Zionist movement to more pragmatic men, like Chaim Weizmann, it became easier for the Baron and the Zionists to cooperate. In 1916, the land for Kefar Giladi, Hamra, and Tel Hai was bought by the Baron and the Zionist organization together.

Arthur Ruppin, the intensely practical head of the Zionist organization settlement department, was opposed to the establishment of the three settlements at that time. It was in the middle of the First World War, he argued; the Jewish community in Palestine had been depleted by deportation, conscription, and famine. Now was not the time to embark on new ventures. He was answered by Israel Giladi, a leader of Hashomer: "True, we don't know what the outcome of the war will be. In the meantime, we have to create facts!"

It was a cry that was to be heard frequently in the history of the Jewish community in this country. Today it is the rationale for establishing Jewish settlements on the West Bank of the Jordan, those same settlements which the United States State Department has termed illegal, and which many Israelis do not support.

Let us jump forward a few years to 1920. The war is over; the Turks have lost; the British are in control of Palestine. They have a mandate to carry out the terms of the Balfour Declaration, issued in 1917, the triumph of the diplomacy of Chaim Weizmann. In a letter to the English Lord Rothschild (not to be confused with the Baron), the British foreign secretary had written:

> His Majesty's Government view with favour the establishment in Palestine of a National Home for the Jewish people, and will use their best endeavours to facilitate the achievement of this object, it being clearly understood that nothing shall be done which may prejudice the civil and religious rights of non-Jewish communities in Palestine ...

After the war, the third aliya—the third wave of Jewish immigration—began, and thousands of pioneers poured into Palestine. What with this development and the Balfour Declaration, the Zionist millennium seemed to have arrived. But there was one small fly in the ointment: the British had the League of Nations Mandate for Palestine; the French were awarded the mandate for Syria (including today's Lebanon). Where did the border run? The area north of the Hula Valley, the Finger of Galilee, was a sort of no man's land, with local Muslim Arabs (encouraged, it was said, by the British) trying to expel the French and their Christian Arab allies.

The Jews did not want to become involved in the fight, but, as things turned out, they were not able to stay out of it. Kefar Giladi, Hamra, Tel Hai, and Metulla were attacked by Arab irregulars. After some fighting, the French withdrew northward and the four Jewish villages found themselves virtually under siege. Metulla was evacuated and Hamra abandoned, which left Kefar Giladi and Tel Hai. In charge of the defense of the two villages was one Joseph Trumpeldor.

Trumpeldor was the first Jewish soldier ever to receive a commission in the czarist Russian army. He lost his left arm in the defense of Port Arthur, during the Russo-Japanese War of 1904. In 1912, he came to Palestine and worked on the land. With the outbreak of war in 1914, the Turks, hoping to secure the loyalty of the Jews in Palestine, offered them Ottoman citizenship. A number of Jews accepted the offer, but Trumpeldor had decided that the best hope for the Jews lay in a British victory. He went to Alexandria, where many Jews had been deported, and, joining forces with another militant Zionist, Vladimir Jabotinsky, he persuaded the British to form the Zion Mule Corps, made up of Palestinian Jews. The idea was that these Jews would fight for the liberation of the Land of Israel; but in point of fact the Zion Mule Corps was sent to Gallipoli. Despite their disappointment at not fighting in their own country, the members of the corps distinguished themselves at Gallipoli, Trumpeldor in particular winning the admiration of his British superior officers for his coolness and bravery under fire.

The mule corps was converted into the larger Jewish Legion, which fought on the British side; but in 1917, after the Bolshevik revolution, Trumpeldor returned to Russia, where he set up Hechalutz, the Zionist pioneering organization. By 1919, he was back in Palestine, and when the crisis came in the Finger of Galilee, he hastened to Tel Hai, where he took over the region's defense.

The issue of the Galilee settlements had become something of a cause célèbre in the Jewish community. The official Zionist leadership in Tel Aviv had called for their evacuation, but Trumpeldor and his comrades resolved to stand firm. There was some debate at Tel Hai as to whether they should fight only Arab irregulars, or whether they should be prepared to resist a regular army as well; but the issue became academic when all kinds of attacks multiplied. The one-armed soldier conducted a resolute defense and sent repeated messages to Tel Aviv, calling for reinforcements. He wrote in his diary:

> A new generation of the Sons of the Land of Israel is standing on the frontier, ready to sacrifice their lives . . . and inside the country they are endlessly debating . . . Will help arrive too late?

The answer, unfortunately, was positive. The official leadership did in due course resolve to send help, but by then it was too late.

A measure of the difficulties faced by the settlers of Tel Hai and Kefar Giladi can be gauged by the fact that the French army, with its machine guns and artillery, had been forced to retreat by the Arabs. At Kefar Giladi, the settlers had twenty-five men and women with eighteen rifles; at Tel Hai, eighteen people with sixteen rifles. They had no other weapons and they had only about a hundred rounds of ammunition per rifle.

Apart from being vastly outnumbered, the defenders were at a topographical disadvantage. The attackers poured their fire down into the communal farm of Tel Hai from the surrounding hills, but the defenders held on. At one point, the Arab forces said their quarrel was not with the Jews. Could the defenders assure them that there were no French soldiers at Tel Hai? Trumpeldor invited a delegation in to see for itself, but some of the attackers opened fire while their comrades were inside, wounding Trumpeldor in the stomach. According to accounts by the survivors, his intestines were hanging out and he calmly instructed his companions how to bind them up with a towel.

"These are my last moments," he said. "Tell them to hold out to the last for the honor of the Jewish people." That evening he was taken to Kefar Giladi, but he died on the way. Just before he died, he spoke the words that are carved on his memorial: *"Tov lamut be'ad artzenu"* (It is good to die for our country). Following the death of Trumpeldor and seven other defenders, the villages were evacuated, but they were rebuilt in 1921, when the British regained control of the region. The Jewish claim had been staked out.

The statue of a lion stands above Trumpeldor's grave at Tel Hai, and on the anniversary of his death, youth movement members and schoolchildren from all over Israel come to pay him homage.

Trumpeldor's memory is revered equally by the left and right, a rare distinction in this country of fiery partisan politics. A man of the labor movement, a pioneer, and a believer in the commune ideal, he is obviously acceptable to the left wing. On the other hand the right-wingers note that he was prepared to act in defiance of the Zionist establishment. They respect his military achievements and remember his collaboration with right-wing Revisionist leader, Vladimir Jabotinsky, the spiritual head of the Herut Party, which leads today's cabinet. In justifying settlement on the West Bank of the Jordan, Herut members point to Tel Hai and say, "If it wasn't for Trumpeldor, the Finger of Galilee would also have been lost to us." The right-wing youth movement is called Betar (Brit Yosef Trumpeldor, the Joseph Trumpeldor Covenant).

Ben-Gurion is revered by the left; Chaim Weizmann is remembered by the moderate center; Jabotinsky is the hero of the right. Only Herzl and Trumpeldor are accepted by all parts of the political spectrum.

Today Kefar Giladi is a flourishing kibbutz, farming both its own lands and the former lands of the now nonexistent Hamra; Tel Hai has become an agricultural college, a regional branch of the open university, and a seminary for music and drama. The building where the famous 1920 battle took place has been converted into a museum-cum-shrine. You can sit in the claustrophobic courtyard, built from the black basalt rock of the area, and imagine the attackers shooting at you from the hills above. The museum itself is well worth a visit; it contains maps, documents, and photographs from the heroic period, as well as old weapons and agricultural equipment used at the time.

On a previous visit to the museum, I had been distracted by the sound of loud piano-playing. Peeping behind a door marked NO ENTRY, I saw a familiar bald head bent over a piano. It was my friend Jerry, whom I had not seen for years. We shook hands warmly and went out to sit in the yard.

Jerry, a tall, suave Czech, came to London to work in our Zionist youth movement, Habonim. It was a pioneering movement, dedicated to the ideals of the second aliya, the establishment of farming villages in Israel. Trumpeldor was one of our heroes, and Israeli emissaries like Jerry were supposed to be examples of the sort of person each of us was aiming to become: the idealistic pioneer, dedicated to socialism, simplicity, and folk-dancing. But, if the truth be told, Jerry was far more suited to London than to his ascetic Galilee commune.

He quickly eschewed his open-necked shirt and leather pioneer's jacket for a tie, smart hat, and rolled umbrella. Always immaculate, he spent as much time in the theaters and cafés as he did teaching Hebrew songs or lecturing on Socialist Zionism. One day, he burst into a room where I was conducting a meeting, his shirt all-of-a-sudden open at the neck.

"Quick, Danny, hide these," he pleaded, thrusting his tie and umbrella into my hands. I slipped them under the table, wondering what the hell was going on. A minute later, all became clear: a gnarled little man with a wrinkled brown face entered. His shirt was buttoned against the

British winter, but he wore no tie. A fellow member of Jerry's kibbutz (and a more orthodox pioneer type than Jerry), he was in England on some official business and had decided to visit his colleague in the youth movement.

We laughed together, remembering this incident as we sat in the sun, and Jerry confessed his moral cowardice; but he still justified his action, claiming that it would have damaged his reputation on the kibbutz if his true London persona had become widely known there. However, he remarked, I shouldn't let those second-aliya types pull the wool over my eyes. And he told me the following story.

His first visit abroad, after many years at the kibbutz, had been to Paris, as a member of a trade-union delegation to some international conference. After years of frugality, he had found the bright lights intoxicating, and when the sessions were over, he and some other young bloods had decided to go on the town. The problem was that they had landed themselves in a taxi with one of the old pioneer types. They had driven around Paris for two hours, viewing Montmartre, Montparnasse, Les Halles, and the Left Bank of the Seine, but the old boy had shown no signs of sleepiness. Finally, realizing that they would not be able to shake him off, they decided to brazen it out and told the driver to take them to some famous night club (Jerry rather thought it was the Crazy Horse saloon).

On arriving there, they faced an unforeseen problem. True Israeli pioneers of their time, they wore open-necked shirts, and they could not be admitted without ties. While they were feverishly consulting among themselves in whispers, wondering where they could possibly purchase ties at so late an hour, the elderly pioneer flicked his fingers for attention. Gravely, he produced five ties from his pocket; one for each of them.

"The most humiliating part of all," admitted Jerry, "was that he even had to tie them for us!"

3

Kɪʀʏᴀᴛ Sʜᴍᴏɴᴀ means "the town of the eight." It is named after Joseph Trumpeldor and his seven comrades killed at Tel Hai, but its atmosphere is far removed from that symbolized by the memorial lion. For in a mere forty minutes' walk, we have skipped three more decades — from the heroic 1920s to the turbulent 1950s.

The two decades after the battle of Tel Hai saw the Jewish community in Palestine grow to more than half a million people, living in towns and villages, farms and communes. With the increase in the Jewish population, opposition to immigration on the part of the local Arabs became more violent. The British authorities were hard put to it to balance the two parts of the Balfour Declaration: that which spoke of viewing "with favour the establishment in Palestine of a National Home for the Jewish people," and that which stated that "nothing shall be done which may prejudice the civil and religious rights of the non-Jewish communities in Palestine."

In 1921, Transjordan was closed to Jewish settlement. Vladimir Jabotinsky's Revisionist Zionists did not accept the ban (and their successors, the Herut movement, have never formally relinquished the right to Jewish settlement across the Jordan), but the majority of the Zionists accepted the new situation. It was regarded as a compromise by the Jews, because Transjordan was part of the Land of

Israel and also had been included in the area to which the Balfour Declaration was supposed to apply.

Violent Arab riots, notably in 1929, when the Jewish community in Hebron was wiped out, prompted the British authorities to limit the scale of Jewish immigration into western Palestine, as well, and quotas were established. These limitations were rejected by even the moderate Zionists, and as Nazism gained increasing power in Europe, the Jews organized the Aliya Bet, as a means to bring in illegal immigrants.

Then came the Second World War and the Holocaust. The pogroms, which had prodded the first aliya into action at the turn of the century, seemed like Saturday-night barroom brawls by comparison. One third of the Jewish people in the world, six million men, women, and children, were gassed, bludgeoned, bayonetted, shot, tortured, starved, or worked to death in Europe.

The pressure on Palestine grew, and the desperate Jews were prepared to consider partition of western Palestine with the Arabs, if they could provide a haven in their section for the survivors from Nazi Europe. After the war, as the mandate drew to a close, the British placed the Palestine problem in the hands of the newly formed United Nations, which voted by a two-thirds majority for the partition of western Palestine.

The Jews accepted partition and proclaimed the State of Israel in their part on May 15, 1948. The Arabs rejected partition. Local Arabs took up arms against the Jews, and the armies of five Arab states — Egypt, Transjordan, Syria, Iraq, and Lebanon — invaded the new nation.

In nine months of intermittent fighting, the outgunned, outnumbered Jews managed to beat back the uncoordinated Arabs from their areas — and a good bit more. In 1949, armistice agreements were signed with all the states, except Iraq, and the armistice lines became the borders of

Israel for nineteen years. In the fighting, some half-million Arabs, who had been living in what was now Israel, crossed the borders into Jordan, Syria, Lebanon, and the Egyptian-controlled Gaza Strip, becoming refugees. They were not absorbed by these countries, except to some extent by Jordan, which granted them citizenship, and they and their children live in refugee camps to this day. The large village of Halsa, not far from Tel Hai, was one of the many abandoned by the Arabs in their flight.

Almost 700,000 Jewish immigrants poured into the State of Israel in its first three years, a larger number than the population that had to absorb them. Aside from the survivors of the Holocaust, most of them were driven out of the Arab countries of the Middle East and North Africa, including Morocco, Tunisia, Algeria, Iraq, and Yemen. Other Jews came from India and Iran.

This was the first and last mass immigration to Israel. It was migration on a scale such as Herzl envisaged, but carried out in conditions of chaos he could not have imagined in his worst nightmares. For these Jews were not idealistic volunteers, dedicated to the building of a new society; they were whole communities, mostly backward in Western terms, transplanted against their will into an unfamiliar environment.

There had always been oriental Jews in the Palestinian Jewish community. There had been important immigrations from Yemen, at the tip of the Arabian Peninsula, in 1882, 1909, and 1910. There were Moroccan and Tunisian communities in the country, as well as Jews from Iraq, Iran, and Turkey; but the majority of the Jewish population had always been from Eastern Europe. Now, with devastating suddenness, came a deluge of Jews of a different type: different in background, in culture, in motivation. Large numbers settled in the towns, many were settled on the land in new *moshav* farming villages; but many thousands had to live in transit camps, called *ma'arbarot,* on the fringes of existing towns, or wherever else possible.

In some ways, the new settlers had a tougher time than the very earliest of the pioneers, for they were not prepared for the hardships. I remember even in 1954, when the ma'arbarot were mostly on the way out, the baffled and hurt expressions on the faces of the parents of large families who lived in corrugated-iron huts of under 200 square feet in area. They baked in the summer and froze in the winter. In the hot weather, the dust was everywhere, and the stench overpowering. In the cold weather, they had to struggle through a sea of mud to the nearest tap, twenty yards away. On top of all this, they were supposed to be "grateful" for all that was being done for them. And indeed they should have been, for when else in world history has a host country absorbed a refugee influx larger than its entire population?

But, of course, they didn't see it that way, and they still do not. Today, three decades later, the problems resulting from those years are still with us. It is referred to as the "social gap," "cultural gap," or "economic gap." Only when we are being really daring do we refer to the "communal gap." Israel's record is uniquely good in comparative terms, but most of the immigrants of the 1950s and their descendants have a lower standard of living than those who came earlier and later.

One of the ma'arbarot was established in the deserted Arab village of Halsa, near Tel Hai, and it is this tented camp, founded in 1949, that has become the town of Kiryat Shmona. The town has its problems, but, without sweeping them under the rug (because we shall return to the communal gap several times during my walk), let's strike a positive note. As I walk into the town, I find it, like Metulla, busy with municipal elections. Kiryat Shmona, still inhabited for the most part by the immigrants of the tented camp and their descendants, none of them from democratic countries, is immersed in the democratic process.

I walked down the street and the cars rushed past, taking citizens to vote. Booths had been set up to guide the voters to their local polling stations. Posters and leaflets were everywhere. The incumbent mayor, benign, gray-haired Aloni, appeared to be winning the poster war: his handsome face looked down on me from a hundred hoardings as I went in search of Marsha Brown, whose name I had received from Arik Yaacov in Metulla.

Marsha proved to be a small, dynamic, bouncy American, with a ready smile and tremendous enthusiasm. She had fallen in love with Kiryat Shmona when she lived there as a volunteer youth worker after the Six Day War.

"I made a five-year plan to study in the United States and return," she said. "I made it in seven."

She had trained as a public health worker and was all set to be coordinator of the new family health center, the first of its kind in Israel. At present, she was involved in setting up the project, but she also doubled as part-time English secretary for the local council.

She had an appointment with the deputy mayor at one of the polling booths, so we drove there in her car. It was situated in a school, and we had to pass through three checkpoints, manned by dark, well-muscled young election officials in tight shirts, before we arrived at the actual station.

The supervising committee sat behind a table, checking the voters' lists. A pregnant woman, a kerchief tied round her head, walked slowly in. She voted and smiled at me wearily before shuffling out. She was followed by a chic young lady, in modish blouse and slacks, carrying a baby in her arms. She could have been the daughter of the first woman, but she evidently wasn't, because she had come to the wrong station. She expressed her dissatisfaction (very loudly) with "them."

The deputy mayor appeared and dictated a letter to Marsha in English about the trip of a Kiryat Shmona school dance troupe to the United States. They got stuck over a word and I suggested a solution, which they accepted gratefully. I had no business being at the polling station at all, let alone improving the style of the deputy mayor's correspondence, but it was all taken as perfectly natural. In Israel, everyone's business is everyone else's.

Once, Israel's ambassador in Washington had been on the phone to the prime minister on a highly confidential matter. He paused to recall the name of the undersecretary of state, and a voice supplied it to him. The alarmed premier broke the connection. Following a special inquiry, two phone operators were dismissed.

"The point is not that the operators were listening in," remarked a perceptive observer later, "but that they were trying to help!"

Marsha drove a little yellow car rather like herself: small, bright, and fast. She took me up into the hills above the town and we proceeded north along the security road, outside the fence. She stopped at a good vantage point, where we looked down at the jumble of buildings in the green valley.

"Thirty-six synagogues," Marsha informed me. "Every *hamula* (extended family) has one, and they don't want to give them up. Most of them are just shacks, dating back to the time of the ma'arbara transit camp, but you can't pull down a synagogue."

With a population of 16,000, Kiryat Shmona is one of the more successful development towns, although more than twice that number have passed through. Every year in July the papers are full of stories of the "exodus" from Kiryat Shmona. Pointing out some of the new factories, Marsha told me that there were still not enough employment opportunities; many of the brightest young people leave for the large towns. Laible Hoffmitz has noted in his study of development towns, *The Other Side of Israel,* that these communities have been the reverse of the survival of the fittest. None of the original settlers wanted to be there, and those with the most guts and talent left. It was the weakest who remained. This was certainly true of Kiryat Shmona, though later on, the town did attract people from both Israel and abroad. Marsha is a good example.

I asked Marsha about the relationship between the town and the surrounding kibbutzim. It was good, she said, because the veteran settlements had shown a sense of responsibility. In the early days, they had accepted a sort of sponsorship of the new town and had located both the regional council offices there and the regional industrial zone. There was a paradoxical situation in that the countryside had, for the most part, higher educational and cultural standards and better services than the town, a reversal of the usual situation anywhere in the world. The villagers were the veterans, the establishment; the townsmen were the newcomers, the underprivileged.

Generally, the resentment between town and village in Israel dates back to the 1950s. The kibbutz then had represented the employer. The villagers had labored hard and long to achieve their standard of living and thought they were doing the townsmen a favor in giving them work. The town dweller saw it differently. He resented the higher standards he saw on the kibbutz and was offended that the villagers did not mix with him socially. He was not invited to the kibbutz swimming pool, nor were his children allowed into the well-equipped kibbutz school. This sort of resentment has lessened with the increase in prosperity of the development towns (Kiryat Shmona has two swimming pools today), but it lingers on in some locations. I recalled an incident just before the general election eighteen months earlier, when some youths from the town of Bet Shean had smashed tractors on a nearby kibbutz.

Marsha did not believe that such an incident could happen in Kiryat Shmona. Apart from the help they had always given the town, a number of kibbutzim had recently started special projects. Kefar Blum, a thirty-five-year-old kibbutz with settlers from England and the United States, had adopted one of the town's poor neighborhoods, establishing a youth club and appointing teachers and social workers to help it along. Nothing was going to be solved overnight: there were two and a half times as many oriental Jews in the town as in the region. Europeans, who formed a majority in the villages, were a small minority in town. However, the balance was improving. It was no longer true that the town's population was made up almost exclusively of unskilled labor and that the villages were full of qualified and trained professional people. Today, a far higher proportion of the town's citizens work in the town itself.

The problems were being solved, said Marsha, but she was scathing about the lack of interest shown by successive governments.

"They wake up only when someone is killed here," she said. She showed me the place where a group of terrorists had broken into the town in 1974 and killed sixteen people. She pointed to a nearby school, explaining that the gang had wanted to capture the pupils as hostages, but fortunately it had been the Passover holiday. When no children had shown up, the terrorists simply went to the nearest apartment block and shot it up.

"Of course, every time there's a katyusha or something, all sorts of officials come up here and make promises that they have no intention of keeping," she said scornfully.

An immigration official had advised her against settling in Kiryat Shmona. He had told her that the people there were "animals."

She had subsequently discovered that this particular official had received a rough welcome in town when he was working for another department.

"He admitted the government didn't keep its promises,

so what does he expect?" she demanded. "Who are the animals?"

This, maybe, more than economics, is the real root of the communal gap in Israel: the prejudice. Marsha's story took me back sixteen years to when I had lived in Arad, a new town in the desert, which we shall be visiting on this walk. Shortly after moving in, friends of ours received a letter from their relatives, asking, "Do you have nice neighbors, or are they Moroccans?"

Our friends were able to reply truthfully, "We have very nice neighbors, who are incidentally Moroccans."

At that time, one of the main problems was that the prejudice was not even acknowledged. At least today it is. Since those days, the problem exploded in the "Black Panther" riots in Jerusalem. Of course the young Moroccans who adopted the American name were not real "panthers." They didn't want to pull down Israeli society; they just wanted a fair share of the cake.

*   *   *

That evening Marsha was due to meet with a group of American Jewish fund-raisers at the town's leading hotel. I said I would join her after the meeting, and spent the intervening time wandering around town. I was to see two examples of the young oriental Jew in the next few minutes. First I was stopped by a party of dark young men who assumed that I was a voter. They wanted me to vote for their independent list. Their candidate, a younger man, stood for clean government. He would wipe out corruption, they said. They represented the new generation, who had been born in Kiryat Shmona; they wanted to throw out the old establishment. Their man would speed development, they assured me. He would get the government to invest in the town, and, what is more, tenders when they came would be fairly awarded on the basis of secret bids. No more "jobs for the boys." I finally convinced them that I was not a voter and went to sit in the town square. It was shabby; bottle tops and ice-cream papers lay strewn around the flagstones. I had a beer at a neon-lighted café and listened to the conversations.

"Did you vote?" A girl with flashing dark eyes and a ponytail was querying a swarthy, unshaven youth.

"Yes, I voted."

"For Aloni?" she asked, naming the incumbent.

"*Kus emuhu Aloni, kus umuhum* all of them!" he replied, heaping an obscene Arabic curse on the entire list of candidates.

At the hotel — new, gleaming with lots of mirrors and shiny black Formica — I joined Marsha and her fundraisers in an upstairs room. We all sat around informally on the floor, the beds, and an occasional chair.

"I just want to sum up my feelings about this trip so far," said Erv, the group leader. "My feelings have been dominated by our visit to that kibbutz of Holocaust survivors and its memorial museum. This had an even greater impact than the television series, because I don't believe in Camp David,* and I feel there can be another Holocaust."

"I want to disagree with you, Erv," said a bespectacled botany professor from Boston, who identified himself as Marv.

"You want to disagree with my *feelings?*"

"Yeah."

"How can you disagree with *feelings?*"

"My feeling was much more for the young soldier guarding the museum," stated Marv. "He was about the same age as my son, and my son is just the type to be first over the top."

---

* The Camp David accords between Israel and Egypt, which subsequently led to the peace treaty, had been signed the previous week.

"There's another thing that struck me," said somebody. "Sometimes you think that this country is a mess. You see an unfinished building and you think it's inefficiency. But then it occurs to you that it may have been started by a man who went away to war and didn't come back."

(Despite the patent good will of all those present, I was put in mind of a statement of one of Baron Edmond's officials in 1898:

"In general I do not like these visits from foreigners and outsiders, which in reality rarely have any useful effect, since 99 percent of them have no comprehension of what they are shown; but nevertheless believe it to be their duty to formulate an opinion, usually false, dictated by ideas they had held in advance.")

"We haven't met enough Israelis on this trip," complained a middle-aged matron with bleached hair.

Marsha dealt with the comments and questions patiently, ably assisted by Bob, another young American, tall, with a handsome, concave face and curly hair.

"This is their first day," he told me afterward. "Only a bunch of Americans would discuss their impressions after *one day!*"

Like Marsha, Bob was a new immigrant in love with Kiryat Shmona. What did they love about it? The people, they both replied. Once you got to know them, they were so warm and spontaneous. Bob was an instructor in the local community center, lecturing adults in evening classes and developing hobbies. "I want them to realize their full potential," he told me seriously. He was also working as a sports coach and playing basketball for the local kibbutz.

"Half the team is from town, but the kibbutz has the court," he explained. Country was still ahead of town in sports facilities, yet he was enthusiastic about plans for a new tennis center in Kiryat Shmona.

I went with Marsha and Bob to one of the polling stations. There, the officials wouldn't let us in to watch the count, which was being conducted behind locked doors in the presence of observers from each of the competing lists. My friends from the "clean government" list arrived to change their observer, who, they said, was too naïve. They pretended he had a sick mother and slipped in a sharper customer.

"Don't tell me they can fiddle anything with nine observers present." Bob laughed.

"I wouldn't put it past them," commented Marsha.

"Oh, come on," protested Bob. "Two or three, maybe. But nine?"

We chatted in the cool night air until about one in the morning, when a car drew up and a bumptious twelve-year-old emerged to tell us, "We have majorities in nine out of fourteen stations."

"Aloni's son," explained Marsha.

It was several days before I saw the official results and learned that Aloni, the incumbent, had indeed won another term as mayor of Kiryat Shmona.

4

SWINGING ALONG the road out of Kiryat Shmona, I realized that this was to be my first real day of walking. So far, I had covered only seven miles; today, I was resolved to do twice that. My plan was to proceed south along the main road as far as Rosh Pina before turning westward into the hills of Galilee.

The sky was gray and threatening, but I didn't fear serious rain. I walked on the shoulders of the eucalyptus-lined road, which were alternately soft and gravelly. On my right, the mountains rose steeply, their summits hidden from view. On the left-hand side of the road, fields of cotton and pasture with free-range cattle alternated with citrus groves. A herd of Brahmin cattle, driven by a young lad, kept pace with me for some minutes before veering off to the east.

The whole area on the left had been Lake Hula, surrounded by swampland. Infested with malaria, it had been one of the most challenging regions settled by the early pioneers. One of the earliest villages, Yesud Hamaala, settled in 1883 by a group of Polish immigrants, had suffered greatly and had been rescued by the Baron. He had planted eucalyptus trees and drained some of the marshes. Over the years, additional areas of swamp had been reclaimed, but it was not until 1951 that the whole lake and surrounding area were drained.

Dozens of farms and villages have since been established
in the Hula Valley, but some people regard the Hula
project as an ecological disaster. Of the 20,000 acres reclaimed one thousand were set aside for a nature reserve,
and on an earlier visit I had been fascinated by the profu-
sion of bird and animal life there. Later, though, it was neglected, and much of the wildlife died out. In 1970, the Nature Reserves Authority had decided to rehabilitate the
park. It had been closed to the public and was due to reopen in two months' time. I planned to make an unauthorized visit on my way past.

As I walked along, I was reminded of how we used to
collect funds in the youth movement for the Hula drainage
project. I went collecting with Shosh, now a respected wife
and mother in the nearby kibbutz of Kefar Hanassi, but in
those days a fiery young Zionist ideologue. We progressed
from door to door in one of the predominantly Jewish dis-
tricts of London until her pitch was word-perfect. When we
rang the bell at an opulent mansion, a young lady leaned
out of an upstairs window, hugging a towel to her bosom.

"I'm having a bath and the phone's ringing," she cried.
"What do you want?"

Shosh was undeterred.

"Israel is short of arable land," she shouted up. "In addition to this, the swamps in the Hula Valley represent a notable health hazard . . ."

"What did you say?" interrupted the puzzled woman.

"Many of the villagers are suffering from malaria," continued my indomitable companion. "But a project is now
underway to drain the marshes and reclaim the land for
farming . . ."

"I'm afraid I must answer that phone," cried the woman,
and we never saw her again.

I had been walking for about two hours, and had finally
adjusted the straps on my rucksack to my satisfaction, when

the rain started. It was only a light shower and I decided to ignore it. Born in England, I have always been amused by what I regard as the Israelis' exaggerated fear of rain. However, a mile or so farther on I did seem to be getting rather wet, so I decided to take shelter under a eucalyptus tree. The eucalyptus may have been a great marsh-drainer for the Baron; but as a rain shelter it was a distinct washout. A little farther along, I came to a clump of oak trees. They looked more promising, but they were enclosed by a wire fence. A notice informed me that they were the last remnants of an enormous oak forest that had once spread over the Hula Valley to the foothills of Mount Hermon.

By now the rain was coming down in torrents, very cold torrents. I didn't dare stop, even though I was soaked to the skin, because I thought I would freeze to death. Even the cars stopped, drawing up by the side of the road, waiting for the storm to pass. But not I: I pressed on, my glasses steamed up inside, covered with raindrops outside, cold, wet, and miserable. Something cold and solid settled on my cheek and I licked it into my mouth. Ice: it had begun to hail. Suddenly, I heard a voice shouting, "Fool, degenerate, idiot! What the hell do you think you're doing?"

I looked across the road, barely distinguishing the outline of what I took to be a hut. I waded across and entered.

"Are you mad?" The voice belonged to a dark young man with a quiff of black hair falling over his forehead.

"Are you trying to kill yourself?"

"You really will think that I'm mad when I tell you what I'm doing," I responded belligerently. "I'm walking to Elat!"

"Okay, okay," he said a trifle defensively, "but not in the rain, for God's sake!"

He made me some hot tea on his primus, while I stripped off some outer layers of clothing in a futile attempt to dry them. My windcheater had proved to be useless; my rucksack no better, my shoes had become papier-mâché. I drank two glasses of hot tea, the scalding liquid coursing down my throat. I felt almost human.

My rescuer's name was Hezi, and he lived in a moshav cooperative called Margaliot in the hills to the west. The village had been founded by immigrants from Morocco in the early 1950s; it was clearly an example of the partial success story of these moshav villages. If some of the development towns and the slum areas of the large towns illustrate the failure of Israel to absorb the mass immigration of the fifties, then the villages demonstrate one way absorption has been achieved, at least on an economic level. As I walked through the country, I was able to see visible evidence of the prosperity of these farming villages in the tractors, combine harvesters, cotton-pickers, sophisticated irrigation, and pesticide equipment, but above all in the large, luxurious houses being built alongside the original simple dwellings.

If Hezi was any indication, there had been some success on the cultural level also, for he informed me that he was finishing his bachelor's degree in modern Jewish history next year. He had completed his military service, toured Europe, and was now in charge of the village citrus groves. He was down today to arrange for the picking of the orange harvest. The rain, he informed me, would put back the picking by at least a week. I asked him where he was studying, and he told me he attended evening classes at the Tel Hai Field College. He was studying just for the interest of the thing; he had no intention of leaving farming for teaching, or anything like that. He looked after the family smallholding in addition to the village citrus groves.

I asked him whether he did not feel cut off, living in a little village high up in the Galilee hills. Not at all, he protested. He had easy access to Kiryat Shmona, Tiberias, and even Haifa. Many good shows and concerts could be enjoyed at the local kibbutzim and, of course, at the Tel Hai college. He noted that he could easily sell his farm if he wanted to; there were people queuing up to join the village. It was a good living these days. The days of struggle to make enough to eat were long past. He had grown up as a farmer, but there were agricultural instructors to tell the newcomers what to do, and everyone got by. Today, also, there was less physical labor involved. Much of the work had been mechanized. Feeding the chickens, for example. When he had been a child, the farmers had humped sacks all over the place; now the bran arrived in bulk and was put straight into a huge hopper, which fed the troughs directly. The same was true of cattle feed, and no one milked by hand anymore.

The rain stopped, but I was downcast when I set out again. I had put off the walk until November for a number of good reasons. Now I had the feeling that I had left it too late. The real winter in Israel comes in January and extends through April, but there can be rain in November and December. It seemed that 1978 was going to be one of those years. Even if I didn't get pneumonia that day — and it seemed increasingly likely that I would — my walk was threatening to become a fiasco. My mood was not improved by the sight of a dead dog that had been horribly squashed by a truck. It was only the first of many slaughtered animals that I was to see on our roads.

I plodded on, my shoes squelching depressingly, pausing every now and then to look hopefully at the sky. Early that morning, it had been bright to the south. Just get a move on, I had said to myself, and you'll be okay. Now, perversely, the sun shone over Kiryat Shmona; where I was going, it was gray-black. I passed the entrance to the Hula nature reserve, all thoughts of a visit there now abandoned, and the turning for Yesud Hamaala. Thinking of that pioneer village and the sufferings of the first pioneers seemed to put my own misery in a proper perspective.

The young enthusiasts from Poland had been warned by

the Jews of Safed that the site was unhealthful; the Bedouin who lived nearby all had malaria. They would not listen: there was rich, well-watered land for farming, and fish from Lake Hula. At the outset they had lived together in a large dilapidated building, which they shared with their livestock.

"The fleas, which were almost as large as flies, literally ate their flesh," wrote a contemporary. "There was no escaping them. It was impossible to sleep outdoors owing to the cold and rain."

The building clearly had to be abandoned, so the pioneers resolved to build themselves huts woven of reeds, like those the local Bedouin inhabited. They found the right type of reeds after some searching, but the support poles could be found only on the other side of the Jordan River. They crossed the river and cut their poles, but when they tried to bring them back, they were stopped by an Ottoman toll-keeper on the Bnot Yaacov Bridge, who demanded money. Because they had no money, they had to work on his plantation to pay off the debt. They finally returned home and built the huts, but one summer they were all burned to the ground, so the settlers had to go through the whole procedure again. Some years later, the Baron took over responsibility for the village, and proper houses were at last built. There is a moving description of the first night in the first house of Yesud Hamaala:

When the lamp was lit on the first night, and a new light shone through the windows, the settlers congregated outside and turned to one another in amazement — a real lamp! The Jews had light and gladness and joy. For years the settlers had languished in their windowless huts, unable to light a lamp for fear of fire ... Above all the children rejoiced, for they had not beheld such a wondrous sight in all their lives.

From the very first year, settlers died from malaria and one villager went mad with the fever, but somehow they stuck it out.

*   *   *

As I continued southward, the showers fell intermittently. I would no sooner start to dry off and feel more cheerful when another cloud emptied on me. My sodden pack had increased considerably in weight, my feet hurt, and I ached all over.

This was just the sort of situation in which I had anticipated taking a bus or hitchhiking. Before setting out on my walk, I had resolved that I was not going to be a fanatic about it. I would indeed walk most of the way, but if necessary I would make use of wheeled transport. Strangely, I now found myself becoming obstinate. A number of cars offered me lifts, but I splashed along, refusing all aid. I might make diversions by transport (as I already had in looking around Kiryat Shmona), but I was going to make it to Elat on foot. It had become a personal matter between me and the elements.

However, when I arrived outside the veteran kibbutz of Ayelet Hashahar, with its pleasant guest house, I felt I had earned a night of comfort. I passed through the beautiful lawns, trees, and flower beds of the village and booked a room.

The hotel deserves its four stars — but a very special place in hell should be reserved for the man who invented the hip bath. A hot bath was just what I needed, but being neither an octopus nor a chimpanzee with rickets, I found it well-nigh impossible to immerse myself. I twisted and turned for some minutes before, with my back painfully arched and my feet tickling my ears, I managed to get the hot water to most parts of my anatomy. The fan heater was rather better value, and I turned it full on, hanging up my sodden clothes on a strong piece of twine that I had thoughtfully brought along. All the clothes in my rucksack had been soaked almost as much as those I was wearing. My nice new blue rucksack was not, whatever its other fine qualities, waterproof.

I ate an excellent dinner that evening in a dining room as elegant as anything you can find in this country. I enjoyed the hot soup and roast chicken, reflecting that Ayelet Hashahar had come a long way from the ascetic commune of the 1920s. (It had been founded by pioneers of the third aliya, whose ideals were very similar to those of the second aliya.) Logic compelled me to applaud this progress, for I have never seen any virtue in asceticism per se. At the same time, I could not help wondering whether, instead of creating a normal, rather stodgy, hotel, the kibbutz should not have developed something closer to its original spirit and atmosphere. I visualized a rough-stone or pinewood ranch-style dining room, with solid, unvarnished benches and tables. One would serve oneself, instead of being waited on by the girls from nearby Kiryat Shmona, and the meals would consist of a wholesome semivegetarian diet, with plenty of the magnificent fresh fruit and vegetables grown in the region. A member of the kibbutz once told me that the guest house was the kibbutz's best contact with the world outside and prevented the community from becoming too introverted. He was at pains to emphasize that this applied to the waitresses also: they were a direct line of contact with Kiryat Shmona. Somehow it seemed to me a long way from the original principle of self-labor, though I doubt if the waitresses would thank me for my purist approach. The hotel is undoubtedly a good source of employment for some of the town's young women.

By morning, all my clothes were dry and I packed them up in the plastic bags thoughtfully provided for the guests' laundry. The next downpour would not catch me unaware, I resolved.

My walk thus far had covered some twenty miles and one century. In Metulla, I had been reminded of the turn-of-the-century pioneering of the first aliya. At Tel Hai, the museum had reconstructed the heroic period of the second and third waves of immigration. In Kiryat Shmona I had seen the results of the mass immigration of the 1950s. I had already spanned, albeit with gaps, the saga of the modern Jewish state. But now, outside the gates of Ayelet Hasha-har, I looked across the road at the mound of Tel Hatzor, and what I had seen all but faded into insignificance. Facing me was not one, but forty centuries of history, layer upon layer, from the early Bronze Age to the time of the Romans.

I have already noted that the return to Zion was prompted by the sufferings of the Jews in Eastern Europe; and I have told how the anti-Semitism of Western Europe, illustrated by the Dreyfus Affair, triggered the movement for political Zionism. But perhaps I have not sufficiently conveyed to what extent "the Return" was just that — a return of an ancient people to its historical roots.

Space does not permit a full account of the history of the Zionist movement, but at this point, opposite the layers of Tel Hatzor, let us pause and remember that no less a figure than Theodor Herzl, the founder, leader, and inspirer of the Zionist movement, was in favor of accepting a temporary refuge for the suffering Jews of Russia, Poland, and Rumania. He supported a proposal to settle Jews in Uganda and thus split the Zionist Congress apart. Amazed that it was precisely those East European Jews, suffering daily from the pogroms, who rejected the Uganda scheme, even as a temporary haven, and moved by their devotion to their historical homeland, Herzl recanted, emotionally quoting from the Bible, "If I forget thee, O Jerusalem, let my right hand forget its cunning . . ."

Archaeological excavations are carried out all over the world, but only in Israel has archaeology been raised to the level of a cult. In the United States, Ronald Reagan, a former film star, became a presidential candidate; in

Israel, Yigael Yadin, an archaeologist, became deputy prime minister. Yadin had, it is true, been a famous general in Israel's War of Independence; but his main claim to fame, when he entered politics some three years ago, was as the man who had explored the Bar-Kochba caves and excavated Masada and Hatzor.

The word *tel* means an artificial mound, made up of layer upon layer of ancient dwellings. In the case of Hatzor, Israel's largest tel, no fewer than twenty-one fortresses and cities have been built on the same site.

Hatzor existed long before it comes into Jewish history. It was built 4500 years ago, reaching its maximum size in the eighteenth century B.C. In the nineteenth century B.C., Egyptian documents listed it as one of the empire's potential enemies. Excavations revealed many interesting facts about the early communities, but great excitement was caused by the discovery of a well-built Canaanite city of the thirteenth century B.C., which had been destroyed by fire. This, clearly, was the city destroyed by Joshua's Israelites when they invaded the land of Canaan. It is recorded in the Bible that "Joshua at that time turned back, and took Hatzor, and smote the king thereof with the sword: for Hatzor beforetime was the head of all those kingdoms . . . and he burnt Hatzor with fire." (Joshua 11:10-12.)

Let us pause for a moment and put Joshua in context. Around 2000 B.C., a man called Abraham, who lived in what is now Iraq, rejected his religion, based on idolatry, and found belief in the One God. He made a Covenant with God, under the terms of which he and his descendants would serve Him and in return would be His chosen people. He brought his family to the land of Canaan (today's Israel and Jordan), which was promised by God to him and his seed forever.

Abraham, his son, Isaac, and his grandson Jacob lived in Canaan, until, in Jacob's time, famine forced them to migrate to Egypt. Several centuries later, the descendants of

Jacob had grown into a considerable people made up of twelve tribes, descended from the twelve sons of Jacob. Jacob had also acquired the name Israel, and the people were called Israelites.

The Israelites were oppressed in Egypt and a new leader, Moses, arose to lead them to freedom. At Mount Sinai, Moses renewed the Covenant that God had made with Abraham and received from God the Ten Commandments. Moses led the Israelites through the desert for forty years, but it was his successor, Joshua, who led the invasion of Canaan and retook it for the descendants of Abraham.

After Joshua died, there were years of intermittent warfare, with the twelve tribes, each of which had been awarded a region of Canaan, continuing to fight the Canaanites and also a seafaring people, who lived in the coastal plain, called the Philistines. Although there were strong Israelite rulers, called Judges, it became clear that a more centralized administration was needed, and in 1033 B.C., the Israelites' first king was anointed, though he wasn't recognized by them all. Saul was briefly succeeded by his son before David took over and became the first king to be accepted by all twelve tribes. He gained control of the hill country of Canaan, but the Philistines continued to fight him, and we read of their battles in the Bible.

Since their encounter with God on Mount Sinai, the Israelites had kept the Ark of the Covenant with the commandments of God inside. David's successor, his son Solomon, built the Temple in Jerusalem, which David had captured and made his capital, giving the Ark a permanent home. Solomon, famous as the wise king, also rebuilt Hatzor.

Digging down through the layers at Tel Hatzor, the archaeologists discovered the fortress of Solomon ten layers down. It was smaller than Canaanite Hatzor, but it was an important royal fortress, with a casemate wall and gateway characteristic of the period.

The excavations indicated that the Bible was indeed accurate as historical account, for in addition to the layers of Joshua and Solomon, the archaeologists uncovered a city-fort that had been destroyed in the eighth century. The destruction was clearly the result of the Assyrian conquest in 732 B.C. What had happened meanwhile was this: after Solomon's death, the kingdom had split in two, the ten northern tribes becoming the Kingdom of Israel and the two southern ones becoming Judah. Israel was conquered by the Assyrian empire and its citizens exiled. Judah survived on its own for more than a century, only to be conquered and its people exiled by the Babylonians, the successors of the Assyrians. Unlike the Israelites, the people of the southern kingdom were able to remain together and maintain their identity as a people, known as the Judeans, or Jews. The empire of Babylon was superseded by that of Persia, and in 539 B.C., Cyrus, the Persian king, allowed the Jews to return home. They settled in Jerusalem and the surrounding area.

But to return to our tel. Many layers of settlement, right up to the second century B.C., were uncovered, but one mystery still remained: How had all these cities and fortresses managed for water? It was two years later, during a dig at Megiddo, farther south, that Yadin found a clue. A deep shaft at Megiddo led to a tunnel, which led to a spring outside the fortress. The Bible records that King Solomon built Hatzor, Megiddo, and Gezer. Excavations at Hatzor and Megiddo had already shown amazing similarities in the layout and design of the two fortresses. Could Hatzor possess a water system similar to that at Megiddo? In 1968, Yadin took his archaeological team back to Hatzor, determined to find out. After a number of months' searching, they found the answer: a system amazingly similar to that at Megiddo.

I climbed the mound with its superb view over the Hula Valley, the red-roofed cottages and gardens of Ayelet Hashahar in the foreground. Clambering over the excavated walls and ditches, I tried to make sense of the different periods of habitation. Even with my guidebook, it wasn't easy. After visiting many sites in Israel over the years, I have come to the conclusion that to understand a site properly, unless it is a simple location with only two or three layers of settlement, you need a professional. But at Hatzor, the water system was staggering, even to an amateur.

Descending the 123 steps to the source* of the spring (in Hatzor, unlike Megiddo, it is inside the fortress), one is astounded by the sheer scale of the ancient enterprise. The total depth is no less than 130 feet, an engineering feat that is, considering the conditions of ancient times, simply mind-boggling. As I descended from the warm winter sunshine, I left the comparative warmth for the cold clamminess at the spring below. At first, I found the steps going around the four sides of the shaft; then I came to the sloping tunnel. The upper steps are plastered, but the lowest ones are built from the hard black basalt. Apparently they were sometimes under water when the spring was high in winter, but even yesterday's downpour had not brought the level up that much.

I climbed back up the shaft and down from the mound, crossing the road back to the kibbutz to visit the Hatzor museum. An impressive selection of pottery and artifacts from the different periods were on display, but I was most struck by something I saw in the entrance hall. One of the plate-glass windows there had been damaged and new plates of glass had been fixed on either side, obviously to preserve the crack.

The curator explained that the original window had been damaged by Syrian gunfire in the Six Day War. The crack had indeed been deliberately preserved. It was, he

---

* Tel Hatzor is the location for Michener's best-selling novel *The Source*.

said, a reminder that modern Israel could also be destroyed and could become the twenty-second layer of Tel Hatzor.

The excavated tel and the museum are a neat illustration of our twin national obsessions: the compulsion to reach out to our ancient past, and the need to find security for our tortured present.

5

I FELT surprisingly fit as I strode southward from the kibbutz. My suede boots had dried out, apparently unharmed by the soaking, and my pack was lighter now that it was dry. No sign of the feared pneumonia. There were still clouds in the sky, particularly above the hills to the east, where I was bound, but the sun shone and my mood was far more cheerful.

I walked past modern Hatzor but did not enter the town on this occasion. I had visited there a couple of times in my kibbutz days. It had been a typical example of an unsuccessful community, with mean housing, few local employment opportunities, and a high proportion of welfare cases. I knew that it had not changed significantly in two decades. It had started as a ma'arbara transit camp on the fringes of the farming village of Rosh Pina. In 1952, when it was decided to make it permanent, the villagers, settled on their land for seven decades, were unwilling to absorb a community larger than themselves, consisting exclusively of settlers from North Africa. Hatzor was mistakenly established as an independent entity. Being wise after the event (never a difficult exercise), one can see that either Rosh Pina should have been forced to accept the newcomers, or the immigrants should have been transferred to Kiryat Shmona.

Hatzor has few local industries, so most of the citizens work in the surrounding area. In the early days, half the potential wage-earners were on welfare, but at least this has improved. The population today is around 6000. As in the case of Kiryat Shmona, many more have passed through — more than three times the present population — but unlike the town farther north, it has not attracted either new immigrants or settlers from other parts of Israel. Decent schools, new housing, and a swimming pool have been built, though the facilities are still inadequate. It is a vicious circle: people leave because of the inadequate services and opportunities, and because there are not enough citizens, there is insufficient demand for something better. Even Hatzor's picturesque and peaceful setting in the Galilee foothills has not proved an attraction, for the buildings are unimaginative and the apartments themselves are small.

Rosh Pina, next door, has at least a sort of tumbledown charm of its own and continues to attract new inhabitants. Its history goes back to the first aliya. In 1882, thirty families from Rumania, led by one David Shuv, settled on their newly purchased land and started to build houses and cultivate the soil. In the early years they came into conflict with local Bedouin, who used the village water supply for their cattle and stole crops from the fields, but the settlers overcame these problems. A deal was struck whereby the Bedouin could water their livestock and the villagers could use Bedouin lands for grazing their own animals. The fields were guarded by two Jewish watchmen, who won the respect of the locals. Malaria and yellow fever took their toll, because the only medical treatment available was from a pharmacist in Safed. One of the founders of the village, Yaacov Bendel, has written how eye inflammation was treated with a compress of asses' dung, and diphtheria by fumes of quicklime.

Nevertheless, in 1887 Baron Edmond had found it one of the most encouraging projects in Palestine. The villagers were hard workers, and the Baron had been pleased to grant them money to enlarge their holdings. Rosh Pina, he felt, contrasted favorably with settlements farther south.

I have already remarked on the name of the village. For a time Rosh Pina, the foundation stone, lived up to its name, but there has been little progress since the early days. Many of the original houses are still standing, their sleepy charm attracting a number of new inhabitants from Israel and abroad; but a sizable proportion of these have tended to be cranks and misfits. One group, which arrived some years ago, was led by a woman who believed that she was a reincarnation of Jesus Christ. At some point her followers were supposed to kill her (though not, it seems, by crucifixion*) and were prevented from doing so only by the intervention of the police.

However, along with the eccentrics, a number of genuine artists and craftsmen have been attracted to Rosh Pina. At the top of the main village street stands an enormous four-story structure, built of black basalt rocks, which once was a hotel. Aryeh Porat lives there with his wife and child, making original bracelets and way-out musical instruments.

Getting into the building was quite an achievement. A dizzying climb up a rickety wooden outer staircase brought me to the second floor, where I found Dinah, Aryeh's dark, attractive wife, and their eight-month-old daughter. Suspicious at first, Dinah quickly became friendly once I explained that I had met Aryeh previously and had come to see his work. Over a cup of coffee, she told me that they had founded a college-commune some three years earlier for "Arts, Crafts and Self-Knowledge." Like many such institutions, the commune had a drifting population, which eventually drifted away altogether. Aryeh and Dinah had been on their own for more than a year, and she thought it

---

* Lest the reader think that this idea has been entirely abandoned, I should mention that about ten years ago the Jerusalem police prevented the attempted crucifixion of a man. "Crucifixion is not allowed in Jerusalem," noted the police spokesman at that time.

would remain that way. The point was emphasized by Aryeh when he arrived.

"Perhaps we'll try to restart the school," he told me. "I like teaching, but we'll never have a residential college again." Dinah added that sometimes undesirables attempted to squat in the building, which they rented from the Israel Lands Authority.

"Once Aryeh had to stand with a wooden stake in his hand to scare away an unpleasant intruder," she recalled.

Aryeh — ragged blond hair and tousled beard, startling blue eyes — had been shopping with his donkey. Unfortunately, he had neglected to ensure that the eggs had been properly packaged, and he presented his wife with a slimy brown paper bag, which she refused to accept. It dropped onto the floor, and Dinah bent to clean up the mess with a patient smile.

"A donkey is a donkey," Aryeh said, laughing, by way of explanation. The other supplies were in good enough condition, and we passed into the next room to look at his musical instruments. I was riveted by the view. From the second-floor balcony, perched above Rosh Pina, I could see the whole Hula Basin and the rift valley as far south as the Sea of Galilee, winking pale blue in the distance. The red roofs of the village were scattered untidily below. Clumps of greenery and houses marked the other villages among the yellow scrub. To the north towered the majestic peak of Mount Hermon, its summit wreathed in cloud.

Aryeh could make any instrument sound good. He picked out a tune on a rather stubby banjo, which he had made himself, and then showed me his latest invention, the Sutul (from the Hebrew *mastul,* "stoned"). It was triangular, with wire strings of varying thickness and an empty corned-beef can for a soundbox. He started picking and twanging the strings as if it were a guitar, but then he produced a smooth, curved piece of wood, which he used alternately as a bow and a xylophone hammer. Adjusting the strings from time to time, he produced some unusual and attractive music.

"I'm not really an innovator," he confessed, hauling out a huge black-bound book about Africa and showing me a picture of an African instrument not unlike the Sutul.

Downstairs in his workshop, I watched Aryeh making a bracelet. He took up an old, ornamented fork (which he told me was about one-third silver) and heated it red-hot. Twisting the prongs of the fork in intricate patterns, until he had a pleasing tangle of metal that looked like a miniature head of Medusa, he doused the whole thing in cold water. The next stage was to cut the fork in two, but in such a way as to leave one half with a projection that fitted into the slot of the second half. All this he did by eye, scorning to take measurements. He then bored holes through both slot and projection with a fine electric drill, once more relying on his eye. He worked with precision, making the hole wider at the ends in order to be able to lock in the improvised hinge. As he worked, he kept up a stream of patter.

"This is my therapy: work. If I don't work, I get nervous and irritable. When I work, I feel good. This makes me feel alive. All this could be done by machines, but I get my pleasure out of doing it by hand."

He then beat both halves of what had been the fork into a curve that would fit around the wrist, using a hammer and resting the bracelet on a lead surface. The lead, he explained, was firm enough to hold the fork, but soft enough not to damage the pattern of the twisted tines. He fitted the hinge, made a slot for the catch, and then heated the whole bracelet to white heat. This oxidized the whole bracelet, turning it black, but he then polished the outer parts so that the silver contrasted with the black under the pattern. It had taken him a little more than an hour. He was delighted when I bought the bracelet for my wife and another one for my daughter.

Although Dinah and Aryeh are not vegetarians, lunch

was naturist in style: rice, shredded cabbage, raisins, nuts, and home-cured olives. We were joined by Marcel, a skinny, sickly lad with a fuzz of beard. He had come from Paris two weeks earlier and was trying to learn art from Aryeh. I asked him if he was a student. No. What then did he do? Nothing. A shrug.

Before I continued on my way, Aryeh showed me around the rambling wreck of the house. He and his family inhabited only three of the twenty-odd rooms. The rest of the place was a mess: doors hung from their hinges, windows were without glass or often even without frames, the walls were cracked and peeling. Graffiti remained from the art school days: FULFILLMENT THROUGH WORK was painted in purple on one wall. LOVE IS ART was scratched in a door. Aryeh told me he was preparing the place for winter, installing a wood stove and putting in double-glazing in their three rooms. I looked at the sheer drop from a third-story balcony and asked him what he was going to do when his little black-eyed daughter started to crawl.

"She'll have to learn." He shrugged.

I picked my way gingerly down the outer staircase.

*   *   *

Aryeh had suggested that I proceed directly up the valley behind his home to Safed, but I decided to double back and walk through the Mount Canaan forest, a rather pretentious name for the woods above Hatzor. On my way I passed through an olive orchard, where several Bedouin women were beating the trees with long poles, knocking the olives down onto sheets that had been spread on the ground. A typical black Bedouin tent had been entirely covered in transparent plastic sheeting. It gleamed in the sun, horribly ugly; but I imagine the Bedouin preferred to be dry rather than picturesque.

Climbing up through the pine woods, I found myself sweating, and I initiated the endless internal debate that was to continue throughout the walk: Should I remove my jacket or not? Remove it, I reasoned, and it would rain. Keep it on, it will remain dry. Five minutes' more climbing and it came off. The dirt track wound steeply up the hillside, with only the endless stretches of pine on all sides. Like most woods in Israel, the Mount Canaan forest was planted by the Jewish National Fund. This organization has done sterling work in a wide variety of land-reclaiming projects; but its tree-planting program is a trifle unimaginative.

The Jewish National Fund was one of the ideas presented to the first Zionist Congress called by Theodor Herzl, but it was established only in 1907. The JNF still exists today, and many — possibly a majority — of Jewish houses around the world contain the little blue boxes in which small sums of money are deposited for building the Jewish nation. Together with the Baron at the outset, dominant as time went on, the fund purchased most of the land where Jews settled in modern Palestine. Today its land has been turned over to the Israel Lands Authority, and its activities are mainly concerned with development and reclamation work. One of its notable activities, both formerly and today, is the planting of trees. The Zionist gospel says that the land was neglected for two millennia, and goats stripped the trees, which died out. As a result, the soil eroded and the land became desert. Hence, tree-planting became the symbol as well as the practical expression of land reclamation. The JNF has planted well over 100 million trees. Those of us brought up in a Zionist youth movement have developed an almost mystical attitude to trees. In my garden at home, one of the pine trees is keeling over at a preposterous angle, a potential danger to life and limb — but my wife will not permit me to cut it down.

But to return to the present walk. I saw that the woods were full of plaques, announcing who had financed the various sections of afforestation. One copse had been planted in honor of Israeli leaders; here I noted the names of Abba Eban and Golda Myerson. This set me thinking. David Ben-Gurion, Israel's first prime minister, had insisted on the national leaders' Hebraizing their names. Abba Eban had been Aubrey Eban, and Golda had become Israel's fourth premier as Golda Meir. Well, Golda was not particularly Hebrew, but I couldn't imagine Golda as Zehava (the nearest Hebrew equivalent). How come Aubrey was already Abba at a time when Meir was still Myerson? Then I remembered that Golda had been our first ambassador to Moscow. She probably hadn't altered her name until she came back to serve as minister of labor.

I pressed on through the endless greensward until, with a startling suddenness, a gap in the trees revealed a stunning view of the Hula Valley to the east, the patchwork of fields, green, gold, and brown, framed by the pines. Stopping to enjoy the scene, I became aware of the pain in my legs; the steady climb had taken its toll. Higher up, the trees were thinning out, and I took a short cut across some rough scrub, startling a deer, which bounded across the clearing in front of me. Nijinsky was supposed to be able to float in midair. Surely he must have taken lessons from a deer: this graceful creature seemed to hang for a full second before touching earth.

Another hour of tough climbing and I emerged, exhausted, from the woods, to find a couple of villagers reclining on a mattress while they drank their coffee. They were guarding a herd of cows that were contentedly cropping the grass around them.

Safed, they informed me, was just down the road. I was amazed at my own map-reading. My feet were now very sore; I hobbled over the lip of the hill and down into the town. The sky was gray, threatening rain, but I only had about a mile to go. I made it with difficulty.

6

SAFED is one of my favorite places in Israel. In the summer when you climb out of the muggy plains into the town you feel like a diver coming up for air. Safed is small enough to be intimate, but not so small that it is incestuous. Everyone knows everyone else, yet you can mind your own business if you want to.

Not mentioned in the Bible, it was originally built as a Crusader fortress in the twelfth century A.D., commanding the highway from Damascus to Acre. It was one of the main Jewish centers in pre-Zionist Palestine, one of the four "holy cities" of Judaism, the others being Tiberias, Hebron, and of course Jerusalem. The first Jews moved into Safed after their expulsion from Spain at the time of the Inquisition in 1492. By the sixteenth century, it had become one of the main centers of Jewish learning in the world.

Rabbi Joseph Caro composed the *Shulhan Aruch* in Safed, completing it in 1563. The comprehensive code of behavior by which the religious Jew regulates his life, it contains details of daily religious observance, dietary laws, Sabbaths, festivals, marriage, divorce, and mourning. In it you will find such diverse information as the rate of interest that can be charged for a loan, or how soon you are permitted to return to your wife's bed after completion of her menstrual period.

While the codex was tabulating such mundane affairs,

Rabbi Isaac Luria, known as "the Ari" (the Lion), taught *kabbalah,* Jewish mysticism, as set out in the *Zohar,* the *Book of Splendor.* The *Zohar,* a commentary on the first five books of the Bible, assumes that every letter has a special significance, containing a deeper meaning in addition to the obvious one. It is thought to have been written by Rabbi Simon Bar-Yochai, who is buried nearby in Meron. Two synagogues named for the Ari are the oldest in Safed.

Jumping the centuries, we find David Shuv coming to Safed in 1881 to buy the land for the village of Rosh Pina. He recalled that "there was no hotel in Safed in those days, nor was there a road. No wheeled conveyances were to be seen there at all. People coming to live in Safed — or rather to be buried there, for only aged folk journeyed to that town — traveled by donkey or mule from Beirut or Haifa."

I have mentioned how, with the growth of the Jewish population of Palestine, the local Arabs grew increasingly violent in their opposition. In 1929, during the same series of riots that caused the death of fifty-nine Jews in Hebron, twenty were killed in Safed and thirty-odd wounded, many of them children and old people. In 1936 and 1938, there were even more serious Arab riots, which also caused loss of life in Safed, but on a smaller scale than before. More Jews and Arabs lost their lives in the skirmishes that preceded Israel's War of Independence in 1948, and in that war Safed became a key town for the control of Galilee.

On November 29, 1947, when the United Nations General Assembly voted by a two-thirds majority to divide western Palestine into Jewish and Arab states, the scheme, as I mentioned earlier, was accepted by the Jews and rejected by the Arabs, who immediately began attacking Jewish towns and villages. Although the full-scale invasion of the new State of Israel did not take place until the end of the British mandate and the official proclamation of statehood in May 1948, there were already 3000 Syrian and

Iraqi troops besieging Safed before the British army pulled out. Even without these additional troops, the 2000 religious Jews of Safed were heavily outnumbered by their 10,000 Arab fellow citizens.

The time has now come to consider the War of Independence — not in detail; that would be a book in itself — but a little more carefully than we have done up to now. On the face of it, the Jews of Palestine were barely a match for that country's Arabs. In fact, as we have seen, Israel stampeded the Palestinian Arabs to flight and fought off the regular armies of Syria, Iraq, Transjordan, Egypt, and Lebanon, as well as troops from Saudi Arabia, to say nothing of the irregular Palestinian groups. Massively outnumbered and completely outgunned, the Israelis won their war.

At the time, many Jews took this victory for a miracle, for a sign that the Master of the Universe, Who had seemed to abandon them in Nazi-occupied Europe, had not completely forsaken His people. It may be interesting to consider some other factors involved, the first of which is that the Jews were not quite so outclassed as it seems. Ever since the days of Hashomer, the Jewish self-defense organization, the Jews of Palestine had devoted much of their talent and resources to military affairs. After the fall of Tel Hai, in 1920, they formed the Haganah, to which almost every able-bodied man and woman in the Jewish community belonged.

In the Arab riots of 1929, 1936, and 1938, the British were responsible for keeping order. Not only were the Jews not encouraged to defend themselves; they were forbidden to do so. However, as the situation deteriorated, the Jewish settlement police was formed to help the British troops, and at certain times the British even helped to train the Haganah. One British officer, Orde Wingate, a fiercely pro-Zionist Bible-lover, helped to train the night squads, in which Moshe Dayan and the late Yigal Allon (subsequently

Israeli generals and cabinet ministers) served. During much of the prewar period, the Haganah smuggled in arms and equipment in defiance of the British authorities.

With the outbreak of the Second World War, many Palestinian Jews joined the British army. In 1947, there were considerable numbers of Jewish officers and soldiers who had fought in battles against Arab gangs and had served in the British forces. In addition to the Haganah, there were two smaller forces, made up of different factions of Jabotinsky's Revisionist movement, the Irgun Zvei Leumi (led by Menahem Begin, today Israel's prime minister), and Lehi (also known as the Stern Gang). Every Jewish town and village had cells of the Haganah and, in some cases, of the other groups.

The Jewish forces were highly organized and well led — but the same cannot be said of the Arab armies. There was open rivalry between Egypt and Transjordan, each of which wanted to be the one to conquer Palestine and particularly Jerusalem.

Nevertheless, even when we take into account the sizable numbers of trained Jewish soldiers and the woeful lack of coordination on the part of the Arabs, the Israeli victory in 1948 was a considerable achievement. In cost 6000 lives out of a community of 600,000; almost everyone in the country lost at least one relative or close friend, many far more than that. There are numerous stories of heroism, of small garrisons holding out against overwhelming odds.

At Degania, a kibbutz on the Jordan River, the Syrians launched an infantry attack, supported by eight tanks and ten armored cars. The Jewish defenders were equipped with a few rifles, Sten guns, and "Molotov cocktails." Four of the tanks were put out of action by these bottles filled with kerosene, thrown from distances as short as ten yards, and the Syrians retreated. Similar instances occurred in some forty villages around the country.

The Jews had one very powerful factor going for them, which they called their "secret weapon." It was *ain brera,* which means in Hebrew, "There is no alternative!" The Jews had nowhere to retreat to. They had come out of the Holocaust in Europe; there was no going back. There was, quite simply, no alternative to winning.

The battle for Safed presents us with another example of what happened all over Israel in 1948; the Jews refused to budge. The departing British, evaluating the military balance, advised the Jews to withdraw. They were met with what seemed to them blind obstinacy. Their advice spurned, the departing British soldiers handed over all the best locations to the Arabs. Among the positions occupied by the Syrian, Iraqi, and irregular Palestinian forces were the old Crusader fortress, which dominates Safed, and the impregnable British military position, the Taggart Fort, on a hill outside the town.

Despite their brave resistance, it looked as if the Jews would ultimately be forced to retreat — but then there occurred one of those incidents of which myths are made. In trying to encourage his forces to hold out a bit longer, the local commander is said to have exhorted them over the radio to use their secret weapon, the *alef-bet.* He meant *ain brera:* there was "no alternative" to standing firm. According to the modern legend, the Arabs who intercepted this message thought the letters *alef* and *bet* stood for atomic bomb!

That spring night, there was a terrible thunderstorm of the sort that Galilee produces all too well. At the same time, the Jews were trying out their new weapon, the Davidka, a primitive mortar made of water pipe, the inaccuracy of which was supposed to be compensated for by the fearsome noise it produced. It seems that the intercepted message, the thunderstorm, and the Davidka did the trick. No one can be certain that the Arabs really believed that the primitive Jewish army of 1948 possessed nuclear weapons. What is certain is that the following morning the Jews were astounded to discover that their enemies had abandoned not only the positions they had been attacking, but the Taggart Fort outside town, as well.

*   *   *

The sky was turning pale yellow, casting a luminous glow over the ancient stone buildings, as I limped downhill through lanes and alleys, twisting and turning until I arrived at the familiar high wall of the courtyard of a house in the old town. I knocked loudly on the iron door, and a petite, attractive woman shouted from an upper balcony, "What are you doing so far north?"

It was Rachel, the wife of my friend Mike Leaf. She came down to meet me.

"You've changed your hairstyle," I told her. "It suits you." She smiled shyly and led the way through the yard and up the stairs. Theirs is a crumbling old Safed house, dating back some 400 years. Mike rebuilt it with his own hands and almost broke his back in the process.

Entering the living room, I was brought up sharp by a devastating painting: on a naked battlefield, lit by explosions, a young Israeli soldier slumps forward in agony, his rifle abandoned by his side. His identity disc hangs down in front of a large bandage that covers most of his chest and stomach. A red stain is spreading over the bandage. Many of Mike's paintings in various styles covered the walls, but it was this one, ironically entitled *Your Place Is with Us at the Front*, that dominated the room. I knew that the picture was autobiographical, for Mike was wounded in the Sinai Campaign of 1956.

At the end of the 1948 war, Israel signed armistice agreements with Egypt, Transjordan, and Syria, and the armistice lines became the de facto borders of the new state. Is-

rael now had quite a bit more territory that the UN had assigned to it and was determined to hold on to it on the grounds that it had acted in self-defense. The Arab countries were not about to accept this. They demanded that the Arabs who had fled during the fighting be allowed to return to their homes, and refused to accept the legality (or even the actual existence) of Israel. Transjordan annexed those parts of western Palestine which it controlled and changed its name to Jordan. Egypt occupied a narrow band of territory in the southwest, which came to be known as the Gaza Strip. Numerous attacks were launched into Israel, causing loss of life and damage to property. In 1954, after some years of passivity, Israel started hitting back, raiding into Jordan and Egyptian-controlled territory.

In 1956, President Nasser of Egypt, who had ousted King Farouk in a military coup four years earlier, nationalized the Suez Canal, provoking the ire of its owners, Britain and France. Not long afterward, he closed off the Israeli Red Sea port of Elat.

Acting in concert, Israel invaded Sinai, and Britain and France attacked along the Suez Canal. The Anglo-French operation was something of a fiasco, but the Israelis captured the Sinai peninsula in 100 hours. All three attackers found themselves assailed at the UN, and the United States and the Soviet Union exerted joint pressure on them to withdraw.

Mike had been a member of the paratroop unit that was dropped behind the Egyptian lines in Sinai two full days before the Israeli armor and infantry began their attack. In an assault on an Egyptian machine-gun nest ("I tried to fuck them; but they fucked me!"), Mike received a burst of automatic fire in the stomach. It was before the days of helicopter-borne medical services, and he was lucky to get out of it alive. Many of his paintings have a strong antiwar slant.

Mike's adventures had begun long before that fateful parachute drop. Like many another member of our Zionist youth movement, he joined our pioneer training farm in England, but unlike the rest of us, he had arrived from southern Africa, working his passage on a ship that passed through the Suez Canal (risky in 1951). When he finished his agricultural training, he returned to Africa to say good-by to his parents, and this time he took an even more hazardous route, walking and hitchhiking from Morocco to what was then Southern Rhodesia.

He eventually arrived in Israel on a normal commercial flight. However, he soon made up for this conventional behavior by volunteering for the army's newly formed paratroop unit. He quickly got into trouble, ending his sapper's course by blowing up the camp latrine. He spent some time in a military jail for that one, sentenced by the man who is today Israel's chief of staff.

"They'd been crapping there since the time of the Turks," Mike likes to explain. "Imagine it, man. Everything covered in shit!"

This, then, is Mike Leaf: adventurer, war hero, near-pacifist, and licensed buffoon, with something of the adolescent about him still. Tremendously good-natured, he is entirely unpredictable, and no one, not even Mike, knows when he is going to break out and go on a binge. Rachel, his second wife, was born in Morocco. She possesses a patient nature, ideally complementary to his mercurial character. If she doesn't stick to him, no one will.

"Here he comes," said Rachel, as the key rattled in the metal front door, behind which they sometimes lock themselves in for weeks when Mike is working all-out. He entered, caught sight of me, and shouted; "Get your trousers back on, you fucker, I've got friends with me."

The friends were Aryeh Porat, who had come up from Rosh Pina to his Safed shop, and a bearded American called Tom. Mike himself was, if not exactly clean-shaven, beardless, his long, dissolute face wearing his usual broad grin. (Mike is definitely one of those people who grins rather than smiles.) He looked pale. He was dressed in jeans and a sheepskin vest.

We sipped Rachel's mint tea, and Mike talked enthusiastically about my walk. He himself walked frequently all over Galilee. He had just completed a hike from Safed to his parents' home near Netanya on the coastal plain. He suggested that he would join me over part of the route, and we agreed he should travel down to the southern desert when I arrived there. I would be needing a companion in the empty spaces.

When Aryeh and Tom left, Mike brought out some of his most recent paintings. He was experimenting with classical Japanese style: a great feeling of space, with the focus on one foreground detail. He told me that he was learning Japanese from a university lecturer who lived nearby. He and Rachel planned to spend a year in Japan some time. It was, they said, a compromise. Rachel wanted to go to the United States; Mike wanted to go to "the east." They had finally settled on Japan.

Mike and I had been members of the same kibbutz, and while we ate supper we got into an argument about communal life. Mike had gone right off the idea.

"If Socialism is all washed up, then what's left?" I demanded.

"I prefer a right-wing regime," declared Mike belligerently. "And don't forget you're talking to an ex-Communist."

Cooperative living and equality could not be combined with freedom, he maintained. Freedom — complete freedom to do just as you liked — was the most important thing.

"You know, mate, when I visit the kibbutz, I have nothing to talk about any more. After the first two minutes, I sit there feeling idiotic. I can't talk about the cotton crop of the village or the price of bananas. They've become bourgeois, stodgy, establishment. Maybe there was something there once, but no more!"

Politics were no good. He was delighted by the low turn-out at the recent municipal elections and looked forward to the day when only 5 percent of the country would vote. Only bastards took part in politics, he asserted.

* * *

The following morning, Mike came part of the way with me, guiding me through the ancient network of lanes, with their uneven paving, to the studio of his friend Victor, a genial, bearded sculptor from Russia. Mike and his comrades scorn to live in the official Safed artists' colony, with its tourist-infested studios and galleries, preferring their own very individual neighborhood in the old town above the cemetery.

As I hobbled downhill, taking the dirt track to the right of the new municipal hospital I was stiff and footsore from the previous day's walk, but the pain wore off during the day. The hospital, a gleaming modern building, has brought modern medicine to Upper Galilee — a long way from the pharmacist in David Shuv's time. The track took me downhill through another pine forest, until, rounding a bend, I saw the Sea of Galilee — rich blue, flecked with golden sunlight, cupped in hazy purple mountains. I stopped to enjoy it for a moment, taking a drink from my water bottle. I was aiming for Akbara, an Arab village off the beaten track, on the way to my former kibbutz. From there, Mike said, I should ask the way. A number of Arab women with shopping baskets walked by, and before very long I was among the rudimentary buildings and corrugated-iron huts of the village. With the sewage flowing in the streets (if they could be called streets), Akbara was an eyesore, a festering boil. The village had no electricity or water mains.

Mention has been made of the Arabs who fled across the borders in 1948 and became refugees. The villagers of Akbara represent another, far less common, phenomenon: that of Israel's *internal* Arab refugees. Most of the refugees live in camps in Jordan, Syria, Lebanon, and the Gaza Strip, but a number of Arab villagers were evacuated during the fighting of 1947–1948 and settled in different locations inside Israel. In some cases — the most famous being the Maronite Christian villages of Ikrit and Birim on the Lebanese border — the villagers have demanded the right to return to their original homes, so far without success.

The Akbara villagers had lived in Kaddita, on the other side of Safed. They claim that their relations with the Jews of Safed were always good and that they were promised to be allowed to return after the war was over. Today, Akbara stands as a living reproach to Israeli society. Unlike the other Arab villagers in Israel, the people of Akbara have not shared in the country's prosperity. Mike, who knows the village well, says the villagers are quite well off. They have made money from a transportation business and from working in Safed and the surrounding area. Their living expenses and their living standards are low. They have made no effort to develop Akbara, whose original inhabitants fled to Syria, and they are bitter about not being allowed to return to Kaddita. They have received no help from the government, which has still not made up its mind what to do about them. The lack of help and the poor living conditions have led to more bitterness, and some of the young men of the village have been imprisoned for belonging to terrorist organizations. Mike told me that he would join a terrorist group if he were an Akbara villager.

Whatever their general attitude to the state, I found the

locals extremely friendly to a Hebrew-speaking stranger. Hussein, a handsome lad of about sixteen wearing a clean white shirt, directed me in flawless Hebrew to climb the cattle track on the hill opposite; he walked with me part of the way in order to point it out. Down in the valley, I found myself unable to make out the track, so I secured the help of Ibrahim, who was tending a flock of sheep. He could not have been more than eleven years old.

The weather had improved considerably and the few clouds still in the sky were white. But the sun was rather hot for November, and my climb up the hill was the toughest so far. My thighs and calves were screaming; my feet sore as hell. The barely defined cattle track wound up the almost perpendicular slope, the scuffed red soil among the gray rocks the only indication of a path. I forced one leg in front of the other, taking an occasional sip of water, but not stopping until I had reached the top. If the bloody cows could do it, so could I!

At the summit, my back to an electricity pylon, I enjoyed the rest and the view. On the right, the wooded slopes rose toward Safed; below me, the huts and hovels of Akbara blended with the scenery, picturesque from this distance. Beyond Akbara were the rolling Galilee hills, and on my left the slopes swept down to the blue Sea of Galilee far below. The voice of the Akbara muezzin, considerably amplified (possibly recorded), echoed across the valley, calling the faithful to prayer.

I rose and started to walk over the burned yellow scrub, following the line of pylons, as I had been told. The yellow grass was interspersed with gray-blue thorns and purple thistles. With a breeze in my face and the surface of the lake glinting in the sun, I felt as if I were walking across the roof of the world.

Whether it was the satisfaction of the climb, the improvement in the weather, the beauty of the scene, or a lingering ebullience from my time with Mike, I do not know; but suddenly I was singing "The Sound of Music," the words of which I hardly know. Despite the weight of my pack, I skipped and danced, reaching my crescendo — "De-dum-de-de-dum of a thousand years" — when I found myself face to face with a stolid employee of the Israel Electric Corporation, part of a team that was stringing wire between the pylons. A truck with his workmates stood nearby.

"Just . . . er, out for a walk," I said, rather desperately. He was poker-faced, with a brick-red complexion, mustache, blue linen cap.

"Very healthy." The tone was dry.

"Yes, I love walking," I babbled on. "What are you men doing?"

"You can see." He pointed to the wire. "Building the country." The implication was obvious: not like some he could mention.

I stumbled along for another mile, my feet very sore, and then the track started to descend. It was with some relief that I spotted the concrete water reservoir of the kibbutz and realized that my day's walk was almost over.

One more obstacle: the kibbutz Brahmin beef herd. Brahmins are supposed to be docile, but I negotiated the field swiftly, my sore feet forgotten, and climbed over the gate into the orchard. *My* orchard. Here I had watered and weeded, pruned, planted, and picked so many years ago. Feeling wonderfully relaxed, I walked through the trees to my kibbutz.

7

I HAD NOT ALWAYS felt so relaxed at Amiad, a prosperous commune situated halfway between the towns of Safed and Tiberias. In fact, it was here that I had spent one of the most tension-racked years of my life.

The kibbutz (plural, kibbutzim) is at once the creation of and the personification of the second aliya. It owes its existence not to a doctrine but to a situation, for, since the very first days, ideology took second place to work. It was simply (as one of the pioneer generation once told me) the best way to organize poverty.

Let us return briefly to Degania, the village that in 1948 fought off the Syrian army with Sten guns and kerosene bottles. In 1909, a group of Jewish pioneers settled on the banks of the Jordan just south of the Sea of Galilee, establishing a commune in which all property was collectively owned, work was collectively organized, and living arrangements were communal. There was no money in the community; no hired labor was employed; no member could engage in trade. Produce was marketed by the group as a whole, which also made all purchases.

In the stifling heat of the Jordan Valley, the ten men and two women groped their way toward a new form of life. They had no blueprint, just a few principles, and they resolved each problem as it emerged. The basis of the settlement was equality: from each according to his means; to each according to his needs.

More communes were established, their members inspired by the ideals of Socialism, which they brought with them from Russia, or by ideas of social justice expounded by the Biblical Prophets, or by yet other principles. In the words of the philosopher Martin Buber:

> There were various dreams about the future: people saw before them a new, more comprehensive form of the family; they saw themselves as the advance-guard of the workers' movement, the direct instrument for the realization of Socialism, the prototype of the new society; they had as their goal the creation of a new man and a new world. But none of this ever hardened into a cut-and-dried program.

From the modest beginnings by the Jordan, there developed a network of more than 200 kibbutzim, flourishing agricultural settlements, which today also maintain some of Israel's most sophisticated industries.

I have already mentioned Habonim, our Zionist youth movement in England. We saw the kibbutz way of life as our highest ideal. Growing up as we did in the cynical years after World War II and the massacre of Europe's Jews, our ideas did not fly as high as those of the founders of the first communes; but we did see the kibbutz as an instrument for building the new State of Israel, for practicing a form of Socialism, and for living on terms of equality and respect with our fellow men. Not for us the armchair Zionism of those who merely gave money to Israel, nor the armchair Socialism of the theorist. We determined to be genuine sons of the soil — productive and practical as well as idealistic.

On my first visit to Israel, in 1954, I had indeed found flaws in our Garden of Eden. I have mentioned that the kibbutzim, responding to the needs of the hour, gave work to thousands of new immigrants, mostly from the oriental countries. I saw this as exploitation, my feelings further injured by the fact that the hired hands were oriental Jews. There were other faults relating to the difference that always exists between theory and practice, but my basic faith in the kibbutz way of life was not challenged. Not so my wife, Angela. She was critical of the way that young children were brought up on the kibbutz, of the childrens' houses, where the kibbutz offspring lived with their peer groups from birth. She felt that the young children should sleep at home and spend more time with their parents than the two hours' visiting-time each day. She sensed a dissatisfaction on the part of many women kibbutz members, which she believed came from a frustrated desire to look after their own children.

I did not really understand her feelings until our first child was born in England and I recognized the importance of our relationship with him. As a result of all this, we arrived at the kibbutz with our two-year-old Etan (the son who is now in the army) and built-in doubts about one of the central principles of kibbutz life.

With the instinct of a two-year-old accustomed to having his own way, Etan waged a guerrilla war on our nerves. He would cry when we left him at night; he started having nightmares; and he took to running away from the nursery to our room in the middle of the night. He developed a phobia about the donkey at the children's farm, saying it wanted to eat him. Once he told me that a horse had eaten his mother. He laughed at that one.

Was the boy conning us? I do not know. I do know that Angela and I never ate together in the communal dining hall because one of us always had to sit with him until he was asleep. A concert, movie, or evening with friends was always interrupted by the need for constant visits to the nursery. We used to brood over the problem during the long, hard hours of our working day.

We were not, of course, the only parents with problems,

but the others for the most part took their children's problems casually, and this made us feel worse. We passed through torturing periods of self-doubt: Were we neurotic? Was our child becoming abnormal because of us? To try to find the answers to these questions, we paid a visit to a child psychologist at a neighboring kibbutz. It was a well-established village, some four decades old, and I remember feeling that every building, every tree, every flower of the utopian community, was a reproach to our doubts.

The wise, white-haired psychologist listened to us carefully. When we had finished, she told us that, though she was no longer sure about Socialism, the kibbutz had proved to be the best instrument for achieving Zionism. Zionism meant creating a home in the land, and this, in turn, meant stability, which was fundamentally the most important thing for a child. With regard to our specific problem, her suggestion was to take Etan home to sleep in our room until further notice.

Shortly afterward we went for a vacation by the sea, taking our son with us. He seemed to become normal again. His proximity to us created a healthier atmosphere for us all. We came to the conclusion that the psychologist was right: we should take him home to sleep, but for good. We would leave the kibbutz.

It is difficult for me to remember, today, eighteen years later, just how agonizing a decision that was. I quote an extract from a diary that I kept at the time:

> Don't they realize how absolutely impossible they have made it? God in heaven, I am committed absolutely. There will never be anything like this again for me. Why did they have to make it so impossible?

It sounds somewhat hysterical, but I think it expresses accurately the nature of our commitment. The kibbutz way of life was supposed to be the fulfillment of all our dreams.

Etan provided an ironical footnote some years later, when he was eleven. He had greatly enjoyed a visit to the kibbutz and wanted to know why we had left. When we told him, he was scathing: "What idiots you were! I would have got used to it!"

*   *   *

Walking through the orchards after my hike from Safed, I recalled the days when I used to work there. Now, in early winter, the trees were bare of fruit, but the foliage was still thick. Soon the leaves would fall and the time for pruning would come. We used to prune the trees, the branches forming a delicate, pink tracery against the blue sky. Bundled up against the cold wind, we would snip our way down the rows, thinning out the centers of the trees to allow the branches to spread out. It was uncomfortable work: one hand frozen, one on fire, the neck developing a crick. But we gossiped as we worked, and every now and then we would break for a sit-down and a snack of oranges.

Blossom time, with the pink and white flowers bursting forth, was the signal to prepare the irrigation pipes, for the apples, pears, peaches, and plums would not grow without constant watering during the long, dry summer months. Today they use light plastic pipes, but in the early sixties we used to drag heavy metal pipes between the trees and set them up in the different rows. It was exhausting work and I was hard put to it to keep up with my friend Basil, who, though thin as a rake, possessed limitless stamina after years in the job. But work was the key to acceptance in the kibbutz, and I strove to match him, back bent, my breath coming in gasps and grunts.

We rose early in order to get the balance of the work done before the heat of the day, and breakfast would come as a welcome relief in what was, for us, midmorning. We usually finished by midday, took an afternoon siesta, and returned in the early evening to switch off the water. Often we would hitch up a trailer and take the whole family to turn off the irrigation. They always enjoyed the trip, more so later in the summer when the fruit began to appear on the trees.

We wore sneakers at work because our feet were always wet. I used to leave mine on the porch overnight and, in the morning, I was always careful to give them a kick before putting them on, in order to dislodge the mouse that made its home in my left shoe. The left sneaker was always well heated by the mouse, and, as a result, my left foot would remain warm all morning, in marked contrast to the cold clamminess of my right foot. I always used to hope that the mouse would find a mate who would take up residence in the right sneaker.

At breakfast, or during other breaks in the work, we would discuss everything under the sun. Often we would talk about the kibbutz and its problems, although I tended to shy away from talking about family life, where my personal involvement was too acute. On other topics I would take the offensive, for example over the question of the hired hands from nearby Hatzor. What sort of Socialist society was it, I demanded, that exploited workers like any capitalist business? Stolid Dutch Elhanan, our foreman, saw nothing wrong in it. The business of the kibbutz, as he saw it, was to make money for its members. Provided the workers received a fair wage, where was the exploitation. The kibbutz members had labored hard and long to build up their farm. They and not the Hatzor workers had invested the money in planting and nurturing the orchard.

I have already noted the problem from the other point of view, when discussing Kiryat Shmona. I mentioned how, from the time of the mass immigration of the early 1950s, the kibbutzim gave work to the newcomers and the latter often resented what seemed to them the superior attitude of the kibbutz veterans. The decision to take on the hired hands was not made easily. Israel's prime minister at the time, David Ben-Gurion, had no doubts in the matter. The main task of the kibbutz movement, he said, was to build the nation. Any other consideration was secondary. But the kibbutz movement had come a long way from its pragmatic origins. If it had started almost without an ideology, it had developed one along the way. There were three distinct kibbutz federations, one of which was openly "Marxist." The question of hired labor gave rise to agonizing discussions throughout the movement; although the majority came down on the Zionist side of the fence, there were many who rated their Socialist ethic as of equal value.

Today, almost two decades after the time about which I am writing, the kibbutz movement is still trying to eliminate the use of outside workers. Few hired hands are employed in the agricultural branches now; the problem is focused on the growing industrial sector of the kibbutz. One solution is to make the hired hands partners in the enterprises in which they work; another is to transfer ownership of these factories from the kibbutz to a regional authority. Certainly today the kibbutzim do not provide the only sources of employment in the countryside. As we saw in Kiryat Shmona, there are local enterprises in the towns, though numbers of townspeople still work in the local kibbutzim, such as at the Ayelet Hashahar hotel.

But to return to our work-break discussions of eighteen years ago. I was confronted with a simple question: Had I the right to condemn hundreds of people to unemployment to salve my Socialist conscience? There could only be one answer.

Another topic concerned the use of pesticides. During the months that I was busy with irrigation, my friend Geoff would, night after night, wrap himself in a rubber suit and mask and spray the trees with the strongest of poisons. I would accuse him of destroying the balance of nature; he would reply that I could not judge Israel by the standards of England. In a Mediterranean climate, the pests multiplied by the hour. I would lament over the corpse of a finchlike *nahlielli,* its vivid blue and yellow feathers beautiful even in death. Geoff would counter with the imperative of defending his produce against the voracious little bird.

These arguments would help the days to pass, but they were only interludes. Ultimately, I had to face the problem of physical labor, a problem for which my Socialist-Zionist ideology had ill prepared me. Physical work was boring. True, there were times when my mind was full of great thoughts, for work can be a stimulus to thought; but most of the time I found that my mind was a blank, as I carried out some monotonous, repetitive task. There were times when I felt like screaming from boredom.

Physically, I found I went through several distinct changes. At the outset there was a feeling of well-being and exhilaration from working in the open air. This was followed by weeks of utter exhaustion, when I could not stay awake over a book, watching a film, or even during a conversation. I eventually emerged from this tunnel of tiredness feeling fit and well. I was proud of my ability to work, aware of my bodily fitness. I felt that I had proved myself.

Harvesting was a more social activity. Apart from the hired hands there were groups of volunteers, both from Israel and abroad: naïve young Americans who sang Hebrew songs and constantly took problems to their rabbi; cynical young Israelis who sang:

> *Haavoda hi kol hayeinu,*
> *Aval lo bishvileinu.*
> *(Work is all our life,*
> *But not for us!)*

For them Tzionut (Zionism) was a joke, but underneath it all they were groping for a sense of purpose. Many of them would find it in the army, volunteering for the paratroops and other special units. Meanwhile, we picked fruit together, eating enormous quantities. Plums and peaches were, of course, popular; but it is the taste of a fresh apple, straight off the tree, with the morning dew still on it, that lingers.

I came out of the orchard and strolled along the shady paths of the kibbutz, between the lawns and flower beds, soon encountering Geoff, whose current job at Amiad is that of landscape gardener. He was tinkering with a small tractor-lawnmower, but he was happy enough to break off and make ribald comments about my appearance. Though I had let him know beforehand about my walking plans, either he had not believed me, or he hadn't fully understood, because my rucksack and water bottle provoked his mirth.

At Geoff's suggestion, I left my equipment in his room, having first ascertained that his dog (a cross between a collie and a German shepherd) was tied up outside. Like his master, Tim is basically good-natured but inclined to be unpredictable. While we ate our lunch in the comfortable, spacious dining hall, I had a momentary flashback, not to the time when I had lived there, but farther back, to 1954, the time of my first visit. I saw a younger, bearded Geoff washing the dust off himself before coming in to eat in the wooden hut that served as a dining room in those days.

"You know," remarked Geoff, a stocky, humorous Cockney with glasses and a graying goatee, "if you're going to write about Amiad, you must realize that kibbutz life has changed a great deal since your day."

I knew that it had. For one thing, the children now slept at home with their parents, at Amiad and many other kibbutzim. Interestingly, it was the second generation, themselves raised communally, who insisted on this innovation. The new system may have solved our problem; but the old way had suited Geoff and his wife, Celia. Geoff had been more concerned about the social tensions that are inevitable in so small a community, the problems that overflowed from work into social life.

"The days when you dreaded meeting somebody with whom you had had a fearful row, the days when your stomach seemed to have tied itself in knots with tension — those days are over for good," he told me. The kibbutz now possessed the social machinery for defusing tension, often preventing it from developing in the first place. Committees and tasks were now structured in such a way as to obviate many of the blow-ups that had occurred so frequently in the past. Many of those with central tasks in the kibbutz had studied the behavioral sciences; in extreme cases, group therapy and psychological counseling were available.

"If you asked me to sum it up in a sentence," said Geoff, "I would say that ideology has been replaced by public relations."

He went on to tell me about the absorption committee, of which he was chairman. Amiad had succeeded in attracting several families over the past few years and, with a membership of 160, it was now on a demonstrable growth curve.*

In my day, Amiad had been through a difficult period, losing large numbers of its members. For some years it stuck at around 90 members. The takeoff point for a kibbutz

* In this, Amiad is typical of the kibbutz movement as a whole. In the 1920s and for three decades after, the kibbutz way of life set the tone for the whole country. Its unique position of power and influence, illustrated by the remarkable high proportion of kibbutz members at all levels of civilian and military leadership, was steadily eroded after the mass immigration of the 1950s. Today, the kibbutz is making something of a comeback on the general wave of rural prosperity, as town-dwellers search for pleasant environments.

seems to be a membership of around 120. Today, with 160, Amiad has a total population of some 400; that includes children, parents of members, and volunteers.

Economically, Amiad was always a success. The founding group were trained farmers, and they knew their way around. They not only knew how to work effectively; they knew which doors to push, where to find loans, how to extend credit. They first made money from tomatoes and bananas, which they grew on land some ten miles away, down by the Sea of Galilee. They were among the first in Israel to grow apples on a large scale, and they again led the field with their Brahmin beef herd. But their greatest success came almost by chance.

Kohner, one of the original group, who had come to the country as an infant from Germany, turned out to possess a remarkable talent for invention. Lacking formal education, he nevertheless has a mind of great ingenuity, and the kibbutz has backed him to the hilt. His first effort was modest enough: a fruit-picking trolley in the form of an elevated wheelbarrow, which the kibbutz patented and sold. It almost doubled the daily norm for fruit-picking. His next invention was plastic wheels for irrigation pipes, which, particularly when combined with the light plastic pipes developed at another kibbutz, have revolutionized irrigation in Israel and many other countries.

But the indefatigable Kohner was only beginning. He then got to work on a system of filtration that has saved countless man-hours of work. Water is rarely pure, and when I worked at Amiad, much of our time in irrigation was spent in unblocking water-sprinklers. This is now a thing of the past. Amiad filters can be found in the United States, Europe, Australia, Hong Kong, Korea, Taiwan, and a number of Arab countries (which, of course, purchase them through a third party). Kohner's latest accomplishment is a device for fertilizing crops via the irrigation system, by-passing sprays and other methods of distribution. All these systems are manufactured in the kibbutz factory, which has become a big business, with exports alone totaling over half a million dollars a year.

I asked Geoff how this expansion had affected the problem of hired labor. Hadn't the kibbutz been forced to take on many more workers? Strangely, the reverse had been true. Many former hired hands had now become independent subcontractors, setting up workshops back in Hatzor to produce parts for the new equipment. The factory also gave employment to parents and older kibbutz members, who were finding it increasingly difficult to work in agriculture.

Sitting there with Geoff in the dining hall, certainly as pleasant and well appointed as the best type of restaurant, I found myself considering its changed role in kibbutz life. In the earliest days, members would not drink so much as a glass of tea in their own rooms, whereas today many families regularly take entire meals in their homes. The dining hall is still important. Many regard it as the last bastion of communal living; others see it as the curse of kibbutz life — the ultimate in lack of privacy. One kibbutz member once told me that in his view all kibbutz dining halls should be burned to the ground.

The days when the dining hall also played the Good Samaritan role, when any weary traveler could draw up a bench and take potluck, are also long past. If you have a friend at the kibbutz, you can wangle a free meal, but unauthorized visitors are likely to be shown the door — if they are noticed.

When I was a member, an old couple turned up at Amiad one day in the summer. He was bald and short-sighted, with rimless glasses and a neatly trimmed white mustache. He was dressed in a light cotton shirt; his trousers (in the fashion of old men) came almost to his armpits.

She was an elegant old lady, gray-haired, with a smile of
great sweetness, wearing a floral dress. Before long they
were part of the permanent kibbutz scene, eating in the
dining hall, relaxing on the lawns, walking hand in hand
along the paths.

They had been in Amiad about a week when the kibbutz
secretary approached me and asked if I knew who they
were. Why on earth me? I was indignant. He was apolo-
getic. Because my family and I were the newest members,
he had assumed that they belonged to us. I thought for a
moment: Who had arranged for their room? They must be
sleeping somewhere. Well, it seemed that Mosh had got
talking to them on the bus, and Haim had struck up a conversation with them in the kibbutz. Each of them had assumed that they were friends of the other. Haim, a member
of the accommodations committee, had assigned them a
room.

For two days we all wondered what to do about them,
until the problem was solved as naturally as it had arisen.
Another visitor arrived at the kibbutz: Geoff's mother, from
London. The "mystery couple" ran into her in the dining
hall, to their visible embarrassment and her fiendish delight. The next day they were gone.

Geoff's mother, black eyes glinting like currants in her
leathery brown face, held court at tea on the lawn.

" 'Course I know them." She smirked. "Lily Goldman
and Fred Marcus."

"I don't understand," said Geoff's wife, Celia. "Is she a
widow or something?"

"I should be such a widow." The old girl laughed.
"They're both married — but not of course to each other!"

*   *   *

Conveniently, I had arrived at the kibbutz on Friday,
which would give me the Sabbath to rest up, after the first

stage of my walk. As usual, Friday night supper was celebrated in that very secular community with a special meal,
served on white tablecloths: wine, blessings, and Sabbath
songs. Geoff's youngest son went on ahead to make sure
that nobody grabbed the family's traditional place or
filched the pickles. On my way in, I was held up talking to
old friends, but I eventually arrived at my place and was
able to enjoy the traditional chicken soup and chicken.

After the meal, Geoff and Celia invited some of the kibbutz veterans to their room, and it didn't prove too difficult
to persuade them to talk about the old days.

Vodak, balding and barrel-chested, has always held an
important position in the community. After many years as
farm-manager and treasurer, he is currently managing the
factory. His gentle, dark-haired wife, Rochele, was the most
sympathetic of the childrens' care staff whom we remembered from our time. Dandy is taller than Vodak, with
graying hair and mustache. Outgoing and an extrovert,
with his own special brand of deadpan humor, he is the
military commander of Amiad. His wife (also, confusingly,
named Rochele) is lively and talkative.

Early in 1946, their group had been sent to a site called
Jeb Yussuf, more or less as a punishment. They were a unit
of the Palmach, the elite corps of the Haganah. (The members of the Palmach were drawn largely from the kibbutzim and their youth movements.) One of their comrades
had broken silence on a night maneuver and was ordered
home. Since it would have meant his passing alone through
hostile, Arab-controlled territory, the group protested
the decision, but the order was confirmed. At this, they
rebelled and said they were all going home with the
defaulter.

The leadership of the Palmach was determined to teach
them a lesson. The Jeb Yussuf site was important because
of its position on the Tiberias-Safed road, but it possessed
no earth or water. Huge quantities of stones had to be

cleared from the area of the old *khan* (inn), and water would have to be trucked in. A tough place to establish a kibbutz, and just the job for those cocky youngsters.

The two men described the hours of backbreaking toil. They had a mule and the occasional use of a tractor, but most of the stone-clearing had been done by hand. The women, added Rochele D., had also cleared stones at first, but later they found that they were of more use to the group if they worked on jobs outside the settlement.

"We were better paid than the boys," she recalled. "In fact, we really supported the kibbutz in the early days."

"The most annoying part of it," added Vodak wryly, "is that the work was useless." The area they cleared has remained empty to this day.

Amiad grows its crops in three locations: down by the Sea of Galilee, where the bananas are grown; a few miles to the south of the village, where the orchards are; and in the Hula Valley to the north, where they have citrus groves. The beef cattle graze on the surrounding hills, sometimes going north in the summer. The beautiful kibbutz gardens are grown in soil that has been trucked in.

"In those days," explained Vodak, "Jewish National Fund officials believed that crops could be grown anywhere if only the stones were cleared, but here at Amiad there were simply more stones underneath."

Now it was Dandy's turn to contribute, with stories about their fights with local Arabs and with the British mandatory authorities. There had been no village at Jeb Yussuf, but there had been tribes of Bedouin camped nearby. The Jewish National Fund had bought the land for Amiad from landowners in Safed. The town Arabs had taken the money, but then stirred up the local Bedouin against the young settlers. There were numerous clashes, but always with sticks, stones, and bare fists; never with firearms.

"We always used to win, even though we were outnumbered," recalled Dandy. "It wasn't that we were tougher or braver than they; we were organized. When they attacked, they seemed to be incapable of cooperation. We used to take on the groups of attackers one at a time and beat the hell out of them!"

The story could be taken as a parable of the Jewish-Arab struggle. In the War of Independence, the Jews were able first to win the battle for Galilee, then partly to win the battle for the center and Jerusalem, and in the last stage to conquer the Negev. In the Six Day War, the first two days were devoted to Egypt, the next two to Jordan, and the last couple of days to taking the Golan Heights from Syria. Even in the Yom Kippur War, that relative triumph of Arab coordination, Israel (after its initial setbacks) held the line in the south and dealt first with Syria, before turning to its counterattack on Egypt. Jordan did not enter that war directly at all, although it might have posed some nasty problems for Israel had it done so. Thus, in every conflict Israel "took on the groups of attackers one at a time and beat the hell out of them," simply because the Israelis were better organized.

Once a squad of British soldiers had come to confiscate their weapons, but the kibbutzniks had buried them outside the living compound. Near their huts, they had buried all kinds of scrap metal. The British arrived with their mine detectors and spent two days digging up the scrap.

"Then they brought the dogs in." Dandy laughed. "We hadn't managed to bury all the weapons properly, so we shoved some into the onion patch. It seemed to work, because, though the dogs were suspicious, they didn't discover the arms."

Later, when the fighting between the Jews and the Arabs developed in earnest, some kibbutz members stole a tanker-truck from the British army to bring in the water. As long as the mandate was in force, the tanker, with its British markings, had remained immune from Arab attack.

The real war began when the British pulled out, but the fighting had been to the north and east of Jeb Yussuf. The men were mobilized to the front, and the women kept the farm going by themselves.

After the war, the group found itself on an arid site with no water, no soil, a small vegetable patch, chickens, and a few odd cows and goats. Looking to the future, they concluded that they would have to leave Jeb Yussuf; there was no possibility of building a permanent village there.

"We didn't want to seem negative," said Vodak, "so we said we would stay on three conditions — conditions that we were sure could not be met. We demanded running water, land down by the lake, and a tractor. To our utter amazement, we got all three!"

The water had come from the spring at Akbara, and the refugee villagers had actually helped them to lay the line. Dandy was able to confirm what I had learned about Akbara, but he strongly opposed the idea that they should be allowed to return to their original village.

"Arabs used to live in a lot of places and so did Jews," he said. "We can't start changing everything around again. Where would it all end?"

* * *

I spent Saturday morning relaxing on the lawn outside my friends' kibbutz home. The weather was fine and a few hours in the sun did wonders for body and mind. My pessimism about the weather was banished, and I began to think about the next stage of my journey. My original idea had been to walk down to the Sea of Galilee via Moshav Almagor, where an army friend lived, but now I thought of varying my trip with a horse ride down to the lake from the nearby Vered Hagalil (Rose of Galilee) ranch. So that afternoon I went over to the ranch to make the arrangements, and, at the same time, to visit the moshav.

Although there are a considerable number of private

farms in Israel, in the old villages like Metulla and Rosh Pina and those in the citrus belt on the coastal plain, most of Israeli agriculture is communal or cooperative. The first moshav was founded at Nahalal in the Jezreel Valley, in 1921, by a group who left the first kibbutz, Degania, because they found the communal life stifling. Not enough scope was given for private enterprise, in their view.

The moshav (plural, moshavim) is a cooperative smallholders' village, where each member has his own tract of land. Some land is also held in common, and there is central planning and marketing; but the moshav way of life is essentially an individualistic one. Neighbors may share a tractor or a pesticide spray, but usually the arrangement does not last for long. In a good number of moshavim, the husband takes a job in town, leaving his wife to work the farm with hired hands — often Arabs from Israel or the West Bank. Some moshavim, those near the large towns, have become garden-suburbs.

Almagor is a genuine moshav, with all the members working their own land, albeit with help from local Bedouin and neighboring Arab villagers. But undoubtedly the cooperation falls short of the ideal. In theory, there is a system of mutual help for emergencies, as when the husband is sick or in the army. However, when we served together during our periods of reserve duty, my friend was always telling me that this or that crop was going to waste in his absence. His wife, who had three young children to care for, could not do much on the farm. In the period after the Yom Kippur War, we were mobilized for prolonged periods. It was irksome for all of us, but especially damaging to the small-business men, including the moshav members. Despite this, my friend was strongly opposed to the Sinai disengagement accords, which separated the forces of Israel and Egypt. The agreement, negotiated in the famous Kissinger "shuttle," cut our annual periods of army service from over three months down to one; but my friend, a fervent supporter of the right-wing Herut Party (which now heads the government, but was then in opposition) denounced it as a sellout.

When I had first visited the site on a trip from Amiad in 1961, Almagor had been at the drawing-board stage. Huge boulders of basalt were already being cleared from the area, and we were covered in the fine red dust thrown up by the bulldozers. We traveled with an armed escort, because the area was under the constant threat of Syrian guns on the Golan Heights. Now, as I approached the prosperous village, with its lawns and trees, the contrast to that time was impressive. I found out where my friend's house was, learning at the same time that his wife had just given birth to a baby daughter. I knocked on the door and my friend, opening it, blinked in surprise. Although we had served together, we had not seen each other for a number of years, having both been transferred to different units.

"*Mazal tov,* Tooli," I said, shaking hands. "How's the new daughter?"

Tooli Perl is the biggest man I know. Only six feet two in height, he is built like a tank. In the army, he would amuse us by using his hand as a bat when he played table tennis. Many were the vigorous political arguments we had, the two of us becoming purple in the face with anger. He could easily have picked me up with one hand and hurled me across the room, but never for a moment did I have reason to suspect that he would, even when I swore at him.

He introduced me to his wife (who came in a more conventional size), and she at once offered me a cup of coffee.

"I'll make the fire, Tooli," I said, "if you'll brew the coffee." We both laughed, and he slapped me playfully on the shoulder, almost dislocating it. When we had patrolled together in the Gaza Strip, it had always been my job to kindle the fire.

My first meeting with Tooli had been at the Allenby
Bridge, across the Jordan River, in the Yom Kippur War.
We had been mobilized as soon as the Arabs attacked, but
we had been kept waiting at our base near Jerusalem all
day. "To see whether we would be needed," we told ourselves and each other, with that ludicrous overconfidence
that affected us all at the time. At nightfall we were sent
down to take up positions along the Jordan, and a few of us
found ourselves under Tooli's command, manning an outpost on the bridge over the river. The first few nights were
tense: it was not clear at that stage of the war whether the
Jordanians would join in the attack. In the event, Jordan
sent help to Syria, but didn't open up on its own account.
Lucky for us: we were in front of the front line.

During those days, Tooli's confidence and calm were invaluable. A couple of the more nervous types were replaced; the rest of us used to make jokes to cover up our
nervousness. I reminded my companions of the tank that
had been preserved at Degania, to commemorate the heroic
stand at the kibbutz in 1948. I said that we would have the
same for us. There would be a plaque, reading: *From here,
Tooli Perl, Shimon Ravid, Daniel Gavron (pause) . . . fled in October 1973.*

On another occasion, while talking to base on the field
telephone, we demanded additional supplies. What was
missing? "Running spikes" was our facetious reply.

It was during that first week that I held direct talks with
Jordan. I was on late-afternoon watch, trying to remain
alert as the insects hummed in the thick vegetation and the
sluggish brown stream flowed past. The dusty wooden
bridge was deserted, and there didn't seem to be a war on.
Suddenly, a Jordanian major (I could make out his insignia
through my binoculars) appeared on the far bank, leading
a party of soldiers toward the bridge.

After inspecting him through the glasses for some time, I

decided to try a friendly wave. His reply was swift and suc-
cint: a universally understood handsign meaning, "Screw
you!" I shook my head vigorously and stretched out my
hand in a conciliatory gesture, palm upward. He nodded
deliberately and repeated his sign. I tried a shrug, two
hands stretched forth in supplicaton — even a kiss. It was
to no avail; whatever I did elicited the same obscene gesture
from the major.

*   *   *

Tooli's wife gave us iced coffee, with large dollops of ice
cream in it, and we talked, bringing each other up to date. I
congratulated him on the victory of the Likud in the general elections the previous year. I told him that his attitude
had been an illustration of the strength of the ousted Labor
Party in its hold on the country. I reminded him that in
1973 he had told me that he was voting for the Likud only
to strengthen the hand of Golda Meir, at that time prime
minister, in her struggle against her own party's "doves."
He hadn't really believed that his own people would get
in, but now there had been a revolution. He must be
delighted.

"I couldn't even celebrate properly," he grumbled.
"They're all Labor Party at the village." He went on to tell
me that, like many Likud supporters, he was doubtful
about the peace policies of his government, wondering
aloud whether they were not giving away too much.

His farm, he told me, was doing well. Apart from his
peppers and tomatoes, his long-term investment in avocados was due to start paying off. He had experienced a
nasty moment during the summer, when a field fire had almost reached his trees, but it had been stopped just in time.

Fires are the the scourge of Upper Galilee, as I remembered from my own time. One afternoon I had been awakened from a deep sleep to fight a fire near where Almagor

now stood. We had used wooden-handled rubber paddles to beat out the flames, because the fire engines could not reach the blaze. All afternoon we had fought the fire across the thorns and basalt rocks. Afterward, I had spent an hour picking the thorns out of my sandaled feet, which taught me to wear long trousers and boots for subsequent fires.

*   *   *

Back in the kibbutz, I watched a group of my friends practicing an East European Hasidic folk dance for a wedding the following week. If they enjoyed the performance as much as the rehearsal, it must have been a happy occasion.

8

I SET OUT LATE from Amiad and arrived at Vered Hagalil in time for an early lunch. The smell of horse manure contributes to the pleasant ambience of the ranch house, which is situated behind an irrigated paddock of bright green grass that contrasts with the autumn scrub. I sat down in the restaurant, furnished with rough pine, and was at once brought a carafe of cold water, pickles, and hot *pitta* (flat Arab bread.)

"What do you have to drink?" I asked.

"The water is good," came the unexpected reply. I ordered an Israeli beer (none of the usual nonsense about only foreign brands being available) and reflected that this was one of the most agreeable eating places in the country. Originally an American, Yehuda Avni left his moshav in the south to found Vered Hagalil in 1965. He offers good food and comfortable, though not luxurious, accommodations, but his special thing is horses. Horse-lovers come from abroad and all over Israel to take rides in Galilee: westward to the Mediterranean, north along the Jordan to Mount Hermon, or simply down to the Sea of Galilee.

Lunch was indeed good: ice-cold borscht, tangy and served with sour cream, was followed by an excellent steak and as many cups of strong black coffee as I wanted.

"My God, that's my cousin Shirley!" I exclaimed, pointing at a drawing of a horse above the bar. "I mean, Shirley *drew* the horse," I amended, noticing Yehuda's startled face.

"Oh, Shirley comes here often," remarked Avni. She would. Shirley is a fanatic about horses. Older and stronger than I (still), she used to force me to play "horses" when we were kids back in England. Many were the hours boringly spent "cropping" the grass with our fingers or neighing idiotically. Shirley would certainly have been amused to see me sitting astride the fine brown mare provided by Yehuda Avni.

Leading us off was Melody, a good-looking, athletic American blonde, whose smile revealed a set of teeth that looked as if they could bite right through my wrist, if I had it in mind to try any funny business. Also along for the ride were the teen-age daughter of an American journalist (braces on her teeth and a seat on horseback like a cavalry officer), and Clive, an English kibbutz member, a novice like me, who had been sent to the ranch by his kibbutz to learn about horses.

After riding along the side of the road toward Almagor, Melody opened a gate and we turned southward down a dirt track to the lake. It was a lovely day, with a brisk, cool breeze and only a few white clouds in the sky. To the east, the stern, brown Golan Heights rose steeply; to the west, the gentle yellow slopes of Galilee; in front of us, the blue lake in its cup of hills, with clumps of green eucalyptus along its shores. Up to now, I have called the lake the Sea of Galilee, its common New Testament name, most familiar, I suppose, to the reader; but the modern Israeli name, which in point of fact dates back to the Old Testament, is Lake Kinneret, from *kinor* (a harp.) One theory says it is shaped like a harp, but there is also a legend which says that the lapping of the water is as sweet as the music of the harp. Of the many descriptions that have been written of the lake, I would like to quote that of geographer George Adam Smith.

Sweet water, full of fish, a surface of sparkling blue, tempting down breezes from above, bringing forth breezes of her own, the Lake of Galilee is at once food and drink and air, a rest to the eye, coolness in the heat.

However, let me tempt the wrath of George Adam Smith's many admirers by saying that I selected the quotation for its beauty rather than its accuracy. Lake Kinneret is hot — bloody hot, not to put too fine a point on it — and the air is muggy, even in winter. Nevertheless, on this winter day I was more than content with the gentle ambling motion of the horse. Arriving at a level stretch of ground, Melody announced that we were going to canter. I was ill prepared for this, having anticipated a little gentle trotting at the most.

"Did you say canter?" I sang out in a high, nervous voice. "I mean, like *canter?*"

"Sure," she replied cheerfully. "Follow us." She and the teen-ager were away like the wind, relaxed and graceful, at one with their horses. Clive and I went after them, clinging on with arms and legs, shaken like a couple of sacks of potatoes. Without visibly slackening her pace, Melody turned in the saddle and laughed at us.

"Copy her," she ordered, pointing at the young girl.

"She knows that she can stop if she wants to," Clive replied through gritted teeth. I looked down at the flint and basalt rocks and kept my mouth shut.

The canter came to an end at last, and we dismounted to take a look at the ruins of ancient Khorazin, built from the local black volcanic basalt. Jesus of Nazareth preached here, but apparently without much success. The New Testament records: "Then began he to upbraid the cities wherein most of his mighty works were done, because they repented not: Woe unto thee Chorazin! woe unto thee Bethsaida!" (Matthew 11:20–21.)

We inspected the remains of the synagogue (built 300

years after Jesus, but believed to be on the same site as the one in which Jesus preached). The pedestals of ten of the original fourteen columns were still in place, and we could see parts of the broken pillars among the yellow thorns. The basalt was engraved in one place with a creature supposed to be a Lion of Judah.

Mounting again, we passed through fields of green peppers, citrus groves, and orchards of avocados, the leaves a dark, shiny green. Melody pointed out the pink church on the Mount of Beatitudes, where Jesus preached the Sermon on the Mount — not of course *in* the church, which was built only in 1937. She told us sternly that we had not been making fast enough progress (Clive and I had refused a couple of canters) and consequently would have no time to visit the church.

Our next stop was at Kefar Nahum (Capernaum), on the shores of the lake, where Jesus started his ministry. Once again the ruins of the synagogue date to the second or third century A.D. It was near Capernaum that Jesus saw Simon Peter and his brother Andrew fishing, and called on them to be "fishers of men." Among the fine carvings is one of a seven-branched candelabra, the original of which was in the Temple of Jerusalem. Today it is the state emblem of Israel.

A little farther along the shore we came to Tabgha, the site of the miracle of the loaves and the fishes, where Jesus reputedly fed a crowd of thousands with five loaves of bread and two fishes.

According to the New Testament story, there were 5000 people present and the scraps afterward filled twelve baskets. Of all the reported miracles of Jesus, this one always seemed to me the hardest to explain, until I heard the following ingenious and simple suggestion: when he started distributing the food, Jesus broke the ice. Others, who had been shy about bringing out their food, also began to share with their neighbors, and so it went on.

Lake Kinneret is, of course, very much Jesus country, so I would like to try to put the founder of Christianity in some sort of historical perspective. At Tel Hatzor, we were able to follow the history of the Jews until they returned from Babylon 539 B.C. at the behest of the Persian King Cyrus. Following their return from exile, the Jews lived in the small nation of Judah around their holy city, Jerusalem. In the fourth century, they came under the rule of Alexander the Great. Despite his Hellenizing mission, Alexander made an exception for the Jews, whom he allowed to preserve their own way of life, and this liberal state of affairs continued after the splitting-up of his empire, when Judah was administered by the Ptolemies of Egypt. However, in 200 B.C. the Syrian Seleucids took over the region, and in 167 there was a strong drive to Hellenize the Jews; their religion was suppressed and their Temple desecrated. Later on this walk, I shall talk about the nationalist revolt against the Seleucids in more detail. At this point, I'll note only that the revolt was ultimately successful and led to the establishment of a larger Jewish state than before, including Judah, Galilee, and other regions.

During the next century Judah experienced varying degrees of independence, playing the Seleucids of Syria off against the Ptolemies of Egypt and vice versa. When Rome became the dominant power in the eastern Mediterranean, Judah became Judea, a province of the Roman Empire. The successors of the Hasmoneans, who led the anti-Seleucid revolt, had now been usurped by a new royal family, Jewish converts from Edom, to the east of the Jordan. When Jesus was born, one of these, Herod the Great, ruled a Judean state that, although subservient to Rome, covered more territory than at any time since the mini-empire of David and Solomon. However, many Jews did not regard Herod as their true king, looking on him as a vassal of Rome. After Herod died, his successors ruled different provinces of Judea; but Judea proper and Jerusalem were administered by a series of procurators, governors from the lower middle class, who enriched themselves at the expense of the province. More than economic exploitation, though, it was religion that sparked off the various rebellions which culminated in the great Jewish war against Rome of 66 to 73 A.D. described by the Jewish historian Flavius Josephus.

The Jews were not an easy people to rule. It will be remembered that they believed they had a Covenant with the One God and that they were His chosen people. His laws were far more important than those of Rome. Furthermore, they believed that the End of Days, foretold by the Biblical prophets, was at hand. At any moment, the Messiah would arrive and usher in the golden age. The kingdoms of the earth (including, of course, the Roman Empire) would be shattered and the kingdom of God on earth would be introduced: the dead would arise; the lion would lie down with the lamb.

That the Jews really believed this is clear from the literature of the time, which includes the Book of Daniel (purportedly written about the exile in Babylon, but really about this period), the Apocrypha, and the Dead Sea Scrolls (the literature of the ascetic sect, probably Essenes, who lived at Qumran on the shores of the Dead Sea).

Jesus of Nazareth was only one of the many prophetic Jewish figures of the time. Judea was teeming with different sects and movements. At the time of his crucifixion, there was no reason to believe that he would be particularly remembered. Indeed, it can be asked whether he really existed as a historical figure at all. The Gospels, it must be noted, were written far later, and I for one am not convinced by the so-called Slavonic Additions to Josephus' *Jewish War*. Josephus was a turncoat and a cynic. Can we really see him writing this sentence? "It was at that time that a man appeared — if 'man' is the right word — who had all the attributes of a man but seemed to be something greater."

The historian was a realist, a worshiper of Roman power. Would a man of the character of Jesus have made him so ecstatic? I doubt it. But, as in the case of Moses, I am not convinced that the question of Jesus' authenticity is relevant. What is clear is that the figure presented in the Gospels is a remarkably enlightened one. His message that one should love one's enemies is advanced even for today. Rabbi Hillel, who lived in Judea when Jesus is supposed to have lived there, was once asked to sum up Judaism "while standing on one foot." He answered: "Do not unto others that which is hateful unto thee." He was quite openly paraphrasing the Book of Leviticus, in which God, through Moses, commanded the Children of Israel: "Thou shalt love thy neighbor as thyself." But Jesus went beyond this:

"Ye have heard it hath been said, Thou shalt love thy neighbor, and hate thine enemy. But I say unto you, Love your enemies, bless them that curse you, do good to them that hate you, and pray for them which despitefully use you . . ."

Nevertheless, I think it may be convincingly argued that it was not Jesus who was responsible for the success of Christianity.

Roman society of the first century A.D. was ripe for a more sophisticated religion. Greek and Roman mythology can be admired to this day, but the religion of Jupiter, Mars, and Apollo was feeble intellectual meat for the intelligent Roman. A large number of upper-class Romans (and particularly their wives) secretly practiced Judaism and other eastern religions. Some modern scholars even see in this fact a contributory factor to the Jewish war against Rome. They believe that the Greek freemen, the administrators of the Roman Empire, saw a threat from Judaism and deliberately provoked confrontations in order to be able to smash it.

Whether this theory is correct or not, the outcome of the war was just that. Following the defeat of Judea, the destruction of Jerusalem, and the burning of the Temple, Judaism became a dead letter for the outside world. But it is doubtful whether in its original form it could have caught on, anyway. Judaism, as we have seen, is based on the idea of a contract between the One God and His chosen people. It demands strict and continuous observance of an endless list of rules and regulations, starting with circumcision for the male, continuing with scrupulous observation of complex dietary laws, the supervision of which is the task of the female, and going on to encompass almost every facet of living.

Saul of Tarsus, who changed his name to Paul and became a member of the Christian-Jewish sect, adapted the religion to the prevailing Hellenistic culture of the times. He removed much of the tedious religious observance, obliterated the Covenant with the chosen people, and converted the sect into a universal religion, acceptable and even attractive to the intelligent citizen of the empire. Jesus became the Messiah of the Gentiles, but the Jewish people did not accept this profound moralist. Apart from being a preacher, Jesus was probably a nationalist leader, possibly a radical, but not, I submit, the real founder of Christianity. The first Christian was Paul. The roots of Christianity are to be found around Lake Kinneret; its development took place elsewhere.

*   *   *

We stopped at a water trough, and my horse (frisky beast) put one hoof in, blew bubbles, and sloshed her head around in the water. She was having a great time. We had two more sessions of cantering, during which I clung on like grim death and told myself not to be childish. Melody was familiar with the route, I reasoned; she had taken out novices before and knew what they were capable of. So I reasoned. The ride came to an end by the lakeside, and in bidding the others good-by, I wished Melody good luck.

"I always have had," was her confident reply. "I put my faith in the Lord, and He hasn't ever let me down!" The capital *H* was clearly audible. I broke out in a cold sweat, realizing that she had relied on Him to save me from the rocks. Then I shrugged. After all, He had.

On the shore of Lake Kinneret, I was in the great Syrian-African rift, which in Israel includes the Hula Basin, the Kinneret, the Jordan River, and (farther south) the Dead Sea and Red Sea. The Kinneret and all the valley southward is below normal sea level, which is why (with apologies to George Adam Smith) it was warm and muggy even on that winter afternoon.

Right by Tabgha is the Karei Deshe youth hostel, where I was determined to spend the night. The land hereabout was bought by a group of German Christians in 1866. Most of the early settlers died of malaria, and all attempts at agriculture failed. For the next few decades it served as a missionary center, but just before World War II, a German espionage unit was established there under the cover of an archaeological dig. The British authorities expelled the Germans and used the place as a convalescent home for British officers and officials. The Israelis inherited it and turned it into an agricultural research station, with special emphasis on pasture and beef herds. The early experiments with beef failed — this was before they brought in the Brahmins — and so in 1961 Karei Deshe became a youth hostel. The hostel was the brainchild of Shlomo Ilan, who had been administrator of the experimental station. He also ran a plant nursery there, which he still maintained although he was now entirely blind. One of my reasons for staying at the hostel was to meet him, for his knowledge of the area is unequaled.

The jumble of old buildings that made up the youth hostel was set in thick rhododendrons and other shrubs, many of them subtropical and typical of the area. The luxuriance of the vegetation and the thick warmth of the air was encouraging my incipient hay fever; but I cooled my blisters in the lake, checked in, and enjoyed a cold beer in the yard outside the dining room.

I was just about to ask someone where I could find Shlomo Ilan, when he appeared. It was unmistakably he: dressed in shorts and summer shirt, thick mane of hair, gray beard, he walked slowly and deliberately, holding his white cane and followed by a group of young men. The effect was of an Old Testament prophet with his disciples. In point of fact, the young men were a party of evangelists from different countries on a tour of Galilee. Their guide had brought them to hear a lecture from Shlomo Ilan, but the old man suggested that they should pitch in right away with questions.

An earnest young German asked him what he thought of Germany. He smiled, noting that he himself was from Germany, having arrived in Palestine in 1930. Speaking a good, if pedantic, English, he said that in his opinion the Germans had been afflicted with a sort of collective national insanity during the Nazi era. It could happen to any people, he warned, though he believed that there was more cruelty in German folklore than in the literature of other peoples. He went on to tell us how, during the Second World War, he had been part of a special unit designed to penetrate the German army and sabotage it from within. The group was made up entirely of German-speaking Jews. They possessed German army uniforms and spent many hours learning army routines, drill, and customs. Happily, the German army never arrived in this country.

The questioners moved on to current affairs, and he fielded questions about Israel and the Palestinians with skill and moderation, giving a graphic description of the flight of the Arab refugees in 1948, as he personally had witnessed it.

His Galilee kibbutz had been surrounded by Arab villages, which were daily being reinforced by armed Arabs. Isolated and cut off from other Jewish villages, he and his friends had watched the buildup through their binoculars. They had set up a lookout post on the bridge across one of the Jordan tributaries, which was the only route out of the kibbutz, and had beaten back a number of Arab attempts to take over the bridge. They were not sure how long they could hold out; the ammunition was getting low and Arab numbers were visibly increasing. Outgunned and outnumbered, they knew it was only a question of time before their village was captured.

On guard one morning, he had been sure that the final showdown had come; huge numbers of Arabs were approaching the bridge. The Jews held their fire as long as possible, and then something happened that completely dumfounded them. The stream of humanity by-passed the bridge and continued eastward. Looking through their binoculars, they saw whole families, their possessions loaded on donkeys and carts, streaming eastward. One of the kibbutz members, who had enjoyed good relations with the local villagers, managed to talk to a family. They told him that they had been ordered to leave by the Arab Higher Committee, the representative body of the Arabs of Palestine, in order to clear the way for the advance of the Syrian and Iraqi armies. They had been assured that they could return in the wake of the victorious Arabs — and return not only to their own homes, but to the Jews' houses also.

"I know it sounds scarcely credible," he said. "I'm not sure I would believe it if I hadn't seen it with my own eyes." He smiled and added, "Of course, I wasn't blind in those days."

No, he replied in answer to another question, he did not think that the Jews had a divine right to the land; he did not even (he excused himself) believe in God. The right to the land came from the use that the Jews had made of it. The development had benefited the Arabs as well as the Jews. With regard to the West Bank, which had been acquired by Israel only in 1967 and was still under military government, pending an eventual decision about its future: he was against its being incorporated into the State of Israel. However, he argued, there could be Jewish towns and villages there, provided they were not built on land owned by individual Arabs. The local Arabs could benefit from the presence of the Jewish settlements. He recalled the case of Carmiel, near Haifa. Some Arab land had been appropriated for the new Jewish town, and Israeli Arabs had strongly opposed this. Today, Carmiel gave employment to large numbers of Arabs and the protests had consequently died down.

Following him up to his room, I introduced myself to him and his wife. Anxiously, he asked me how he had done with the group, and I was able to reply truthfully that he had handled them well.

Lots of people brought groups to see him, he said. Often he talked about the Kinneret, but sometimes, like tonight, he never reached that topic.

Karei Deshe had been all his life for many years. He still worked in the nursery and the gardens, although his blindness, which had started two years ago as a result of diabetes, was a handicap.

"I am president of the World Association of Blind Gardeners," he told me proudly.

Originally, he and his wife had been kibbutz members, but they had left because she wanted to bring up her own family. We ate delicious grapefruit and discussed the problems of kibbutz life. He knew the people at Amiad well from his time at the experimental station. He understood that they had a good beef herd today. Akbara, yes, he knew the problem intimately: a big blunder, or rather a series of blunders. There probably really wasn't enough land for agriculture. The solution would have been to turn Akbara into an Arab suburb of Safed. It could have become a model for resettlement instead of a disgrace. He had put forward the idea to officials of the Ministry of Agriculture, but found them indifferent.*

I spent much of the following morning with Shlomo Ilan in the plant nursery behind the hostel. He still seemed to know all the plants, relying on smell and memory. He says he doesn't always get it right. Unfortunately, his sense of touch is badly affected by his diabetes. He plans to spend less time in the garden than hitherto and to write a book about the Kinneret region.

"I cannot learn Braille because of the diabetes," he told me. "But I'll manage without: I'll dictate the book."

*   *   *

My next stop was the Kinneret Limnological (lake study) Laboratory. It is right by Karei Deshe, but there is no way through, so I had to walk the long way round. It was a pleasant enough stroll, but it was midday before I found myself walking through the bougainvillaea to the laboratory building.

Tommy Berman, a deadpan Czechoslovakian-born Scot and a member of Amiad, had started the laboratory in 1967, after the Ministry of Agriculture had become con-

* Since my walk, the case of Akbara has received the sort of public attention that it deserves. Following a news conference held by the villagers in Tel Aviv, several newspapers carried long feature articles about the village. An official of the prime minister's office was quoted as saying that the situation in Akbara was "unacceptable to the government." A resettlement project in other Galilee Arab villages has been stymied by hostile reaction from the locals, although some half-dozen Akbara families have decided to solve their problem in this way. The possibility of Akbara's becoming a suburb of Safed is still, apparently, on the agenda. To me it seems the logical solution.

cerned about the quality of the water in Lake Kinneret. At the time, Tommy was just back from the United States. He had originally left the kibbutz to spend a year in America; eight years later he had returned with an American wife and a Ph.D. in microbiology. We sat on the lawn by the water with Terence, his fat, good-natured dog, while he explained the odd mixture of science and politics that had made the establishment of the laboratory necessary.

Israel had launched a large-scale program to carry water from the Jordan River to the parched lands farther south. There had been a comprehensive plan, worked out by an American expert, but this had become impracticable because of the division of Palestine between Israel and Jordan. After fruitless attempts to get the Jordanians to cooperate, Israel had decided to go ahead unilaterally but to take only its own share of the river's water. However, when the Jordan project had been harassed by Syrian gunfire, causing a series of incidents that reached the UN Security Council, the Israelis decided to pump the water directly from Lake Kinneret, out of the range of Syrian guns. It involved extra expense, because the water was being taken from a lower altitude and had to be pumped up into the hills before flowing south. The political advantages, though, outweighed the economic liabilities.

The new project quickly ran into difficulties. The Kinneret water was too saline for the orange groves on the coastal plain. Two of the saline springs that fed water into the lake were diverted in an open channel, joining the Jordan River south of the lake. This did indeed solve the salinity problem, but the authorities became concerned about the general quality of the lake's water. It was, after all, Israel's largest reservoir, and now it was supplying a good bit of the water being used for domestic as well as agricultural purposes.

So Tommy had been charged with establishing the Kinneret laboratory. Today, he told me, some twenty people

worked there, including five senior scientists. He was no
longer in charge, working half time at the lab and half time
as kibbutz secretary. A white launch chugged into the bay;
it had been collecting water samples from different parts of
the lake. The scientists had found the lake to be, on the
whole, in a healthier state than they had feared. One of
their main concerns had been that the use of chemical fertilizers by the surrounding farmers was putting too much
nitrate into the water. This had been, of course, aggravated
by the Hula drainage scheme, which had added considerably to the area fertilized. In fact, the lake was found to have
its own denitrification process, which had reduced this danger measurably.

I asked him outright whether the Hula drainage scheme
had been an ecological disaster. Definitely not, he said. It
had been necessary from a health point of view, quite apart
from the farmland reclaimed. Today more was known
about ecological problems, and the scheme would probably
have been carried out in a different way. At the time, the
engineers had implemented the scheme without consulting
the biologists. Now the situation was different: the biologists were brought into the picture early on.

The laboratory was currently assessing two power
schemes. One program was to build a hydroelectric power
plant near Moshav Almagor. Here the problem was simply
to assess how much water could be diverted from the Jordan without upsetting the balance of nature and changing
the quality of the water entering the lake. Tommy personally was far more concerned about a project for mining
peat in the Hula Valley. Enormous quantities of peat were
to be dug from depths of between 100 and 600 feet, which
in effect would result in a new Lake Hula. Although the
burning of this fuel could provide up to a third of Israel's
energy needs, Tommy described the ecological implications
of the scheme as "horrific." Given the current political situation, the uncertainty of oil supplies, he acknowledged that

the pressure to put the project into operation would be considerable. The laboratory was working on ways to reduce the ecological damage to a minimum. He was confident that the biologists would be listened to.

We went inside, where he showed me an algae-measuring machine. One of his current projects was to alter the balance of the different types of algae in the lake. At present the dominant alga was eaten only by St. Peter's fish. Since this is the most famous and tasty of the Kinneret fishes, I told him that the situation seemed ideal to me. In fact, though the St. Peter's fish is the best known, it is a minority in the lake. Most of the algae were not eaten at all; they decayed, polluting the water with surplus organic matter. If more generally edible algae were encouraged, the fish population of the lake would increase, more of the algae would be eaten, there would be less decay, the water would be cleaner, the catches of the fishermen would improve, and everything would be better all round.

In the middle of his explanation, the phone rang. New York was on the line about kibbutz business. Wearing his other hat, Tommy told his caller that she would have to return and sort out her personal problems. She was not to worry about the kibbutz; first she must decide what she herself wanted. The kibbutz would do its best to help. He himself would meet her at the airport.

Outside again, we looked at birds through his binoculars. There were gulls and cormorants and small coffee-colored birds, which I couldn't identify. He pointed out one sitting on a wire.

"Walk toward it," he advised. I did so and saw what he meant. The back and wings flashed aquamarine in the sun as it flew off. "It's been a good year for kingfishers," he remarked.

*   *   *

Walking along the shore of the lake southward, I was soon brought up by a wire fence with a large notice: PRIVATE. NO ENTRANCE. PROPERTY OF KIBBUTZ GINNOSAR. TRESPASSERS WILL BE PROSECUTED!

I was more than just annoyed; I fumed for several minutes. It was bad enough when private property–owners were selfish; I expected better from a so-called Socialist society. I know I was being unfair. Ginnosar has extensive banana plantations, and agricultural thefts have been growing recently. In this location, people on holiday probably invade the orchards and gardens frequently. Nevertheless, it did set me thinking about the humbug that exists in kibbutz life, along with the admirable features, and I remembered a story that I had once heard about that very kibbutz.

I was told it by Robert, a suave, German-born ex-member (now, unhappily, dead), who had served in senior positions at the kibbutz. One day he had decided to leave. As is usual in such cases, great efforts were made to persuade him to change his mind. One of those who came to talk to him was a cabinet minister in the government of the day. What with service in the army, study abroad, and political activities, this member had actually spent all of six months at the kibbutz in the past two decades. After listening attentively to Robert's reasons for leaving, he had nodded and said, "I understand you only too well, Robert. I know it isn't easy, but look at me: I've stuck it out!"

*   *   *

Walking along above the open canal, which takes the saline water from the northern springs to the Jordan south of the lake, I fell into step with an Arab from the nearby village of Wadi Hamam, who told me a sad story. His first wife had died some years ago and he had remarried. The problem was that his new wife was from the village of Kafr Kana, almost fifteen miles away, and she refused to come and live in his village. His children from his first wife were in Wadi Hamam; his wife was in Kafr Kana; and he was commuting between the two. He did not feel that he would be able to go on like that much longer, nor could he see a solution to his problem. Saying good-by, he branched off toward his village and his children.

Over to the right towered the cliffs of the Arbel, honey-colored in the afternoon light. Once in 1960 I had been in charge of a youth tour of the country, and we had descended those cliffs in the late afternoon. It was an irresponsible decision — though not mine — and darkness had fallen before we reached the bottom. Rarely have I experienced such a deep sense of relief as when we were all safely down.

It was in the caves of the Arbel that Hezekiah lived with his followers in the early days of Roman domination. Described by Flavius Josephus as a "bandit chief," he was the father of Judah of Galilee, mentioned in the Gospels, a nationalist rebel against Rome. Judah's son, Menahem, captured Masada in the Jewish war against Rome in A.D. 66, and Menahem's nephew, Elazar, commanded Masada in the heroic siege of A.D. 73. The suicide of the defenders of Masada (to which we shall return later in this walk) is a famous story. Less well known is the saga of Hezekiah, without doubt a nationalist rebel, despite Josephus' label. He was pursued by the young Herod, who later became Herod the Great, and was besieged in the caves of the Arbel. He and his followers killed their families and themselves rather than fall alive into Herod's hands. Was this the example that inspired Elazar to follow the same course at Masada a hundred years later? I have always thought so.

*   *   *

Tiberias deserves a complete book to itself; but I have already lingered too long on history and will try to be brief. The original Jewish settlement was at Hamat, south of the town. Tiberias itself was built during the first century A.D. by Herod Antipas, the son of Herod the Great, and named in honor of the Roman emperor Tiberius. For many years the Jews considered it an abomination, because it was partly built on the Hamat cemetery; but later it became an important Jewish center, as we have noted — one of the four holy cities, along with Jerusalem, Safed, and Hebron.

After the fall of Jerusalem in A.D. 70 Galilee became the main area of Jewish settlement, and Tiberias was the center of Jewish learning. It was here that the so-called Jerusalem Talmud was compiled in the third century. The first five books of the Old Testament, the Penteteuch, are the Law of Moses, the Torah, which religious Jews believe were dictated to Moses on Mount Sinai. They were supplemented by the commentaries of case law, which for many years were not written down. This "oral" law was committed to paper in the first century B.C. because the rabbis feared it would otherwise be forgotten. Called the Mishna, this codex was completed only some 200 years later. But that was not the end of the story. The Hebrew Mishna was, in turn, amplified by the rabbis' commentaries, called the Gemarah, written in Aramaic, the everyday language in Judea of the Second Temple period. The Mishna and the Gemarah form the Talmud, a vast compilation of Jewish law and tradition.

There were two versions of the Talmud. The Babylonian Talmud, as its name suggests, was compiled in Iraq, where a large Jewish community remained since the time of the Babylonian exile. The Jerusalem Talmud, despite its name, was compiled in Tiberias.

Great men are buried here: Rabbi Akiva, spiritual leader of the final Jewish revolt against Rome of A.D. 132; Yohanan Ben-Zakkai, founder of the Yavne academy, which preserved Judaism after the great defeat at the hands of the Romans in the first century; Rabbi Meir the miracle-worker, a famous second-century scholar. But the most famous of all was Maimonides (the Greek patronymic form of his name). Rabbi Moses Ben-Maimon, often called by his acronym, the Rambam, was the great twelfth-century scholar and physician who served as court doctor to Vizier El-Fadil in Cairo. He is believed to have treated Saladin himself, and there is a legend that Richard the Lion-Hearted tried to procure his services. Maimonides was not only the greatest physician of his time, he was one of the greatest Judaic scholars of all time. His *Mishne Torah* remains the best simple exposition of the Talmud, and his *Guide for the Perplexed** has never been surpassed as an explanation of Jewish philosophy.

The legend says that Maimonides, who was born in Spain but moved to Egypt, asked to be buried in the Holy Land, so when he died his disciples loaded his coffin onto a camel. The camel, after walking all the way from Egypt, finally knelt down in Tiberias. The disciples took this as a sign that their master wished to be buried here.

*   *   *

Throughout this walk (which was only just beginning) I was tempted to linger, for there was so much to see. Galilee was chock-full of history from Biblical times to the most recent period. I had to keep reminding myself of my purpose, which was to cover all of Israel. Tiberias was a case in point. I could have remained there for days; but I resolved to press on through the town and reach a kibbutz farther

* As I write these lines, President Sadat is on a visit to Israel. President Navon gave him a copy of this work in Arabic, Hebrew, and English, noting that it was originally written in Arabic. Thanking him, Sadat called the book "a treasure, a real treasure."

south. It was not to be: two miles outside the town I found myself among the ancient ruins of Hamat. In all honesty I must record that it was not history that detained me. Modern buildings have been erected above the thermal springs, famous since ancient times for their healing qualities. I was still footsore from the unaccustomed exercise — even more sore from my horse ride — and I could not resist the temptation to enter the large, elegant Hamat Thermal Recreation Center, built just next to an excavated Roman-style bathhouse of the third century.

It was very smart indeed: gleaming black marble, huge, tinted plate-glass windows, and red carpets. The brochure showed a sexy, blond masseuse, but I had my doubts and elected to take a simple bath without trimmings. In the event I proved right, for the only masseur in sight was a rather grotty male. I also eschewed Scottish and Vichy showers (whatever they may be) and plunged straight into the warm pool. If there is anything more relaxing than a full-sized swimming pool filled with water at 90° Fahrenheit, I would like to know about it. I swam around, luxuriating in the warmth.

It put me in mind of a stretch of army service on the Suez Canal, when we had traveled down one Saturday to thermal baths on the Sinai coast near A-Tor. It had been toward the end of the stint, and we were all becoming snappy and irritable. After three hours of wallowing in the hot water, we were relaxed and good-humored. The effect lingered on for the four days we still had to serve.

Here in Tiberias, I swam around until a fellow bather showed me how to lean against the spouts of water that fed the pool, letting the water massage my back and neck. My companion was a middle-aged man from Netanya, who had come especially for the thermal treatment. He was suffering from a slipped disc. Notices around the pool warned one that more than twenty minutes was potentially injurious to health, so I got out and dried myself under a hot-air machine. Then I sat and wrote up my diary.

By the time I left the baths, it was too late to continue my walk, so I returned to Tiberias and put up at the Church of Scotland hospice by the lake. A less Israeli place would be difficult to imagine; the ambience was entirely British, and very genteel British at that. I was delighted with my spotless bedroom in the massive basalt building, the white-painted bedroom furniture of fifty years ago, the peace and quiet.

There was free tea in the upstairs lounge, where I watched a classical concert on television in the company of three gray-haired ladies; two very serious, one with a jolly smile. The concert came to an end and in strident contrast we were offered the Israeli hit parade. The serious ladies buried their noses in their Bibles, but the jolly one seemed to be fascinated by the gyrating disco dancers.

I read myself to sleep with a volume of fourth leaders from the *Times* of London. One leading article defended the institution of Santa Claus and his reindeer; another spoke up for the rights of the common sparrow.

In the morning, I enjoyed a breakfast of teacakes and strong English tea. I sat next to a sprightly, seventy-year-old Englishman, who told me that he was visiting Israel for the first time since he had served here in World War II. He was enjoying himself so much that he kept extending his trip.

"I wish I had stayed on in nineteen forty-five," he told me. "I should have joined a kibbutz."

*   *   *

The climb out of Tiberias is very steep, particularly with a pack; but one is amply rewarded by the fine view of the lake at the top of the hill. Sipping a cold drink on the terrace of a café, I enjoyed my last view of the Kinneret, the hazy blue hills to the east, the rich green vegetation of the veteran kibbutzim on its southern shore, the golden sheen of the sun on the blue water.

The road westward across Lower Galilee is paralleled by an abandoned road along some six miles of its course. Consequently, I made good progress on a firm, level surface, without the bother of the passing traffic, which was some fifty yards away. The hills here are gentler than those farther north, covered in many places with silvery-leaved olive trees.

I stopped briefly at a brand-new olive-canning factory — all conveyor belts, stainless steel, and huge, black plastic containers for storing the olives in bulk. The kibbutznik manager told me that it was a joint project of a number of kibbutzim in the area. At present, it was only running itself in. The factory would eventually process fruit from the whole area, including that grown by the Arab villages. In due course it would produce olive oil as well as canned olives.

"Can we expect to buy local olives in the shops now and stop importing from Greece and Argentina?" I asked.

"You can't stop free commerce," replied that sturdy Socialist.

                    *   *   *

Over to my right was the bumpy hillock of Karnei Hittim, the Horns of Hittim, where the great Saladin (his real name is Salah e-Din, but I'll use the name by which he is best known) scored his first decisive victory over the Crusaders.

My feelings about the Crusaders had run the full gamut from starry-eyed admiration to contemptuous revulsion. Raised at a British boarding school on the novels of Sir Walter Scott, I had first seen them as, quite literally, "knights in shining armor," going off on a heroic mission to liberate Jerusalem from the infidel. Later, when I began to learn about Jewish history, I saw them as a sort of mediaeval Gestapo, proto-Nazis of the worst kind. The truth, surely, must lie somewhere in between.

The Crusades were inspired by a sermon preached in 1095 by Pope Urban II, who urged Christians everywhere to liberate the Holy Land, which was polluted by the infidel. His call met with an amazing response, and vast armies marched through Europe toward Palestine. On their way, the Soldiers of Christ wreaked vengeance on those whom they believed were Christendom's enemy, the Jews. Jewish communities were massacred from Lorraine to Worms and along the Rhine Valley to Prague. When Godfrey of Bouillon fought his way into Jerusalem in 1099, the streets ran with Jewish blood, and the survivors were locked in their synagogues, which were then set on fire.

Small wonder, then, that the Jews supported the Muslims, who had allowed them to live in comparative tranquillity. The center of Muslim power at this time was in Egypt, which controlled the Holy Land up to the time of the early Crusades. In 1174, a young Kurd named Saladin came to power in Egypt, and soon, with a brilliant combination of intrigue and military prowess, he extended his control to Syria and Iraq, completely surrounding the Crusader kingdom. In 1187, he crossed the Jordan River in a drive against the Christians, and in July of that year, a Crusader force marched out of Tiberias to meet him in battle at the Horns of Hittim. Saladin set the scrub and thorns of the hill on fire. While the Crusader knights roasted in their cumbersome armor, they were hacked to pieces by the more lightly armed Muslims. Remembering my own experience with Galilee field fires, I looked up at the hillock, still covered by the yellow brown scrub and thorns, and could easily visualize the scene.

Saladin pressed home his advantage, taking Jerusalem in

October; by the end of the following year, the only remaining Crusader foothold was at Tyre on the Lebanese coast. The Third Crusade, in 1191, succeeded in establishing Crusader rule over Jerusalem and parts of the land, but all in all the Christian kingdom survived for only about a century. It couldn't have been as black as I have painted it. Some of the knightly orders were selfless in extending medical services to the surrounding countryside and welfare to the poor. In Rhodes, for example, the Crusaders are remembered with gratitude.

A number of Arab thinkers have made much of the fact that Crusader rule lasted only for a century and argue that Jewish rule in Palestine today will last no longer. The Jews, they say, are foreigners who have come from Europe fired by a religious ideal, like the Crusaders. Their "kingdom" is as fragile as that of the Christians in the twelfth century.

This reasoning is fallacious. The Jews' devotion to the Land of Israel never waned all through the centuries. Jews never ceased to pray for a return to Zion, and, more important, they never stopped coming. There was no time when there were *not* some Jews in Palestine. Particularly after the defeat of the Crusaders, groups of Jews and individual Jews came to the land in every decade. As we have seen in the case of Safed, Jews came to live in the Holy Land or to die there. The modern return, though revolutionary in concept and different in scope from what had come before, must be seen as a continuation of a process that has never stopped. Furthermore, Zionism cannot in any way be compared with the Crusades. The Jews returned to settle and work the land, not to lock themselves up in massive fortresses.

This said, I would caution that Israel still has to prove itself. Today, the ideals of the second aliya are betrayed by the hysterical scramble for consumer goods. The principle of self-labor has been steadily eroded since the Six Day War in 1967, with the availability of Arab labor. The settlements currently being established in the West Bank are all too like Crusader castles. These are themes to which I will return during my walk.

*   *   *

I passed by the religious kibbutz of Lavie, which has taken the name of a Second Temple–period Jewish town on the same site, and turned left through a wood of pine and olive trees. The pines were, of course, planted by the Jewish National Fund, but the olive trees date back to the Arab village of Lubia, the inhabitants of which had fled across the border in 1948, after an unsuccessful attack on the nearby Jewish village of Sejera, now renamed Ilaniya. It was there that I planned to spend the night. Walking through the pleasant woods, I suddenly experienced a blinding headache. I rested in the shade and drank most of the contents of my water bottle. The pain disappeared as suddenly as it had arrived.

On the far side of the woods, I was rather put out to discover that the footpath to Ilaniya, marked quite clearly on my map, had been plowed over. It added only a mile or so to my walk, but, after the morning ascent from Tiberias, it seemed a lot.

9

AT THE ENTRANCE to Moshav Ilaniya, I found a crowd gathered around a horse that had been run over by an army jeep. The animal was lying on the ground; its eye had a glazed look and I didn't think it would remain alive for long. From the conversation, I gathered that its side had been badly gashed and already stitched up by the vet, but there was also concern about a possible fracture.

"You won't be able to race him now," said one of the bystanders.

"I don't care," replied a solid woman in a red, polo-necked sweater. "I just want him to live."

She told me that the horse belonged to her son, currently in the army. She didn't know how she would face the boy if his foal died. It had got loose that morning and must have bolted across the road, she said. Her husband arrived, towing some straw bales behind a tractor. They unloaded the bales and started trying to prop up the animal with them. I found it difficult to watch and slipped away to find my friends Vic and Shirley Ziv.

The progress of the Ziv family in Israel had paralleled our own. They too had been kibbutzniks in Galilee (at a different kibbutz) before settling in the town of Arad in the Negev desert. Like us, they had left the desert town after about a decade, but where we had come to Jerusalem, they had joined the new-old moshav. Originally built on Roth-

schild land in 1902, the village had declined and only recently had been revived as a moshav cooperative. Vic and
Shirley had inhabited a picturesque hovel, dating to the
time of the Baron, for two years, but now they were living
in a brand-new moshav home.

Like a number of friends of mine, Vic had opted to be his
own boss, and the moshav way of life was a convenient way
of achieving this. In Arad, I had watched him work his way
up from junior clerk to a competent storeman and purchasing agent. I had also seen how less competent people
(with the right connections) had been promoted over his
head. Vic never grumbled about this, explaining his move
to Ilaniya as a "search for greener pastures." He had, as he
put it, become "dried up" after a decade in the Negev.

Shirley had become an enthusiast of natural foods and
was keen to grow fruit and vegetables herself. Vic was out
when I arrived at their house, and Shirley soon had me in
the garden, which she proudly showed me. I was impressed:
she had tomatoes, eggplant, green peppers, and artichokes.
Avocado trees had been planted, although they would not
bear fruit for some years.

"All organic," she proclaimed. "It's all organic: no
sprays, no fertilizers except for natural ones!" Chickens,
dogs, and cats wandered freely in the yard; half a dozen
goats were penned up nearby. Shirley told me that the
goats provided all their milk. The chickens, rejects from a
kibbutz hatchery, supplied all their eggs.

Vic arrived while we were inspecting the garden and
took me down to his four-acre plot in the valley below.
Every moshav member had four acres of irrigated land and
another area of land without irrigation. Because Vic's business was bees, he had not claimed his right to the extra
land, concentrating on his irrigated plot. At the present
time, he was growing flowers for export and green peppers.
The peppers looked fat and juicy, but Vic explained disap-

pointedly that they had been affected by a blight — some type of worm — that had cut the crop in half. He had been hoping for a handsome profit; now he would barely cover his costs. No, it was not because of any refusal to use pesticides. He smiled. Natural methods were confined to the home plot. On his four acres, he obeyed the instructions of the agriculture experts. Instructors visited the village on a regular basis and, as a new member, he needed their advice.

He managed for the most part without outside labor, thanks to the very considerable help given by Micha, his seventeen-year-old son.

"In fact," he confessed, "when we work together, *I* am helping *him.*"

They could not, however, manage the harvest on their own. The picking was done by Arab women from the formerly Bedouin village of Shibli nearby, although the Ziv family worked alongside the women. He had not bought a tractor, he told me, preferring to hire one of his fellow villagers to do the plowing and fertilizing. At picking time, he rented a tractor and trailer.

Eventually, honey would be his main source of income. In partnership with a former instructor, he was building up to 200 hives. Right now, he claimed, he was not making money. He supplemented his income by serving as the cultural affairs secretary of the village, hiring films, arranging for concerts and visiting performers, and organizing the occasional party.

Everything was organized centrally through the moshav, which was quite reasonable about extending credit. Thus, seeds or saplings, tractor rent, fertilizers, and pesticides were all paid for on credit through the village, which even covered the expense of the Arab labor at harvest time. Conversely, all his produce was marketed through the moshav, which debited his income for whatever services and materi-

als he had taken. With the comprehensive agricultural instruction available, he thought he couldn't go far wrong;
but making money — that was something else again.
Meanwhile, I observed, he had a decent standard of living,
pleasant house, and garden, plenty of food. Wasn't the system wide open to abuse?

Vic thought not. As long as he worked hard at reasonable
projects, the moshav was reasonable about credit; but if he
consistently engaged in risky ventures, or failed to work his
plot at all, the tolerance would end. There were a couple of
problem families at the moshav; still, most of the members
were now doing quite well.

After a lunch of farm vegetables, milk, eggs, and honey,
Vic took me for a walk around the village. Up on the hill
stood the old Hashomer building, today a youth farm. It
was in 1907 that the first Jewish guarding organization was
founded secretly, bearing the name Bar-Kochba, after the
leader of the A.D.132 revolt against Rome. Within a few
years, it had come out into the open with its new name,
Hashomer. Its first contract was for guarding Sejera, the
farming village and Rothschild training farm. Hashomer
was never a large organization, yet it placed the task of
guarding Jewish villages firmly in Jewish hands and did a
great deal to convince the Arabs of Galilee that the Jews
were not easy targets. The members dressed in Arab
clothes, rode Arab horses, and became adept at understanding local customs.

After a Bedouin of the Zbeih tribe stole a Greek rifle
from Hashomer, Hashomer retaliated by stealing a bull
from the Zbeih.

"Perchance you have seen a bull wandering in your
fields?" asked a tribesman who had come to the Hashomer
farm.

"Perchance you have seen a Greek rifle that fell off one of
our carts and rolled into your tents?" came the reply.

The hint was well taken and the property was exchanged. The members of Hashomer lived hard lives on the borders of poverty, guarding at night and working as agricultural laborers by day. Their difficulties were fully shared by the women members, who worked and guarded alongside the men. Itzhak Ben-Zvi, who later became Isarel's second president, was a founder of Hashomer. Ben-Gurion, as a young pioneer, had lived and worked in Sejera. In August of 1909, he suffered a knife wound during a Bedouin attack on the village.

This highly pragmatic man, who was to become Israel's founding father, had arrived in Jaffa in 1906. He wrote a lyrical description of his first night:

> I did not sleep. I was among the rich smell of corn . . . A dream was celebrating its victory. I am in the Land of Israel, in a Hebrew village in the Land of Israel, in a Hebrew village called Petah-Tikva.

He never achieved a rank higher than corporal in the Jewish Legion, but from the time of his Hashomer days, he was always involved in defense matters. Later, when he became prime minister, he also retained the defense portfolio.

Vic took me to see the house where Ben-Gurion had lived in 1909. The house and courtyard must have looked much the same in those days: ducks paddled around a muddy yard, which was enclosed by walls of black basalt. The original house still stood; the old dairy now served as a hay store. The modern dairy was out of sight behind it.

The present owner, the son of the man who had employed Ben-Gurion, shook hands with a firm grip. He was a broad-shouldered, weather-beaten farmer, who looked as if he had been on the land for generations. He started by saying that he wouldn't talk; he had nothing to add to what I could read in the books. But of course he did talk.

Ben-Gurion had been a leader, an organizer, he said, not a worker. His father had told him that physical labor had bored Ben-Gurion and that the man who was to become the nation's leader had not been much good at it. Ben-Gurion and his comrades were only employees at Sejera, he noted. They had been attached to the Hashomer farm nearby.

He took me across his yard to show me the rusty mule plow he had driven in his youth, but he had no nostalgia for the "good old days." He was all for progress. Vic (he laid a calloused hand on my friend's shoulder) and the other newcomers were every bit as good as the old pioneers. He was proud of his modern dairy, and the only thing holding up the rebuilding of his house was the plan to turn all the buildings into a museum of the Hashomer days. His house would be incorporated in the complex, he explained, but it would be modern — as modern as Vic's.

I asked him what he thought of the current peace process. He had been born in the Galilee; had grown up with the Arabs. Could the problem be resolved?

"I believe that there will be peace," he declared, scratching his chin and obviously relishing his role as guru. "In my experience, the Arab is a realist. You know that in the old days we always had to get the roof on the house. Once the roof was up, the Arabs accepted the established fact and didn't try to pull it down.

"Sadat is a typical Arab realist: he knows that the Israeli 'house' is well and truly up, roof and all."

He went on to say that there had been enough fighting. His own brother had been killed in the defense of Sejera in 1948. He had left the village after that, not thinking to return, but he had come back. The past would be forgotten and both peoples would work to build a better future.

"The time has come to enjoy life," he concluded. "What did one work for, if not to give one's children a better life?"

That afternoon I went with Vic to the Bedouin village of Shibli, situated under the towering inverted cup of Mount Tabor. In the days of the Judges, Deborah and Barak had assembled the tribes to fight the chariots of Sisera on the mountain. Later, Christian tradition says that the transfiguration of Jesus took place at the summit. Saladin had a fortress there in his war against the Crusaders, and, in 1921, the Franciscan order built a basilica there to mark the transfiguration. Today there is a monastery and hospice on the summit. The village of Shibli (or, to give it its full name, Arab a-Shibli) is situated on the northern slope. Two other Bedouin tribes have also settled down and built villages on the slopes. Before the days of Hashomer, the Bedouin of Shibli had served as guards at Sejera.

Vic and I were warmly received in the house of Muhammad. His living room, painted vivid green and furnished with Formica-covered furniture, was decorated with tinsel.

We sipped hot, sweet tea, as Vic broached the purpose of his visit: the hiring of a team of Arab women for his pepper harvest. There were some of the usual preliminaries, during which Muhammad explained how busy he was but how he would be pleased to help Vic out. He would do anything for Vic, he said, even if it were well-nigh impossible. Not so with regard to the other villagers, he grumbled. You couldn't rely on them, but for Vic . . .

The conversation turned to technical matters: how many women, how many buckets, clippers. Vic would be on hand with tractor and trailer, and the boys would work together with the women.

"I think they appreciate that," Vic said in an aside. "Some of the other members just leave the Arabs to get on with it."

On the way back, Vic told me that a rival contractor had undercut Muhammad, which was the reason for the Arab's annoyance with the village. The other man was indeed cheaper, but he worked with teams of young girls, who didn't take the work too seriously. Muhammad's old women, said Vic, could be relied on to pick cleanly and not leave any vegetables in the field.

That evening, Shirley disclosed a strange fact about Ilaniya: the women did not have the vote in the village. The principle of the arrangement was logical enough. In village matters, each farm had a vote; but she had discovered that a woman could cast the farm's vote only if she had written authorization from her husband. Although the moshav is less of an innovative society than the kibbutz, it is still supposed to be a new, progressive way of life, so I was amazed to learn of this aberration. Shirley was furious about it, the more so as her attempts to bring up the matter for discussion were always thwarted. She vowed to continue the struggle for women's rights in the village.

Oded, the Zivs' younger son, was amazed at my idea of walking through the entire country and fascinated with my maps. A mischievous kid, but with a pleasant disposition, he was determined to be of help. He kept dashing off to consult friends, returning to look at my maps, until finally he announced that he knew a special overland route to the Nazareth road and would be up especially early in the morning to put me on the way.

The following morning, he took me on his brother's motorbike around the back of the village. We drove down a leafy path, bumped over some waste ground, and somehow got across a plowed field. He took me to the corner of another field and gave me careful directions: I was to follow the path around to the corner of the fence and then cut diagonally across the next field. Soon I would come to an overgrown cart track, which led to a footpath, which in turn led to the Nazareth road. I thanked him and bade him farewell.

Following his instructions to the letter, I arrived five minutes later at Ilaniya's second road, two minutes' walk from the Zivs' house in the normal course of events. Still, the boy meant well, and I did reach the Nazareth road.

10

I MADE GOOD TIME along the road to Nazareth and was soon walking through the village of Kafr Kana. In the early years of Jewish settlement, observers used to write of how the new villages stuck out like sore thumbs in the landscape of the Holy Land, whereas the Arab homes blended wonderfully with the scenery. There is something in this contention, although today the older Jewish kibbutzim and moshavim are developing a beauty of their own. An Israeli with an inferiority complex about the Arab talent for merging with the environment should walk into Kafr Kana from the north and feast his eyes on the workshops, garages, kiosks, and other corrugated-iron structures that line the road, interspersed with garbage dumps, rusting vehicle chassis, and an incredible assortment of general litter. The ugliness is particularly offensive because, off the main road and in the village proper, the narrow, high-walled streets and stone houses are a delight.

At the Church of the Wedding, a pleasing, four-turreted building with a large statue of the Madonna above the entrance, I was received by a tubby friar in a brown habit, who asked me to wait while he did his shopping. I sat in the sunny, marble-paved courtyard and wrote up my diary. The friar proved fluent in Italian and French; despite seventeen years in the country, he spoke no Arabic or Hebrew.

He didn't speak English either, so we communicated in what I hoped was French.

Under the altar in the church was an opening into the room believed to be the place where Jesus turned water into wine at the wedding. I peered dutifully into the cellar, but could not see anything of interest.

The climb up the steep hill to Nazareth was difficult and frustrating. Although I had been walking for more than a week, my feet and legs were still very sore. It was only five miles beyond Kafr Kana, according to the map, but the road seemed never-ending. In addition, I kept passing through small villages that I thought were the outskirts of Nazareth. At last, after about a half-dozen false arrivals, I was rewarded with the sign WELCOME TO NAZARETH.

As in the case of Safed, most of the town slopes down into a central valley. There was no problem about directions because I could see the pink and red Church of the Holy Sepulcher quite clearly. The steepness of the stepped streets forced me into a half-trot, and within a matter of minutes I found myself in the street where my friend Mansur Kardosh has his toyshop–cum–snack bar. When I entered, he greeted me effusively, embracing me and pumping my hand. I accepted his offer of a drink, downing two beers almost without thinking.

I had first met Mansur in 1965, when he came to lunch in our house in Arad. What was a Christian Arab from Nazareth doing in the Negev desert? He had been the secretary of an Arab nationalist party called El-Ard (The Land), which had been declared illegal on the grounds that it did not recognize the State of Israel. Nineteen sixty-five was an election year, and Mansur Kardosh, along with three of his colleagues, was exiled from Nazareth for the duration of the election campaign. Although he was bitterly sarcastic about being exiled under the same British mandatory regulations that had been used against the Jews before 1948, he always said afterward that he had been lucky to be sent to Arad, because he made a lot of friends there.

My wife and I were the first ones to invite him home for a meal, and he never forgot it. At the very most, I was risking mild social disapproval in inviting this Arab "extremist" to lunch; but in his paranoiac state at the time, what he termed my "humanitarian gesture" seemed to him an example of civic courage on a par with that of a Solzhenitsyn or a Sakharov.

In addition to being exiled to Arad in 1965, Mansur was restricted to Nazareth for some years after the 1967 war. The restriction was eventually lifted, but recently he was served another order, banning him from travel to the West Bank. Because these matters are so shrouded in secrecy, it is difficult for me to assess honestly whether Mansur is a danger to Israel's security. In Mansur's version of events, he has been persecuted only for his views, which admittedly are pretty extreme.*

The Israel-Arab conflict is one of those intractable problems in which each side feels it has a monopoly of justice. It was, I supposed, inevitable that the Arabs living in Palestine should have rejected the Zionist return. If there is a case in history of an indigenous population welcoming an incursion, I do not know of it, and it would have been strange indeed had the local citizens accepted the idea that the Jews were returning to their ancestral homeland.

At the same time, it cannot be denied that the Jews were impelled by strong forces, possibly the strongest forces ever applied to a people.

We have followed the history of the Jews as far as Roman

---

* After these lines were written, Mansur was arrested and detained for two weeks on suspicion of being in contact with a hostile organization. He was subsequently released, and, as of now, no decision has been reached on whether to bring him to trial. On the phone, he told me that he had had "a nice discussion" with his interrogators, adding, "You have another paragraph for your book!"

times, when Jerusalem was destroyed and plowed over. Jews were banned from their former capital, which became the Roman garrison of Aelia Capitolina. Judea became Syria Palaestina. The Roman (later Byzantine) administration lasted for 600 years, during which sizable numbers of Jews remained in Judea, although the majority were dispersed to all corners of the empire. It was during this period that the Jerusalem Talmud was compiled in Tiberias.

In A.D. 638, Palestine was conquered by the Arabs and, aside from the relatively brief interruption by the Crusaders, it remained under some form of Muslim administration until the end of the First World War. The majority of the population were Muslim Arabs; but there was never a time when the land did not have a Jewish community. Although the Arab-Jewish idyll painted by some Arab sympathizers is false, it is true that, as in the rest of the Muslim world, the Jews fared better than they did in Christian Europe. There are Jewish scholars who maintain that the Arabs living in Palestine are converts descended from the original Jewish population. This is probably about as relevant as the theory that the Jews are descended from the East European kingdom of the Khazzars. The Jews feel themselves to be descended from the ancient Judeans, and the Arabs in Palestine regard themselves as Arab in every way.

We have seen that the Arabs of Palestine were hostile to the Jewish immigrants from the outset. There were examples of friendship and cooperation. Arabs did sell land to the Jews. King Feisal of Iraq even met with Chaim Weizmann and welcomed Zionism as a sister-movement to Arab nationalism. But the general response was one of hostility.

It was Nahum Goldmann, one of the few veteran Zionist leaders still alive today, who said that the tragedy of the conflict was that Zionism and Arab nationalism grew up together, with Zionism just a bit ahead. Had Zionism come fifty years earlier, the creation of the Jewish state would have been almost unopposed, at least on a national scale. On the other hand, if *The Jewish State* had been written fifty years later, Zionism would never have got off the ground.

Palestinian nationalism is, of course, a recent phenomenon. Although it was the Palestinians who resisted the Jewish incursion (the Jews did not, after all, come to Iraq or Egypt), there was no specific Palestinian consciousness. Until the Six Day War in 1967, the case against Israel was an Arab case: the *Arab* refugees had been driven from their homes in 1948; Israel was a threat to *Arab* independence, an intruder in the *Arab* world, a dagger pointed at the *Arab* heart. The famous United Nations Security Council Resolution 242 doesn't mention Palestine or the Palestinians — only the refugees.

In 1967, Israel's borders were the armistice lines of 1949, which represented the positions of the armies at the close of the 1948 war. The Jewish state was in possession of those areas of western Palestine awarded to it under the United Nations partition plan of 1947, plus extra land won in the war.

The Arab states had never ceased to express their hostility to Israel at two levels. Formally, they demanded that Israel withdraw to the 1947 lines (lines the Arabs had themselves obliterated by their attack), and also that Israel take back the Arab refugees who had fled from their homes in 1948. At a different level, they proclaimed that the Jewish state was illegitimate per se and had no right to exist. The Jews, they said quite openly, "should be driven into the sea."

For its part, Israel was not prepared to consider returning any of the extra territory it had won in war; nor would it take back the refugees, who, it claimed, were not its responsibility. Apart from the fact that the refugee problem had been caused by the Arabs themselves, Israel argued, it had taken in an equivalent number of Jews from Arab lands.

There was at one point an Israeli offer to take back 100,000 refugees, though nothing ever came of this. There has also been an ongoing dispute concerning the numbers of refugees; but, without going into the details of this, it can be observed that the numbers have obviously increased over the years.

Despite the continuing conflict, hotted up every now and then by military flare-ups, the Six Day War came with devastating suddenness. Egypt, the key Arab state, had much of its army tied up in a civil war in Yemen. In Israel, Levi Eshkol had replaced Ben-Gurion as prime minister and was regarded as politically more moderate than Ben-Gurion. As Israel celebrated its nineteenth Independence Day, war was far from everyone's minds, although the chief of staff did mention to the premier some suspicious Egyptian troop movements.

Yet in the space of a few weeks, Egypt's President Nasser had concluded a three-way alliance with Syria and Jordan, expelled the UN buffer force in Sinai, filled the peninsula with Egyptian troops, cut off shipping to Israel's Red Sea port of Elat, and was openly challenging the Israelis to fight.

Not without initial hesitation, Israel took up the challenge and won a victory that stunned it as much as it stunned its opponents. The armies of Egypt, Syria, and Jordan were routed, and the Israelis found themselves in control of large new territories. In the south, the Egyptians had been forced out of the Gaza Strip and the entire Sinai peninsula. In the north, Israel had captured a chunk of Syria known as the Golan Heights, from which the Syrians had persistently shelled Israeli settlements in the Hula and Jordan valleys. To the east, the Jordanians had been expelled from what came to be called the West Bank of the Jordan, the area of western Palestine that it had annexed in 1949.

The Israeli government resisted calls for the incorporation of the newly won territories into the state. Except in the case of East Jerusalem, which was swiftly annexed, the territories were held in the hope that they could be traded off in exchange for peace and recognition. As Moshe Dayan, then the defense minister, put it, he was "waiting for the phone call from Amman and Cairo."

Unfortunately, the call never came; the Arabs did not want the deal. At a summit meeting in Khartoum, the Arab leaders resolved: no talks with Israel, no peace, no recognition.

A disillusioned Israel began to establish settlements in those parts of the new territories it considered to be strategically important. Complicating the issue, a new religious movement, Gush Emunim (Movement of Believers), began to establish unauthorized settlements on the West Bank, ancient Judea and Samaria. This movement rejected the return of any land to the Arabs, particularly any part of the Land of Israel.

Sometimes the Gush won post facto recognition by the government for its villages; sometimes not. The present Israeli government, which agreed to return all Sinai to Egypt and to dismantle settlements there, is committed to retaining the West Bank, and it supports Gush Emunim and its settlements.

The Arabs radically changed their tactics after the 1967 war. For the first time they began to talk about the "national rights of the Palestinians." Yasir Arafat's terrorist movement, El-Fatah, moved into the headlines of the world's press and took over the Palestine Liberation Organization, which had become almost defunct. The PLO called for the destruction of Israel by armed force, but it no longer talked about "pushing the Jews into the sea," as it had for two decades. It now defined its aim as the replacement of Israel by a "secular state for Muslims, Christians, and Jews."

One could say that the Palestinians have replaced the

Arab refugees as the Arab stick with which to beat Israel. But in a very real sense the conflict has returned to its roots: the struggle between the Jews and the local Arabs (Palestinians) over the piece of land between the Jordan River and the Mediterranean Sea.

It would be nice for the Israelis to present the case as one between them and the Arabs. After all, the Arabs have twenty-two states. Palestine represents less than 1 percent of all Arab land. In this context, the Israeli case is overwhelming. But the fact remains that there is a chunk of real estate — the Jews call it the Land of Israel; the Arabs call it Palestine — to which two peoples lay claim. Paradoxically, it is the Jews who are responsible for the Palestinian national consciousness; Israel has created Palestine, which was previously southern Syria.

Back now to the "extremist" views of my friend Mansur Kardosh. In those conversations we first held in Arad in 1965, he used the term Palestinian nation. It was the first time that I had heard of the concept. He and his friends, he explained, wanted a Palestinian state on the West Bank of the Jordan and in Gaza. It was not true that they did not accept the State of Israel; Israel was a reality that could not be denied.

His ideas seemed to me to be wildly unrealistic. The West Bank was then part of Jordan; Gaza was ruled by Egypt. If he wanted a Palestinian state there, what did it have to do with Israel? He replied that Israel should simply agree to the idea; he and his friends would see to the rest. Unrealistic as his ideas were when he first expounded them, they were theoretically possible two years later, when Israel found itself in control of the West Bank and Gaza.

Shortly before the 1967 war, there was a letter, appealing for restraint, published in the Israeli English-language newspaper the *Jerusalem Post*. Mansur Kardosh was one of the signatories. I rather admired him for that, since most nationalist Arabs were at that time gleefully anticipating the annihilation of Israel. I must say that Mansur has been consistent in his abhorrence of violence. Not that he has ever condemned a terrorist act as such. But he has always argued that violence is wrong and that the Palestinians, as the weaker side, were likely to get the worst of it in any violent confrontation.

We did not see Mansur again for many years, until my wife and I visited him in Nazareth three years ago. He received us warmly, as did his schoolteacher wife, Yvonne. We had a pleasant lunch together, but we couldn't stay off politics for long. He was by now a firm supporter of the Palestine Liberation Organization. I said that I understood his support for that organization; but how did he justify the PLO covenant that called for the destruction of Israel? His reply was that Israel was to blame for the PLO's extremism. The Palestinians were realists; they knew that Israel could not be destroyed. But Israel was the strong side; it had to make the first gesture. If Israel recognized the PLO and agreed to negotiate with it, that organization would become moderate overnight and accept the idea of a West Bank–Gaza state.

Since that visit, I had been receiving various pieces of literature from Mansur. Some of it was merely appeals for scholarships and so on, but of late the tone had been getting more strident. The Sadat peace initiative was described as a "sellout"; the Camp David agreements were a "betrayal of the Palestinians." For this reason I had been a little uncertain of my welcome, but I needn't have worried. When I asked whether I could stay the night, he replied, "Welcome, my dear friend, welcome. You must know that you always have a home in Nazareth."

Distinguished, gray-haired, fair-skinned, Mansur freely admits that his family could be of European origin. Kardosh could be a Rumanian name, he says, laughing, but one thing is certain: he is a Palestinian. No doubt; but in point of fact, Mansur is also very Israeli. His informality, casual clothes (open-necked shirt even in winter), his boisterous person-to-person, first-names-only approach, add up to a personality far removed from the more formal and reserved West Bank Arab.

He gave me a seat behind the bar and we immediately became engrossed in an argument about the Camp David accords, which had been signed two months previously. I was surprised at the vehemence of his opposition; after all, many on the Israeli side were concerned just because the agreement seemed to point to a Palestinian state. Sadat, I said, was fighting hard for the Palestinians. Mansur shook his head in disagreement: Sadat was putting on a performance for internal consumption.

"You mean for the Arab world?" I asked.

"No, for consumption inside Egypt" was the reply. "He's in trouble there."

I suggested to him that the Palestinians now had their best-ever chance. They would not get their state right away, but if they played their cards right, they would get something very like it. No, he insisted, the autonomy plan was a sham. There was no point even discussing it. Palestinians and Israelis should meet only on what he called "terms of absolute equality." I pointed out that the logical candidates to run the autonomous regime would be the mayors of the West Bank towns. Nearly all of them were avowed supporters of the PLO. How could he possibly object to that? He smiled once more, shaking his head in disagreement.

"For God's sake, Mansur," I burst out in exasperation, "there you go again, missing your chances! Don't you see that this has been the pattern from the start? We Zionists were always prepared to compromise — to settle for half the cake — and we have a state today. You've always insisted on getting everything and have ended up with nothing!"

"We are stronger today than we were ten years ago," he retorted. "Why should we change the policies that we've been pursuing if they've made us stronger?"

"You know what, Mansur?" I countered. "I'm going to bring my right-wing Israeli friends to talk to you; they'll be encouraged."

One of the customers in the shop came over and told me that I should not take Mansur too seriously. He didn't represent anyone, said this man. Most of them felt differently. Mansur smilingly introduced him to me as "one of our quislings."

"Mansur is wrong," said the man. "Zionism is a strong movement and we Arabs have to come to terms with it. Mansur thinks that American imperialism is using Zionism, but the reverse is true." He saw my frown and added hastily, "Oh I'm not talking about *The Protocols of the Elders of Zion** and that rubbish. We are educated people here, but you Zionists are powerful. You are international."

Mansur took me upstairs to his apartment, where I shook hands with Yvonne, the headmistress of a local Christian school.

"It's nice to see you again, Mr. Gavron," she said in her gentle voice. "What a shame that Mrs. Gavron could not come with you." (None of the Israeli informality here: Mansur calls me "Danny" and I call them "Mansur" and "Yvonne"; but to her I am always "Mr. Gavron.")

I sat and watched television with Baha, a delightful eight-year-old with a passion for toy pistols. He made me

---

* *The Protocols of the Elders of Zion,* fabricated in Paris at the end of the nineteenth century by agents of czarist Russia, "revealed" an international Jewish conspiracy to dominate the world. They quickly fell into disrepute, even in Russia, but they have resurfaced from time to time. Nazi Germany revived them, and even today they appear in various Arab countries and in South America.

realize how much I was missing my own nine-year-old Assaf.

Mansur came up from the shop and we sat out on the terrace, as the sun went down, drinking coffee and smoking. The terrace overlooks part of the town, and my friend pointed to some apartment blocks up on the horizon. It was the Jewish suburb of Upper Nazareth. I had to admit to myself that it seemed to glower over the Arab town like a watchdog.

"You see," he declaimed. "It is sitting on my head."

"That's all very well," I said. "But Nazareth won't be in your Palestinian state. Even if you get your West Bank–Gaza state, Nazareth will still be in Israel."

"Let us imagine that there is peace," he replied. "Ten, even twenty years of peace and friendship. After that time, couldn't Israel allow a bit of autonomy for Nazareth?"

"That's just the sort of talk that frightens the most moderate Israelis off the idea of a Palestinian state," I told him.

Mansur launched into a tirade against the United States, the number one enemy of the Palestinians. The Americans and the reactionary Arab regimes wanted the Israeli-Palestinian conflict to continue, at least to the end of the present century, to safeguard the oil business.

I suggested that it was more logical to suppose that they wanted stability, but he shook his head. Once the conflict between the Jews and the Palestinians was solved, he said, the reactionary regimes would fall. That was what the Americans feared most of all.

I challenged him about Yasir Arafat's trips to Moscow. Didn't he realize that Soviet domination of the Middle East was the worst possible thing?

"Why should I fear the Russian bear, when the American animal is already biting my shoulder?" he asked, holding his shoulder and wincing to give emphasis to his remarks. In a way, he mused, he preferred the present government to that of Labor. At least Begin and his auton-

omy scheme would keep Hussein out of Nablus and Hebron. It was clear that Mansur's nightmare was the return
of Jordanian rule to the West Bank.

*   *   *

A fellow guest at dinner was Raiq Jarjura, a young lawyer
who had just stepped down as deputy mayor of Nazareth.
A graduate of the Hebrew University of Jerusalem, Raiq
was as fluent in Hebrew as he was in English. (Mansur af-
fects not to know Hebrew, although I suspect that he knows
quite a bit.) Younger than Mansur, Raiq belonged to an alliance of Communists and intellectuals that had first won a
landslide victory in the municipal elections three years previously and had just repeated it last week. Raiq himself was
not a candidate this year.

Mansur was originally well known as an anti-Commu-
nist, but as our conversation showed, he was moving toward them. The Israeli Communist Party was originally a
classical Marxist party of Arabs and Jews, but most of the
Jews have left it and it has become increasingly an Arab
nationalist party. Nevertheless, the leadership (including
the present mayor of Nazareth) are convinced Marxists,
loyal to Moscow, and many Arabs with nationalist senti-
ments could not bring themselves to join. The solution was
the alliance of Communists and intellectuals, which, as we
have seen, won the elections twice running. Things move
fast in Israel, and the Communists and their allies — the
extremists of yesterday — are today regarded as the relative
moderates. Their place on the fringe has been taken by two
other groups. The Ibn el-Balad (Sons of the Village) openly
support the PLO, even the rejectionist front of that organization. They believe Israel should be replaced by a state for
"Muslims, Christians, and Jews." The Progressive National
Movement is considered by some to be even more extreme,
but its official platform is more moderate, calling merely
for self-determination for Galilee and the Arab triangle (an

Arab-inhabited region inland from the coastal plain near Netanya), as well as for the West Bank.

Yvonne served us a magnificent dinner of lamb chops and a kebab, made of mixed minced beef and lamb, flavored with cinnamon and garnished with pine nuts. We drank a good (Israeli) red wine.

Over the meal, Raiq spelled out his position: the Jews had to acknowledge that the land belonged to two peoples, the Jews and the Palestinians, and that it had to be shared. Israel should initiate talks with the PLO, which he, like Mansur, claimed would become moderate as soon as it was recognized. Unlike Mansur, who always laughed at Israel's worries about security, citing its great military strength, Raiq acknowledged the genuineness of Israel's security concerns. Mansur claimed that Israel had a superiority complex. No, said Raiq, he thought it was really an inferiority complex. Raiq had, of course, been exposed to Israeli Jews far more than Mansur. Apart from the friends he made in Arad, Mansur's contacts with Jews had been confined almost exclusively to members of the security services.

Raiq also strongly disagreed with Mansur's suggestion that the present Israeli government was better than its predecessors. It was the worst possible government, he said. However, he was at one with Mansur in denouncing the Israel-Egypt peace moves, and any suggestion that the Palestinians could be represented by anyone other than the PLO merely provoked their joint mirth.

I put the point to Raiq about Nazareth not being part of a Palestinian state. His reply was that a fair basis for discussion between Israel and the PLO would be the 1947 UN partition plan.*

---

* This is, of course, the plan mentioned earlier for dividing western Palestine between the Jews and the Arabs. The Arabs rejected the scheme and invaded Israel in 1948. By the end of the war, Israel had more land than had been provided for under the plan. Nazareth and other parts of central and western Galilee were slated for the Arab state. This Arab state, of course, never came into being; it was annexed to Transjordan, which changed its name to Jordan.

I tried to draw them out on the subject of Lebanon, because both men are Christian Arabs, but they refused to see it my way. In their view, the civil war there was not between Christians and Muslims; it was between the Israeli-backed capitalists and the poor.

I asked them about the younger generation of Israeli Arabs. What did they think of the Ibn el-Balad and the Progressives? Ibn el-Balad was a 1978 version of his own El-Ard, said Mansur. Not that he agreed with all their statements ("They even criticize the PLO," he observed in a rather shocked tone), but it was his old movement in a modern guise.

As the evening progressed, I found that we could discuss general principles amicably, even though we differed. But the temperature rose noticeably when we got to specific issues. Zionism and Palestinian nationalism were good topics, but once they raised the problem of land expropriations for Jewish settlement in Galilee, or I criticized a PLO terrorist act, the gulf between us widened into a broad river of mutual distrust. Some sharp words passed between us on these matters. Still, when he got up to leave, Raiq shook hands warmly and said that, with men of good will on both sides, all the problems could eventually be solved. How about a united Israeli-Palestinian front against the reactionaries? I asked semihumorously. Both men took the possibility seriously.

Yvonne came in to announce that she had given up her bed for me. I protested vigorously, particularly when it turned out that she was being shunted off to the children's room and I would be bunking down with Mansur; but she wouldn't take no for an answer. After she had shown me the freshly made-up bed, I bowed to the inevitable, reflecting that, after all, this was the well-known Arab hospitality.

"Don't mind if Mansur snores," she joked.

In the morning, she brought freshly squeezed orange juice to my bedside. After a generous breakfast, it was down to the shop for farewells. I shook hands with young Baha, slapping our right hands together, Arab-style. Before I departed, Mansur introduced me to some friends as "the man who invited me in Arad."

"What did you guys do to him in Arad?" one of them asked. "He never stops talking about his time there." We continued to chat for a few minutes, and it became clear that their views were similar to Mansur's. I could have extended the discussion, but it was time to leave.

"*Shalom,*" I said in Hebrew, not really thinking.

"*Shalom,*" replied those Palestinian nationalists, without a trace of hesitation.

*   *   *

Walking through Nazareth, I was struck by the ambivalent nature of the town. With a population of 40,000, about half Christian and half Muslim, it is Israel's largest Arab town. It is a distinctly Arab town, yet somehow it is also very Israeli. Not just the Hebrew shop signs, together with the Arabic. There is something about the atmosphere — the rush and bustle, the dreadful driving, the eating in the street, the essentially friendly informality — that is characteristically Israeli. Nazareth is a friendly town, whether you speak Hebrew or English (I alternated), for it is very much the tourist center.

There are half a dozen hotels, numerous restaurants, countless souvenir shops, ranging from the air-conditioned elegance and steep prices of Mazzawi's to the sidewalk stalls. I stopped to buy a drink and was asked whether I was an American. No, English, I replied on impulse, and at once had the price of my drink reduced by a pound (five cents). Was this a protest against American support for Israel or a derisory comment on the state of Britain's economy? I shall never know.

As I walked through Nazareth — so Arab, so Israeli — I

thought about the alienation of people like Mansur and Raiq. Could we have done better? I am sure the answer is yes. I am sure more can be done to make the Israeli Arabs feel a part of Israel. And yet, a minority in their position, the state of war, our frenetic drive to absorb our variegated population — all these factors would probably have produced a feeling of alienation whatever we had done. I shrugged, but the shrug was not an answer.

*   *   *

I visited the newly rebuilt Roman Catholic Church of the Annunciation, built on the site where Christians believe the Archangel Gabriel announced the coming of Jesus. I found the modern pink and red stone building rather garish. The lower church is constructed around a sort of marble pit, where the priest sits, with the congregation above him. Upstairs, there is a more conventionally designed church, with brightly colored mosaics from all over the world. There were African and Japanese versions of Jesus, as well as the more conventional European and Semitic types.

Farther up the road was the Greek Orthodox Church of the Annunciation. It was a much older building, dark and cool, with Mary's spring running inside. Somehow, it possessed an air of sanctity that the newer church lacked.

*   *   *

After a long search for a bookshop, I found a souvenir shop that sold books. I bought a reprint of Colonel Wilson's *Land of the Galilee* (first published 1880) as a present for Mansur.

The shopkeeper, a Mr. Abunassar, engaged me in conversation while his wife gift-wrapped the book. A Christian from Lebanon, he told me that he could not imagine living anywhere else than Israel (Israel, he said; not Nazareth). He was a Catholic, he informed me. He used to pray in the old Church of the Annunciation, but he did not like the new one, asserting that it was more like a casino than a church.

"The priest sits below in that pit," he complained. "Tell me, how can he avoid looking up the women's skirts. And if he does that, let me tell you, sir, he is not thinking about God!"

11

THE DESCENT into the Jezreel Valley was as pleasant and easy as the climb into Nazareth had been tough. The road looped down through the pine woods (named for Lord Balfour, who issued the Balfour Declaration) to the level plain below.

We are in Old Testament country here. In connection with Mount Tabor, I mentioned Deborah and Barak. I could add the name of Gideon, one of the best-known Judges in the period between Joshua and King Saul, the first known exponent of the Israeli principle of quality over quantity.

At En Harod, to the southeast of where I now walked, a large army flocked to his banner to fight against the Midianites. He thinned them out, first sending home all who admitted to being afraid. This still left 10,000 men, so he made them drink at the spring of En Harod (still flowing today and a favorite spot for picnics) and selected only 300 — those who, instead of bending down to drink directly from the spring, scooped up the water with their hands, thus showing that they were on the alert for a surprise attack. In a brilliant night raid on the Midianite camp, Gideon panicked the enemy and won a stunning victory. It was perhaps the first time, but not the last, that Israel's elite troops used daring and imagination to defeat a far larger enemy.

Not far from here, Saul consulted with the Witch of Endor (modern En Dor) before his disastrous defeat at Mount Gilboa — and let us not forget that the Israelites also lost many battles. But why just Deborah, Gideon, and Saul? Josiah, Jehu, Jezebel, and Naboth are four other names that come to mind here. My thoughts were back 3000 years and more as I marched down the road.

Then, through an opening in the trees, I came on a sight so common in modern Israel — the patchwork of fields, fishponds, and orchards; the fields mostly brown after the winter plowing; the orchards dark green, or, where newly planted, forming a geometric pattern; the young saplings like sentinels in their straight rows.

It had not been like that in 1921, when large tracts of the Emek Yesra'el (Jezreel Valley) were bought up by the Jewish National Fund. Known simply as the Emek, it was the largest continuous tract of land purchased thus far by the returning Jews. Its epic conquest was the task of the third aliya.

If the second aliya established the pioneering ethos and invented the kibbutz, it was the third wave of immigration that consolidated these things, adding the cooperative moshav for good measure. The third aliya was inspired by the Hechalutz pioneering movements, established by Joseph Trumpeldor in Russia and by Ben-Gurion and Ben-Zvi in the United States. The vast majority of the pioneers came from Eastern Europe, once again "encouraged" by the anti-Jewish persecution there, notably in the Ukraine; but a few came from America also. The third aliya was no less highly motivated than the second, and it was far better organized. The pioneers who now arrived in Palestine had been trained on farms in their countries of origin. Pioneering youth movements, similar to the classical European movements, such as the German *Wandervoegel,* emerged. Like their European comrades, the young Jews hiked in the woods and fields, lived the simple life, and searched for their cultural roots. Unlike them, they had a concrete aim: pioneering settlement in the Land of Israel.

The most radical of these movements was Hashomer Hatzair, later to become orthodox Marxist in philosophy. Its first kibbutz, Bitaniya, was famous for its attempt at a total revolution in human relations. Its atmosphere was recently brilliantly re-created in a play, *Night of the Twentieth*, the best locally written and produced theater that I have seen. All night the young fanatics bare their souls before their comrades in an attempt to achieve perfect communal harmony. Even private sexual relationships are vicariously shared by the whole group. Several of the old-timers wrote to the newspapers to protest at what they called the distortion of the play. One of them was the late David Horowitz (subsequently governor of the Bank of Israel), who was a member of Bitaniya. Nevertheless, his own memoirs (not yet available in English) tend to confirm the picture painted by the play. His characterization of his former community: "A monastic order without God."

In 1921 more than fifty-one square miles of the Emek were purchased. The only Jewish settlement in the area was the village of Merhavia, founded a decade earlier. Merhavia, to which most of the Bitaniya group was later transferred, had been an unsuccessful cooperative experiment, based on the ideas of Dr. Franz Oppenheimer.

Oppenheimer had put forward his scheme as an alternative to the kibbutz, where the principle of equality was somewhat modified. The farm was supervised by an agronomist, and the workers were paid according to their productivity. It was intended that at a later stage the members would form a producers' cooperative and that artisans and professionals would ultimately join the community.

Although Dr. Oppenheimer himself, who visited Merhavia, advised them not to apply his ideas too rigidly, the cooperative failed just because its members lacked sufficient imagination to be flexible. There were the normal objective difficulties, but where the pragmatic kibbutz managed to survive, the cooperative did not. There was jealousy over the inequalities: the combination of large farm and individualist economics did not work. The Oppenheimer cooperative was not, it seems, "the best way to organize poverty."

In the same year the Emek was bought, a new form of cooperative was formed that did succeed, the moshav. We have already visited two moshavim and noted their success as a form of life. It appears that the more individualist approach did succeed when combined with the family farm. Whereas Oppenheimer had visualized a large farm supplemented by family farms, the moshav was based on the home farm supplemented by collective enterprises.

Apart from the creation of the moshav, the early 1920s also saw, in the Emek, the emergence of the large kibbutz. In the interests of simplification, I have described Degania as the first kibbutz. In fact, it was the first *kvutza*, envisaged as a large family, with a maximum size of some sixty members. Degania and the first communes simply split up like amoebae when they became too large. In the Emek, at En Harod, the first kibbutz (large kvutza) was formed, with no limit placed on its size. Today, there is no distinction between the two forms, and all the communes are called kibbutzim; but there are still some villages that prefer the more intimate size (though none as small as sixty) and others that strive for enlargement. The smaller kibbutzim limit their membership to between 200 and 300, whereas some of the larger ones have memberships approaching 1000 each, which, with children, visitors, and parents, means a community of over 2000.

Between 1921 and 1924, 20,000 immigrants entered the country. The majority were pioneers, although not all of them could settle on the land. Some formed themselves into mobile work-teams, the most famous of which was Gedud Ha'avoda (the Labor Battalion), to which a number of men who later attained positions of leadership in the country belonged. They helped the kibbutzim and moshavim to transform the Emek (partly scrubland, partly swamps infested with malaria and other diseases) into the cultivated farmland that it is today. It was the story of Metulla and Yesud Hamaala, of Rosh Pina and Degania, all over again.

As I walked down into the Emek, this saga of development was much in my mind. A natural coward, I am the last person to undervalue martial bravery, but I cannot avoid the feeling that in modern Israeli history too much emphasis has been placed on warfare and too little on pioneering. Although the building-up of the land could not have been achieved without self-defense, there is a certain amount of truth in the remark that it is easier to die for a cause than to live for it. For me it is the dull, gray, grinding day-after-day effort of building and cultivation that is the real epic of our recent history.

One of the fishponds flashed in the afternoon sun, and my thoughts became less solemn as I recalled an incident, many afternoons ago, when I went boating in a kibbutz fishpond with my friend Vic.

We got into the boat and, taking the oars, I pulled strongly for the center. It was a beautiful day, and we enjoyed the peace and the sound of the water slapping against the bows. We hove to out in the middle, where Vic stripped down to his underpants, announcing he was going for a swim. Fortunately for him, he planed off the boat in a flat racing dive. When he stood up, the water came only about halfway up to his knees!

Until that time, I had always thought that the fishponds were deep, like artificial lakes; but it seems the shallower the pond, the easier the fishing. In some types of pond, the fish are netted; in others, the water is simply drained away, enabling the fish to be literally shoveled up.

*   *   *

After about four miles, I left the road and struck off westward through the woods toward Kibbutz Ginnegar, where I intended to spend the night. The sun was low in the sky as I passed an Arab herdsman with a mixed bunch of sheep and goats. The black goats wore bells around their necks, which clanked musically as they walked: a romantic scene.

I skirted a vast plowed field, proceeded through extensive citrus orchards, the dark green trees heavy with yellow grapefruit, passed by the dairy, the cows outside swishing their tails at the flies, and walked by a huge building, which I later learned was a factory for the manufacture of plastic sheeting. In fact, the Ginnegar factory turns out the widest single-sheet polyethylene film produced anywhere in the world. Here I encountered a pipe-smoking kibbutznik taking his daughter for a walk in her push-chair. After receiving directions from this man, I walked through the kibbutz to my friends' home.

Ginnegar is solidly impressive. Founded on a swamp in the first drive of Emek settlement in 1922, by a group that broke away from Degania because of a shortage of land, it has retained something of a kvutza approach, its membership remaining at fewer than 300. The Degania group was joined by others who had tried unsuccessfully to form a settlement south of Zichron Yaacov. Ginnegar today, with its well-grown trees and tended gardens, its thick lawns and ivy-covered houses, has a very permanent look. If it ever did stick out like a sore thumb in the landscape, those days are long past.

I had not seen Aliya Zarchi and her mother, Shoshana, since their visit to England twenty years ago, but they welcomed me with considerable warmth. Over coffee and cake, I learned that Shoshana had retired from her work in Tel

Aviv and come to live at the kibbutz. She had obviously settled in well, and I was reminded of a study, by the late Yonia Talmon, which suggested that old people settled down better in a kibbutz if they were outsiders. The kibbutz veterans felt guilty about cutting down their working hours in that very work-oriented society, whereas outsiders, who brought their pensions with them, felt quite at home.

By the time I had finished taking a most welcome shower, Yaacov arrived from painting his mother's house. His clothes were speckled with white paint.

If I were to append here a physical description of Yaacov Zarchi and an account of his attributes, I would be laying myself open to the accusation of drawing a caricature of the ideal *sabra* (native-born Israeli). When he worked as an emissary to our youth movement, he had some difficulty in comprehending our rather masochistic British-Jewish humor, but this is not to say that he lacks sensitivity or is incapable of thinking intelligently about subjects outside his own field. A schoolmaster for ten years, he returned to the university to take his M.Sc. in zoology and now specializes in the genetics involved in chicken-breeding. He spends half the week at a genetics laboratory in Acre and the other half at the regional hatchery owned by Ginnegar and two other kibbutzim.

He told me that his teen-age daughter, who had just come in, was doing a research project for her matriculation on the founding of the kibbutz. She had unearthed some interesting documents about the settlement attempt of the Zichron Yaacov group. He showed me a photostat of a paper listing their assets, including two mules, a donkey, plows, harness, and foodstuffs. Value: fifty pounds sterling. Today, the turnover of the plastics factory alone was almost $10 million a year.

I mentioned to Yaacov how impressed I had been on my walk by the Baron's villages. Hadn't the role of the first aliya been underestimated? Although a child of the third aliya, he readily agreed that this was so. The early villages had indeed exploited Arab labor and had often indulged in an inappropriate, bourgeois style of living, but they had laid the foundations for what came afterward.

"How do you think the men of the second and third aliyot survived?" he asked. "They were around the early villages. Without them, they couldn't have been such heroes!"

Despite the sarcastic implication of this last phrase, Yaacov reiterated how tough it had been in the Emek in the 1920s. Almost all Ginnegar's founders had suffered from malaria, including his own parents. Many of them had died of it. Even he could remember the time when much of the Emek had been an evil-smelling swamp.

Yaacov's two sons, both ex-army, came in with their girl friends. The older one, Ron, had served in the same unit as my son; it turned out that he had just missed being Etan's commanding officer. He was very taken with the idea of my hike and hastened to give me helpful advice. I should try to keep on soft surfaces. Cross-country was best, but along the roads I should stick to the shoulders. Hard surfaces, he explained, tired your feet more quickly.

On the way over to the dining hall, Aliya told me that Ron had volunteered for an extra year in the army.

"Well, at least he earned himself some money," I suggested.

"What good is that to a kibbutznik?" she asked scornfully. Ginnegar, I noted, was an old-fashioned kibbutz. When they come out of the army, most young Israelis like to go abroad. At Amiad and other kibbutzim I know, they are given money for this purpose by the kibbutz; but the kids often elect to earn some money for themselves in a town job. Staying on for extra time in the army is one way to do this; apparently at Ginnegar it wasn't considered the thing to do.

She went on to tell me that Ron had no plans for going abroad. Nor did he wish to study, as so many kibbutz off-spring do. He had spent six months helping out at a new kibbutz and now he was back at Ginnegar, working in his branch, serving as a youth leader for younger children in his spare time. He had been going with his current girl friend for some years, she confided.

"I don't know why they don't get married," she complained, in the manner of Jewish mothers since time immemorial. I have no doubt that the founders of Bitaniya, now living at Merhavia just down the road, talk the same way today.

In the dining hall, the Zarchis were hospitable and attentive. Did I like the yoghurt? This cheese was good. Did I have enough to eat? Try some of this sausage.

I explained that I did not eat milk and meat together. Kashrut, the Jewish dietary laws, forbid this, citing a Biblical passage about not boiling the kid in the milk of its mother. But this is the only law of kashrut that I observe. I have absolutely no objection to eating the forbidden pork but would die sooner than drink milk with it. The idea simply makes me sick. An illogical hang-up, I told Yaacov.

He rejected this, saying that he was coming to have more interest in tradition as time went on. Raised in a strictly secular society, he found himself observing Jewish customs. The previous year, he had been doing his stint of army reserve duty on Yom Kippur, the Day of Atonement. In the army, most of the officers are either Israeli-born or from families of European origin. The oriental Jews, who make up more than half the enlisted men, tend to dominate at the noncommissioned-officer level. A remarkably high proportion of the officers are from kibbutzim and moshavim, and few of them fast on Yom Kippur. Last year, Yaacov, a deputy company commander, had decided to fast and to participate in the prayers. Aside from his finding it a

worthwhile experience in itself, the more traditional oriental Jews under his command had shown great appreciation.

"You know," he told me, "after the Yom Kippur War,
Shai, my younger son, asked me straight out why we Jews
are here in Israel. He's the sort of kid who questions everything. I realized then that the only honest answer was that
Israel is the continuation of the Jewish experience. Other
things — pioneering, the kibbutz, the new way of life —
they're just by-products."

After supper, Shoshana took me to her room to show me
her latest hobby: montage art. The pictures, built up of cut-
outs from journals, were really fine. This was an evening
occupation, she told me. In the mornings she worked at the
special old people's adjunct to the plastic sheeting factory.
"I've become a production worker in my old age," she told
me with a twinkle.

I recalled an argument that we had had in 1957, when
she was visiting England. I had criticized the Sinai Campaign of the previous year, suggesting that Israel had been
wrong to gang up with England and France in attacking
Egypt. Looking back from the vantage point of today, one
can see that it was the start of the process that was to alienate Israel from the third world and from "progressive" circles generally. Possibly it was unavoidable.

"I know that Israel had to defend itself," I had said, "but
many of us in the movement can't stomach the thought of
being on the 'imperialist' side."

Yaacov had taken my point, but not Shoshana. "You are
not real Zionists!" she had cried.

*   *   *

The following morning I walked down to Yaacov's hatchery, where, twice a week, 50,000 chicks are born. Yaacov
and half a dozen others were sorting the fluffy yellow crea-

tures, which were traveling down the conveyor belt, by gender. It was a swift procedure, thanks to the genetic engineering of Yaacov's other place of work, the Acre laboratory. They had developed a breed, he explained, in which the female chicks had longer wing feathers than the males. Thus, they could be sorted at a glance, and no expertise was required by the sorters.

A current project at Acre was an attempt to breed a heavier bird with less food. At present, he told me, it took three kilograms of food to grow a one-kilogram chicken. This was a better ratio than for beef or lamb, but it could be improved, he thought. They were aiming for a ratio of two to one.

I reminded him of the story of the man who decided to cut down on food for his horse. Every day he gave him a little less, until, as he put it, "I was just getting him used to eating nothing at all, when the bastard died on me!" Yaacov assured me that his own experiments were less ambitious.

In the inner room of the hatchery, vast trays of eggs were being kept at the right temperature for the three-week gestation period. The trays were in constant movement, tilting from side to side.

"We watched the hens sitting on their eggs and noticed that they constantly turned them over," explained Yaacov, noting that nature was still the best teacher. Apparently the movement prevented the white of the egg from sticking to the shell.

Back in the sorting room, a young woman was examining chicks through a special microscope. These were another variety of chick; they had not been bred with differing wing feathers. The sick animals were placed on one side. They staggered around drunkenly. If they did not improve, they would be destroyed. He mentioned that Vic and Shirley had recently taken some rejects. I told him that I had seen them and they looked all right to me; but he claimed that they would always be substandard.

I saw a large plastic bag full of still-living creatures and learned that they were being taken to feed the wolf at the Ginnegar children's zoo. I was invited to breakfast, but, squeamish townsman that I am, I declined firmly and fled from that Brave New World of poultry.

I now struck up through the woods and fields to the town of Migdal Haemek. With a population of 13,000 and several successful local industries, including textiles, cosmetics, beer, and leather goods, it is one of the more promising of the new immigrant towns of the 1950s. Quite a few immigrants and Israelis have joined the predominantly oriental community of the founders, but the town still has social and educational problems. At Ginnegar I learned that youngsters from Migdal Haemek had only last month stolen eight stereo sets from the kibbutz bachelor quarters. In the early days of the town, there had been such a bad problem of unemployment that the local union hall had been burned down in a violent night of rioting. Obviously things must have improved since those days, but I thought I could understand those underprivileged kids, growing up in a festering rural slum, resenting the well-off kibbutzniks and seeing nothing wrong in depriving them of some of their considerable property.

As it happened, I was surprised: Migdal Haemek was in no way a slum. Some neighborhoods were a bit shabby, but for the most part it was clean and tidy, with broad, tree-lined streets and modern schools. The view down into the Emek was superb.

I bought a sticky sweetmeat from a street vendor and turned westward down the road to Nahalal. An hour and a half later I found myself opposite the entrance to the first moshav. I did not enter the village but rested nearby in the shade of an olive tree.

Looking across at the orchards and cultivated fields, I

tried to visualize the scene so eloquently described by one of the founders, Shmuel Dayan, the father of Moshe Dayan. A group of them had come to the site of their new village, a location where both Arabs and German Christians had tried to settle but had succumbed to malaria.

We stood motionless. We looked at the hill and beheld a large cemetery with hundreds of graves close together. The youngest of us whispered, "But don't we want to live?" The second said, "This is where we will settle!" The third suggested a plan for draining the swamps. We thought of Hadera and its swamps. And when we descended from the hill, we knew in our hearts that we would indeed build a village there.

Opposite Nahalal I turned northward up a dirt road, walking for a couple of miles through open countryside, with nothing to keep me company but the jet aircraft screaming overhead. I passed a few dilapidated stone hovels, which I took to be the village of Zarzir. It was not mentioned in the guidebook, but it was marked on the map. The dirt road turned west, and after a mile, I came to a relatively modern village with ornate houses, all of them sprouting television aerials. The houses had obviously been built during the last few years, but the village was not marked on the map. I decided to check the mystery after I got home. In fact, I received the answer farther south, as I shall relate in due course.

I did not see any adults, but I was almost mobbed by a bunch of Arab schoolchildren who were playing football in a field by the side of the road. My mistake was to take a photograph of them. They crowded around, pawing me and jumping up and down in their enthusiasm. Clearly friendly, they were nonetheless very excited and almost beyond the limit of self-control.

I have long been used to Arab or Bedouin children with

light brown, or even blond, hair, but my attention was riveted on one youngster, about eight or nine years old, with
the brightest red hair I have ever seen. I am still wondering
about the genetic origins of that flaming carrot top. A distant whistle sounded, and the children, disciplined again,
streamed off toward a low wooden structure that must have
been their school.

At first sight, Bethlehem in Galilee is just an ordinary
moshav village, with the simple houses of the founders replaced by more elaborate structures, just as they are everywhere else. But when you arrive in the main street, you
meet a row of what can be described only as stately man-
sions. Built of stone, three- and four-storys high, surrounded by lawns and apple orchards, they look more like
the homes of British landed gentry than the houses of simple moshavniks.

These stately homes were built by the German Templars,
members of a Christian reform movement, who first settled
in Haifa in 1869 and also built colonies in Jerusalem and
Jaffa. Some four decades later they founded Bethlehem in
Galilee and the neighboring village of Waldheim, today
Alonei Abba. When Merhavia was established in 1911, the
Templar communities admitted the Jewish village into
their milk cooperative. A member of Merhavia was to write
later:

> I heard from them about their sufferings during the early
> days of their colonies. I said to myself, What have we to com-
> plain about? We live in luxury, compared to what the Tem-
> plars went through in their early days.

Relations between the Jewish settlers and the Templars
were not to remain so idyllic. In 1939, on the eve of World
War II, the British authorities expelled the German colo-

nists, many of whom had shown open sympathy for the Nazis.*

Instead of dismantling their houses, the Jews who founded the moshav of Bethlehem in Galilee in 1948 took them over. Today, the renovated homes are among the most spacious and pleasant in the country. Modern Israelis, even the rich, simply do not build on that sort of scale.

I bought some bread, sausage, and apple juice in the village store (also a converted Templar building) and ate it sitting in the sun on the lawn outside. After lunch, I continued my walk to Alonei Abba, where the villagers do not live in the Templar houses, using them only for public buildings. One is a cultural center, another is used for offices, and a third serves as the village health-fund clinic. There is also a beautiful, ivy-covered church, which has been preserved and surrounded by fine gardens. Once again, this building would be normal enough in a European setting, but stands out strangely in the landscape of modern Israel.

I got into conversation with two of the villagers, who took me to see an enormous, stone-built pool, half-covered with water lilies. It must have been all of fifty yards long.

"In winter it serves as a reservoir," they told me, "but in the summer, we clean it up and swim there."

They must have been pulling my leg.

About a mile past Alonei Abba, I lay down to rest in the middle of an olive orchard and almost fell asleep. Puffy, white clouds moved across the blue sky, the sun shone, the birds sang. My feet and legs were feeling better than before; it was my best day of walking so far. In the woods near Basmat Tivon, a Bedouin village, I met the first pedestrian I had seen in open country. An air force officer, he was ap-

* Last year, a collection of helmets, swastikas, uniforms, insignia, and Nazi literature was found in the locked cellar of a house in Jerusalem's "German Colony." The cellar had not been opened in four decades.

parently simply going for a walk. I had encountered a number of Arabs, but they were always with herds of livestock. This was the first man walking for the pleasure of walking.

If Migdal Haemek had been a pleasant surprise, Kiryat Tivon proved to be something of a disappointment. Built by the Yekkes, German Jews who arrived in Palestine in the 1930s, it contained tidy streets lined by neat rows of houses and carefully tended gardens; but there were also a number of shabby neighborhoods, litter, tatty notice boards, and smashed public telephones.

The pioneering third aliya of the early 1920s was succeeded by the predominantly urban, middle-class fourth aliya, many of its members from Poland. After them came the German Jews of the fifth aliya, also urban and middle class. They arrived in the wake of Hitler's rise to power.

The Yekkes are still the butt of numerous jokes in Israel because of their rather ponderous formality, their demand for order and efficiency, and the inordinate number of professors and Ph.D.s among them (and their insistence on the use of their titles). A number of them settled in kibbutzim and moshavim, although most of them settled in urban environments. Their neighborhoods have a reputation for neatness and order, in contrast to the anarchic ambience of the Eastern Europeans who preceded them or the oriental Jews who came after them.

Because my walk was planned to take me through the outlying areas of the country, the kibbutzim, moshavim, and new development towns, my account of Israel is tending to stress the early pioneers on the one hand and the mass immigration of the 1950s on the other. I probably don't do justice to the Yekkes and other middle-class immigrants, who created much of the country's economic and industrial infrastructure.

However, Tivon, a Yekke creation, did not entirely, as I say, live up to its reputation as the garden-city of Galilee.

Because there was no public phone in working order, I walked miles out of my way to the house of my friends, only to find that they had moved. One of their former neighbors, a genial captain in the merchant marine called Marani, simply loaded me into his car and took me to their new home. (I wasn't cheating on my walk, because I traveled back the way I had come.) Marani's action was typical of a certain type of Israeli, who is almost intrusive in his desire to be helpful. I should note that he had arrived home after a month at sea just minutes before I knocked on his door, but this did not prevent him from going out again immediately to help a complete stranger.

Joey and Judy Englesberg received me with the hospitality that I am afraid I had started taking for granted. They insisted that I sleep in their son's room; the boy would double up with his brother. After supper, Joey, a keen hiker, pulled out his maps, I pulled out mine, and we considered the next stage of my walk. After mulling over the various possibilities, he suggested that I go to see Hagar, the taxidermist at the kibbutz seminary of Oranim on the outskirts of town. She knew the countryside well and might also be able to give me a contact in the Druze village of Daliyat el-Carmel, which I intended to visit.

I mentioned my disappointment with Tivon, and Joey noted that it wasn't the Yekke suburb of the 1930s. It had become a normal part of Israel, with all the negative and positive features that this involved. It was still, they maintained, a good place to bring up children. With a population of some 14,000, Tivon seemed to me pretty ideal. It was big enough to support a couple of high schools, several youth clubs, and a couple of cinemas, as well as a reasonable variety of shops. Judy mentioned that the older children and soldiers home on leave found it a bit dull. They tended to travel to the bright lights of Haifa or even Tel Aviv for entertainment.

Their teen-age son came in at that point, as if to illustrate Judy's remarks. He had been to Haifa to see three films for the price of one, a special program designed to cash in on the high school teachers' strike, which had started while I was on my walk. He at once turned up the radio, where a song from the movie *Grease* had just come on. Like all the kids I had encountered, he was a strong Travolta fan.

Their parents were busy watching a British television soap opera, *The Brothers*. In Israel, where there is only one channel, watching the box is a communal cultural event. Everyone watched *The Brothers* (Joey and Judy were no exception), and we settled down to an evening's viewing.*

---

* An enterprising Israeli charity brought the cast of this show over for a series of personal appearances. To their evident amazement, they were received as pop idols and mobbed by enthusiastic and sometimes hysterical crowds.

12

To the south of Tivon, a grassy, wooded slope is the site of the finest set of catacombs in the Holy Land. The hillside is honeycombed with tunnels and caverns. Here are tombs with stone doors, marble-lined burial chambers, decorated with fine carvings and frescoes. It was the tombs that first attracted the attention of the archaeologists, but their excavations turned up an important town of the second century A.D., indicating that this is the site of ancient Bet Shearim.

After the end of the Jewish war against Rome in A.D. 73, Jerusalem was destroyed and the center of Jewish learning moved to Yavne in the coastal plain. But after the last Jewish rising, led by Bar-Kochba, was crushed in 135, the Jews were forced to move out of Judea altogether. It was then that Galilee became the center of Jewish life. At different times, there were academies at Shfaram and Sepphoris, but Bet Shearim was the main center, and it was here that the Mishna was compiled by Rabbi Yehuda Hanassi, who died in 220. After his death, the majority of Jewish scholars moved to Tiberias.

Farther west from Bet Shearim, set among the lawns and pine trees, beneath the steeply rising slopes of Mount Carmel, is the Oranim kibbutz seminary. Hagar, puffing a cigarette as she sat among her stuffed birds, was not very helpful about the route. She waved vaguely at Mount Carmel and told me I should keep north of the Mukhraka church, something I knew from looking at the map. She was far more helpful on Daliyat el-Carmel, suggesting several names, but finally deciding on Azzat, the head of the local health-fund clinic. He would definitely be in his office, she said.

I walked south along the road toward Yokneam, looking hard at the hillside for something like a track; but I was almost past the Mukhraka, which I could see high above me, before I found one. Climbing the steep path, I soon came to a tiny hamlet of tumbledown stone buildings. There were also a few fruit trees, two horses, and three donkeys, but the village was too small to be marked on the map. I rested in the sun beside a cave, the entrance of which had been built up as a doorway. Lined with straw, it looked comfortable and dry. It was clearly used as a stable.

After a rest and a drink from my bottle, I pressed on up through the Carmel forest. This was no Jewish National Fund pine plantation but a natural wood of oak and hawthorn, one of the very few in the country remaining from ancient times. The oaks were small and stunted by European standards, but by Israeli reckoning they were very old. The steepness of the path forced me to pause and drink more frequently than usual, but another hour and a half saw me at the fork in the path for which I had been aiming. Straight on up led to the Mukhraka church; right to Daliyat el-Carmel. The gray, square, stone church was almost perpendicularly above me. I decided that it was worth a visit.

The path was by now even steeper, and I found that I was climbing rather than walking, using my hands to help me up between the trees and rocks. Someone, probably the Nature Reserves Authority, had obligingly marked red blazes of paint on the rocks to indicate the trail. I would not have made it without them. The rucksack dragged me backward, but I left it on. I was sweating with the effort. The last 300 yards were strewn with a litter of beer cans, Coke bottles, plastic bags, cigarette cartons, and other rubbish. Awful. But then I was over a gray stone wall and inside the church courtyard.

If Bet Shearim was the center of Jewish life in the Mishnaic period following the fall of the Second Temple, I was now right back in the Old Testament, for the Mukhraka (Arabic for "place of burning") is believed to be where the prophet Elijah confronted the priests of Baal.

We are in the period after the kingdom of Saul, David, and Solomon. Israel has split into two kingdoms, sometimes warring, but, in the time of Elijah, allied to each other by marriage. Israel's King Ahab married Jezebel, daughter of the King of Tyre, making an alliance with the seafaring Phoenicians. Their daughter Athalia has married Yehoram, King of Judah, thus forging a three-way relationship. On the surface, this should have been an ideal situation. Relations between the Phoenicians and Israelites had been cordial since the time of King David. The King of Tyre had supplied Solomon with much of the material for building the Temple of Jerusalem. The three-way alliance was indeed a success, and a profitable trading relationship developed through the Phoenician connection; but the increase in wealth led to social and religious corruption.

When the Israelites had conquered Canaan under Joshua, the land had been allocated among the twelve tribes, and within the tribes it was distributed to the individual families. Although the families could and did sell their land, according to their economic circumstances, the Law of Moses stipulated that the land return to its original owners every fifty years. This ensured the maintenance of a relatively just society.

King Ahab, extending his land in the Jezreel Valley, needed to purchase a vineyard from a man named Naboth, but Naboth refused to give up what he rightly called "the heritage of his fathers." Under Mosaic law, his refusal should have ended the matter, but Queen Jezebel was not troubled by Jewish customs. She persuaded the elders of the Jezreel district to bring Naboth to trial for treason, find him guilty, and execute him.

Ahab then went to the vineyard to take possession, but there he was confronted by Elijah, a wild-looking man dressed in animal skins, who thundered, "Thus saith the Lord, In the place where dogs licked the blood of Naboth shall dogs lick thy blood . . ."

It was an uncanny repetition of a scene that had taken place more than a century before, when the prophet Nathan had confronted King David, after the latter had engineered the killing of Uriah the Hittite in order to get his hands on Uriah's wife, Bathsheba. In both cases the king was humbled by the prophet.

Even if we do not accept the Biblical accounts as pure history, the prophets of ancient Israel are an extraordinary phenomenon. With no official standing whatever, either by election or appointment, they imposed their will on kings, generals, and even priests. Before Elijah, Moses, Deborah, Samuel, and Nathan were among those who earned the title. National leadership did not obviate the possibility of one's being a prophet as well as a king. During King Saul's better period, it was asked: "Is Saul also among the prophets?" Among the successors to Elijah were such figures as Elisha, Amos, Isaiah, Michah, and Jeremiah.

They were stern religious leaders, who acted as the conscience of the nation. They railed against materialism and corruption, summoning the peoples of Israel and Judah back to the Law of Moses. They stood up for the poor against the rich, favored simplicity over opulence, proclaimed justice and equality.

"What doth the Lord require of thee" demanded Micah, "but to do justice, love mercy, and walk humbly with thy God?"

They prophesied God's punishment on Israel and Judah because of the corruption of their societies; but because God was merciful there would ultimately be a renewal. Isaiah, who lived during the period that the Judean state was approaching its end, forecast the End of Days, when "out of Zion shall go forth the law, and the word of the Lord from Jerusalem . . . and they shall beat their swords into plowshares, and their spears into pruninghooks: nation shall not lift up sword against nation, neither shall they learn war any more."

To this day, that remains an unrivaled expression of the quintessential dream of mankind. The destruction of Israel and Judah and the exile of their peoples were, of course, seen as God's punishment.

We have noted that at the time of Jesus, the Jews thought that the age prophesied by Isaiah was at hand. Two millennia later, the pioneers of the second aliya drew their Socialist inspiration from the prophets of ancient Israel.

But it is time that we returned to Elijah, confronting King Ahab in Naboth's vineyard. Ahab was discomfited, but not Jezebel. She continued to sabotage the Law of Moses, spreading the religion of Baal, with its sacred prostitution and child sacrifice. Elijah continued his denunciations and forecast a three-year drought as God's punishment for the evil in the land.

According to the Biblical account, it did not rain for three years, and it was at the end of this period that Elijah resurfaced to confront the prophets of Baal on Mount Carmel. He suggested that each party prepare an altar with a sacrifice on it, but no fire under it.

"Call ye on the name of your gods, and I will call on the name of the Lord, and the god that answereth with fire, let Him be God."

The challenge was accepted, and the priests of Baal cavorted all day before the altar with their sacrifice, to no avail. In the late afternoon, Elijah built an altar of twelve stones for the twelve tribes of Israel, cut up his sacrifice, and placed it in position. He then did a strange thing: he poured water all over the sacrifice and the altar.*

Then he uttered his prayer: "Let it be known this day that Thou art God in Israel and I am thy servant."

The sacrifice was consumed in fire, and the people fell on their faces, crying, "The Lord, He is God!"

Elijah, if we are to believe the Biblical story, was not too magnanimous in his victory. He took all 450 of the prophets of Baal to the brook of Kishon and slew them there, upon which a thunderstorm signaled the end of the drought (and apparently the Lord's pleasure at the slaughter!). Elijah, it may be noted, did not get rid of Jezebel or her religion. It was left to Elisha, his successor, to root out alien forms of worship from the Holy Land.

I ascended the roof of the Mukhraka church to enjoy what is possibly the finest view that Israel has to offer. To the west, the undulating pine forests sweeping down to the sapphire-blue Mediterranean. To the north, the hills of Galilee rolling all the way to Nazareth. South and east, the breathtaking panorama of the Emek, spread below like a map, its towns and villages, fields and orchards, its fishponds flashing in the sun, right across to the hills above Tiberias. Surely I can see half of Israel on this crystal-clear November day!

From the Mukhraka, I made good time along the road to Daliyat el-Carmel, easily finding the health-fund clinic, where Azzat worked. Stocky, balding, with clipped mustache, Azzat told me that he had established clinics both in Daliya and the nearby Druze village of Issfiya. His work as a health-fund official came after many years of military service.

---

* There is no obvious reason for this, unless Elijah was simply *shvitzing*. Could he have had access to a supply of kerosene?

Despite clashes between the early pioneers and Druze in Metulla and Safed, the Druze have been for the most part Israel's "good Arabs." They fought on the Jewish side in 1948 and serve in the army and border police in large numbers to this day. They have been a persecuted minority in the Arab world ever since they broke off from mainstream Islam in the eleventh century, accepting the claims to divinity of the Egyptian Caliph El-Hakim Abu Ali el-Mansur. For this reason, they tend to live in inaccessible mountain ranges, in Mount Lebanon, in Jebel Druze in Syria, and on the Carmel and western Galilee in Israel.

The first Druze villages were established on the Carmel in 1590, following a revolt against the Turkish sultan. About three centuries later, the villages were destroyed, after they had participated in a revolt against Egypt's Muhammad Ali; but 1860 saw the Druze in flight from Lebanon. They re-established Daliya and Issfiya.

Druze women do not wear the veil. Upright and handsome, many of them wear modern clothes today, even trousers. The older men wear white keffiya headdresses, but without the black headbands worn by the Arabs, and often grow impressive mustaches. The young men are indistinguishable from Israeli Jews, and, indeed, many of them affect Israeli names, such as Rafi or Ilan. There is a definite tendency toward assimilation into the Jewish society, although this is a minority movement at present. I knew a young Druze who married an American Jewish girl, despite the fact that he was already married back in his village. He had met the girl in Elat and, when I last knew them, he was leading a double life. His American wife knew about his Druze wife, but back in the village they were said to live in ignorance of his other alliance.

Azzat told me that all his sons were serving in the armed forces. Druze are conscripted into the army just like the Jews, and many of them elect to stay on as regular soldiers. Azzat told me that he had been in the supply convoy trying to relieve the siege of Yehiam in western Galilee in 1948. The convoy was ambushed, and forty-six men, including eight Druze, were killed.

I asked Azzat whether young Druze were not being affected by the atmosphere of radicalization in Israeli Arab society. Muslims are not conscripted to the army, although a number of them do volunteer to serve as regular soldiers. I had heard that some young Druze had undergone a process of conversion to Islam to avoid conscription. In Azzat's view, this movement was insignificant; just a few young hotheads and Communists making a noise. Communists? That's right; they didn't believe in Islam any more than I did. The vast majority of Druze, he insisted, were loyal Israelis.

As for Daliyat el-Carmel, everything was under control. Not only were there no Communists here; there were no criminals. There had been a Daliya youngster in jail, but the village elders had petitioned the authorities and obtained his release. The Druze preferred to settle these matters among themselves.

I was skeptical. Was everything in the Druze garden so lovely? I asked. By no means, he replied emphatically. Druze agriculture in Daliya was a thing of the past. Once the village had supplied all the olives for the Atlit olive presses, but the youngsters didn't want to work on the land anymore. Most of the men served in the forces or worked away from home. It was not a healthy situation. There were a number of plants and workshops in the village; but these employed mainly women.

As we talked, Azzat was processing the clinic's patients, checking and stamping forms, directing clients to the doctor or appropriate nurse. One of the nurses was a Christian Arab, he told me, but the remainder of the staff were Jews. A Druze girl had trained as a nurse and had done well, but she had not liked the work. Now she was back in a workshop.

I asked him whether he minded talking about the secret Druze religion. He did not mind at all, he replied in all sincerity, but he couldn't tell me very much because it was a real secret. The *sheikhs*, the elders, guarded the details. How could he possibly believe in a religion that he knew nothing about? I demanded. He trusted the elders, he explained. All he knew was that he must not murder, lie, or steal, and that he must deal fairly and honestly with his neighbor. It was quite sufficient, he intimated.

Azzat introduced me to Dr. Yaeli, a new immigrant from the Soviet Union, who lived in Haifa and commuted daily to Daliya. Although it was already an hour when other clinics around the country would be closed, Dr. Yaeli kept her taxi waiting until she had seen all the patients. Here and at the Good Fence, I thought.

Dr. Yaeli told me that she enjoyed her work. The Daliya villagers were good people, she said, and appreciated what she did for them. They did not complain. She had come to know most of them personally, at least the mothers and children. Azzat had taught her Hebrew and was now starting on Arabic.

It was time to be on my way — but in which direction? Azzat suggested En Hod, an artists' village on the coastal plain some four miles westward. Since it was already into the afternoon, I accepted his proposal. On my way to the pine woods, I passed some terraced fields, but they were not being cultivated. For more than a mile, I walked along an old cobbled road, finding it very hard on my feet. It brought me to a sort of stockade, filled with sheep, where the young Druze guarding them told me it was the former road to Moshav Kerem Maharal. I had come too far south.

It was four o'clock, uncomfortably near sunset, but I was now so sure of myself that I stopped to enjoy the view. The ruins of the Atlit Crusaders' castle were silhouetted against the sea a long way below. The pine woods sloped downward, framed by the cliffs, and I thought it was an allowable hyperbole that this area had been named "little Switzerland."

Starting off again, I quickly came to a clearing with no exit: a dead end. I began to make haste to retrace my steps, but I still could not find the path. Although I could make out En Hod not far below, I was not sure I could get down there without coming to one of those sudden drops that are a feature of that part.

It was an ironical situation: I had come safely through Galilee, much of my route off the beaten track, only to find myself completely lost within sight of the Haifa–Tel Aviv road. Deciding that it would be safer to walk uphill than down, I began to climb toward some lights over and above to the right. By now I was worried: I was having to fight my way through a thick undergrowth of thorns, and the climb was so steep that I had to remove my rucksack and drag it up behind me. I was sweating — and not only with exertion: the rocks and thorns were a barrier I wasn't sure I could pass through. It was getting darker by the minute and I contemplated settling down for the night; but I had arrived at the sewage stream of the houses above, and the smell was intolerable.

For a further fifteen minutes, I clawed my way upward in the thickening dusk, to be rewarded at last by the lights of a house just above me. More climbing, then over a wall into a garden. I walked around the front of the house into the village street. Not a soul was about. I later discovered that I was in Moshav Nir Etzion, but there was no one to tell me that at the time. Once a dog barked at me. Then silence. I walked out of the village and down the road until I reached the busy Haifa–Tel Aviv highway. The Galilee part of my walk was over.

Part II
The Coastal Plain

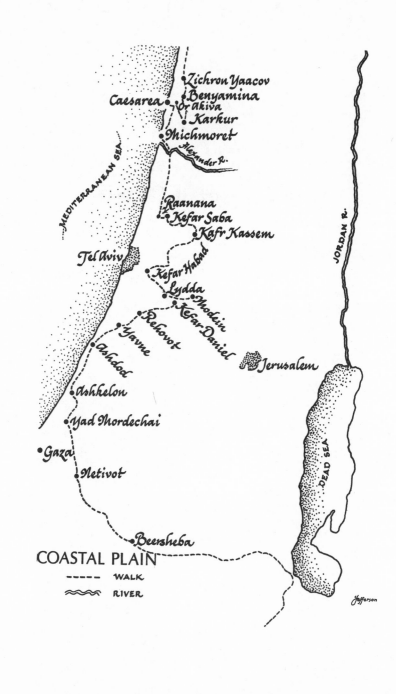

Zichron Yaacov
Benyamina
Caesarea • Or Akiva
Karkur
• Michmoret

Alexander R.

Raanana
• Kefar Saba
• Kafr Kassem

Tel Aviv

• Kefar Habad
Lydda
Modiin
• Kefar Daniel
Rehovot
Yavne
Ashdod • Jerusalem

• Ashkelon

• Yad Mordechai

• Gaza

• Netivot

• Beersheba

MEDITERRANEAN SEA

JORDAN R.

DEAD SEA

COASTAL PLAIN
- - - -   WALK
~~~~   RIVER

Jefferson

13

THE SUN WAS SHINING brightly as I walked across the sands, banishing my irritation. It had been a trying morning. First, my rucksack strap had come undone as I walked toward the sea along the line of the Washingtonian palm trees, introduced to Atlit by agronomist Aaron Aaronson. Then, I couldn't find a piece of wire to fix it, although most of the time pieces of wire were ten-a-penny on the roadside. Finally, my plans to visit the Atlit Crusaders' fortress, so captivating from above, were stymied; it turned out to be a military area.

I have already noted that the Crusaders lost control of Palestine to Saladin toward the end of the twelfth century. Subsequently, they gained control of the coastal plain, setting up their headquarters at Acre, farther north. In 1218, they built an important fortress at Atlit, which they held until they left for good in 1291. Atlit was, in fact, their final point of departure. To forestall a possible return of the Crusaders, the Muslims dismantled most of the fortifications; but much of it remained intact until 1837, when an earthquake completed the work of destruction. I should still have liked to see it.

In 1903, Baron Edmond bought Atlit and the surrounding swampland. The first villagers built evaporation pans for the production of salt, a function the pans still fulfill today. During the First World War, Atlit was the center of a pro-British spying organization, of which more later. In the Second World War, it was a British naval base, and after the Allied victory in North Africa, it became a prisoner-of-war camp. After the war, illegal Jewish immigrants were detained there.

Who were these illegals? In the years before the war, and, of course, for the duration of the conflict, the British clamped down severely on Jewish immigration to Palestine. The British authorities were concerned not to alienate the Arabs, so they acted against the Jews. They were worried that the Arabs might support the German side, but obviously there was no danger of the Jews supporting Hitler! It was a reversal of the situation in the years before the Balfour Declaration, when the British had been angling for Jewish support.

To the Jews, the cold logic of the British position seemed callous indeed. Jews were desperate to leave Europe, and they had nowhere to go. Every country in the world imposed quotas restricting the number of Jews they would allow in. Palestine, the so-called National Home, was also closed to them.

The Haganah set up Aliya Bet (B-aliya, as opposed to A-aliya, the legal variety), an incredibly complex operation for smuggling Jews out of Nazi Europe and into Palestine. Getting the immigrants past the British blockade was often harder than getting them out of Europe, but the operation continued throughout the war.

After the war, the British would still not allow the survivors of the Holocaust to enter Palestine. Aliya Bet stepped up its activities, bringing in thousands of illegals in a miserable collection of leaky and inadequate vessels. Sometimes the immigrants managed to land. Often they were stopped by the British, either to be sent back to Europe or interned on Cyprus. The "lucky" ones were detained in Palestine, many of them in Atlit.

In one of the famous stories of the time, a Haganah force broke into the camp and broke out again with 200 illegals. At the same time, a convoy of trucks was traveling south past Atlit. Naturally, the British chased the trucks, which turned out to be empty. The illegals made their escape on foot.

*   *   *

It was a morning of mistakes. My next one was to walk right past the Atlit village restaurant, one of the best in the country, in order to eat at the nearby kibbutz guest house. I not only missed a meal in Atlit; the guest house was closed for the summer. I walked down toward the beach somewhat disgruntled.

At this point (as I have already mentioned) my irritation vanished as I walked along the firm sand. The salty breeze blew in my face, the gulls swooped and screamed, a flock of late storks bunched, hanging almost motionless in the clear sky. The Carmel range was now on my left, and I could see quite clearly the large openings of caves in the cliffs. My friend Elijah had lived in one of those caves, but their history went back much earlier.

Most archaeological sites in Israel are of the Bronze Age and later, going through the Biblical, Second Temple, Byzantine, Muslim, and Crusader periods. The Carmel caves are different. In the late 1920s, an Anglo-American expedition discovered skeletons there belonging to an intermediate type between Neanderthal man and *homo sapiens*. Weapons and jewelry of stone and bone were found nearby, as were the bones of elephants and rhinoceros, dating back more than 100,000 years.

Proceeding southward, I passed the Atlit war memorial, where the son of a friend of ours is among those commemorated.

We had come to know David during several successive

summer holidays. When we first met him, he was a robust, young-looking forty-year-old, sunburned, shoulders back, chest thrown out — a bit of a *shvitzer* (boaster), as we Israelis say.

"I was a champion swimmer in Manchester," he informed us, as he shouted instructions to the children in his charge and splashed the teen-age girls. We used to call him "David the Swimming Champ" in an ironic but affectionate tone. He became a fixture of our summer holidays.

Then, in 1974, a quiet, stooped man approached us on the beach and asked us how we were. I looked at my wife in puzzlement. Suddenly it dawned on us: it was David. He was no swimming champ now, but a man who had folded in on himself, who had literally shrunk in size.

"You haven't heard," he informed rather than asked us. His son had been killed in the Yom Kippur War of the preceding year. It was a hideous story. Initially, the boy had been reported missing, and for long months his grief-stricken parents had dared to hope that somehow he might still be alive. When his remains were finally discovered, he had to be identified by his teeth. David recounted all the ghastly details.

I had never seen a man so transformed by sorrow. He died a few months later, of cancer they said. I think he died of a broken heart. He didn't bother to fight the disease; he simply lost the will to go on living.

I suppose that the real tragedy of this story is the death of the son, a young man deprived of the chance to live; but it is of David I think when I pass the memorial, for me an unbearable illustration of the cost of our continuing conflict.

The Yom Kippur War was traumatic for Israel. This year once again, on the anniversary, national and military leaders felt compelled to remind the people that it was the Arab side which asked for a cease-fire at the end of the conflict, that Israel won the war. But in a very real sense it was Israel's first defeat.

Not that Israel lost the battle. Attacking on Yom Kippur, when the whole country was shut down and even normally nonobservant Jews were fasting, many of them in synagogue, the Arab side did gain some initial advantages. The Syrians advanced across much of the Golan Heights, captured by Israel in 1967, and threatened Galilee. In the south, the Egyptians crossed over the Suez Canal in large numbers, taking all but one of the forts along the Israeli-controlled side of the waterway.

Taken by surprise, at first almost overwhelmed, faced by some of the most formidable technology ever mobilized in war, Israel's counterattack, which took its forces to a point sixty-three miles from Cairo and to within shooting distance of Damascus, was epic by any standards. Although Israel's losses were greater than in any conflict since the 1948 war, they were small compared with those of Syria and Egypt. In terms of equipment, the Arab side lost almost three times as much as Israel. Despite the presence of Egyptian forces in the Sinai, Israel's territorial gains on both fronts were decisive. Yet all this failed to obliterate the trauma of those first few hours. A bitter joke of the time said: The Arabs have learned to fight from us; we have learned to make propaganda like them.

No other war has provoked such doubts, so much soul-searching and breast-beating. War was considered an insufficient word to describe what had happened: it was an "earthquake." The search for a scapegoat led to the appointment of an inquiry commission and the ultimate destruction of the careers of the chief of staff and two of his senior colleagues. The subsequent protest movements, many of them led by demobilized soldiers, ultimately brought down the government. Many Israelis accepted the statement of their president, Ephraim Katzir, who coined the phrase "We are all guilty!"

Outside observers have suggested that it was Israel's arrogance that had been punctured, that the myth of this country's invincibility was shattered. Such theories show a misunderstanding of Israel's essential sense of vulnerability. Israelis have always been all too conscious of being outnumbered by more than fifty to one. This generation has grown up in the shadow of the slaughter of Europe's Jews. It knows not only that a Holocaust can happen; it *has* happened. Nothing in history even remotely parallels the Jewish experience. No other people has lost one third of its membership.

When the Six Day War broke out in 1967, considerable numbers of normal, intelligent Israelis really believed that they were about to die in a mass bloodbath. The relief after the swift, spectacular victory in that war may have led to a kind of drunkenness; but almost everyone assumed it would be followed by negotiation and withdrawal. The so-called arrogance, really a kind of hopeless fatalism, came with the refusal of the Arab side to talk.

Israel's thesis has always been that it cannot afford to lose even one war. It is a variant of the *ain brera* (no alternative) doctrine of 1948. Israel can win as often as it likes; but if the Arabs win, that is the end. Until 1973 this was almost universally accepted in Israel. Thus, when Moshe Dayan said in 1967 that Israel had prevented the destruction of the Third Temple, it was not jubilant arrogance; it was the relief of one who had seen the millennium face to face.

The trouble with the Israel-Arab conflict is that it has been a struggle between two inferiority complexes. The Arabs have felt humiliated by their failure to wipe out a minuscule country composed of the world's rejects, the more so as they always regarded their own Jews as a minority to be tolerated and pitied at best. The Israelis have always been acutely conscious of the numerical, political, and economic superiority of the Arabs. Neither side believed in its heart of hearts that it was the stronger, and that is why neither side could take that first real step toward peace.

Long before the Yom Kippur War, I remarked jokingly to a friend, "Why the hell don't we admit to the Arabs that we've lost the conflict, that they're stronger, and that we surrender? Then they'll be happy and give up the war against us."

Of course, something comparable to this did happen in the Yom Kippur War. During the second week of that war, a fellow soldier timidly suggested, "Maybe we ought to leave it like this, with them on our side of the canal? Then they'll salvage their pride and make peace."

Sitting in our outpost on the Jordan River, we all jumped on him. The Arabs have to be taught a lesson, we said. We have to get to Cairo and Damascus this time!

But my small, balding, undistinguished army mate was right, and we were all wrong. It was indeed his "victory" in the Yom Kippur War that gave President Sadat the self-confidence to come to Jerusalem. The other Arab leaders, who never achieved even his limited success, are still staying away.

As for us Israelis, well, maybe the shock treatment did shake us out of our preconceived notions. One of Israel's most perceptive commentators, General Chaim Herzog, called his book on the war *The War of Atonement,* and not only because it was launched on Yom Kippur.

*   *   *

It was difficult to remain with these somber thoughts as I walked along the shore in the sunshine. Two children sped past on their bicycles, their dog scampering after them. There were so many happy memories of our holidays at nearby Moshav Habonim. Days in the sun, lazy days, swimming, snorkeling, evening films outside on the village lawn, barbecues on the beach, and sing-songs around the campfire.

I passed a shipwreck, the metal hulk buried in the sand,

and I knew that I had almost arrived. The wreck was about thirty feet long. It was reputed to have been a refugee boat, bringing in illegals in 1947. I don't know about that: it couldn't have brought very many. One of our kids once called it "the fish-wreck" in his childish English, and fish-wreck it has remained. In the summer it used to be half-covered by water and we would wade out to it. It was an adventure for the children, but once Jera, my brother's son from England, after clambering aboard with unaccustomed daring, had found the sea tugging at his feet.

"Help, I'm being killed!" he shrieked as he jumped over-board.

I arrived at our beloved bay to find four men fishing in the sea with very long bamboo poles. They told me that they were from Nazareth. I sat on the rocks and watched them. They did not seem to be catching very much, but that didn't seem to worry them. They were clearly enjoying themselves; from time to time shouts rang out in Arabic.

Inland about a mile away, I could see the houses of Mo-shav Habonim, our vacation village for a number of years. Although most of the memories were, as I have mentioned, of summertime, our first visit there was in autumn, and we had very special reasons for enjoying it.

We had been living in the town of Arad in the desert for more than six years, and the green lawns, balmy nights, and subtropical vegetation were a welcome contrast to the arid southlands. It had been a difficult year. The previous autumn, we had moved up to a new house we had built on the hill above the town. We had expected to be part of a new neighborhood, starting with at least twenty families; but after we were already settled in our house, most of our friends announced that they were putting off their move until the spring.

Thus it was that we found ourselves almost totally iso-lated on a bare desert hill, with no road, no street-lighting, and the next-door neighbor about a hundred yards away across the wilderness. It was some three months after the Six Day War, about the time that the Arab terrorist organizations, notably El-Fatah, restarted their operations against civilian targets in Israel.

About a month after we moved in, terrorists blew up the natural-gas pipe that passed through our back garden. Four of our windows were shattered, and my wife was showered with glass; but there was no other damage. I was fifteen miles away, working at a temporary job down at the Dead Sea, when it happened. The gas burned with a spectacular flame, and half the town was up at our house taking pictures. But at nightfall they all left, leaving us to face the darkness alone. I cannot say that we felt happy those first few nights, but Angela took it in her stride — until the gas company came and repaired the pipe.

"It was as if they were deliberately setting up the target again," she told me when I came home.

Our "winter of discontent" was not without its lighter side. One evening we had some people to dinner, including a number from abroad and a Tel Aviv attorney. Over coffee, I tackled him about the possibility of getting some compensation for the damage caused by the explosion. Should I sue the local council or the gas company? He thought there was a case for either or both. Where actually did the explosion occur? In the garden, eh? Just down there? Not nice, not nice at all. (Pause.) Well, he rather thought they ought to be getting along. It had been very nice. Thanks for the dinner. Ninety seconds later they had swept away in their large car and we were alone in the night. We were used to it by then and could laugh. Angela said grimly that she would remember that technique for getting rid of lingering guests.

After a year on that hill, our visit to Moshav Habonim was therapeutic. It was so civilized. We climbed up on the roof of the cultural center and looked down on the lights of a dozen neighboring villages. The train went past our window at regular intervals during the night, hooting and waking us up. We loved it.

On our first morning there, Etan and I rose early and spent five hours snorkeling. A decade ago, the Mediterranean was less polluted, and we spotted a wide variety of fishes.

"The best day I have ever had," said my eight-year-old son.

There were many other good days. For six consecutive years, we rented a modest moshav house, and each holiday was better than the one before it. Undoubtedly, one of the main reasons for the success of our vacations was the presence of our friends the Plotkins, members of the moshav. It was to their house that I now repaired to receive a most welcome cup of tea.

From them, I learned that the village was prospering, earning good money from avocados and other subtropical fruit. It had also acquired some new members — bad news for us, because there would be no houses for rent in the summer. But I was glad to hear that the village was cresting the wave of rural prosperity.

Later that evening, I called on two other friends, Beryl and Hanan, and Hanan reminded me of an argument we had had six months earlier about the prospects of peace with Egypt. He had maintained that the differences between us and the Egyptians were too wide. He still believed this, saying that he did not really believe the Egyptians wanted peace; they just hoped Israel would withdraw from the territories taken in 1967. He said that Egypt was giving full support to the PLO, which wanted to get rid of Israel. I disputed this and said that Egypt was primarily interested in the Sinai. If Israel showed a reasonable attitude toward withdrawal from the West Bank, the Egyptians would leave us alone to settle it with Jordan or the Palestinians or both.

There was nothing original about this argument, and I mention it only to illustrate a curious point. My walk was undertaken during the Israel-Egypt negotiations that did eventually lead to the peace treaty. These talks were arguably the most fateful in our nation's thirty-year history; our future depended on their outcome. In a country the size of Israel, you cannot cop out. If there was war, my son would be in the front line; Hanan's daughter could become a widow. Everyone in the state is directly and materially affected. And yet, people had switched off. In this very political country of ours, the negotiations were a nonevent. Apart from my evening with Mansur Kardosh (and we always talk politics), the peace process had come up only when I mentioned it first. People were talking about their personal affairs, the local elections, the development of their town or village, even the general purpose of Zionism — not the current peace process.

Maybe the whole thing was too new an experience; possibly Israelis were so used to the siege that they thought it would go on forever. Or was it that they were afraid to hope, frightened of the bitter disappointment of failure?

I really do not know the answers to these questions, but possibly a clue was provided in Hanan's final remark to me.

"I hope that I'm wrong and that there will be peace," he said. "I hope that there are things I don't know about."

That could be the key phrase: "things I don't know about." Jewish history (and in particular modern Israeli history) has conspired to make the Israeli — citizen of the most open democracy on earth, where everybody knows everything — believe that there are all sorts of secret factors, all manner of behind-the-scenes deals in national and international events. Maybe. I am enough of an Israeli to half-believe that myself.

14

FROM MOSHAV HABONIM, I walked south along the railway line with the banana plantations on one side and some experimental fishponds on the other. There are freshwater ponds all over the country that breed carp. Here, an attempt is being made to breed saltwater fish in ponds. After a couple of miles, I turned east toward the Haifa–Tel Aviv road and soon found myself in citrus country. Taking advantage of the situation, I picked a juicy grapefruit for breakfast. I enjoyed it, but from then on confined myself to oranges and tangerines. Grapefruit is fine for breakfast, with toast and coffee to follow, but on the road, I found that the bitter taste lingered on.

Opposite the citrus orchard was a field with long lines of plastic-covered tunnels, about waist-high. Closer inspection showed that flowers were being grown in them. Plastic sheeting (much of it manufactured in Ginnegar) has revolutionized farming all over the country. Wherever I went I was to find different types of hothouses, from simple covers held up with iron hoops to elaborate structures with temperature and moisture regulators.

Near the Arab fishing and farming village of Furedis, I was invited to photograph two elderly men with a small flock of goats. Grizzled and toothless, wearing baggy linen trousers, with a keffiya wound around his head, Mustafa was a retired quarryman. His goats and fruit trees supplemented his pension, he told me, and he counted himself well-off. He pressed me with an invitation to coffee, but I declined.

I walked up the steep hill into the town of Zichron Yaacov, arriving at the Carmel wine cellars, founded by the Baron, where I persuaded the elderly lady, who acted as a sort of local guide, to show me around. I viewed the enormous vats, the modern plastic and stainless-steel equipment, the bottling plant; but I found myself more interested in the photographs of the early days, which showed the first workers at the winery, their casks, horses and carts, and primitive equipment. I was assured that, despite all the new equipment, the wine was still stored in oaken casks. Originally concentrating on the sweet red wine used for the Friday night Sabbath blessing by Jews all over the world, the cellars now turn out a wide range of European-style table wines.

In 1882, a group of Rumanian pioneers bought some land on the Carmel, around the site of a deserted Arab village. They were particularly hopeful about a fertile-looking plain to the south of the village. They had brought seed with them, which they planted, but the seeds rotted in the marshland and malaria struck hard at the villagers. In 1883, twenty-nine of the hundred inhabitants died of malaria and cholera.

The following year, Baron Edmond, who was just getting involved in settlement, came to their rescue, and in 1887, his officials decided that viticulture was the answer for this location. The winery was established. Large investments were made and a synagogue was built. Despite the conflicts that arose between the Baron and the pioneers, they called their village Zichron Yaacov (memory of Jacob), after Baron Edmond's father.

The Baron's officials had quite rightly spoken out against the life style that was developing in the village, with Arabs being used not only as field laborers, but even as domestic servants. This practice was stopped. The other reason for conflict concerned the Hebrew language. The Rothschild officials tried to encourage the use of French as a modern, civilized language, whereas the villagers were devoted to the revival of Hebrew. I had a very personal interest in this particular aspect of the story, because one of the champions of Hebrew was Rabbi Zeev Yaavetz, who lived in the village during the last years of the nineteenth century.

Yaavetz, an eminent Hebrew scholar and a historian, who published a fourteen-volume history of the Jews from a religious standpoint, was my great-grandfather. He was something of a family totem, and I was determined to take this opportunity to find out something of his early life. My guide informed me that Yaacov Epstein, the son of one of the founders of the village, was the local expert on the pioneer days. I would find him at the local council offices.

A secretary informed me that my man was having a meeting with the mayor, but I did not have to wait for long. Small, alert, with bright eyes behind his spectacles, Epstein strode from the mayor's office. His face lit up when I told him why I had come.

"What an amazing coincidence!" he exclaimed. He drew out a wallet from which he extracted an ancient photograph of a black-bearded young man with flashing eyes.

"Yaavetz?" I asked. The only picture that I had ever seen was of an elderly scholar with a snow-white beard, which hangs in my aunt's home in London.

"Yaavetz," he replied with satisfaction. "I have just secured a small grant from the council to have this picture enlarged for our museum." He promised to tell me all about Yaavetz.

I followed Epstein out of the municipal building and down the main street. Zichron Yaacov has grown into a small town, one of the prettiest in the country. It was expanded in the 1950s with the arrival of the oriental Jewish immigrants. More recently, a number of Israelis have built private houses there, attracted by the superb views of Galilee to the north and east and the panorama down to the sea on the west. The hilltop climate is relatively cool, and there are several beaches within a few minutes' driving time.

Yad Lerishonim, the Founders' Memorial, is at the southern extremity, overlooking the cultivated plateau, which used to be swamp. A beautiful little museum, established and maintained almost singlehandedly by Epstein himself, it contains a fine collection of photographs, maps, and documents of the early period. Epstein led me over to a group photograph, obviously of a school, and pointed to the same young bearded man whose picture he had shown me earlier.

"That is Zeev Yaavetz" (dramatic pause) "and he left because of her!" He indicated a dark-eyed beauty in the same picture, thick hair piled high, dressed in a flowing white garment. My interest pricked up; I sensed an ancient family scandal about to be disclosed.

"Oh, no," he shook his head. "It's not what you're thinking; it was because she was chosen to be the headmistress of the school."

Yaavetz had served as headmaster, but the Baron's men had sent this young lady to Paris. When she returned, it was resolved to appoint her headmistress. Yaavetz had said, "Either me or the Frenchwoman!"

The Baron's men had influence, so he had resigned. Ironically, recalled Epstein, the "Frenchwoman" (as they all called her, although in point of fact she was a daughter of the village) had never become the principal. The opposition by the villagers was so strong that finally another rabbi had been brought in to take up the position — but by then Yaavetz had left.

Epstein told me that my great-grandfather had been

very much loved in Zichron. He had stood up to the Baron's men for the rights of the villagers and had mediated a number of disputes between them. He had also served as a respected mediator in disputes among the settlers.

"Did you know that Zeev Yaavetz started the custom of tree-planting on Tu B'Shvat?" he threw at me.

Tu B'Shvat, the fifteenth of the Hebrew month of Shvat, which falls in early spring, is the New Year of the Trees. It has become an important festival in Israel, where afforestation has played a major role in land reclamation. Every kibbutz, moshav, and school has tree-planting ceremonies on that day, with special songs and dances.

"Before Yaavetz," said Epstein, "we simply went to synagogue for prayers on Tu B'Shvat and ate fruit. It was Yaavetz who said that we must plant trees. We started in Zichron, and soon it was taken up by all the other villages."

My previous knowledge of my great-grandfather's achievements had been confined to his history and his fight for Hebrew. He was responsible for adapting two Hebrew words to modern usage: *kvish,* meaning highway, and *tarbut,* in the sense of culture. His conflict with the "French-woman" has to be viewed in the context of the struggle for Hebrew waged by the early pioneers. Its success, the envy of those trying to revive Gaelic and Welsh, must be attributed to the tenacity of the pioneers, and in particular to the obstinacy of one man, Eliezer Perlman, who came to Palestine in 1881.

While lying ill in a Paris hospital, Perlman learned from a fellow patient, a Jerusalem inhabitant, that the different Jewish communities there communicated in Hebrew. Jews from Morocco and other Arab countries who lived there could communicate with their European fellows only in Hebrew. He also learned the Sephardic (oriental) pronunciation, which was in use in Palestine.

On his way to Palestine, Perlman started to speak Hebrew to his wife, forcing her to answer in the same language. Arriving in Jerusalem, he became assistant editor of a Hebrew newspaper. A few years later, when a new boys' school was opened, he prevailed on the principal to adopt Hebrew as the language of instruction, and obtained a teaching post there.

When the Ottoman authorities offered Turkish nationality to all who wanted it, Perlman took out papers in the name of Ben-Yehuda (son of Judah).

"Now I was legally and officially a citizen of Jerusalem," he exulted. "I bore the Hebrew name of Ben-Yehuda . . . I felt that I had been reborn."

Even at home and with his friends, Ben-Yehuda sternly refused to speak any language other than Hebrew. Although his wife was ill when giving birth to their first child, he refused to engage a home-helper in case the child's language be polluted by a non-Hebrew speaker. Quite recently his daughter recalled in a radio interview a frightful row between her parents resulting from her mother's singing a Russian lullaby.

Ben-Yehuda composed the first comprehensive dictionary of modern Hebrew and was undoubtedly the outstanding figure in the revival of the language, but it was a struggle waged by many of the early pioneers. Zichron Yaacov played its part. It was here that the first Hebrew Teachers' Association was founded, in 1902. It should be stressed that Hebrew has fulfilled a vital role in the unification of modern Israel. I have dwelt on some of the divisions in our society; but I have no doubt that a basic unity does exist and that the Hebrew language is one of the most important factors which brought it about.

Dutifully, I followed Epstein around the remainder of his museum, a personal effort in more ways than one. There were innumerable photos of Epstein on horseback, Epstein in Arab headdress, Epstein cross-legged on the ground conferring with armed colleagues and Bedouin sheikhs. He pointed to the picture of a rabbi who had been murdered by local Bedouin.

"They paid for that with blood," he declared, not without satisfaction. "Now it can be told."

Relations with the people of Furedis, on the other hand, had always been very good. Others had tried to incite them against Zichron, but to no avail. During the 1948 war, he personally had gone to Furedis to tell the Arabs not to flee.

"Don't leave, I told them. Epstein guarantees your safety!" He thumped his chest to emphasize his remarks.

Leaving the museum, I paid a brief visit to the house of the Aaronson family, which commemorates Zichron's best-known celebrities.

Aaron Aaronson became world-renowned as an agronomist after he discovered wild wheat, the "mother of wheat," in the region of Mount Hermon. Invited to the United States, he made a notable contribution to the acclimatization of wheat in the colder, northern region. His achievements made possible the establishment of an experimental station in Atlit, with American funds. He introduced many species from abroad there, including the Washingtonian palms I have already mentioned.

Shortly before the First World War, he founded an organization called the Gideonites, named after the Biblical Gideon. The members planned to revolt against Ottoman rule and to set up an independent Jewish state. With the outbreak of war, the Gideonites merged themselves into Nili (initials for "the glory of Israel will not be false," in Hebrew), a spying organization on behalf of the British.

Using the Atlit experimental station as their base, they were successful in collecting information about the Turkish forces and passing it to the British in Egypt. As an agronomist, Aaronson had considerable freedom of movement both inside and outside the country, particularly when he was called on to deal with the great locust plague of 1916. But his sister Sarah was no less effective. Frequently dressed as a Bedouin woman, she went all over the country, collecting intelligence. One of the means of conveying this to the British was by signaling to warships off Atlit.

Late in 1917, the Nili spy network was uncovered and many of its members were captured. Sarah refused to flee and was arrested in her Zichron Yaacov home. Horribly tortured, she refused to divulge anything. Hot stones under her armpits, savage and repeated beatings on the soles of her feet, thumbscrews — none of these managed to break her down. When her elderly father was stripped and beaten in front of her, she merely exhorted him to be brave and to remember his ancestors. Finally, she managed to get permission to go to the bathroom, where she had concealed a pistol, and shot herself in the mouth.

Wandering through the pink stucco house and its shady courtyard, I was reminded of a previous visit, when we had caught sight of Sarah's sister, a very old lady by then, frail and white-haired. The room of Sarah can be viewed, much as it was then, and there is a display of Aaron's botanical specimens.

*   *   *

That afternoon, I walked up to Bat-Shlomo, a tiny village of twelve families that has remained unchanged for seventy years. In the 1950s a moshav of the same name was established nearby, with the hope that the two communities would eventually merge, but the original hamlet has remained resolutely separate, a picturesque place with old stone houses and cows wandering down the only street.

I enjoyed a cup of tea and a brief chat with one of the founding families, the Edelsteins. Their son, a third-generation farmer on the same land, came in from plowing and supplied me with a good crack that Moshe Dayan had made when he was the minister of agriculture: "There are three ways of losing money: gambling, women, and agriculture. Gambling is the quickest; women the pleasantest; but agriculture is the surest!"

I laughed, but challenged the truth of the statement, citing the manifest prosperity in the countryside. He claimed that the affluence was recent, following decades of hardship. He doubted whether agriculture was a good investment when compared to other things. Someone who played the stock market could increase his investment more quickly, and even the purchaser of a house or apartment made better profits. Every government had funneled enormous sums into agriculture, which was in fact subsidized. The farmer was handed a lot on a plate. Young Edelstein had been to the United States and seen farms where the owner had had to dig his own wells. In Israel, water was brought to the fields.

Many crops were becoming prohibitively expensive. Fruit, for example, could be grown only with Arab labor. Jews were not prepared to do the work. That was why the kibbutzim were going over to mechanized crops, like cotton. On this, at least, his remarks were inaccurate. I had seen citrus groves in Ginnegar; avocados at Moshav Habonim. Amiad still maintained extensive orchards and was experimenting with a new fruit called actinidia. I put it down to the old tradition of Arab labor continuing in the first villages, although it would be wrong to suggest that they were the only ones that took advantage of Arab workers.

* * *

I stayed that night with Yossi and Solly Snir, former neighbors who now lived in the house of a fellow writer, Hillel Halkin. In contrast to the American-born Halkin, who had relished every Zichron character, the Snirs had little patience for their fellow citizens. It had been the same in Metulla, where Aric Yaacov, formerly from New York, loved the villagers, whereas the Israeli-born Hamizrachi had found little to commend them. Sabras, I conclude, have no time for the pioneering saga. Yossi — pragmatic, intelligent — laughs at sentimentality. About Bat-Shlomo, he asked me, "Didn't they ask you who was winning the war, the Jews or the Arabs? They're not part of the State of Israel!"

There had been no real mixing in Zichron Yaacov between the veterans and the immigrants of the 1950s. There were two separate communities, as if they belonged to separate species. A friend of the Snirs, newly settled in Zichron, recalled that during the Yom Kippur War, she had been refused milk for her baby. "Zichron villagers first" had been the rule at the local grocery store.

Metulla, Sejera, Zichron, Bat-Shlomo: everywhere I had found villagers odd to the point of eccentricity. I suppose that the first settlers would not have stuck it out at all if they had not been extraordinary people. It was Chaim Weizmann who said, "You don't have to be mad to be a Zionist, but it helps!"

15

Baron Edmond de Rothschild's tomb is outside Zichron Yaacov on a hill called Ramat Hanadiv (hill of the benefactor), which overlooks the fields and orchards on what used to be the malarial swamp. In 1954, an Israeli warship brought the Baron's remains to be laid to rest in a natural cave, which is today surrounded by beautiful gardens. The order to bring Baron Edmond's remains for reburial in Israel, in an official state ceremony, was given by the prime minister of the time, David Ben-Gurion. The wheel had come full circle, as the former second-aliya pioneer paid tribute to the Father of Settlement.

Walking down the hill into the plain below, I realized that I was finished with mountains until I reached the Negev. My route would now take me more or less straight down the cultivated coastal plain, with no more serious climbs or descents until after Beersheba.

I would now be passing through the most densely populated part of the country, although I would be avoiding Tel Aviv and its surroundings. It is a paradox that most Israelis today live in the plain, whereas in historical times the Jews were a hill people. Their enemies, the Philistines, lived in the plains, and even later on they were concentrated in the hills, whereas the Romans and Syrian-Greeks lived in such centers as Caesarea. Some of the proponents of annexation of the West Bank point to this historical anomaly, suggest-

ing that the Jews have more right to live near Nablus, for
example, than in Tel Aviv. The historical Land of Israel,
they note, was in the mountains. In due course we shall
be returning to these questions. At this point, let me be
content with registering my opinion that if there is a lesson
to be learned from our history, it is that Israel, or Judea,
existed in different shapes and sizes, according to the situation at each particular time in history. Thus, in the time of
David and Solomon, it stretched over much of what is
today Syria and Lebanon, as well as Israel and Jordan.
Conversely, following the return from Babylon, Judah was
confined to a small area around Jerusalem. The modern return of the Jews was to regions where they were able to
purchase land from the Arabs. This tended to be in the
plains, many of which had degenerated into swamps.

The weather was holding as I walked through grape and
citrus country toward Benyamina (named for Baron Edmond, whose Hebrew name was Benjamin). The soil had
turned red, the *hamra* soil said to be the most suitable for
citrus, and I treated myself to a couple of particularly juicy
tangerines from a nearby orchard.

About halfway between Zichron and Benyamina, I came
across an interesting industrial plant. Largely automated,
and employing only three workers, it recycled used plastic
(polyethylene bags, transparent sheeting, and other items)
to manufacture insulation granules and black plastic pipes.
The piping was not strong enough for irrigation; it was
used for holding electric wires inside walls. The granules
could be compressed into blocks for the insulation of walls
or ceilings. One man was cutting up the waste material
with a band saw, and two others were feeding it into hop-
pers. It emerged at the end of a series of tubes and water
troughs, either as granules or in the form of a continuous
black snake of tubing.

I wondered why such plants cannot be established near

every town and village in the country. It would keep the
countryside clean, utilizing material that is not only
wasted, but that is usually left around as an eyesore. I have
no idea of the economics of such a plant — the machinery
looked modern and expensive — but presumably it had
been worth somebody's while to make the investment. I
applauded the unknown man, a real benefactor of the
countryside.

Benyamina is a sleepy village of citrus and flowers, the
latter grown mainly under various types of plastic covering.
The main road is lined with tall palms, and signs of moder-
nity are few and far between. Even the railway station has a
pleasing, archaic quality about it. A delightful white cot-
tage, surrounded by a green lawn, bears the legend SHOE
SHOP.

The walk was pleasant enough, except for the sight of my
fifteenth dead dog. There had also been cats, mice, birds,
and hedgehogs — all casualties of society's champion killer,
the automobile. I continued south along the road to the
joint township of Pardes Hanna–Karkur, created by the
merging of two villages. Karkur, started by a group of London Jews in 1912, is mainly famous as the site of growing
pineapples under glass.

Leaving the road, I struck across the sand dunes to Or
Akiva. A tough but stimulating walk. I struggled up the
soft slopes to attain the hard, flat surface of the plateau,
sweating and panting and wondering where on earth I had
got the idea that I was finished with climbing. That walk
was as bad as an army training march, except that I could
set my own pace. Although the area is not marked as a nature reserve, it is without human habitation and consequently filled with a plentiful variety of bird life. Despite
the rains of the previous week, the ponds and valleys were
dried up, with the exception of one shallow pool, where the
seagulls congregated. Emerging onto the main road, I ob-

served several notice boards: DO NOT APPROACH: DANGER OF DROWNING. SOFT SANDS: DANGEROUS! And so on. *Now* they tell me, I said to myself.

Or Akiva is one of the least successful development towns of the 1950s. It started life in the normal way as a ma'arbara transit camp for immigrants. Experiments to convert it into a fishing village and an agricultural settlement failed. The bad living conditions and the unemployment of the early years have left their mark, and the town is currently the holder of the national record for juvenile delinquency.

I had first seen it in the early 1960s, when it was already a small town, but not a pretty one. Mean apartment blocks, dirty shops, and litter-filled streets affronted the eye. The community was badly governed, with a corrupt and bickering town council. In 1971, the government stepped in and appointed a committee of civil servants to run the town for three years. Since that time, sizable sums of money have been invested in trying to make Or Akiva a better place to live in. This is evident as you enter the new main square, which is lined with modern shops and cafés, and a large cinema. Colorful plastic benches and a children's playground have been installed. The new apartment blocks are far pleasanter and the neighborhoods better maintained. In several locations, visible efforts have been made to clean up. Many of the original transit-camp shacks are still standing, but in most cases, these now serve as garden huts for quite affluent private houses.

A few minutes' walk down the road, and I was in a different world: the garden-suburb of Caesarea, possibly the most luxurious neighborhood in Israel, and a glaring contrast with Or Akiva, which provides it with daily-maids and gardeners. Almost all the houses in Caesarea are second homes, owned by Jews from abroad and Israelis from Tel Aviv and Jerusalem. The existence of Caesarea so near to Or Akiva vividly illustrates how far modern Israel has strayed from the egalitarian vision of the early pioneers. Walking between the rows of opulent villas with their well-tended gardens, most of them empty now that it was winter, I considered the factors that had led to the emergence of a wealthy class in this country.

I have already mentioned the fourth aliya. Between 1924 and 1926 some 60,000 Jews, more than half from Poland, arrived in the country. No less than 80 percent of these middle-class immigrants ended up in the three main cities: Jerusalem, Haifa, and Tel Aviv. Reinforced in the 1930s by the Yekkes of the fifth aliya, these immigrants, some of them wealthy, created the country's industrial infrastructure. The Jewish community in Palestine now had a capitalist class.

Nevertheless, the Israel that came into being in 1948 was still an egalitarian society by any standards. There were some rich men, and the mass immigration of the 1950s brought in a large class of underprivileged, but it is fair to say that there was still no really wealthy class in the country. On my first visit to Israel in 1954, I saw very few private cars on the roads. Indeed, even today, many Israelis refer to a private car as a "taxi," because those were almost the only automobiles on the roads aside from trucks.

Paradoxically, it was the Histadrut, the General Confederation of Labor, that was mainly responsible for the emergence of a capitalist society in Israel. The Histadrut had been founded in 1920 as a unified body to represent the country's workers. It took over a number of public works and started its own enterprises, but was also a general trade union. Acting in the correct trade-union tradition, the Histadrut demanded better standards of living for its members. The Labor Party, Mapai, dominated the government as well as the labor federation, and so it initiated a search for capital to finance modern industries that could provide high wages.

Some of the first investors were Jews from abroad; but local wealth was created, and private building contractors made money building houses and luxury apartments for the newly emerging affluent classes. Another source of capital that flowed into Israel at this time was German reparations. Western Germany paid out compensation to the individual victims of Nazism and also made national restitution to Israel as the country that had absorbed most of the survivors of the Holocaust. German reparations fueled much of the industrialization of the early sixties. Many Israelis see the reparations as the start of the degeneration of Israel's Socialist society. The effect of the payments was felt even in the kibbutzim, where members suddenly found themselves the recipients of large amounts of capital. Quite a number left their settlements and bought homes in the towns; but most remained in their villages, and the problem arose as to what to do with the money. Some kibbutzim insisted on the money going to the community as a whole. In many places, however, it was argued that the reparations had been paid over because of personal suffering, and the recipients were allowed to spend the money on themselves.

All over the country, Israelis began to own cars and other consumer items that they had not previously dreamed of possessing. The whole process was accelerated by the Six Day War and the industrial and commercial expansion that followed it. Cheap Arab labor from the newly occupied territories of the West Bank and Gaza now became available, and the Israeli Arab community had also grown swiftly since 1948.

The wages earned by the Arab workers raised living standards both in the Israeli Arab community and in the West Bank and Gaza. This has been a good thing both for the Arabs themselves and for Israel, but the consequences for Israeli society were mixed. On the one hand, there was a general rise in living standards, but on the other, there was too much conspicuous affluence. A nouveau riche class emerged, and the social gap, which had of course always existed, widened. One problem was that most of the rich were of European origin. Some oriental Jews also became wealthy, but the vast majority of them were in the poorer classes. And here was another paradox. The Histadrut's demands for higher living standards initiated the creation of capitalism, but now it became apparent that much of the industry was, in fact, Histadrut-owned. Many of the luxury apartments were being built by the Histadrut's building company. The Confederation of Labor was one of the biggest capitalists in the country! Furthermore, labor relations have been worst in the public sector. Almost all the strikes in Israel have occurred in government concerns, Histadrut-owned industries, or the civil service.

Although I had seen plenty of Jewish workers on my walk, the principle of Jewish self-labor seemed far away as I walked through Caesarea that afternoon. And yet, even as I regretted the passing of the simple, modest society of the pioneers, I was forced to ask myself whether Israel could have survived as a simpler and hence more primitive society. Wasn't mechanization and technical advancement essential for purely military reasons? Could Israel have maintained its position without the development of a military technology, which had to be supported by an industrial infrastructure of some sophistication?

I stopped in front of the home of the late Focca Hirsh, reputedly the most opulent villa in Caesarea, with a separate servants' apartment, a kidney-shaped swimming pool, and almost an acre of grounds. It is being offered for sale at a little over half a million dollars, including furniture and art treasures. And at this point I was forced to take stock and regain a sense of proportion. Is this wealth? Are these people "super-rich"? I thought of the great estates in Europe, of the landowners of thousands of acres, of the houses with hundreds of rooms. Measured against almost any standards other than those of the pioneer Jewish community in Israel itself, this country is still an egalitarian community. I thought of the houses in Or Akiva down the road and was forced to admit to myself that the differences between them and the Caesarea villas were often more of style than of quality.

There are an estimated 300,000 disadvantaged urban-dwellers in Israel, but, apart from some exceptional pockets, there is no real poverty, certainly no starvation. Where individual poor people fail to obtain assistance, it is either through ignorance or inefficiency, not because the help is not available. Operation Renewal has been launched by the present government to try to wipe out slums and deprivation; but even the inhabitants of the depressed neighborhoods say it is educational and social facilities that are really needed, not new buildings. Human rehabilitation is the need of the hour rather than slum clearance.

Yet, strolling down toward the Caesarea harbor, I felt a pang of sorrow that such beautiful second homes can exist in Israel while so many live in substandard first homes. I may tell myself to have a sense of proportion, but I find that my yardstick is still that of the 1920s.

In all honesty, though, I must record that these feelings did not prevent me from enjoying a memorable late lunch (almost an early dinner) at the exclusive Tower restaurant above Caesarea beach.

I began with *kubbe* (meat-filled rissole with cracked-wheat casing) and *tehina* (ground sesame sauce). This was followed by a superb gray mullet, fresh out of the sea and simply grilled, to avoid any interference with the natural taste. I ordered half a bottle of white wine to go with it and ended up with excellent Turkish coffee. Good as the meal was, it was the setting that made it memorable. The sun was descending into the sea, turning the battlements of Crusader Caesarea into a darkening silhouette against the flaming orange sky. The waves lapped against the jetty; I did not want to move.

Of course it was not the Crusaders who founded Caesarea. Indeed, though their remains here are some of the most impressive in the country, the Crusader fortress covered only a small part of what had been Roman Caesarea. Originally fortified by the Phoenicians in the fourth century B.C., it became important when the Edomite usurper of the Hasmonean line, Herod the Great, became King of Judea. I have noted that many of his Jewish subjects regarded Herod as a Roman vassal. One of his most Roman traits was his passion for spectacular building. He renovated the Temple of Jerusalem, making it one of the sights of the ancient world. He built an elaborate palace in the capital and also constructed fortress-palaces in the desert, the most famous of which was Masada. Here, on the coast, he built a large city and called it Caesarea, in honor of the Emperor Augustus. The deep-water port, constructed with two stone breakwaters, is impressive even by modern standards. The city also boasted a marketplace, a large theater, and a hippodrome that seated 20,000 people. A six-mile-long aqueduct brought water from the Crocodile River farther north.

Caesarea was the scene of numerous dramas. Herod's grandson, Herod Agrippa, was stricken in the theater here with the so-called Herod's Disease, in front of an adoring crowd of spectators. The story is told both in Josephus and in the New Testament. When the popular king appeared in the theater to cement his alliance with other eastern kings, he was hailed by the people as a "God." According to both of our sources, his punishment for failing to reject this appellation was the same illness that had killed his grandfather, a particularly revolting infection of the intestines and bowels. He was dead in less than a week. I think that if one takes into consideration the undoubted fact that he was shoring up an eastern alliance against Roman domination, the conclusion that the last King of Judea was poisoned cannot be ruled out.

Peter the Apostle is said to have baptized the centurion Cornelius here, and it was to Caesarea that Paul was first brought for trial. In A.D. 63, a clash between Jews and Syrian-Greeks in Caesarea led to the massacre of 20,000 Jews by Roman soldiers and triggered off the great Jewish war against Rome. Later still, following the suppression of the Bar-Kochba revolt of A.D. 132–135, Rabbi Akiva, spiritual leader of that rising, was tortured to death in the Caesarea dungeons.

Caesarea had, in fact, been the capital of Roman-occupied Judea after the Herods, and the various procurators who administered the country lived there. One of the most interesting artifacts found by the archaeologists is a shard inscribed with the name of Pontius Pilate. To skip the Byzantine and Persian periods: Caesarea was taken from the Muslims by the Crusaders in A.D. 1101, but it was only after Richard the Lion-hearted retook it from Saladin in 1191 that it was seriously fortified by them.

Much of the Roman harbor and the impressive amphitheater have been reconstructed. The massive walls and deep moat of the Crusader fortress have been excavated. The aqueduct has been reclaimed from the sand that covered it for generations, although of course it no longer supplies water to the town. On previous visits I have enjoyed superb concerts in the amphitheater and on one occasion I saw a spectacular performance of Saint-Saens's *Samson and Delilah* there. I have searched in the sands beneath the aqueduct for ancient coins, but have never found any. I have dived off the ancient stone jetty of the harbor into the clear, deep water. Sitting with these memories, looking out over the towers and battlements in the gathering dusk, I found it, as I say, very difficult to think of leaving.

I contemplated sleeping somewhere in the vicinity, but finally resolved that I would walk off the meal. At the back of my mind was the nagging feeling that I ought to be making more progress. As in Tiberias, I reminded myself sternly that I had promised myself to cover the whole of Israel, even if each individual location did demand a book to itself.

As one turns southward, he finds the beauty of Caesarea insulted by the looming twin towers of the new Hadera power station. Fortunately, it had become dark, and as I walked at a brisk pace along the shoulder of the main Haifa–Tel Aviv highway, I could see only the winking red and blue lights on the towers, high up in the sky. Down below, construction work must have been continuing, for the night was intermittently lit up by purple flashes of welding torches, as if the devil himself was busy in his workshop, wreaking this monstrosity on our beautiful landscape.

It may have been the vehicle exhausts, for the road is a very busy one, but I rather think it was the kubbe and tehina. At all events, I felt very sick on that walk. I forced myself to continue, hoping that the exercise would improve matters, but by the time I arrived at the village of Michmoret I felt very bad indeed. Michmoret offers rented rooms to vacationers, and I was looking forward to a shower and comfortable bed. Unfortunately for me, it was off-season: at house after house I was informed that accommodations were closed for the winter.

The November night was relatively mild, so I staggered down to the beach and rolled myself up in my sleeping bag under the stars. I woke in the cold, gray morning (the sunsets in Israel are beautiful; not the sunrises), feeling very much better. There was no breakfast to be had on the beach, which I shared with the seagulls and a couple of dogs, so I walked out of Michmoret toward the east. I had had enough of the highway and decided to cut across to the less busy inner road south. I found myself walking along the banks of the Alexander River. At first polluted and evil-smelling, it improved farther east, where the eucalyptus-lined stream teemed with bird and animal life. The path led me under the railway line and I sat under the bridge, watching an otter (or nutria) playing and swimming in the water. A train thundered high overhead and the animal dived from sight.

Walking through plantations of young avocado trees, the saplings protected by tents of sacking, their trunks painted white to protect them from the sun, I emerged from the countryside onto the road near the village of Kefar Vitkin. Here I met a group of children out on a nature hike. They were escorted by their teacher, who toted a carbine. It was the first group of Jews I had seen in open country since setting out on my walk. True, I was walking most of the time during the week in termtime, when most children are in school and their parents are at work; but it was also at a time of a strike by the country's high school teachers, and the secondary schools were all closed. Many of the pupils were presumably pursuing their studies at home; others, along with their teachers, were probably working at temporary jobs. But I should have thought that at least some of them would have taken the time to explore the highways and byways of their country.

The Jews were, it seems, in their towns and villages, on their tractors, at their factory benches, or in their cars. They had left the woods and hills, the fields, paths, and glades to the Arabs. A Martian, newly descended on earth, keeping away from the main centers of population through natural caution, would almost definitely conclude that Israel was an Arab country.

Kefar Vitkin, a prosperous moshav founded in 1933, is well known in Israel as the first port of call of the *Altalena* in 1948. A lengthy book has just been published on the *Altalena* affair, and Menahem Begin, Israel's prime minister, almost lost his life aboard the ship, so a brief recap is in order.

It is the last week of June 1948. The state of Israel is just over one month old. The two dissident Jewish military organizations, the Irgun (led by Begin) and the Lehi are in the process of being merged with the Haganah to form the new army, the Israel Defense Forces. But the merger has not yet been completed. An independent Irgun is still operating in Jerusalem, and some of its units are claiming that the new army discriminates against them. The situation is delicate.

The first of several truces in the 1948 war has been declared, and the country is full of United Nations observers. War is to break out again soon, but for the time being the Jews (Israelis now) are forbidden to bring more arms and equipment into the country.

Into this finely balanced situation sails the *Altalena*, a ship carrying Jewish volunteers who have come to fight for the new state, but also loaded (quite literally) with dynamite. For the ship is an Irgun vessel, acquired in Europe while that organization was still independent.

The arms are desperately needed. Negotiations between representatives of Prime Minister Ben-Gurion and Irgun leader Begin have been only partially successful. They have agreed that 20 percent of the arms on board will go to the beleaguered Irgun forces in Jerusalem, but they have not yet agreed about the disposal of the remainder of the equipment. The ship arrives at Kefar Vitkin, a Labor village loyal to the government. It is partly unloaded, but it is spotted by UN observers and puts out to sea again. Later it arrives off Tel Aviv.

Begin goes on board. The government orders the ship to surrender; ultimata are presented and lapse. The army (in fact, units of the Haganah) opens fire on the *Altalena* and sink it. Jews have killed Jews; there is a threat of civil conflict in the air. Begin himself narrowly escapes death after one of his colleagues throws him to the deck of the ship and sits on him. He is the last to leave the ship. Still under his control, the Irgun backs down from confrontation.

Today Menahem Begin is prime minister and his Herut Party, in the Likud, leads the government; but the *Altalena* and all it symbolizes is as live an issue today as it was then. It was, of course, only the last in a series of clashes between the Irgun and the Haganah, but it was the culminating one. After it, the Irgun, already in the process of disbanding, ceased to exist as a separate unit.

For the Labor movement, the incident was the final assertion of governmental authority, the expression of determination to quell insurgency and to allow a democratic state to come into being and survive the 1948 war. To Begin and his colleagues, it was the ultimate in hypocrisy and deception, the absolute proof that the ruthless Ben-Gurion would stop at nothing to get his way. It was the Irgun, they argue, that showed national responsibility by refusing to fight back and by abstaining from shedding Jewish blood.

The debate continues. The discussion in the Knesset, Israel's parliament, over the Israel-Egypt peace treaty may have been long and dramatic; some of the debates over religious issues or economic policy have been acerbic; but if you really want to get the members shouting, put down a motion on the agenda that in some way relates to the Haganah-Irgun clashes of the 1940s. Then you will see the real fireworks.

*   *   *

I arrived at the inner road south and walked through the heart of Israel's citrus country, keeping to the paths through the groves, which ran parallel to the highway. Despite the softness of the sandy surfaces, my legs and feet were still painful after two weeks of hiking.

Stopping for breakfast at a roadside café, where I had hot *burrekas* (cheese-filled pastries) and two superb cups of coffee, hot and bittersweet, I picked up a local journal entitled *In the Sharon and Samaria*. Some local news items caught my eye. Negotiations were proceeding for the formation of a municipal coalition in Givat Ada. Tal Brodie, the American immigrant basketball star (and a local folk hero), had initiated a new coaching scheme in the locality. In Hod Hasharon a new athletics club had been established and a Sharon region residents' committee had been formed to oppose the Camp David accords. My contemplation of these items was interrupted by a burly man in a roll-necked sweater, who demanded to know from the café at large: "What has B—— done wrong?"

He was referring to a senior military officer who had been suspended from his post and was due to go on trial for conduct unbecoming with a female non-commissioned officer under his command.

"What do you mean?" demanded the restaurateur, a dark, handsome man with a neat black goatee and tinted spectacles.

"I want to know what he did that was so terrible." The admiral's defender was a large man with a heavy, florid face. I decided that he was a building contractor, one of the nouveaux riches.

"Would you like something like that to happen to your daughter?"

"I didn't say that, but this isn't new."

"I didn't say it was new. I just think the time has come to put a stop to that sort of thing," stated the restaurateur. "Anyway," he added, "the girl has guts!"

"That's just where you're wrong," asserted a young gas-station attendant. "I think that she was put up to it. How come she woke up only after a year and a half?"

"These things take time."

"Nonsense," insisted the attendant. "She enjoyed herself first of all and then went sour."

"I don't know about that," replied the other. "You may be right, but I'll tell you one thing: I don't mind two soldiers screwing if they want to, but a man with a rank" (he tapped his shoulder) "he shouldn't take advantage of his position."*

I made good progress that day, but I was limping painfully by the time I reached Raanana, a village that has become one of the more pleasant Tel Aviv suburbs. Arriving at the home of my friends Bimbo and Denise, I said, "I spent last night on the beach, so today I decided to find somewhere civilized. However, I have reconsidered and come to spend the night with you."

"He's been working that one out all day," Bimbo told his wife. Wrong: I had been working on it only for twenty minutes.

Bimbo Bardan (whom Denise is trying to train us all to call Ben) is a bespectacled, humorous Welshman, who served for many years as an Israeli economic envoy in Geneva. Now he was working for himself and had just returned from a year as economic adviser to the government of Kenya. He was full of praise for Nairobi, which he said was a pleasant place to live in. Despite some inefficiency and corruption, he said Kenya compared favorably with most other African countries, though he was worried about what would happen when Kenyatta died. He felt the large and very prosperous middle class had a way of life worth

---

* The officer was subsequently acquitted on technical grounds, although a three-man military tribunal said it believed the girl's testimony. He was allowed to resign from the navy.

defending, which militated against violent change, but the situation was not entirely predictable.

One of the built-in advantages of the Bardans' comfortable apartment was an unlimited supply of hot water. It could not have come at a better time; I wallowed in a deep, very hot bath for almost an hour.

This revived me to such an extent that I accompanied them to visit friends of theirs, an optometrist from England and his wife, whom I had met once before. They had lived for some months at an immigrant absorption center in Arad, where they had found it somewhat difficult to adapt to local customs. One of the man's complaints had been that the local children had burned his son's handkerchief. I had expressed shock, along with confidence that this sort of thing did not often happen in Arad.

"Bloody sure it doesn't," snapped back the reply. "I'm sure that the other kids don't *have* handkerchiefs!"

This evening, they were full of accounts of their son, who had been accepted to study medicine at the Hebrew University. It was the same boy whose handkerchief had gone up in smoke. My general impression was that the family's absorption into our primitive society was well on the way to success.

16

In Raanana I was in the metropolitan conurbation around Tel Aviv, and I wanted to get out into the country again. My plan was to walk eastward and then take a line south, not far from the old border between Israel and the West Bank of the Jordan. My route took me through Kefar Saba, a pleasant little town with tree-lined streets and public gardens. After a bit I turned right, through citrus groves, along a path I hoped would bring me to the Arab village of Kafr Kassem.

Kafr Kassem had become famous (or rather notorious) in the Sinai Campaign of 1956. When the war against Egypt started, the Arab villages in Israel had been put under curfew. A group of Kafr Kassem villagers, returning from their day's work, inadvertently broke the curfew, and a local army unit opened fire on them, killing forty-seven.

It was described by Prime Minister David Ben-Gurion as a "shocking tragedy," and strenuous efforts were made to compensate the families. An official committee of inquiry was established, and the soldiers responsible were put on trial. Sentences ranging from seven to seventeen years were imposed by the military court; but after various appeals and pardons, the longest period actually spent in jail by any of the perpetrators was three and a half years.* The in-

* The recent actions of Israel's chief of staff, General Raphael Etan, in reducing sentences passed on soldiers convicted of killing civilians and prisoners in the Litani operation, have caused sharp criticism in the country. Many

cident caused a good deal of heart-searching in Israel, and
at the trial the principle that a soldier is not obligated to
obey illegal orders was established.

The precedent was later used in the case against Adolf
Eichmann, when the Nazi war criminal was put on trial in
Jerusalem for his part in the murder of millions of European Jews. His plea that he was merely obeying orders was
not accepted. It was, in fact, during the Eichmann trial in
1961 that I first made contact with Arab villagers from
Kafr Kassem. I was living at a moshav nearby, and some of
the Arab villagers were hired to help us pick our cauliflower
crop. While we were hacking away together at the vegetables, amid the rain and mud, the Arab foreman told me
what he would like to do to Eichmann, illustrating his
words vividly with his knife on an unfortunate cauliflower.
Still relatively new to the country, I was rather surprised to
hear an Arab expressing himself so vehemently on the subject of the Nazi Holocaust. I have since learned that many
Arabs tend to tell their Jewish fellow citizens what they
think the Jews want to hear. They seem to look on it as a
kind of sport, a way of laughing at the majority.

*   *   *

But to return to the walk. I had not gone far through the
orange trees when I met Mahmud, an elderly Arab, dressed
in traditional cotton trousers and tunic, who was collecting
firewood. I asked him for directions and he suggested I wait
for him to tie on his load so that he could show me the way.
His high wood pile secured on his donkey cart, he wound
his keffiya around his head and climbed on top, taking my
rucksack with him.

---

attributed the pardons to General Etan's personal attitude toward such offenses. Unfortunately, the case of Kafr Kassem would seem to support the
belief that the killing of Arabs by soldiers is not too serious an offense in
some official circles in Israel.

He told me that he was from the West Bank town of Kalkiliya, although once he had owned an orange grove in what was now Israel. However, he said, now there should be peace. Why should he and I wish to harm each other? His Hebrew was a bit better than my Arabic.

For the next half-hour I walked beside him through the orchards and past a couple of Jewish villages, until we came to a parting of our ways. He pointed out the route and let me have my pack. I cut along a dirt road going across the fields, and about twenty minutes later I emerged on the Kalkiliya–Rosh Haayin road, which was fine. However, I soon discovered that I was a mile north of the village of Jaljuliya, instead of three miles south of it, which was anything but fine.

Let it be clearly stated that I set out on this walk determined to be independent of timetables, to forget clocks and watches, to wander happily wherever my feet and my inclinations took me. Not for me the rush and bustle, the compulsion to hit targets, the importance of keeping appointments. Yet now that I was faced with the prospect of walking four miles more than I had wanted, I cursed the absent Mahmud richly. Did the fool not know north from south, or east from west? Ah, what did a few hours matter to a dull-witted countryman? For some moments I shook my fists and danced with rage in the road. Then, forcing myself to calm down, I pulled out my map to try to see what had gone wrong. It wasn't long before I saw that the mistake had been all my own. I had gone hopelessly wrong in Kefar Saba, continuing east, instead of branching off south. Far from misleading me, the maligned Mahmud had rescued me from wasting even more time. If not for that shrewd peasant, I would have walked an extra eight miles.

Passing Jaljuliya, I noticed a number of passenger trucks parked in the village. I presumed that these were for transporting West Bank Arabs to work in Israel, clearly a good source of income for the villagers. There was also a gas station, but only for diesel fuel and kerosene — a real working-class fuel station, with no fuel for effete automobiles.

My feet were very sore as I walked along the roadside, and I was very angry about it. (It seemed to be my day for being angry.) Why, after two weeks of walking, should my feet still hurt? I had noticed over the days that the different parts of the body took turns in feeling painful. Thus, I might start out with muscle soreness in the calves. When this wore off, there would be a blister on the heel. I would walk that one off to find the straps of my rucksack biting into my shoulders, and then it would be the toes. Now, suddenly, on the road south of Jaljuliya, it was my arches. Why them, for God's sake? They had been all right up to now. I had learned a hard lesson: walking with a pack is always an effort. Leaving Kiryat Shmona, I had told myself that by the time I got to the center of the country I would be fine; that my feet would have hardened, that I would feel fit and would stride out with pleasure. Crap! The fact that there was nothing to be gained from self-pity did not in the least prevent me from indulging in it, but I pressed on toward Kafr Kassem nonetheless.

The village lies two miles east of the road, and I was just wondering whether I had it in me to keep going when a horse and cart came by. I rationalized: one, Kafr Kassem was a slight diversion from my road south; two, I wasn't traveling by car. Gratefully, I climbed in and was driven to the village. The carter was an old man and not too communicative, but just before we arrived, he stopped next to an enormous red Oldsmobile.

"That belongs to our new mayor," he told me.

Dark, handsome, with an aquiline face, long hair, tight trousers, and sports shirt open almost to the waist, Abdul Rahim looked young to be a mayor. He was, he informed me proudly, the youngest Arab mayor in the country, although at thirty-eight he was older than he looked. We sat outside in the sun in the shabby town square and chatted. A waiter brought us strong, black, cardamom-flavored coffee, together with glasses of cold water.

Abdul Rahim told me that he had won 45 percent of the vote under the new system of direct personal elections for mayors. He had been a member of the previous council, but, disgusted by the wheeling and dealing, he had resigned. I asked him whether it would be any better now. After all, he would still have to form a coalition. That was so, he conceded, but his election had given him authority. His nearest challenger had scored fewer than half his votes. He felt that this proved the workability of the new system.

National and international issues had played no part in the recent elections, he explained. There was one issue: development. There had been no public building in the village during the period of the previous council and very little since the 1960s. The infrastructure was designed for a village of 5000; today Kafr Kassem was almost twice that.

"Look." He gestured at the tumbledown buildings around the square. "No town hall, no post office, no proper shops, and a shack for a cinema. We need more electricity, running water, a new sewage system, roads — I'm not even talking about industry. First things first."

I mentioned the building activity I had observed on my way into the village. What were those new apartment blocks? Wasn't that public building? Abdul Rahim seemed puzzled: What apartments? There were no apartments in the village. With something of a shock, I realized that the "blocks" were in fact private houses. Even Caesarea had not possessed anything so grandiose.

I shouldn't deceive myself, he said. The large houses were inhabited by *hamulot*, extended families. Most didn't have electricity, and their owners were up to their ears in debt.

Did he think he could get things moving? He was sure

that he could. It was a question of putting pressure on the Ministry of the Interior. He had good contacts; he spoke good Hebrew; (he did indeed — far better than mine!); he was forming a regional committee together with representatives of neighboring settlements, such as Taibe, Jaljuliya, and Rosh Haayin. They wanted the ministry to set up a local office. At present they had to go to the nearest bureau at Rehovot, which was too far away. Rosh Haayin? I expressed surprise. Why not? he demanded. They had good neighborly relations. Many of Kafr Kassem's problems were similar to those of the Jewish township, populated by Jews from Yemen, which had also suffered from slow development.

"You want to know what my aims are?" he asked. "I want my villagers to have the same rights and services as the Jews in Petah-Tikva. Why not?"

He launched into a stream of complaints: a Jewish farmer could get a loan to buy a tractor in three months; it took the Arab a year. Many of the villagers got fed up with waiting and took loans at exorbitant interest to buy equipment. Wasn't it just a case of the Jews being better at fighting the bureaucracy? Maybe it was, but that didn't justify it. The Jewish farmers also had better assistance from agricultural instructors, he claimed. A university professor was conducting experiments in his fields, but he said that he didn't benefit directly from them. He also complained that the man didn't know a word of Arabic.

"He told me that he couldn't get it into his head." He laughed. "I told him to change his head!" Really, he went on, wasn't it a disgrace that Jews didn't know Arabic after thirty years of life together in one country? Had I noticed that many West Bank Arabs already knew Hebrew after only eleven years of contact with the Jews? On this last point I had to admit that he was right.

He continued with his catalogue: he was growing tomatoes and groundnuts for export. He earned dollars, but he saw only Israeli currency. How did he know he was getting a fair price? I told him that most Jewish farmers would probably say the same thing. Apart from that, he had the biggest car that I had seen in Israel.

By now, we had been joined at our table by a number of young men, who were listening intently to our discussion. I asked him whether his election had been a vote for a new generation, a revolt against the establishment. Only to a certain extent, he thought. He had, in point of fact, succeeded his own uncle. One of the young men told me that he worked as a taxi driver with a Jewish company. He complained about land expropriation. Kibbutz Givat Hashlosha had been built on Kafr Kassem land, he claimed.

"How much land?" Abdul Rahim asked him. The man shrugged. "Why make a point without carrying it through?" demanded the mayor. He turned to me: "Four thousand dunams" (a thousand acres). "I'm prepared to accept what happened in the nineteen forty-eight war, but it's going on all the time. I'm afraid they'll take more of our land."*

Others at the table raised the question of a Palestinian state emerging from the peace process. Kafr Kassem, Israeli since 1948, would not be a part of it, of course, they said with smiles that seemed to indicate regret. Did he want to be outside Israel? I asked Abdul Rahim.

* Kibbutz Givat Hashlosha was partly established on land that belonged to Kafr Kassem villagers who fled in the 1948 war. Land belonging to absentees is taken over by the state. In the particular case of Kafr Kassem, there is another piece of land expropriated by the state. It is a tract of 750 acres of stony land. The law says that this land, of no use for agriculture, is the state's. The local villagers claim with some justice that the land, which they cultivated between the rocks in traditional Arab fashion, is theirs. I have learned from a reliable source that these 750 acres will soon be returned to the village; but after so many years of disappointment, the villagers are still suspicious.

"I was asked that the other day by a Scandinavian journalist," he said. "I can tell you just what I told him: it's an
irrelevant question. Have we been invited to negotiations?
Has anyone mentioned us? Carter, Begin, Sadat? We are
not involved in the process!" He reiterated that he wanted
to concentrate on concrete issues, such as land, assistance,
development, services, and a fair deal. Why shouldn't Kafr
Kassem have industry? Why shouldn't the village women
work in factories like the Jewish women, instead of in the
fields?

The talk drifted to other matters. One of the company
showed me with pride the afternoon paper, which had a
feature on Kafr Kassem's soccer team. Now top of the third
league, they were all set to get into the second league. It was
clearly a considerable source of pride for the youngsters.

"We have one foot inside," exulted one of them. "In
time, we're going to make the national league — you'll
see."

And finally I asked the mayor about that tragedy
twenty-two years ago. He would have been sixteen at the
time, and it must have made an indelible impression on
him.

"I'll tell you what I think." He talked slowly, weighing
his words with care. "In the nineteen forty-eight war there
was chaos. I'm prepared to accept anything that happened
then; but in nineteen fifty-six there was a government, a
prime minister, a minister of defense; it should never have
happened. It cannot be explained away.

"There is a memorial to the fallen at the entrance to the
village. The anniversary of the tragedy was last month, and
the whole village was there. It was quiet — no noisy demonstrations — but we remember."

As I walked out of the village I looked for the memorial,
but I failed to locate it, despite the directions I had received. To the east, across the former armistice line, I could

just make out the settlement of Elkana in what was formerly Jordanian territory.

This walk was deliberately confined to Israel as it was during its first nineteen years. On no occasion did I cross the armistice lines of 1949, the "Green Line," as it has come to be called. But the new Jewish settlements, established in territory occupied in the Six Day War, are very much a part of our modern reality, and they cannot be ignored.

When I did visit Elkana, a tiny fortress of small, square blockhouses, hemmed in by barbed wire and the gray rocks of Samaria, it was by helicopter. I traveled then with an American Zionist group, escorted by a cabinet minister. The chopper put us down outside the perimeter fence, and as we walked up the hill, a bunch of children marched down with their teacher, singing, "Samaria is ours in the Land of Israel." It was slightly theatrical: they were right on cue.

"These children are our guarantee of peace," exclaimed the cabinet minister. He went on to explain his thesis that Israel was far too narrow. Measured to the former border, it was less than ten miles wide; but it was really even less than that because the belt of Israeli Arab villages, such as Kafr Kassem and Jaljuliya, effectively cut the Jewish strip to under six miles. An ex-general, the minister expressed his opinion that this was quite simple indefensible. Military settlement was not enough, he continued. You could not measure security only in soldiers and guns. Only civilians with their children, and their "desire to see the other side of the hill," would guarantee the region for Israel. These were the real pioneers of today, he said, inviting us to see the conditions under which they lived.

We entered one of the homes: the two-room apartment was indeed crowded for the family of six that occupied it; but the stylish modern furniture, woven rugs, coffee-table books, stereo set, and two (!) televisions belied the aura of

Spartan dedication. Furthermore, the householder dodged a question about whether this was his only home. It is well known that many of the pioneers who live in these villages possess comfortable homes in Tel Aviv or Jerusalem.

We stood on a promontory to hear a talk from a young, intense, skullcapped American immigrant. He began by explaining the security aspect of the village, but he was soon put down by the minister, who told him brusquely in Hebrew that his job was to talk about his devotion to the Land of Israel; the minister would deal with security.

The youngster switched scripts with evident ease, explaining that Elkana was named for the father of the prophet Samuel. This land had belonged to the tribe of Ephraim. The Jews had always lived in the hills. They had more right to Elkana than they did to Tel Aviv. If Zionism was the return to the Jewish homeland, how could anyone dare suggest that they could not return to the very heartland of Jewish history?

Elkana was built on rocks, chimed in the minister — this was manifestly true — and no land had been taken away from the Arabs. All the Jewish settlements in Samaria were being built on land that the Arabs did not own and could not use. He was angry about a recent television program that had said the settlements were being constructed on agricultural land.

"Look at the agricultural land," he kept shouting, pointing at the rocks. "Look at the wonderful farming land!"

Somebody asked about the source of livelihood of the village, and our lecturer said that at present all the male settlers commuted to jobs in the Tel Aviv area. There was no land for agriculture, but there were plans to establish light industries. There were 300 presently in the village, including children. Another seventy families were ready to come if housing could be made available.

Elkana is one of the settlements of the religious-nationalist Gush Emunim. Although it was established by the previous Labor-led government, many of the movement's villages were set up in a partisan manner and recognized only after they were already on the ground.

It started with the Etzion region, south of Jerusalem. In the War of Independence, the four villages in that sector were overrun by Jordan's Arab Legion. Many of the villagers were killed; others were taken into captivity. The survivors subsequently established new settlements in other parts of Israel or joined other villages. But after the 1967 war, when the area returned to Israeli control, some of the sons of the former villagers determined to re-establish Jewish settlement there.

The Labor-led government of that time was a broad coalition, with different shades of opinion represented in the cabinet and differing attitudes toward the newly captured territories. It had moved to annex East Jerusalem to Israel, but the rest of the new areas were left in a state of suspension. There were those who felt that, as integral parts of the historical Land of Israel, the new parts should be integrated into the state. Others felt that they could eventually be traded for peace.

The youngsters had chosen their site well. Even the more dovish cabinet members remembered the heroic (if unsuccessful) defense of the Etzion bloc in the 1948 war. The villages had been Jewish and built on land purchased by the Jewish National Fund. Furthermore, the area was contiguous with Israel. Whatever became of the West Bank, Gaza, the Sinai, and the Golan Heights, the Etzion region could be incorporated into Israel with only a minor border adjustment. The village was recognized and granted full assistance.

The next unauthorized settlement was in Hebron, a town in the heart of historical Judea, but also in the heart of the Arab-populated West Bank. In the spring of 1968, a group led by the redoubtable Rabbi Moshe Levinger rented the Park Hotel in Hebron for ten days in order to celebrate Passover in the city of the Patriarchs.* They stayed for six months.

After months of soul-searching discussions, the authorities moved the group to the military government compound in Hebron. Subsequently, Kiryat Arba, a Jewish suburb of Hebron, was built for them. Today its solid apartment blocks are regarded by some as concrete proof of the success of Jewish settlement in the West Bank, although, in fact, most of the householders are renting their flats instead of buying them, as is usual in Israel.

With the refusal of the Arab states to negotiate, the idea of trading territory for peace seemed less likely, and the government's ambivalent attitude remained unchanged. Attempts to settle in Samaria, in the northern part of the West Bank, were prevented by the army. At the same time a relatively liberal military regime administered the Arab citizens. On the one hand, there was a strong policy against subversion: suspected terrorists were rounded up; their houses were blown up. On the other hand, the local inhabitants were allowed to run their own affairs without too much interference; they were permitted to work in Israel; and the bridges across the Jordan River were kept open to two-way traffic and trade.

The government began to establish its own "security" settlements in the new areas, but away from Arab population centers. The new villages were set up in the Golan Heights, the Jordan Valley, and the Sinai.† But Kiryat Arba stood as a precedent for settling the Arab-populated areas as well, even though it was said that the "city of the Patriarchs" was a special case.

* Abraham, Isaac, and Jacob are believed to be buried there in the Machpela cave, sacred to Jews and Muslims alike.

† The Sinai settlements are now being dismantled under the terms of the Israel-Egypt peace treaty.

Then came the shock of the Yom Kippur War. If it made some Israelis doubt the effectiveness of territory as a guarantee of security, it only confirmed it for others, among them the religious youths who had settled in Etzion and Kiryat Arba, and who had tried (so far without success) to settle in Samaria.

Gush Emunim was a new phenomenon in Israel. Although religious Jews had played a part in the Zionist enterprise, it was quite definitely a minority role. There were a number of religious kibbutzim and moshavim, but for the most part, the rabbis had opposed Zionism. A number of extreme religious sects still do, and even the Agudat Yisrael Party, which has four members in the Knesset and supports the present government, cannot be termed Zionist.

Now Gush Emunim proclaimed that it was assuming the mantle of true Zionism and declared that it was launching a drive to settle Jews all over the West Bank, the historical Judea and Samaria. The doctrine that emerged showed Gush Emunim as a reincarnation of the patriotic movement of the Second Temple period. The members declared that Israel was now in the initial phase of the Messianic age, that the return of the liberated territories was God's sign to His people.

In more settled times, the Gush (if it had emerged at all) would have made little headway; but Israelis were reeling from the shock of the Yom Kippur War. Many traditional Zionists were re-examining their beliefs, assailed by doubts about the future path of the Jewish state. In this situation, the certainty projected by the Gush leaders was extremely attractive to many Israelis. A number of political leaders who should have known better hitched a ride on the Gush Emunim bandwagon.

If the previous government was ambivalent in its attitude toward the Gush, the current government at first gave them its full support. Unlike the Labor Party, which draws much of its support from the kibbutzim and moshavim, the right-wing Likud coalition has no settlement movement. It was delighted to adopt Gush Emunim.

*   *   *

It is time to return, not yet to our walk, but to our helicopter trip around Samaria. Our next hop took us to the town of Ariel, a community of 600 families, only some of them members of Gush Emunim.* The gun-toting young settlers informed us that there was a large waiting list. Ariel is a good illustration of the Gush theory that if it points the way, others will follow, for it is an open secret that the actual numbers of pioneers that the religious movement can mobilize is severely limited.

The attraction of a place like Ariel is evident enough. Housing prices in the large cities have become prohibitive for most young couples. The development towns of Galilee and the south are hours away from the conveniences of the central region. To move to Ariel, at a nominal rent, the settler doesn't even have to change his job: he is less than an hour away from Tel Aviv or Jerusalem.

Our next stop was Elon Moreh, and here both the government and the settlers have run into trouble. At the time I write this, the Israeli supreme court has ordered the evacuation of the settlement. The government has agreed, but it is still uncertain what the settlers will decide.† When we paid our visit, the court had not handed down its decision; but following an appeal from a group of Arab villagers who owned part of the land on which the village was built, it had ordered a temporary freeze on development. The young settlers were indignant: "Abraham pitched his tent

---

* The cabinet minister said 800 families, but he was corrected by a local settler who said 600 families. In fact, there were 172 families there at the time!

† After much procrastination, the settlers were evacuated to the nearby site of Jebel Kabir, where there were no private Arab land claims.

at Elon Moreh; Joseph is buried nearby. If we give up this place, we may as well give up the whole Land of Israel!"

There was a dramatic pause and the villagers began to chant:

"*Am Yisroel hai!*" (The people of Israel lives!)

There is some significance in the pronunciation of Yisroel (Israel), which was articulated in the old Ashkenazic manner, for it can be argued that Gush Emunim is an alien growth in modern Israel, a throwback to the pre-Zionist era.

The comparison of the Gush Emunim settlements to the Crusader fortresses has already been made. The massive walls and deep moats of the Crusader castles have been replaced by barbed wire and reinforced concrete, but the isolated, closed-in communities of the Gush, with their religious fervor and siege mentality, have much in common with the Crusader society. Another possible comparison is with the Jewish community of pre-Zionist Palestine: studying the Bible and the Talmud; unproductive and supported by handouts.

Partisans of the Gush would, of course, suggest other comparisons. They look back to Trumpeldor's defense of Tel Hai, carried out against the official Zionist policy of the time, or the tower-and-stockade kibbutzim of the 1930s, when villages were put up over night to forestall Arab opposition. The objection to this comparison is twofold. First, both Tel Hai and the tower-and-stockade settlements were built on land legally purchased by the Jewish National Fund, whereas the Gush villages are on conquered or expropriated land. Second, the early settlers reclaimed and farmed the land; they did not commute to factory benches in Lydda or offices in Tel Aviv.

For all its emotional and historical associations, modern Zionism has been a pragmatic movement. As I pointed out to Mansur Kardosh in Nazareth, the Zionists always knew how to say yes, even when what was being offered fell short of their ideal. When the British put forward a partition plan in 1938 that would have given the Jews the coastal plain north of Tel Aviv, the Emek, and eastern Galilee for their state, the practical Ben-Gurion agreed. The plan came to nothing because the Arabs rejected it. In 1947, Israel accepted the highly unsatisfactory UN partition plan.

Gush Emunim, with its all-or-nothing extremism, is the mirror image of the Palestine Liberation Organization, which still dreams of the removal of Israel by force. There is a grotesque symmetry between the ideology of the Gush and the PLO. Both want a single state between Jordan and the Mediterranean (albeit with different names); both strive to undo the "miracle" of 1948, when the Jews managed to obtain a small state of their own, with a small Arab minority.

It is true that Ariel is more attractive than Kiryat Shmona and that the hills of Samaria are historically more Jewish than the coastal plain; but at this time the Jewish state that emerged in 1949 is about all that the present Israeli population can handle. Israel has absorbed Nazareth and Kafr Kassem (more or less); it cannot absorb Nablus and Hebron. The fact must be faced that Zionism has only partly succeeded: the Jewish state has been created; but most Jews have remained in America and Europe.

*   *   *

And now the time really has come to return to the author, walking westward away from the old border toward the Rosh Haayin pumping station. Built by the British to pump the local spring water to Jerusalem and subsequently sucking fluid from the Yarkon River to the north, it has now become a way-station for our old friend, the water of Lake Kinneret.

Over to the right was the hill of Afek, a grassy slope

around the Muslim fort built after the expulsion of the Crusaders, now a favorite spot for picnics. In the period of the Judges, the Israelites lost an important battle here against the Philistines. In an attempt to boost morale, the Ark of the Covenant was brought from Shiloh, but it was captured by the enemy. According to the Biblical account, the Philistines found the Ark too hot to handle — pestilence and misfortune broke out wherever it rested — so the Israelites got it back.

In the fourth century B.C., when Alexander the Great conquered the Holy Land, the priests of the Temple of Jerusalem came out to Afek to give him their blessings. According to the tradition, it was this meeting that convinced Alexander not to enter the Temple and not to interfere with the Jewish religion.

*   *   *

I had a late lunch at a roadside café outside Petah-Tikva, staffed by three Galilee Bedouin. The eldest, in his final school year, was earning money during the high school strike; but the two younger boys were dropouts, one of them only ten years old. There are, unfortunately, holes in Israel's system of compulsory education, particularly in the Arab sector.

17

It was Friday when I left Petah-Tikva, and I had already decided to spend the Sabbath at the ultra-religious village of Kefar Habad. Despite the fact that both movements are religious, no comparison can be made between the Habad movement and Gush Emunim: they are birds of an entirely different feather. The Habad sect was founded in the eighteenth century, and (although its leader has, in point of fact, forbidden the return of any part of the Land of Israel to "the Gentiles") its primary interest is in religious observance.

The Habad movement is one of a number of Jewish Hasidic sects that hark back to the ghettos of Europe. Most of these groups are non-Zionist — or even anti-Zionist — and keep themselves very much to themselves, emerging only to stage violent demonstrations against what they regard as desecration of the Sabbath (driving, sports). What distinguishes the Habad members from their fellows is their firm belief that every Jew can be brought to the Torah, the religious law, as itemized in the first five books of the Bible.

There is a certain amount of legally enforced religion in Israel, even though the 1948 Declaration of Independence specified freedom of religion and conscience, as well as full equality for all citizens, irrespective of religion.

Because of the nature of coalition politics, the religious political parties — even the anti-Zionist ones — have been able to impose some religious observance on the nation at large. There is radio and television on the Sabbath, but no public transport. Personal status is in the hands of the religious authorities, which means that an Israeli can be married, divorced, or buried only in Jewish, Christian, or Muslim ceremonies. Moreover, these rules tend to discriminate against the poorer sections of society, for the rich can drive their cars on the Sabbath if they wish, and go abroad to be married in a civil ceremony.

In all these matters there is a status quo that represents a compromise between the religious and secular parties in the Knesset. But this status quo is fluid, and when they feel themselves in a strong bargaining position, the religious parties press hard to gain ground. They led the fight for the amendment to the abortion law, making legal abortions in Israel much more difficult to obtain. They also campaigned for the cancellation of plans for building a sports stadium in Jerusalem, on the grounds that the emporium represents "Hellenism" and will facilitate the desecration of the Sabbath by staging soccer games. On the other hand, they do not feel strong enough to legislate against Sabbath soccer as such.

But the Habad members believe in persuasion rather than compulsion. You can see Habadniks in the development towns and the villages, in the poor neighborhoods and at bus stations. They visit night clubs, coffee bars, discothèques, army camps, and prisons. They ask householders to affix *mezzuzot* to their doorposts, and persuade passersby to "lay *tefillin.*"*

* The mezzuza is a cylinder containing a minute scroll with Biblical texts proclaiming the unity of God. It commemorates the time when the ancient Israelites marked their doorposts with lamb's blood to avoid the ten plagues, inflicted on the Egyptians, prior to the Exodus under Moses. It is believed to possess protective qualities.

Tefillin are little boxes containing similar texts. They have to be "laid" — that is, strapped to the arm and forehead — while a man recites special prayers.

Every door of a house should have a mezzuza; a man must lay tefillin every day. Both articles are supposed constantly to remind the Jews of their obligations to the one God.

A year ago, when I was doing army service in the Sinai, two Habadniks arrived at our isolated outpost, just before Rosh Hashana, the Jewish New Year, with vodka and biscuits. After talking to us about the significance of the forthcoming holiday, they led us — all five of us — in a rousing sing-song, lasting almost an hour, before moving on to the next outpost. It was quite a party.

I had made no prior arrangements to stay at Kefar Habad, but I was fairly confident that I would get a warm welcome. The village is situated close to Ben-Gurion International Airport and, as I drew near, plane after plane was coming down to land in time for the Sabbath.

Scrambling down a grassy bank below the main road, I found myself on a quiet lane leading to the village. It was green and peaceful after the main road. As I walked between the rows of modest houses, the birds were singing in the trees. I didn't know much about Kefar Habad, but I knew enough to ask for the *Yeshiva,* the religious seminary, and it was there that I encountered Yossi Schneerson, a slim, brown-faced, sixteen-year-old villager. He was dressed in what I later learned was the Habad "uniform": black suit, white, open-necked shirt, and a snappy, black, narrow-brimmed hat over short side-curls. (This is in contrast to other ultra-religious Jews, who tend to long side-curls, broad-brimmed hats, and ornate tunics, and wear *streimals* — fur hats — on Sabbaths and holidays.)

"Who sent you?" asked Yossi, assuming I had been recommended by one of their field workers.

"No one," I replied. "I'm engaged on a walk through Israel. This morning, when I set out from Petah-Tikva, I thought that your village would be the best possible place to spend the Sabbath." (This was a slight embroidery of the truth; I had thought of the idea about a week before.)

"Wonderful!" he exclaimed. "That is what we call *hashgaha ishit,* personal supervision. The Holy One, blessed be His Name, sent you to us."

"I could move on if there's no room," I suggested. "It's still a couple of hours until Sabbath . . ."

"What?" He was scandalized. "Turn away a Sabbath guest? Never!"

He took me into the yeshiva, a modern but cold and shabby building. This lack of comfort was to be the pattern at Kefar Habad; they had no time for such physical things as warmth or cleanliness. Not that there was any lack of hygiene; just that they have better things to spend their time and money on than polished floors, gleaming paintwork, comfortable furniture, or central heating.

After finding me a bed in one of the dormitories, where I left my pack, Yossi took me to meet his family. On the way he explained to me that, although he was a local villager, he lived most of the time at the yeshiva, where there were numerous students from outside the village (and from abroad). His father was a farmer but also had a job as school supervisor with the Ministry of Education.

Their house was being prepared for the Sabbath: what seemed like dozens of teen-age daughters were mopping the floors; countless little boys and girls were being scrubbed and put into clean Sabbath clothes. My impressions, as I soon discovered, were not so exaggerated: Yossi has fifteen brothers and sisters!

A handsome woman, with a kerchief on her head in the fashion of religious women, emerged from the house.

"I would like you to meet my mother," said Yossi. I gaped: the fresh-skinned, clear-eyed woman could not possibly be the mother of sixteen children! I pulled myself together and stuck out my hand.

"We say hello without shaking hands," explained Mrs. Schneerson, with such directness and charm that I didn't even feel myself blushing at my faux pas. She welcomed me to the village and gave us coffee and cake. Then it was back to the yeshiva for Sabbath preparations.

"You can have a shower if you like," Yossi told me. "I go to the *mikveh,* the ritual bath."

"I'd love to come to the mikveh," I assured him.

"Wonderful!" exclaimed the boy again. "You're showing the right spirit. I told you that the Holy One, blessed be His Name, sent you to us."

Religious Jews are extremely modest about the human body. In the religious neighborhoods of Jerusalem, notices are posted ordering the visitor to dress modestly. Girls with bare arms, or in trousers, are likely to be spat on, or even stoned. For this reason, I was amazed at the lack of self-consciousness at the mikveh. I was embarrassed amid the mass of naked, white male bodies, which had never seen the sun; the men were not. It was I who cast my eyes down; they behaved perfectly naturally.

We showered first under streams of very hot water, of which there seemed to be a limitless supply. Proceeding to the ritual bath itself, about four yards square and very crowded, we walked down the steps until we were shoulder-high in the water, and then immersed ourselves totally. I tried to repeat the prayers that I heard Yossi reciting. You are supposed to perform the ritual immersion three times, but Yossi did it three times three. Not to be outdone, I also submerged myself nine times.

"Purification, that's the idea," Yossi explained on the way back to the yeshiva. "We are commanded to purify ourselves. It is especially important today, the Sabbath, but I do it every day."

Back in the dormitory, I met several other students, white-faced and serious, little tufts of beard starting to sprout. Yossi took a suit and hat, identical to the ones he was wearing, from his locker — these were his Sabbath clothes — and changed taking considerable care to conceal himself beneath a blanket. On our way to the synagogue, I asked him about his self-conscious modesty when he changed, compared with the carefree manner exhibited in the mikveh. When one was able to be modest, one should be, he told me. He was not fanatical about it, though, and in the ritual bath it was simply impractical. As we walked through the building for *maariv*, evening prayers, I tried to enter into the spirit of the place, imitating Yossi by touching my hand to each mezzuza as we passed it and then kissing the hand.

The synagogue was bare and very large; it contained dozens of small tables with prayer books on them. The hall was full of young, black-suited figures, praying fervently, swaying back and forth as they chanted. I asked Yossi if there was any significance in this swaying of the body. He told me that some people believed it was the spirit trying to get out but that in his view it was merely a custom.

After the prayers were finished, Yossi handed me over to an older man of the same name for a *shiur*, a lesson. Bearded, with a strong, handsome face, alert eyes behind steel-rimmed spectacles, the new Yossi first made a comment on his name: "You will find many Yossis in our generation. Yosef was the name of the previous rebbe and we are all named after him." He went on to explain that "the rebbe" (Yiddish for rabbi) is the leader of the Habad sect. He is known as the Lubavicher Rebbe, or the Rabbi from Lubavich, the Russian town where the Habad sect was founded. The present incumbent, Menahem Mendel Schneerson, lived in Crown Heights, in Brooklyn, New York.

Yossi himself was currently living at the yeshiva in Migdal Haemek. It was part of the Habad program for spreading the Torah. He was not a teacher there, he told me, but a student. However, he did try to help his fellow students at the seminary, who were mainly oriental Jews from Migdal.

Yossi then proceeded to expound Habad Judaism to me in a forceful manner. The essential belief in Judaism, he said, was the primacy of head over heart. Man was the only creature who looked upward. His head was above his bowels; not on the same level, as in beasts. (I thought of a giraffe, but did not interrupt.) The term Habad was made up of initials for the principles of the movement: *hohma,* wisdom; *bina,* understanding; *da'at,* knowledge. Wisdom was the initial perception, understanding was the mastery of the details, knowledge was the overall conception. All three elements were essential.

Unlike the Christians and Muslims, explained Yossi, the Jews did not depend on one individual for their belief; 600,000 adult males had witnessed Moses receiving the Law from God on Mount Sinai. God had created the universe. Creation, moreover, was a continuous process, so if the Holy One, blessed be His Name, stopped creating for a single instant, the whole universe would revert to nothing.

"What if I simply do not believe in God?" I asked.

"No such thing," replied Yossi confidently. "There is no such thing as a Jew who does not believe." Maybe, he continued, there were Jews, such as myself, who *thought* they didn't believe; but every Jew in his heart of hearts wanted to believe, and the Habad movement was out to help them.

I challenged him about the actions of the Habad followers. How did they presume to force people to lay tefillin?

Laying tefillin, explained Yossi patiently, was a *mitzvah,* a commandment from God. The whole purpose of a Jew's being on earth was to perform mitzvot; that was what the Creator required of him. It did not really matter whether the performer of mitzvot understood what he was doing. The important thing was the performance itself. A famous mediaeval rabbi had even said that it was permissible to use violence to compel people to perform mitzvot.

"Of course we don't do that today." Yossi smiled. "But pressure, persuasion: I approve of that."

The lesson was pleasant and informal. He asked me

about my work with the radio station, and I asked him about his life in Migdal Haemek. Why wasn't he in the army? I wanted to know. For the time being he had exemption as a yeshiva student, he explained. When the time came, he would serve. Habadniks, he pointed out, did serve in the army.*

What about girls and marriage? I asked. He spoke frankly: he was twenty-two years old and he would soon want to get married. He had absolutely no need to meet girls, except for the purpose of marriage. Couldn't he meet girls socially? I asked. Why? What for? He had enough of a social life in the yeshiva. He would meet girls, but only for the purpose of getting married. If he found one whom he wanted to marry, and the feeling was mutual, he would apply to the rebbe for permission.

"You will write to New York?" I asked in amazement.

"Of course."

"What if the rebbe opposes the match and you still want to marry the girl?"

"If the rebbe is against, I stop wanting to marry the girl. More than that: if the rebbe doesn't reply, the question of marriage becomes unthinkable."

"But how can the rebbe possibly know?" I asked.

"The rebbe is the leader of the Jewish people. He takes his responsibilities very gravely. He is your leader, too."

* The Israeli army does not grant deferment for studies, except in the case of very bright students who are studying something that the army can afterward use. They join the academic units. Later, these students serve longer than the normal period. Exception is made for Jewish religious studies at a yeshiva. The idea behind this is that, with the loss of the European yeshivot in the Nazi Holocaust, the Jewish state must do all it can to foster Judaic studies. Many of the ultra-orthodox Jews are openly against the state, believing that Israel should not have been established before the coming of the Messiah. They never serve in the army, a fact that causes resentment in the population at large. Members of the religious Zionist pioneer movements do, of course, serve in the army. I don't think one could call the Habad sect Zionist; but in army service, as in other things, its members pull their national weight.

He launched into a brief account of the history of the Habad movement. I knew that Israel Ben-Eliezar, known as the Baal Shem-Tov (master of the Holy Name), a great rabbi of the eighteenth century, had founded the movement of Hasidism. Originally a secret sect, it had later come out into the open, in opposition to the two main trends in Judaism at that time. It was opposed both to the overly intellectual mainstream of Judaism and to the new movement for reform and modernization, the *haskalah*. Hasidism stressed the joyful aspects of religion and the performance of mitzvot. It recognized the dignity of manual labor and maintained that the simple man could be as good a Jew as the scholar. According to Yossi, it was the Habad movement, based in Lubavich, that carried forward the true message of Hasidism. The present rebbe, ninth in succession to the Baal Shem-Tov, was the seventh Habad leader.

My lesson over, I was handed back to the care of young Yossi, who introduced me to his father, Zalman, gray-bearded, benevolent, his rough farmer's hand giving a firm handshake. He conducted me to his house for the Sabbath meal.

A large table, covered by a white cloth, filled the main room of the Schneerson home. The modest furniture had been pushed aside to make way for it. Two bottles of red wine, a bottle of grape juice, and some glasses were the only items on the table; the crockery and cutlery arrived with each course. Waiting for the family to arrive, the old man asked me what I was doing. I told him about my walk, and he looked at me shrewdly and suggested I might write a book about it. I admitted that the thought had crossed my mind.

He told me that the moshav had some seventy families of farmers and a further four hundred families who had been attracted to the center of Habad in Israel. In addition to these, there were several hundred yeshiva students, most of them from outside the village. Four of his sixteen children would be absent tonight, he explained. Two older daughters were living near the rebbe in New York, and two young teen-age sons were at a yeshiva in Lydda. But this was made up for by the presence of the guests, myself and two girls from Jerusalem, who told me that they were *baalei te-shuva* (irreligious Jews who had returned to orthodoxy).

Zalman filled a large silver goblet with sweet red wine, topping up with a little nonalcoholic grape juice. He held the goblet by the base in the palm of his hand, made the *kiddush*, the Sabbath blessing, chanting the prayer as if he meant it, and then downed the drink at a gulp. Then it was my turn: I read the blessing, rather than chanting it, and earned a snigger from the younger children. Children of all ages sat around the table; the men were at the top, the women (including the guests), at the bottom. The youngest member of the family surveyed the scene from his cot. The teen-age boys took turns in blessing the wine, as we had done, and then the father held up two *halot* (special sweet bread for the Sabbath), which had been concealed under a white cloth, and delivered another prayer: "Blessed art Thou, O Lord our God, King of the Universe, who brings forth bread from the earth."

Each of us received a piece of the bread, sprinkled with salt, and the meal began. The first course, brought in by mother and daughters, was fish in sharp sauce. I imitated the father, mopping up the sauce with bread, thinking that this was the main course. I was wrong. Chicken soup came next. It was tasty and served with noodles; but it was warm rather than hot. This was because it is forbidden to kindle light on the Sabbath. Everything is kept warm on a small gas flame, which was lit before the onset of Sabbath.

Between each course, we sang *niggunim*, Hasidic tunes without words. At first, the father started the singing, but later each of the brothers started a song. I did not know the tunes, but they were easy to pick up, being similar to other Hasidic tunes I did know. There was a sort of compulsion to join in, and I must admit that I was enjoying myself almost as much as the old man.

The younger children were all over the place, sitting on their father's knee or squabbling over places to lie down on the couch behind him. As we continued singing, the father leaned back in his chair, closing his eyes as he sang. A few songs later, he was fast asleep. I could not take my eyes off the mother. In my view of things, a woman who has given birth to sixteen children should be worn out. She was young, bright-eyed, her movements swift and graceful as she handed out the food. The father was eventually awakened by one of the youngest children, who scrambled up on his knee. Zalman hugged the boy, clearly doting on him. Schneour was three today, I was told. The following week, he would be taken to the synagogue to have his first haircut: his blond pigtail would be shorn, though he would be left with side-curls, short, in the Habad style.

Tomorrow, Zalman continued, was a special Sabbath, the one before the new month. To celebrate this, they would be reading the entire Book of Psalms, in addition to the psalms they read every Sabbath.

"How will I manage to read *all* the psalms?" demanded ten-year-old Levi.

"You will read as many as you can," replied his father.

The main course was boiled chicken. The mother continued to produce the enormous quantities of food for the seventeen of us without any fuss. We finished the meal with glasses of tea. More songs, and then I went back to the yeshiva to sleep.

I was up early the next morning, in time to say all the psalms as well as the morning prayers before breakfast. At first something puzzled me about the synagogue, but I couldn't put my finger on it. Then I had it: in most synagogues, the worshiper wraps himself in a *tallit,* a prayer shawl, but here hardly anyone did. I asked Yossi about it and he explained that all the young men wore at all times a small prayer shawl (*tzitzit*) under their shirts. Only married men wore the large tallit also. Because this was a yeshiva, married men were few and far between. I must say that the serious rows of black-suited, black-hatted young men made the hall look pretty bleak.

That morning I had the privilege of receiving a lesson from a Habad elder, Dov-Be'er Kesselman. A frail, narrow-shouldered, gray-bearded sage with a woolen scarf around his neck against the cold, he sat opposite me and repeated the story I had already heard about Mount Sinai, but he went into more detail. What the Creator had given Moses on Sinai was not just the Torah, the five books of Moses, but the entire Bible, Talmud, and all the commentaries. After all, he pointed out, Moses was up there for 120 days — far too long for just five books of the Bible.

I have already explained the generally accepted development of the Mishna and the Talmud, which were compiled by numerous rabbis and scholars over hundreds of years in Judea, Galilee, and Babylon. Now Kesselman gravely informed me that the whole body of case law and commentary, as well as the Bible, had been given word for word to Moses on Mount Sinai. Admittedly, only the Torah had actually been written down; the rest was oral tradition, transcribed only later, when it had been feared that the people would forget it.

The Jews, he reiterated, were on earth for one purpose only: to perform mitzvot, God's commandments. What could possibly mean more than carrying out the Creator's wishes? Half of the 613 mitzvot concerned practices connected with the Temple and could not be performed at present; but soon, when the Messiah comes, the Temple will be rebuilt. On the Temple Mount? I asked. Where else? What about the Muslim shrines that happened to be there? He smiled tolerantly. The Messiah would solve all problems. Nobody would object to anything that the Messiah did.

We are joined by another visitor, Haim, a small-business man from Tel Aviv, who had read about Habad in the papers and who like me, had just turned up. When would the Messiah come? Haim wants to know. Soon, very soon, affirms our sage. The rebbe had said "in our time." Haim prompts: Maybe the rebbe is the Messiah? I am a little worried by his audacity. Kesselman takes it seriously, rattling off a genealogy to prove that the rebbe can trace his ancestry back to King David (a requirement for the Messiah.) The *galut,* the Jewish dispersion, will end. Despite the existence of a Jewish state, he explains, the dispersion is still in force all the time that the Messiah doesn't come. In a moment of perception, I realize that Kesselman really does think that the rebbe is the Messiah, and the borderline between reality and fantasy blurs. I remain seated; but I feel lightheaded and my knees buckle.

Kessleman then launched into a series of parables, long-winded Hasidic tales, all with the same moral: happy the man who performs mitzvot.

A man complains about the weight of the load he is carrying until he learns that the load is diamonds. Then he is happy that the load is heavy. Mitzvot are like diamonds, but more valuable. The Jew is lucky to have that extra load. The *goyim,* the Gentiles, have only the 7 general mitzvot to perform, those pertaining to good neighborliness and decent living. The Jews have 613 plus 7; lucky the Jew with his greater load. There is a repetitiveness about Hasidic teaching that mesmerizes. It was about now that I came to understand a certain point about Habad Hasidism: moral arguments were irrelevant. One was indeed obligated to behave morally, but not for the sake of morality. There was a far more compelling reason: the Creator had commanded it.

After the lesson it was time for the midday prayers. I was fast reaching the saturation point, but, as in my walking, I determined to stick it out. It seemed that I had been reading the prayer book for several days, when the service came to an end and it was time for lunch. Yossi invited me home again, but I told him that I wanted to eat a meal in the yeshiva. He readily agreed and handed me over to Fishel Jacobs, a red-bearded American.

Fishel was a zealous instructor. He showed me how to wash my hands and bless before the meal. I held the full glass of sweet red wine in the palm of my hand and blessed it before drinking it down. For lunch there was *cholent,* the traditional Jewish Sabbath day meal, a sort of stew, based on beans, potatoes, and a little meat, with hard-boiled eggs thrown in. Left on a light that is lit before the Sabbath, it quickly becomes a stodgy mess. Generally I abhore it, but here in Kefar Habad it was so appropriate that I found myself actually enjoying it.

Fishel told me that he had been a karate champion in the United States, with a good chance of a place in the American national team at the Moscow Olympic Games, but he had decided to turn to study of the Torah instead. I looked at his pink face, framed with red beard and side-curls, his black suit and snappy black hat, and tried to imagine him in his white tunic with (presumably) black belt. It wasn't easy. Karate, I suggested, was more than a mere sport; it was also a philosophy, a way of life. He readily agreed, saying that it was a good philosophy (pause) for orientals.

"But you did well in it?"

"Yes, I did," he agreed. "Let me think how I can put this. You work at the radio station. Well, if you get a tape and it's for a different type of machine from the one you have,

I'm sure a good sound engineer will fix something up, but that doesn't make the tape the right one. The right tape for a Jew is the study of Torah and the performance of mitzvot."

I asked him whether he was happy with his decision, and he replied that it went far beyond mere happiness: he had a feeling of complete fulfillment. Was he as fit physically as he had been? He frowned and paused. In a different way, he concluded. I was prompted to ask him about something that had been puzzling me. At this lunch, as at the Schneerson home, vast amounts of food were being consumed, accompanied by sweet wine, fruit compote, and tea. The Habadniks ate and drank a lot, but I had not seen a fat man in the village. Even the older men had trim figures, despite their having, for the most part, no time for sports or other physical activities. The yeshiva students spent fifteen hours per day in prayer and study. Their exercise was confined to jogging to the mikveh and back each morning. The ex-sportsman considered the question at length, but the best he could manage was: "They lead happy, healthy lives."

I still have no explanation, unless it is simply that they expend so much energy on study and worship. I considered this with my fellow outsider, Haim, when we had a few moments alone together. Haim did not know why they were thin, but he thought that he had never seen people more content with their lot. He had not seen an angry man all day. He was amazed at how much they appeared to enjoy life without discothèques, cinemas, television, and other forms of entertainment.

"Last night," he confided, "I sat at the Friday night meal, praying, drinking wine, singing songs: we were all content."

He contrasted the previous evening with his normal Friday night in Tel Aviv — mostly he went to the disco. He told me that he used up a great deal of energy just trying to enjoy himself. Even when he didn't feel like going, he forced himself to go, to keep in with the crowd. He didn't really like the crowd or the disco. There was too much noise, too much drink, too much shvitz. You had to keep up, he said. It was always the latest thing: the latest clothes, the latest car, the latest record, the latest place where "everyone" went.

"I said to myself, what a gloomy Friday night, sitting around the table with a bunch of complete strangers. But then I realized how much I was enjoying myself. I don't know how to explain it — without entertainment, without fun — but I was happy."

He went on to tell me that he had not smoked a cigarette all day. Usually, he had finished a whole pack by Saturday afternoon, yet he did not feel the lack of it.

Well, then, I challenged him: What about throwing it all up and coming to live here? He frowned. No, no, that was going too far. But you had to admit, there was something in it. I knew what he meant.

*   *   *

That afternoon, Yossi took me for a walk around the village. It was a bare half-hour intermission in the constant round of prayer and study. We entered a gigantic synagogue, one of four in the village. A number of elderly men were sitting having a discussion. Yossi told me that it was called *hitvadut,* a sort of mixture of prayer, contemplation, and inspirational discussion. When one of the participants felt called upon to speak, he would address the others.

From the synagogue we proceeded to a special public hall, used for non-synagogue occasions. Schools, groups from kibbutzim and moshavim were received there, explained Yossi. Around the walls were pictures of the rebbe, praying, laying tefillin, dancing, singing, talking to children.

"The rebbe loves children," said Yossi reverently.

Weren't they making a bit too much of a mere mortal? I
asked. Yossi understood the question very well. No, he af-
firmed, they were not making him into more than a human
being. They respected him for what he was, a very great
man. He received hundreds of thousands of letters every
year, and each one got his attention. Letters came from all
types of people, not just his own flock. He would take them
in sackfuls to the grave of his predecessor and stand there,
going through them one by one. Sometimes he stood there
for hours, said Yossi, in the sun, the rain, even the snow.
Not every letter received a reply; sometimes the rebbe
merely offered a prayer (but that prayer, Yossi implied,
went straight along the hot-line to the Almighty).

Later that night — or, rather, the following morning —
at three o'clock, the rebbe was due to deliver a message to
his flock in New York and around the world. All Kefar
Habad would come to this very hall to hear his message,
which would be delivered in Yiddish.

The interlude was over; it was time to return to the
yeshiva for our hitvadut. It was led by my friend of the
morning (*this* morning? My sense of time was slipping),
Dov-Be'er Kesselman. His impassioned harangues were interrupted for sessions of singing, drinking vodka, and eating
pickled   cucumber.   Several   hundred   students   were
crammed into a small hall. They sang the Hasidic tunes,
clapping their hands, stomping their feet, and banging the
table. Knocking back the fiery vodka, I find myself joining
in, shouting the wordless songs, swaying and clapping.
Next to me young Yossi seems in a trance. Across the room,
Fishel the karate champion and the older Yossi are both
red in the face from singing, banging their hands together
in a frenzy. The tempo increases, we sing louder, more enthusiastically yet. We have almost taken wing. Then,
abruptly, silence.

Kesselman: "So many walk in the dark, whereas we see a

great light in the darkness. How lucky we are that we have a great rebbe to tell us what we must do, to inform us of what the Creator expects of us, to guide us in our lives.

"You all know that the rebbe has declared a renewed campaign to make Jewish housewives light candles on Sabbath eve, to fix mezzuzot on Jewish doorways, to get people to lay tefillin and to perform more and yet more mitzvot.

"We must not let the rebbe down; we must not disappoint our rebbe; we have to redouble our efforts. No Jew is too lowly for us. Oh yes, you yeshiva students know a bit; but this does not make you better than other Jews. On the contrary, you are obliged to help those less fortunate than yourselves. We must get to every Jew, whether he is in the discothèque, in the cinema, the street, the prison. We must get to every place where there is a Jew and see that that Jew performs mitzvot!

"Soon it will be the rebbe's birthday. What better present can we give our rebbe than a redoubling of our efforts for mitzvot? Some new dissertations have just been published. Everyone must learn at least one of them by heart. Before the rebbe's birthday you can all learn at least one and some of you can learn two or even three, those of you who are gifted at learning. So let this be our target: at least one dissertation by everyone!"

The frail old man, buoyed up by his own eloquence during his speech, sinks back, exhausted, and the singing starts afresh. But this time, instead of the almost rocklike rhythm, there are plaintive, soulful melodies, soft but passionate. I look around at the men's sweating faces, their simple but profound joy — the two Yossis, Kesselman, Fishel, and so many more. Why can't I believe?

The singing stops and a young student rises to deliver a dissertation, chanting a nasal Yiddish. I cannot understand a word, but he goes so fast that I doubt whether anyone else can either. Once again it seems that it is the act itself rather than the meaning that is important.

And then it was all over. Kesselman had spoken intermittently for three hours. Darkness had already fallen and there were more prayers to be said. *"Shavua tov,* a good week" was the universal greeting.

I said good-by to the Schneerson family (distant cousins of the rebbe, I learned), to Haim, and to Fishel. Yossi's mother gave me the address of a yeshiva in Jerusalem where I could continue my Hasidic studies. Fishel gave me the two-volume *Lubavicher Rebbe's Memoirs,* with the following inscription:

> The radio station may be broadcasting; but there is no purpose unless the radio is turned on. So too the Jewish soul in each and every Jew must be "opened" by studying our Torah to receive anything. Continue to study. Be successful in all your endeavors and remember the Habad Hasidim — Fishel Jacobs, Kefar Habad, 25th Heshvan, 5739.

18

THERE IS SOMETHING very strange about walking out of Kefar Habad toward Ben-Gurion Airport. Israel's main air terminal is no Kennedy or Orly, but even our modest facility has the look of the twenty-first century about it. I progressed along modern highways and concrete overpasses, not really designed for walking, leaving the eighteenth-century world of Isaac Bashevis Singer for the futuristic era of Isaac Asimov and Ray Bradbury. These, at any rate, were my thoughts as I sipped a plastic cup of so-called coffee in the glass-fronted terminal and read a paper to bring myself up to date on the activities of the modern world.

The main news story brought me up with a jolt. It concerned the horrifying mass suicide of the members of the Peoples' Temple in Guyana. Had we come so far ahead of Lubavich? Weren't we possibly lagging behind the Habad followers? Although it was true that had the Lubavicher Rebbe in his phone call that morning proclaimed the coming of the Messiah and called on his followers to commit suicide, many of them would have done so, with four millennia of morality behind him he would have been about as likely to issue such a command as to jump over the moon.

Leaving the airport and walking along the road toward Lydda, I was astonished to find a plastic bag, containing dozens of dead blue and green parakeets. How they got there and what they died of I do not know. It made a macabre variation from the parade of dead dogs and cats by the roadside.

Lydda has never quite made up its mind about what it wants to be, retaining quaint corners from its days as an Arab town, and an inadequate and shabby center from the same period, with modern neighborhoods unconvincingly grafted on. It is much the same as it was when I lived in the area sixteen years ago. Normally, I am a sucker for oriental restaurants, but none of the establishments in town attracted me. I decided on a light lunch, a pizza; but Lydda boasts nothing so modern. In the end I bought an Iraqi *pitta,* a flat flexible bread loaf, almost half a yard across, which I chewed happily all the way to the Herzl forest.

To the east, just on the former border between Israel and Jordan, is the site of the graves of the Hasmonean brothers, leaders of the Jewish revolt against the Hellenistic Syrian empire in the second century B.C. There is no sign of the mausoleum, which was built by the surviving brother, Simon, after all the others had been killed; but the Arabs call the niches in the hillside "the graves of the Jews," and the nearby Arab village is called El-Midiya, which is similar enough to Modein, where the Hasmoneans came from. The huge gray stone blocks that covered the tombs have been pushed aside, and the graves long ago were plundered of what they contained; but the hill commands a fine view of the Judean foothills. Every Hanukah festival, a torch is lit from a beacon near the graves and carried in relays to Jerusalem, where the president of Israel kindles Hanukah lights with the flame.

Hanukah, due to be celebrated in less than a month (along with Christmas), commemorates the victory of the Hasmoneans and, as one might imagine, is a popular festival in modern Israel. Today's Israelis look upon themselves as the successors of the Hasmoneans, as they celebrate the victory of the few against the many, the triumph of the weak against the strong. Sitting by the graves, I considered the Hanukah story, conjuring up the scene in the village down in the valley.

The villagers in the central square of Modein look frightened, though none so terrified as the priest in his white robes, holding a white cockerel ready for sacrifice on the pagan altar. A company of Syrian soldiers is on guard, the men sweating in their leather tunics and under their gleaming helmets.

All at once an old man, sword in hand, strides purposefully toward the priest. Before the soldiers can even move, he strikes the priest with his weapon, killing him. The cockerel squawks and flutters to the ground. As the soldiers spring to life, they are fallen upon by five young men, the Hasmonean brothers, dressed in linen trousers and short tunics, bearded and skullcapped, wielding their daggers with deadly efficiency. It is all over in less than a minute. The old man and his sons stand, slightly dazed, their bloody weapons in their hands, wondering what they have started.

What they had started was the Hasmonean revolt of 167 B.C., but to understand it, it is necessary to go back to the fourth century, when Alexander the Great was on his way to conquer the mighty empire of the Persians. We have already mentioned that Alexander, who Hellenized the entire known world, made an exception for the Jews. There is a legend that Alexander dreamed about the high priest of the Temple of Jerusalem, who told him to conquer Persia. Consequently, when the latter came out to meet him at Afek, he agreed to steer clear of the Temple.

This may or may not be true. More probably, the shrewd general understood — as the lesser men who came after him failed to do — that forcing Hellenism on this small, obstinate people would cause more trouble than it was worth. Alexander's immediate successors, the Egyptian

Ptolemies, continued his liberal policy toward the Jews; but in 200 B.C., the Syrian-Greek Seleucids won control of Judah, and when Antiochus Epiphanes came to the throne in 175, the attitude changed abruptly. Antiochus tried to impose Hellenism on the country by force.

In fact, the Greek culture was starting to make its mark. Numbers of Jews, particularly those of the aristocratic classes, were finding Greek customs attractive. But the king's heavy-handed approach stiffened Jewish resistance. Unlike other peoples, who were able to adapt to Hellenism without much difficulty, the Jews encountered considerable difficulties with the process. Those who adopted Hellenistic practices did so at the expense of their religion. The Jews had their Covenant with the One God, who demanded absolute obedience to His commandments. The theaters, statues, and gymnasia of the Greeks were repugnant to Judaism.

There had been some passive resistance to adopting Hellenistic practices, but the scene in Modein was the first armed act of insurrection. Under the leadership of Mattiahu, an elderly priest of the house of Hasmon, the Hasmonean revolt was in the first instance largely a struggle between loyalist and Hellenist Jews. When the old man died, and his third son, Judah, took over the leadership of the movement, the civil conflict rapidly escalated into a full-scale Jewish uprising against the might of the Seleucid empire.

Judah led the Jewish guerrilla forces in a series of spectacular victories against the vastly superior Seleucid army. In the year 165 B.C., he occupied Jerusalem and rededicated the Temple (which had been converted into a shrine of Zeus) to the One God. A legend says that, in the Temple, the Hasmoneans found only one day's worth of oil for the Menorah, the ceremonial candlestick, but that oil burned for eight days. In memory of this miracle, and to celebrate the purifying of the defiled Temple, the Jews still light candles or beacons for eight days at Hanukah.

This is the legend of Hanukah, celebrated by Israelis and other Jews, but the story does not end here. Judah went on to lose all that he had won. Refusing to accept the limited freedom offered by the empire, he went all-out for total victory, and in so doing lost the support of many of the people. When he was finally defeated at the battle of Adasa, only a few hundred Jewish soldiers remained. They were forced to flee to the other side of the Jordan River.

It was left to the youngest brother, Jonathan, who took over as leader on the death of Judah, to pick up the pieces. He, it seems, learned the lesson that Judah had failed to learn: that however many battles the Jews won, the empire could simply continue sending armies against them. Judah knew when to fight; Jonathan learned when not to.

It took Jonathan almost a decade of slow, patient work to restore the independence of his country, which he then ruled for a further eight years; often fighting, but more frequently skillfully practicing imperial diplomacy. When he was finally outmaneuvered and killed, his brother Simon inherited a stable, independent Jewish state. The Hasmoneans continued to rule until Roman times.

Why is Judah, who ultimately failed, remembered so much better than Jonathan, the real hero? Judah was a straightforward military leader, whereas his younger brother was a master strategist. Where Judah took on the whole empire, Jonathan played his enemies off against each other. He would support the ruler in Antioch, switch to the pretender to the throne, and then switch back to the king again, winning favors for his country at each stage of the game. Judah was called Judah the Maccabee (Judah the Hammer), whereas Jonathan was Apphus (the fox).

The fact of Judah's fame and Jonathan's ignominy tells us something about the way myths are made. People prefer their heroes to be heroic, their legends to be drawn in clear black and white, even if real life consists of varying shades of gray. If Judah is taken as a model, the lesson is that courage is enough, that the weak can prevail against the strong, the few against the many, that sufficient faith conquers all. The lesson of Jonathan is less exciting, more prosaic: a small nation cannot gain all that it wants. It must be prepared to fight for its freedom, but it must know when to fight and whom to fight. In a world of giants, the Jewish pygmy must keep his wits about him. Flexibility and imagination may be more important than stamina and courage. Israelis, when they celebrate Hanukah, are right to remember the brilliant victories of Judah; but they should not forget Jonathan, the leader who used his brains to determine when he should apply his brawn.

19

I PLANNED to spend the night at Kefar Daniel, a village where we had lived for a year after leaving our kibbutz. Then it had been a tiny, isolated border settlement, with one bus in the morning and another in the afternoon. Since that time three other villages had been established in the area, including a new Modein, and the main Tel Aviv–Jerusalem highway now cut across the village fields. Still, approaching it from the back, as it were, through the extensive pine woods named for Theodor Herzl, the founder of modern Zionism, I found that everything looked much the same as it had in our day. I emerged from the trees to enjoy the sight of the village sprawled over its limestone hill in the afternoon sun.

Taking a remembered short cut across the fields, I encountered a bearded tractor-driver. He switched off his engine and sat looking at me. I looked right back. I have no idea why he didn't speak. I remained silent for the very simple reason that I didn't know what to say. Kefar Daniel was at once familiar and strange. As at Amiad, I had lived there a year of my life — but there the resemblance ended. Amiad had remained familiar; we visited every year and maintained friendships with the members. I had never returned to Kefar Daniel in the sixteen years since I left.

"Looking for someone?" The silence was broken.

"That's right."

"Who?"

I had been debating with myself whom to visit there, finally deciding to leave it to chance. Now a decision was being forced on me.

"The Woolfs," I replied. "Miriam and Moshe Woolf." I hoped that they still lived there.

"Fine," he replied. "I'll show you where they live." We walked up the hill together, and he told me that he had been living in Kefar Daniel for seven years. I offered the information that I had lived there many years ago. How long for? he wanted to know. Only a year, I told him. Any regrets? he asked. Did I sometimes feel I had made a mistake? I told him that I never looked back.

Not true. I am an inveterate nostalgist. I always look back, often with regret; but never for a single instant had I regretted our decision to leave Kefar Daniel.

Kefar Daniel is a *moshav-shitufi,* a sort of kibbutz-moshav hybrid, where the farm is collective, as in a kibbutz, but the living is separate, as in a moshav. There are some two dozen villages of this sort in Israel. Leaving Amiad as we did, with deep regret and a continuing belief in the principles of a collective way of life, we thought the moshav-shitufi would be the ideal solution to our problems.

The first moshav-shitufi was founded in 1936 by a Bulgarian group, and a year later some German Jews founded the second village of this type. Most subsequent ones were created by Yekkes, although Kefar Daniel was, in fact, founded by Jews from English-speaking countries. An obvious comparison that suggests itself is with the ill-fated Oppenheimer cooperative at Merhavia in the 1920s; but Oppenheimer's idea was for a graded wage structure, according to productivity, whereas the moshav-shitufi is based on equality. Nevertheless, the actual experience of living at Kefar Daniel indicated that (in the case of this village, at least) the comparison is not so wide of the mark, because one of the major problems there was the inequality between members.

In theory everyone was equal, as in a kibbutz, but there were two major differences. First, variations in the standards of furniture and private equipment are less felt in a kibbutz because the life style is more communal. If everyone eats in (or takes home food from) the same dining hall, it does not matter so much if one member has a gas stove and another doesn't. Second, within any given kibbutz, there is a consistent move toward equality. Today, with the prosperity of the kibbutz sector, material equality has been more or less achieved. Two decades ago there were minor inequities as a result of acquisitions from relatives, German reparations, and so on, but the kibbutz was always leveling up. Thus, if one family possessed a record-player or a sofa, the other families knew that within a short period they would receive the same.

Not so at Kefar Daniel. Many of the veterans from Britain, South Africa, and the United States had beautifully furnished homes; others, from Eastern Europe or the Middle East, who joined later, possessed only the most basic equipment. The formal equality of the wage packet was a mockery. Family A used all its budget on food, outings, and holidays. Family B was forced to save up for furniture or clothes, and consequently had an entirely different diet. Nor could Family B pull itself up by its own bootstraps. One man, who went to work at an outside job during his summer holidays, was expelled from the village for breaking the rules. Another used to slip off to raise money by donating blood.

Criticisms of the setup invited the righteous anger of the village veterans. A moshav-shitufi, one was told, was not a kibbutz; they did not want uniformity. If one family wanted a sofa and the other a refrigerator, where was the harm? The harm, of course, was that one family had a sofa and a refrigerator, and the other family had neither.

However, all this was far from our minds when we arrived at Kefar Daniel on a fine autumn day in 1961. Our worry, it may be recalled, was our son and his inability to adjust to the kibbutz pattern of communal child-rearing. We took Etan to our modest moshav home and put him in the bedroom next to ours with a sublime feeling of satisfaction. From the first night he slept soundly. He seemed to feel an immediate security that even sleeping in our kibbutz room had never given him, as if he sensed that this was a permanent arrangement.

I went to work in the moshav orchards and soon felt at home in the familiar environment. Angela, already pregnant with our next child, was happy keeping house again. The budget was small, the village shop rudimentary — but she managed. She didn't even mind cooking on a primitive paraffin stove or using a dark cavern of an icebox, into which I had to put a huge block of ice each morning. True, the village was small, poor, and struggling; but this only added to our sense of participation, to our feeling that we were carrying out our pioneering principles.

Then things started to go wrong. My first unpleasant memory is of being taken aside by the head of the village absorption committee, who told me off for wearing gloves at work. It was winter and I tend to suffer from chilblains. Wearing gloves improved my work performance, but I was informed that I had made a "very bad impression."

Angela recalls a different incident. A fellow newcomer had told her of a remark by one of the village veterans: "The Gavrons don't have a gas stove or a fridge, but they have enough books for a public library!"

I feel almost ashamed about recording such incidents, but in a small community events such as these can determine one's future path in life. From the vantage point of today, I can see that Kefar Daniel was suffering from the exaggerated introspection that besets all small communities. Even decent people are likely to turn into small-minded gossips when they live in a community of twenty families. This, indeed, was part of the problem; but I also believe, as I have indicated, that there were some basic flaws in the structure of the society.

We were not the only newcomers. There were half a dozen other families from England and South Africa, and we disturbed the surface placidity of the society.

Gerry, a humorous Cockney from London, who had formerly worked as a television repairman, found it impossible to manage on the allowance paid by the moshav. In his jocular manner, he took to describing the village of Kefar Daniel as "a prison camp," and he would make all sorts of elaborate plans for "escape." He pretended to scavenge for food in the dustbins, and when one of the other newcomers got a parcel of tinned dog food for his pet, he asked him if he might have whatever the dog didn't want. We had two particularly decrepit watchmen from a nearby moshav who used to perform guard duty with us. When they came on duty, Gerry would invite us all to watch the "changing of the guard."

Gerry's remarks were often accepted by the veterans with good humor, as were his sudden outbursts of temper and occasional refusal to work. Gerry made them feel virtuous and heroic, so no matter how scathing his language, how sharp his tongue, he was forgiven. Not so Alex, a shrewd ex-London taxi-driver, and me. Not only were our criticisms of the members' work habits or the inequality fiercely resented; we also found ourselves blamed for Gerry's nastiest remarks. We were accused of "putting him up to it." Needless to say, Gerry reveled in this situation: he could say what he liked and we would be shouted at.

Possibly because I was not a new immigrant, I was the

most resented of all, and clearly at some point a decision was taken to "teach me a lesson." I was put on the cotton-weeding machine, a mechanical hoe on the back of a tractor, where one sat at ground level, directing the blades between the rows of young cotton plants. This work was exceptionally uncomfortable, tiring, monotonous, and even dangerous. Gerry refused to do it for more than an hour; no one else did it for more than three successive days. I sat on that bloody hoe for six solid weeks! Foolishly, I was determined to prove that I could stick it out.

I do not intend to chronicle all the petty events of that year. Suffice it to say that as it drew to an end, all six of us newcomer families either had been asked to leave or had decided to go somewhere else.

So this was why I was — to put it mildly — uncertain of my reception in Kefar Daniel. Not that I felt hostility to everyone. Moshe Woolf had been very much a member of what I have called the "establishment," but my memories of him and of Miriam, his wife, were entirely positive.

And, as it happened, the gray-haired, balding Moshe gave me a friendly reception, inviting me to have supper and stay the night. Things were going well for the village, he told me, and indeed the evidence was there on all sides. The houses had been enlarged, a fine new cultural center had been built, the gardens had been extended, and generally the place looked better cared-for. Moshe mentioned that Kefar Daniel, along with a number of other moshav-shitufi villages, had become an associate member of the kibbutz movement. This, he felt, had brought tangible benefits to the village, including a new factory for the production of pianos.

"Some of the villagers were against our joining the kibbutzim," he remarked. "But those of us who know what's what are for it." Under the friendliness I could not help catching the familiar echo of "them" and "us."

Miriam, lively and outspoken, looking much the same, with her fresh complexion and jet-black hair, as she had sixteen years earlier, told me about her hobby as a photographer. While she talked, she bustled around getting the supper. Moshe pulled out a number of albums and I stared at the pictures in amazement; she was really good. Whether they were wedding photos for the village, snapshots of the family holiday in Europe or of local scenes and wildflowers, the pictures were quite superb. It is not just that the technical standard was high (one expects that with modern cameras), but her composition was first class. In my judgment she is in the professional class, but, unfortunately, the moshav rejected her application to attend a course in photography.

On my way to visit another family, I ran into George, a bluff, red-faced American farmer from the Midwest, who has lived in Kefar Daniel for two decades. A Messianic Christian, George lives in Israel with his family because of a profound belief in the Bible.

"What about these peace talks?" he asked me worriedly. "The Jews mustn't give up any of the Land of Israel, you know." In our brief conversation, I learned that George thought that, because of my work at the radio station, I was not only in on all the latest developments, but probably in a position to influence them. I remembered him and his wife as hard-working, decent, pious people, outsiders in the village, but accepted on their own terms. Ingenious and good with his hands, George had always made a notable contribution.

The following morning, I ran into Zvi Klar, who invited me home for breakfast. The skinny, sickly-looking Zvi has remarkable strength and stamina. When I lived in the village, the two of us had conned each other into running a four-mile challenge race. It was one of those affairs where some mild boasting had led to counterboasting and the matter swelled to the point where we found ourselves on the starting-line with the whole village turned out to watch.

I was ten years younger than Zvi and had been a fair long-distance runner at school, so he was a bit nervous at first. He suggested that we jog along together so as not to give the spectators the satisfaction of seeing one of us humiliated. I was agreeable to this, and we ran at a steady clip for about three miles. At this point, with the rest of the route going uphill back the way we'd come, Zvi found he felt very fit, and he invited me to hot up the pace. He won by a couple of hundred yards, to the visible delight of my detractors. Zvi and I had remained good friends and he had gone on to join a local sports club after I left the village. It had been too late for him, though, and he soon gave it up. If he had trained as a young man, I believe he would have become a fine athlete.

Now, over breakfast, he entertained me with his mixture of cynicism and wit. "What do you think of the peace talks, eh? The wily Sadat is breaking the agreement even before it's agreed. With the Russians he at least allowed the ink to dry. Our Polak is no better. And that poor peanut-farmer sandwiched between the oriental and the Polak, eh? Doesn't know what's hit him, eh?"

All this delivered in his music-hall German accent. He went on to talk about the village.

"We want new members; but they must have private incomes. South African millionaires, eh? You think you can manage on the official moshav allowance? Don't make me laugh. Three thousand pounds. There are half a dozen private cars in the village; they run them off the allowance, eh? What do you think?"

I said that I thought one could run a car on 3000 pounds ($150) per month, but that wouldn't leave anything to buy food, let alone clothes and other basic necessities. It seemed, too, that cars were not limited to the rich newcomers; at least one veteran had just purchased one.

"I don't want a car," explained Zvi. "I don't want to kill myself. We have a holiday each year in a decent hotel. I take a taxi — why should I have a good holiday, with good service, and then clamber aboard a bus like an animal, eh? I take a taxi. On the allowance, of course, eh?"

And finally about his current job in the village: "I'm color blind, I know nothing about plants and I'm in charge of the landscape gardening. What do you think? A color-blind landscape gardener. Good, eh?"

I thanked the Klars for breakfast and walked out through the village. It was clear that the sort of deprivation which some members had suffered in our day was a thing of the past. On the other hand, with the arrival of private automobiles, the inequality had reached spectacular proportions.

I found that I had the same ambivalent feelings about the place I had had before: a weird community, but one that works in its way. No regrets about having left; I couldn't have stood the paradoxes.

20

I CROSSED under the highway, which cuts across the fields of Kefar Daniel, walking cross-country toward the smoke-stacks of the Ramla cement factory. The tall chimneys were a convenient landmark for me; but I would resent them fiercely if I were an inhabitant of this area, for they belch out their smoke all day and all night. The apple, plum, and apricot orchards of Kefar Daniel, where I had labored so assiduously, had been uprooted a number of years before. I walked between plowed fields that, I had been told, now grew only cotton. Who sat on the hoe now, or has something more civilized been invented? As I continued west-ward, the soil became paler and I found myself in an area of vineyards. A few farmworkers were repairing the wire frames on which the vines trailed, looking dead, as they always do in wintertime when they've shed their leaves.

Crossing the former Jerusalem road, some miles to the west of the highway, I suddenly recognized the scene of the most unpleasant accident that I had ever experienced. We were driving back to Jerusalem from the airport with my wife's mother, newly arrived from abroad, when the front axle of the car broke, sending it totally out of control: no brakes, no steering, no gears. ("Why didn't you use the handbrake?" asked a friend later). The vehicle could quite easily have veered into the line of oncoming traffic; fortu-nately for us it left the road, overturning into a ditch, but then partly righting itself and coming to rest on its side.

There was no time even to realize what had happened before we were surrounded by dozens of concerned people, who soon pulled us out of the car and stood it upright. None of us was badly hurt, but my mother-in-law had a cut on her head from broken glass, and both her hands were bruised. Our rescuers — motorists who had immediately stopped when they saw what had happened — asked around until they found a car with enough room for us. We were still a little dazed, but we started to enter the vehicle that had been drafted for us, when we were stopped by the driver, an elderly American wearing a skullcap. He pointed to my mother-in-law's swollen hands and suggested that they needed attention. We agreed, but said we could wait until we got to Jerusalem.

Possibly the old man was afraid we would make subsequent claims against him. Whatever the reason, he drove off into the night, leaving us standing on the dark road. Now we were really at a loss, standing alone amid our luggage. But a few minutes later, a van with some rough-looking, swarthy youths pulled up and the driver asked what the trouble was. When we explained, the young men insisted on taking us to the nearest hospital, although it was in the opposite direction from the one in which they had been traveling. They were rather insensitive, making loud jokes about our plight and guffawing at their wit, but they insisted on helping us, and it was only with the greatest difficulty that I persuaded them to accept payment for their petrol.

This was only one of the many times that I have been assisted on Israeli roads. Israelis tend to be interested in their fellow men to the point of intrusiveness, and sometimes one remembers only the latter; but this sort of warmth and human concern is very much a national characteristic. I recalled Hezi on the road south from Kiryat Shmona. His language had been insulting, but his instinct had been to help a fellow being in distress.

The weather was strange, with a silver sun burning hotly out of a gray sky. I found that I was drinking far more than usual. It was undoubtedly a *hamsin,* a dry desert wind. (The word is Arabic for "fifty." There are fifty days of such wind every year.) It was rather late for a hamsin, which usually turns up in autumn and spring. Perhaps it was making a special effort for me, on the assumption that no book about walking through Israel would be complete without the experience of walking in a hamsin!

Possibly it was the weather that caused me to blunder into the army camp. I certainly never intended to, but I must record that I was in and out of the installation about six times. Getting in was easy enough — indeed, I never noticed I was entering until I was actually inside. Once I was there, though, the place seemed to conspire against me, shutting me in with gates and barbed wire.

Eventually I made my escape and continued on my way. More plowed fields, some green with winter vegetables. The crops were being watered with sprinklers, swishing and clapping as they revolved. An unfamiliar sound so late in the year, but, then, the weather had apparently been designed for my walking plans rather than to suit the country's farmers. For some time I walked toward a large structure that puzzled me. Big and shiny, with huge fat yellow pipes snaking down from its roof, it looked like a model for man's first colony on the moon.

It turned out to be the most spectacular hothouse that I have ever seen. It was a vast structure, covered with plastic sheeting, with enormous fans set into its walls and dozens of dials and gauges (presumably for measuring temperature, humidity, and the like). The owner of this impressive piece of equipment, a gnarled, brown-faced peasant with a fine white mustache, informed me that he grew carnations there. I said that I had never known such complex structures were needed. He explained that it was a new experiment.

The carnation-grower was a Karaite from Egypt. His village, Moshav Matzliah, was partly Karaite and partly Moroccan. The Karaites are a Jewish sect, believing only in the Bible and not in any of the later sacred literature. For example, they would not be celebrating Hanukah next month because it is a post-Biblical festival. Matzliah, the name of the moshav, is Hebrew for "succeed." Pointing to his plastic structure and to an expensive-looking villa going up on his land, I made some crack about the name being appropriate and was treated to a ten-minute lecture on the sufferings he and the other villagers had gone through and how the government was still "screwing" them. In fact, that very afternoon the papers were full of a story about a flower farmer who had burned his whole crop because he was compelled to sell his produce through Agrexco, the government exporting authority. I did not make a thorough study of Israeli agriculture, nor did I examine the balance sheets of Israeli farmers; but from my walk through the countryside, I got an impression of fantastic prosperity accompanied by endless grumbling on all sides.*

According to my map, there should have been a path westward to Rehovot, but I couldn't find it. Instead, I struck across open, sandy country, along the line of some electric pylons. I soon arrived at the borders of Rehovot's extensive citrus groves; from there, a cart track led into town. The soil here was almost pure sand. I rested and enjoyed three of the juiciest, tastiest oranges I have ever had.

In Rehovot I had lunch at a small, pretentious restaurant, where I was given a steak that I could neither cut nor chew. The waitress asked whether I wanted it to go back under the grill, but I said I thought it was beyond all possible help. What was wrong with it?

"Madam," I said stiffly, "I happen to have come a long way on foot, but my shoes are not yet in need of repair. I

_____
* This was 1979; there are signs that the prosperity of this period is coming to an end.

cannot conceive of any other use for this piece of material."
I must put it on record that I was offered the choice of any
other main course on the house, but I declined.

Rehovot is the site of Israel's world-class scientific research center, the Weizmann Institute. Originally founded
on a modest scale in 1934 by Chaim Weizmann, an organic
chemist of international renown before he became Israel's
first president, it first concentrated on projects connected
with local agriculture and medicine. A decade later, a
group of Weizmann's friends and admirers began planning
a far larger enterprise, and the Weizmann Institute of Science was dedicated in 1949.

Today it has a staff of 1500 scientists and graduate students, and more than 400 research projects are in the pipeline in such fields as cancer research, immunology, hor-
mones, aging, cell structure, computer science, geophysics,
lasers, atomic particles, astrophysics, and magnetism.

The moving spirit behind the institute in its early years
was a former American show-business impresario, the late
Meyer Weisgal. In addition to raising millions of dollars,
Weisgal used to pace the grounds, picking up discarded cigarette packs and even matchsticks. As a result, the institute,
with its manicured lawns, tidy paths, and well-kept flower
beds, which, in the words of a visitor, "breathes the spirit of
Plato's original academy," does not seem like part of Israel
at all.

Towering above the campus are the twin towers of the
atomic-particle accelerator, one of them topped by an elliptical bulb. One of the scientists using this equipment is
my cousin Avigdor, who agreed to show me around.

Shooting up to the top of the tower in a lift, I marveled
at this country's diversity. Eight miles north, the Habadniks were living in eighteenth-century Europe. Three miles
eastward, a Karaite (who regarded Habad doctrine as new-
fangled) grew his flowers with sophisticated, modern

equipment. Here at the institute, they were carrying out the latest research.

The elliptical structure at the top is nothing more exciting than a lecture room for guests, although the view is impressive: Ashdod and the sea, the towns of Rishon Lezion and Rehovot, the orange groves, and a bird's-eye look at the splendid campus of the Weizmann Institute itself, its beautiful buildings and well-tended gardens. From the egg, we walked down a ramp into the laboratory where the experimental material is introduced into the accelerator. The basic idea, explained Avigdor (taking great care to use terms that a moron like me could understand), was to cause a collision between the nuclei of different types of atoms. By measuring the effects of the collision, scientists learned more about the structure and behavior of matter. He was colliding oxygen atoms with carbon. The stream of oxygen atoms passed down the tower at ever-increasing speeds, shedding electrons on the way, toward a carbon screen at the bottom.

Was that the reason for the tower's great height? I asked. To give the atoms time to speed up? He shook his head patiently. No. The reason for the size of the accelerator was to provide adequate insulation. Fourteen million volts were developed, and that needed a lot of insulating. We went farther down the tower on foot, walking on a circular ramp and pausing to inspect each chamber through which the beam of atoms passed. Needless to say, I couldn't make anything of the mass of wires, tubes, and pipes. In the reaction chamber at the bottom, Avigdor handed me a sheet of transparent material about half an inch across. That was the carbon; the beam of oxygen atoms came zipping down this enormous and complex structure to crash against a nickel-sized bit of carbon.

"What's the point of it all?" I asked.

"Pure research," replied Avigdor, with a smile. "We just

want to know more about what makes the universe tick."
He went on to remind me, a trifle severely, that most useful
inventions had been the results of pure research. Transis-
tors, lasers, calculating machines — he rattled off a list of
examples. Not to be outdone, I quoted Chaim Weizmann's
dying words:

> Those who strive consciously to reach the mountain top
> remain chained to the bottom of the hill. Those who set out
> to achieve something specific in science never achieve it. It is
> those who work for science for its own sake who reach the top
> of the mountain.

Avigdor felt that this was a fair statement of the institute's philosophy, although a great deal of applied research
was also being carried out. Apart from his main work with
the accelerator, he was spending one day a week at another
laboratory, investigating the measurement of radioactivity
in human beings who worked with radioactive materials.
He was hopeful that this work would lead to improved
safety measures.

When we took a break for coffee, I asked Avigdor
whether he felt handicapped in his work because of Israel's
being such a small country. In his field, he replied, the
Weizmann Institute was as good as any similar establishment in the world; but he confessed to a feeling that life in
Israel made effective research difficult. Life was too hectic.
He spent too much time running around, arranging his
daily affairs. He was worried about money, and of course
there were the constant interruptions for military service.
He said that he had done better work in his three years in
the United States at Los Alamos simply because he was relaxed and free to concentrate on his research.

I asked him about his salary, and he quoted a figure that
was more or less the average Israeli wage. A branch man-

ager of a small bank earns about three times as much before taxation. Even to one with my egalitarian outlook, his salary seemed ridiculously small. The Weizmann Institute does not, of course, decide how much to pay its scientists. Like all salaries in Israel (except in the private sector), Avigdor's is decided in nationwide negotiations between the unions and the government. Needless to say, he could earn vastly more abroad — and he admitted that he had received a number of tempting offers.

Changing the subject, I asked him how many people could understand one of his research papers. Probably about twenty at the institute, he thought; another dozen outside it. Only a few hundred in the whole world. Less than a thousand? I prompted. "Well, don't call me a liar if it's one thousand and one." Many others kept up with the general trend of his work through the critical scientific journals. That was how he himself kept abreast of the work of other scientists. I was left with an image of research flying off in all different directions, rather like the atoms he was studying.

I spent the night with Jane and Irrie Foreman, two good friends from the old days, and in the morning Irrie took me for breakfast to the huge milk-processing plant where he works. Showing me around the huge vats, smelling of sour milk ("What smell?" demanded Irrie), where the various cheeses and milk products are made, he explained the rigorous methods used to check the quality of the milk. In the old days, I was told, most farmers had watered their milk varying only in the degree to which they did it. Today this was impossible. Milk had a very stable freezing point. Accurate measurements of this meant that any adulteration was immediately discovered. Once a few heavy fines were imposed, the practice had died out.

"Hit them in their pockets!" said my friend with relish. When the milk arrived at the plant, a number of basic tests were carried out at once for acidity, temperature, and taste. Taste could be tested only by a human being, but it was among the most important factors. Only last week, Irrie said, he had rejected 500 liters of milk from a kibbutz because of the taste. It had subsequently been traced to a changed plastic pipe in the kibbutz dairy.

"I have a lousy sense of taste," confessed Irrie, "but one of the girls in the lab is first class."

Within a few weeks, new criteria for purity were due to be introduced at the plant. Milk with a too high bacteria count would be rejected, and bonuses would be paid for milk with a low count. My friend mentioned the name of a kibbutz with a large number of English-speakers and a good reputation.

"Filthy buggers," he commented, showing me the results of a bacteria count on their milk.

At breakfast, which naturally included plenty of yogurt, sour milk, and different kinds of cheese, Irrie and some colleagues discussed the latest wage negotiations. I can never understand the ramifications of our work agreements, so their talk had a familiar ring to it.

"I see. So we get six percent of the basic and an addition to the increment, which, with the cost-of-living allowance, comes to twenty-seven percent gross . . ."

From Rehovot, I walked along the railway track toward the coast. The track took me past Tel Yavne, situated between the railway line and the road. Few people go past the hill, which turned out to be a bird sanctuary second only to the Or Akiva sand dunes. A drumming sound made me look up, and I saw a woodpecker picking away at a telegraph pole.

Yavne became a center of Jewish learning during the Jewish war against Rome of A.D. 66–73. I have already mentioned that the Hasmonean dynasty continued to rule the Jews until the Herodians usurped it. During the entire period, the clash between the Greek and Jewish cultures continued, and after the death of Herod Agrippa in Caesarea, the Jews found themselves under increasing pressure. Judea was once more under direct Roman administration by the procurators.

These middle-class Romans made a practice of enriching themselves by taxation, which placed an intolerable burden on the Jews, coming as it did on top of the official taxes and the tithes they paid to the Temple in Jerusalem. The small farmers, driven off the land by the large estate-owners, formed a discontented class in the towns. Although a case can be made to explain the Jewish uprising in economic terms, the primary basis of the conflict was, as so often in the past, religious.

The Jewish belief in the imminence of the End of Days has already been mentioned. There is no doubt that they believed that their people were being punished for their sins, for the pervading Hellenism and corruption. They were certain that once their cup of bitterness was full to overflowing, God would intervene on their side and usher in His kingdom on earth. There was no logic in the revolt of the Jews — divided among themselves, outnumbered in many areas by the Syrian-Greek colonists — against the greatest power that the world had ever known.

An eloquent illustration of the Jewish belief in the ultimate triumph of the Almighty has been recorded in the Book of Daniel, when the prophet interprets the dream of the Babylonian monarch Nebuchadnezzar. The king had dreamed of a great image, with a head of gold, the breast and arms of silver, the belly and thighs of brass, the legs of iron, and the feet partly iron, partly clay. The feet were broken by a great stone, which destroyed the image and became a great mountain that filled the whole earth.

Nebuchadnezzar, explained Daniel, was the head. The breast and arms, belly, thighs and legs were the great kingdoms and empires that came after him. (The strongest, presumably, was the "iron" empire of Rome.) But God, the great stone, prevails against all these kingdoms:

"And in the days of these kings shall the God of heaven set up a kingdom, which shall never be destroyed: and the kingdom shall not be left to other people, but it shall break in pieces and consume all these kingdoms, and it shall stand for ever" (Daniel 3:44).

Right up to the fall of Jerusalem in A.D. 70 — indeed, until the sacking of Masada three years later — the Jews continued in their obstinate belief that this time would come.

The siege of Jerusalem by four Roman legions and a host of auxiliaries (close to 100,000 men) lasted for five months in the final phase, until the last outpost, the Temple, was captured and burned to the ground. It was an epic defense, but it would have been more effective had the Jews not spent so much energy fighting each other.

In the year 68, when Vespasian was still the Roman commander in Judea, there is a legend that Yohanan Ben-Zakkai was smuggled out of Jerusalem in a sealed coffin. The Jewish defenders were not permitting desertion at the time, and the only way the disciples of the elderly rabbi could get him out was by pretending that he was dead. The coffin was taken to the tent of the Roman commander, upon which Ben-Zakkai emerged and prophesied that Vespasian would become Emperor of Rome. He asked for permission to found a Jewish academy.

Vespasian reportedly promised to allow this if the prophecy turned out to be true. It did, and Ben-Zakkai founded his school at Yavne. Much of the early work on the Mishna was started ("remembered," in the Habad version of events) in Yavne, before the centers of learning moved to Galilee.

Ben-Zakkai was a leader of the Pharisees, and it may be useful to say something about this movement. In the New

Testament, the term Pharisee has a negative connotation — apparently they had their differences with the early Christians — but it was the Pharisees who developed the Mishna and the commentaries, who built "a fence around the Torah," adapting Judaism to the modern world without abandoning its basic tenets.

If the Hellenistic Jews were prepared to assimilate into the dominant culture of the time, abandoning Judaism, and the zealots thought they could maintain their way of life by meeting the Greek way of life head-on, the Pharisees found a way to accommodate Hellenism to their faith. Without abandoning Judaism, they made use of Greek logic and philosophy to elaborate and explain the Torah. The Habadniks believe that the Talmud, along with the Torah, was expounded to Moses on Mount Sinai; but one is forced to concede that the Mishna and the Gemara speak with a very different voice. The Torah is entirely inspirational: the Law is proclaimed by God through Moses and it must be obeyed. The Talmud argues, explains, amplifies, and persuades.

The very idea of an oral tradition (*halacha*) is Greek, although the Greeks used it in a different way. The *agraphos nomos* was used to contradict written edicts, whereas the Pharisees, as we have noted, used the halacha to build a "fence" to protect their Law.

Today it is often argued in Israel that it was the zealots and extremists who preserved Judaism. If not for their refusal to compromise, it is said, the Jewish people would not be here today. This may be disputed. We have already seen that it was Jonathan, the compromiser, who saved Judaism in the Seleucid period. It was the Pharisees who preserved the Jewish religion in the subsequent era. The religion practiced by all Jews today (except the tiny Karaite sect) is Pharasaic Judaism.

As a Pharisee, Yohanan Ben-Zakkai was a leader of the mainstream of Judaism, and it was his academy at Yavne that brought the religion through the difficult period after the war against Rome, the burning of the Temple, and the forced abandonment of Jerusalem. The heroes of the revolt against Rome perished. It was Ben-Zakkai, the scholar, who ensured the survival of the Jewish people.

*　　　*　　　*

As I proceeded westward, threatening gray clouds appeared in the sky. I was proving less than brilliant as a weather forecaster. Ever since my soaking in Galilee, I had been telling myself that all would be well once I got past Rehovot. Now, for the first time in weeks, rain looked likely. Fortunately, it held off, save for a drop or two; and a little farther on, by the railway line, I found a garden with a plaque dedicating it to the memory of one "Eliahu Dahan of Blessed Memory." I haven't the faintest idea who Eliahu Dahan was, why a garden should have been dedicated to his memory, or who would ever come to this corner by the railway track, miles from any habitation; but I spent a pleasant half-hour resting on the lawn beneath the poplar trees that surrounded it.

Crossing the main road to Ashdod, I walked through an area of scrub and sand dunes, which was marked on the map as a nature reserve. Pleasant at first, with a fair amount of bird life, I later found myself in a fly-infested valley covered with thorn bushes. In the middle of it was a skeleton of a horse, which probably accounts for the flies. I had quite a job to fight my way through the thorns and onto the road.

At the entrance to Ashdod, I ate a first-rate lunch in a self-service restaurant: cheap, clean, tasty — all that such a place should be and so rarely is.

I walked along the main road into Ashdod, past the industrial sector of town. Lining the road were factories for electronics, wool, rayon, metalwork, and motor assembly. Small groups of Arabs huddled by the roadside, waiting to be taken home to Gaza. In town were bright lights, busy shops and cafés, and crowds of teen-agers drinking Coke, flirting, and making calls from public phones. Several cinemas appeared to be doing a brisk trade.

With its tall apartment blocks, busy streets, and general air of bustle, Ashdod has a distinctly urban ambience. Different in concept and much more ambitious than the other development towns, Ashdod may not fit into that category.

Founded in 1956, and planned as a deep-water port, it was conceived from the outset as a major metropolis by Israeli standards. The population is already over 50,000, and its target is 350,000. Although it was established after the main wave of immigration, it started off in classical development-town style, with twenty-two Moroccan families located in temporary huts by the seashore. The development was swifter than usual. Less than twenty miles from Tel Aviv and only some forty from Jerusalem, the project proved attractive to private investors. The Ashdod Development Corporation was set up to coordinate private enterprise; but it soon became involved in land speculation, and the government became a 50 percent shareholder to keep an eye on things.

The two main projects are the electric-power station and the port. Along with the industries already mentioned, they have guaranteed full employment and given jobs even to outsiders.

The port had to be made artificially: a breakwater almost two miles long was constructed, and it was inaugurated in 1965.

More central than Haifa, Israel's main port, it is also nearer to the chemical industries of the Negev. It already handles almost as much tonnage as Haifa and is far more automated, with equipment for handling bulk cargoes on a roll-on, roll-off basis.

Approximately 50 percent of the population are oriental

Jews, mostly from Morocco; about a quarter of the citizens are Israeli-born. Shortly after my walk was over, I served in the army for a spell and remarked to a fellow soldier from Ashdod what a vibrant, lively community it was. He was less enthusiastic, complaining about the rowdiness and dirt.

"At least the public phones work," I said. "That isn't the situation in most towns."

"You must have got there less than a minute after it was repaired!" he retorted.

Ashdod's very success presents problems. Designed to siphon off excess population from the big towns, it has proved attractive to citizens from other development towns, thus contributing to the concentration of people in the coastal region rather than acting as an agent for population dispersal.

There was no problem about finding a pizza in Ashdod: I had the choice of half a dozen eating places. I checked in at the pleasanter of the town's two hotels and took a stroll before turning in. Seeing a crowd of people streaming toward the beach, I decided to follow and soon found myself in a brightly lit public hall by the seashore. I was attending a typical Israeli wedding. No one queried my presence, confirming the impression that an excessive number of guests had been invited. This was usual enough. The tables were laid out with hors d'oeuvres, fruit juice, and wine. The band was playing amplified music, incredibly loud. The bride and groom, seated on a special dais, were receiving their guests. They looked dazed, as well they might.

I have attended a number of these weddings (by invitation, of course), which all too often cost the families far more than they can afford. Too much food, drink, and noise is the order of the day, along with a sort of demonstrative vulgarity that is as distressing as it is pathetic. Some wedding caterer once saw a film with a flambé dish being brought to the dining table. He introduced the custom (copied by all his fellows) of turning out the lights and bringing in the main course, lit by improvised spirit lamps. I cannot say that I have ever enjoyed one of these affairs, and on this occasion I had no business being there, anyway. I fled.

*   *   *

Up early the following morning, I resolved to walk south along the sands to Ashkelon. Under a lowering sky, I soon came to regret my decision, because the soft sand made the going difficult. I sought a firmer surface along the line of the sea, but the waves kept taking me by surprise and washing over my shoes. I picked up a palm branch and used it as a walking stick to help myself along. My pack seemed heavier than usual, and I looked enviously at the young fisherman who kept passing me, sprinting barefoot along the beach and casting his net into the waves, without, however, any visible sign of success.

About a mile and a half south of the town, I came to the ruins of Ashdod-Yam. It was never an important settlement, and there was little to see. It was always a mere outpost for the main city of Ashdod, some three miles inland. Tel Ashdod is less easy to identify than other tels, much of its having been destroyed by subsequent building and farming, but excavations were carried out there between 1968 and 1972. Layers of settlement from the pre-Biblical period to the time of the Byzantines were uncovered; of course, the famous Ashdod was that of the Philistines from the twelfth to the tenth century B.C.

We met the kings of Israel briefly at Tel Hatzor and heard some more about them at the Mukhraka on Mount Carmel. The time has now come to take a look at the development of the unified Israelite state of the eleventh century and at its most important enemies, the Philistines.

In the thirteenth century, there were violent upheavals in

the eastern Mediterranean. It was the end of the Mycenaean civilization; the Hittites were collapsing; and the Egyptian empire was on a downward swing. Originating, according to one theory, in the Aegean, according to another in Asia Minor, the Sea Peoples came sweeping eastward, dealing severe blows to Egypt. One of these peoples was the Philistines, and they settled in the southwest of the land to which they eventually gave their name. Palestine. They formed a powerful confederation of five city-states: Ashdod, Ashkelon, and Gaza on the coast; Ekron and Gath farther inland.

The Israelites had invaded Canaan from the east about a century earlier, and as the Philistines expanded eastward, a clash between the two was inevitable. Initially, it was the tribe of Dan that bore the brunt of the struggle. One of their number, Samson, engaged in some daring counterattacks, but he was apparently attracted by the pagan way of life and married Delilah, a Philistine woman. The story of how she beguiled him into being captured and blinded by his enemies is well known, as is the final act of destruction carried out by the Israelite hero. Israel has been accused of possessing a fiendish plan to bring about the destruction of the world in an atomic holocaust, in the event of a defeat at the hands of the Arab states. Some lurid fiction of this nature has been published, and at least one prestigious journalist has made the suggestion. For some eccentric reason that escapes me totally, this plan is referred to as a "Masada complex." I may be woefully ignorant, but to the best of my knowledge, Samson (who admittedly did, according to the Biblical version, bring the whole temple crashing down on himself and the Philistines) never went near Masada. If Israel did have a Masada plan — and this reflects more on the accusers than on Israel itself — it would involve mass suicide by the Israelis, and the rest of the world would have no role save that of spectator. But we shall come to Masada in due course.

The tribe of Dan was driven out by the Philistines and forced to seek territory farther north. Thus, "from Dan to Beersheba" became the traditional extent of Israel, although, as we have seen, there were times when the Jewish state was larger and times when it was smaller. I have already told the story of the Philistine victory at Afek. I should add that it was to Ashdod that the Ark of the Covenant was first brought by its captors.

The technology of the Philistines was superior to that of Israel. They had superior iron weapons and used advanced techniques of chariot warfare. At one time they were so dominant that the Israelites were forced to come down to the coast even to have their iron farm tools sharpened. At another point, the Philistines reached the Jordan River. The Israelites were forced to unite. In 1033 they elected a king, and the collection of tribes began to emerge into a nation. King Saul waged a successful guerrilla campaign against the Philistines before he was killed, along with his eldest son.

During the reign of Saul, we have another famous Biblical story, that of David and Goliath. Arthur Koestler has described the contest as "grotesque":

> ... the nimble little Semitic tribesman pirouetted around the half-idiotic giant, victim of his pituitary glands, and amid the jeers and cheers of the bystanders, knocked the poor brute out with a jagged stone from his sling.

It is not clear on what authority Koestler alters the Biblical account, which has David choosing five *smooth* stones. Nor can one imagine why the author should have decided that the giant was "half-idiotic." Military champions are not necessarily distinguished for intellectual endeavor, but a certain skill and daring can be assumed. There is no reason to take the story as anything other than an allegory. The same story occurs throughout Jewish history: Gideon at En Harod, the Hasmoneans, the Israel Defense Forces. The moral: Israel is a small country; it must make its own rules of combat and not allow the larger enemy to delineate the game.

David undoubtedly learned the lesson, for when he became king, he hired mercenaries and contracted alliances. As we saw, he took the hill city of Jerusalem for Israel's capital. The consolidation of the nation and the building of the Temple was left to his son Solomon. David is remembered as a remarkable, if flawed, human being and the writer of many beautiful poems, the Psalms; but his significance for Jewish history is that he was the king who united a group of warring tribes into a nation extending from Damascus to the Red Sea and from Amman to the Mediterranean. Small wonder that the Messiah, who is to appear at the End of Days, is of the House of David.

*   *   *

From time to time, as I walked along the sands, I waved at the soldiers manning the lookout posts. By ten o'clock, I reckoned that I must be close to Ashkelon. The sun was now shining and I felt that I had earned a rest. I placed my rucksack in the sand, my camera on it, and my stick and water bottle beside them. Then I spread-eagled myself in the sun.

I was not conscious of dropping off to sleep, but when I woke up, my equipment had disappeared — only the stick and water bottle remained.

It took me several seconds to absorb what had happened. I was dimly aware of a petrol engine starting up nearby. Perhaps I even saw somebody or something out of the corner of my eye — or did I imagine it? When my mind began to function consciously, I thought that I must have placed the rucksack somewhere else, but in searching for it, I found the imprint it had made in the sand: the two holes of the frame were unmistakable. Climbing a sand dune to the east, I saw that I was near one of the roads that lead out of Ashkelon to the nearby beaches.

Looking around, rather desperate now, I spotted an army lookout post some way off. That was it, I concluded; the soldiers had played a joke on me. I rushed up to the outpost and asked the soldiers if they had taken a blue rucksack. For a joke, I hastened to add. An elderly soldier looked at me suspiciously. I was dressed simply in jeans and shirt. I didn't have so much as a jacket.

"Where are you from?" he asked. The stubble glinted silver in his wrinkled brown face.

"I'm walking through the country," I explained, trying to be patient. "I came from Ashdod this morning. I was just resting over there and my equipment was stolen. I thought that maybe one of the soldiers . . . A joke?" I ended lamely.

"How did you get here?"

"Along the beach from Ashdod."

"That's a lie; no one came along the beach!" Some other soldiers came up; all agreed that nobody had walked along the beach that morning. Suspicious and a little nervous, they placed me under arrest, telling me not to move from my place outside their tent. I heard them reporting the incident on their field telephone.

"He speaks Hebrew, but not clearly," the old man said into the mouthpiece. Bloody cheek!

Reporting my appearance was the best thing they could have done: it brought a police jeep in ten minutes. Fortunately, I had my money and my papers on me, so they had not been stolen. The soldiers were muttering about the "lies" I had told them, but the police at once began searching for my possessions. I got into the jeep and we began to comb the area. A couple of young men with a van were questioned, but the pack wasn't in the van or nearby. The police told me that even if they had stolen it, there had been plenty of time for them to get rid of it.

After about half an hour, we drove to the police station,

where I filed a complaint. I decided to return to the dunes afterward. Apparently, kids often stole wallets, handbags, attaché cases, and so forth, throwing them away once they had extracted the money or valuables. Not this time. Four hours of careful searching failed to turn up anything. I met some high school children who were looking at a collection of personal papers, but they were someone else's.

I was upset about losing my lovely new framed rucksack, which had served me so well, and the warm sleeping bag. The camera was a good one and had lots of undeveloped pictures in it. I was sorry to lose my clothes — but all this was nothing compared to my notebook. A hundred and ninety pages of scrawl: the basis of my book so far. I have a fair memory, but what about all my thoughts and ideas?

* * *

Back home on the bus to a warm greeting from Angela, six-teen-year-old Ilana, and nine-year-old Assaf. Then I sat down at the typewriter and bashed away for three days solid. I think I got most of it back — but, then, I'll never know what I forgot.

Apparently, Ashkelon is famous for thefts. At least six people subsequently told me stories about people they knew being robbed there. About a month later the *Jerusalem Post* ran an item about a man whose rental car had been burgled there. When he returned to Tel Aviv, the hire company clerk, noticing the broken lock on the door, said, "I see you've been to Ashkelon!"

* * *

The first immigrants to live in the town were from Yemen. They moved into the deserted Arab town after the 1948 war and were soon joined by others from Morocco, Tunisia, Libya, Turkey, and India; but Ashkelon did not become a classical development town, in the manner of Kiryat

Shmona and Migdal Haemek. In the early years, a group of South African Zionists were attracted to the spot, with its relatively lush vegetation and golden beaches, and their suburb, Afridar, developed alongside the other neighborhoods. Afridar, with its hotels, cafés, and beaches, grew into a pleasant enough tourist center, but the people had little contact with the rest of Ashkelon, which developed about a mile inland.

Casting about for an explanation of the high crime rate in Ashkelon, it suddenly hit me: Or Akiva. If Ashkelon had become notorious for burglary and petty crime, it was Or Akiva that held the current Israeli record for juvenile delinquency. The similarities are striking: in both cases we have the existence of two entirely different life styles side by side. (One could even stretch the comparison to Kibbutz Ginnegar and Migdal Haemek.) Caesarea and Afridar are two of the most pleasant living environments in the country. Or Akiva and Ashkelon are among the less pleasant.

It is logical enough: poverty, as such, does not necessarily lead to crime; the dangerous situation is affluence and relative deprivation in close proximity to each other. Frustrated expectation, rather than want, is the midwife of theft and delinquency.

In the case of Ashkelon, at least, something is being done, for the town is one of the first locations for Project Renewal, the scheme sponsored by the government and Jewish donors from abroad for renovating and improving slum neighborhoods. Ashkelon has been "adopted" by the British Zionist movement. Student volunteers from England are spending periods of up to a year in Ashkelon, as social workers and youth leaders. A group of dentists from Britain has set up a mobile dental clinic. Possibly more significant than these volunteer operations was the election of Eli Dayan to be the new mayor. At thirty-one, the youngest Jewish mayor in Israel, he is himself a product of the Ashkelon neighborhoods. One hopes that the combination of a young, local mayor and resources mobilized from abroad will remedy the situation and that Ashkelon will not be famous for its negative features.

Traditionally, Ashkelon was always known for its delightful beaches and pleasant hotels and even more for the National Park, which provides one of the best backdrops in the country for the archaeological remains. The excavations may not be as spectacular as those of Tel Hatzor, but at least six distinct layers of settlement have been discovered, and they are displayed among the lawns and shady trees of the park.

As at Ashdod, the most famous Ashkelon was that of the Philistines, but the site was also inhabited during the Canaanite, Greek, Roman, Muslim, and Crusader periods. It was first mentioned in Egyptian documents of the eighteenth century B.C. In 332 B.C. it was won by Alexander the Great from the Persians and became a center of Hellenism. During the Hasmonean period it was taken by the Jews. Most of the ruins in the park are from the Greek and Roman periods, but Philistine remains were uncovered south of the area.

I had planned to linger in Ashkelon, but the previous happy memories had been overlaid by a nasty taste.

21

FRESHLY EQUIPPED with an orange-colored rucksack to replace my blue one, I returned to Ashkelon and quickly endeavored to place as much distance between it and me as I could. But it really is an ill wind that blows no good, and a fringe benefit of my enforced rest at home was that I missed the rain that had finally caught up with me again. There was still plenty of evidence of the downpour when I hit the road going south. The ground was soft, though fortunately it was inclined to be sandy, and there were large puddles everywhere. It was still very much citrus country, the orange groves alternating with plowed fields.

A black-clad Arab woman, piling green fodder high on her donkey cart, reminded me that I was near the old border between Israel and the Gaza Strip. I had not been into Gaza for several years, nor had I any intention of going there now. As I walked along, I pondered the difference between Nazareth and Gaza (and, for that matter, between Kafr Kassem and Kalkiliya), and I realized that Israel had not, in fact, tried to make Gaza or the West Bank into a part of the state. In language, custom, dress, and life style, the Arab of Gaza or Nablus is a foreigner; the Arab of Nazareth is not. The citizen of Nazareth is certainly an Arab, but he is also an Israeli. I have no doubt that the Israeli Arab feels kinship with his brother across the border, just as the Israeli Jew feels kinship with his cousins in America;

but that does not make the American Jew into an Israeli or the Israeli Arab into a West Banker. I walked unarmed and unafraid through the length of Israel, making no distinction between Jewish settlements and Arab villages — but I would not do the same in Gaza or the West Bank.

Aside from a couple of brief visits, my experience of Gaza has been as a soldier. I remember that on my first tour of duty there, in 1970, I was amazed by the countryside: the citrus groves, the rolling sand dunes, the cactus and scrub. Previously, I had visualized the area as one continuous refugee camp. There was no shortage of camps, but there were also villages, farms, and open country. Wherever we went, we were accompanied by the rhythmic squeak of the old-fashioned water pumps, for there are considerable underground reserves of water in the strip.

It was a time of constant terrorist activity in the region, and our task of controlling it was a tough one, the more so as we were an ordinary infantry unit, not particularly brave or tough or brilliant. My commanding officer was an engineering technician; my sergeant was a storekeeper from the Dead Sea potash works; the other soldiers were clerks and teachers, crane operators and bus drivers, mechanics and builders.

"It isn't an easy task," said the young operations officer on our first day. He was a regular, gun slung low on his hip, a bit of a bullshitter. "Last time someone threw a grenade at me, I fired back and the 'grenade' turned out to be a stone. Fortunately I missed. You may not be so lucky. You can never know whether you're going to wind up with a citation for valor or a jail sentence."

We were instructed to remain constantly on full alert, but it was sometimes difficult to remember this as we strolled through the sunny countryside. In point of fact, our unit did not lose a single soldier during its tour of duty, but in those days that was a rare and enviable record.

A wide-awake soldier stays alive! This was drummed into us again and again while we went through a snappy retraining course to get us up to scratch, at a camp not three miles from where I now walked. Dressed in filthy fatigues, we stalked and patrolled, crawled in the dust and charged up and down sand dunes. Helmets always worn, ammunition belts strapped correctly, guns loaded, with safety catch ready to be flicked off at a moment's notice. The gun had to be slung *around* your neck, it was stressed, so that if you were attacked by an assailant (and, for example, stabbed), he wouldn't be able to take your weapon too easily. ("How charming," remarked Angela when she heard about this later.)

We were inundated with regulations and instructions: never fire unless fired on first; don't fire into crowds; don't shoot at women or children — ever! The torrent of orders, written and oral, never seemed to stop. We were to "honor and suspect" the local citizen. We must be firm, but never brutal.

There were, of course, different interpretations of these rules. Ali, our Druze scout, thought that firmness meant a sharp blow with the back of the hand if a local did not reply to his questions quickly enough. A teen-ager who cursed him received a thrashing with a bamboo cane. Ali was soundly rebuked for his overzealous attitude and was taken off patrols. He felt very hard done by. I tried to reason with him, but soon realized that he didn't understand what I was talking about.

We lived in a camp that had been formerly used by the Egyptian army of occupation. It was part of a larger complex, which included the local police station and the military government administration. The policemen were all locals. We used to watch them drilling in the compound outside their station. They used antique rifles, and their hobnailed boots struck sparks from the asphalt. The police station was the place to go if we wanted a good cup of coffee. If we wanted to watch a movie or flirt with the girl conscripts, we went to the Gothic military government building, with its labyrinth of corridors. Except when we were on patrol, we were not allowed out of the complex, but most hours of the day and night we were on patrol. Our routines were carefully irregular so that the locals could never know when we might show up.

We patrolled through the streets of the refugee camps, streets so narrow that we could touch the walls on either side as we walked down them. The huts were mean and shabby; the sewage spilled onto the streets. The young children would run after us (keeping their distance) and shout, *"Yahud, yahud"* (Jew, Jew). The women used to go to the street's central tap to collect their water. They balanced the tall earthenware jars on their heads with amazing dexterity. We were fascinated by their graceful, swaying walk, but they looked right through us, as if we didn't exist.

On patrol we kept strict discipline, but when we took rests (always at least two on guard; the remainder with weapons at hand), fierce debates would break out among the soldiers. The corporal, originally from Morocco, who had himself lived in an immigrant camp in Israel in the 1950s, declared that we had to wipe out the camps and give the people a new start in life. Others countered that the camps were none of Israel's business: Why hadn't the Egyptians done anything for nineteen years? Why hadn't the refugees themselves done anything?

"You don't understand," protested the corporal with passion. "This type of environment stifles you. I remember it only too well. For our own good, we have to give them a chance!"

Then it was through the market: loose piles of dates, figs, pomegranates, apples, onions, and potatoes. There were orange and sweetmeat stalls and heaps of loose tobacco. The multitude of bodies pressed against us as we fought our way through. What would happen if someone threw a grenade? No matter; we pressed on. We had to penetrate every corner.

I found night patrols the most frightening. I always felt that someone would jump out of the shadows. We would enter a café, a lighted green cavern, ordering the men up from their cards and dominoes, the coffee growing cold as we lined them up against the wall to check their papers.

I sit with a pile of identity cards, trying to check them against a list of suspects. They all seem to be called Muhammad or Ahmad — quite often, both. I call forward five at random. A bent, white-haired old man corrects my pronunciation of his name and, in the resulting laughter, the tension lowers somewhat.

"If they were all like him, we could patrol Gaza with the youth movements," murmurs one of my companions.

Our actions were necessary — there were terrorist acts almost daily — but I could not help imagining the roles reversed, with Arab soldiers interrupting my quiet evening of cards. Jews, after all, had always been on the other side of that sort of thing. The boot was on the other foot with a vengeance.

As the days passed, our confidence grew and I found that I stopped being afraid. I have always been a timid sort, the man who avoids dark corners and walks away from a fight. If someone fixes me with a hostile stare, I usually drop my gaze. But in Gaza it was different: I was the guy with the gun. I found myself returning hard stares with interest. I investigated every dark corner and I never walked away from anything. Pleased as I was by this conquest of fear, I was nevertheless concerned lest my newly relaxed walk might turn into a swagger.

Although, as I said, we didn't lose any of our soldiers, there were a number of incidents. There was that tense afternoon, with the tires burning in the streets, when a squad of us stood in the center of a stone-throwing mob of youths and children (the little kids heaved rocks the size of fists!) for almost twenty minutes before we received permission to move. When we advanced, the crowd melted away with increasing rapidity, until the best we could do was capture three small boys, who were taken to the local police station for their parents to collect later.

Or there was that Friday night. A soldier chants the kiddush, the wine is drunk and we all burst into song, songs of Sabbath peace. Suddenly, the building trembles, and the roar of the explosion follows a split second later.

"Emergency squad, mobilize!" comes the order, and almost at once the command cars are revving up in the road outside. In half an hour the squad returns: grenade in the town square; no damage except to our Sabbath peace.

Were we too soft? Few of us who went on patrol thought we should be tougher. Calls for the iron fist came from the cooks and mechanics, who left the camp only to go on leave. Our most bloodthirsty soldier was the company barber. It is true that shortly after our tour of duty, ordinary soldiers were not sent to Gaza anymore for a time. Border police and paratroops were called in, and they winkled out the terror gangs once and for all. I doubt whether we could have done it. Gaza has been relatively quiet since then.

Not that our time in Gaza was one of unrelieved gloom: it had its lighter moments. There were two delightful eleven-year-olds who (in defiance of regulations) would come and help with the chores in return for all the food they could eat. In this instance, our commanding officer, a copy-book soldier if ever there was one, was outwitted by our sharp sergeant major, who somehow always managed to conceal the boys.

While the CO was having his breakfast, they would be cleaning the showers and latrines. A sudden change of plan by the CO could result in the boys bolting through the lavatory window. Once, when he made an unexpected visit to the kitchen, the burly cook shoved the unfortunate children into the vegetable chest. Often I was asked to distract the CO's attention during a crucial moment so that the boys could be moved to another part of the camp. I would summon the hapless man to imaginary phone calls, which I then had to explain away; ask him stupid questions, to which I already knew the answers; solicit his opinion on "suspicious objects," which could be seen only from the roof (and which had been there for weeks).

Looking back on it, I suppose the exploitation of the boys to do our dirty work was deplorable. At the time, I saw it in terms of knockabout slapstick, a welcome relief from the unpleasant routine.

My next tour of duty in Gaza was after the Yom Kippur War, in 1974. By then the atmosphere was entirely different. We patrolled in far smaller groups; we were allowed to buy in the shops and drink in the cafés. The children were far better dressed and shouted *Shalom* (peace), rather then *Yahud*. The teen-age girls would flirt, like teen-age girls anywhere, and ask for our help with their Hebrew and English homework. Much of the housing was still deplorable, but here, too, there had been an improvement.

The occupation had been a good one, as occupations go. The local agriculture had boomed, industry had advanced, the standard of living had risen, unemployment had been wiped out by the job opportunities in Israel, education and health services had improved. Being a soldier of occupation was far less unpleasant, but it still wasn't a job that I relished doing.

Well, it probably won't have to be for much longer. In one form or another, Gaza is going to be turned over to its own inhabitants.

*   *   *

Yad Mordechai is named for Mordechai Anielevicz, the leader of the Warsaw Ghetto revolt of 1943, when the Jews of Warsaw, armed with pistols and gasoline bottles, stood out against the German army for eight whole weeks, fighting from roofs, bunkers, and cellars. In the end, the Germans razed the whole ghetto area to the ground. Not one building was left standing; not one Jew was left alive.

The kibbutz has a museum of photographs commemorating the ghetto battle and a large statue of Anielevicz, shirt in tatters, grenade in hand. But it also has a reconstructed battlefield of its own famous stand against the Egyptian army in 1948, with models of soldiers and tanks. At Yad Mordechai, also, the buildings were razed to the ground; but here the similarity with Warsaw ends, for the kibbutzniks returned and rebuilt their village, today a prosperous commune, with a dairy, orchards, beehives, and many field crops. The kibbutz runs a mini-market on the road, and I stopped there for a glass of fresh milk and a bun before continuing on my way.

Walking southeast from Yad Mordechai, I kept to the sandy paths that ran parallel to the road. I recalled that when I first traveled through here in 1954, it was all desert: a rolling, red-brown plain as far as the eye could see. Now the desert had been pushed back with water: acres of citrus, vast green carpets of irrigated crops, plowed fields with water points clearly visible.

I was skirting along the western edge of the Lachish development scheme, one of the most significant projects of the period of mass immigration. In tracing its development, we can learn more about the problems and achievements of the 1950s.

The Lachish scheme was planned and executed by Aryeh Eliav, today best known as a left-wing exponent of negotiations with the PLO, but for many years one of Israel's leading experts in absorption and settlement. Lova (as everyone calls him) is at first glance an unimpressive figure. Small and quiet, his graying blond hair swept back from a high, intellectual forehead, his looks belie his record of action and accomplishment. He joined the Haganah at the age of fifteen, eventually reaching the rank of colonel in the navy, but most of his actions were undercover ones. He was, for instance, very involved in the organization of Aliya Bet, smuggling Jews out of Europe during the postwar period. During the Sinai Campaign in 1956, he donned the uniform of a French army officer and rescued the members of the Jewish community of Port Said, bringing them to Israel. At the height of the Kurdish revolt in Iraq, he visited the Kurdish leader Mustafa Barzani. He served in Israel's Moscow embassy, was a deputy cabinet minister, and played a key role in unifying Israel's Labor Party, before going into the political wilderness to advocate strongly the dovish policies he now espouses. He has also written a number of books on modern Israeli history and current affairs.

In the mid-1950s, when water, pumped from the Yarkon River north of Tel Aviv, became available for agriculture in the south, he was put in charge of the Lachish scheme. He assembled a team of regional planners, agronomists, architects, and engineers, and he insisted that they live on the spot so that, unlike the situation in other development areas, the managerial class would not be commuters from the large towns. Eliav also understood the importance of the human factor. Determined to try to gain some understanding of these new immigrants — so different from the prewar variety who had built the state — he went to live at Moshav Nevatim, to the east of Beersheba, populated by Jews from Cochin in southern India. By choosing to live at Nevatim, he was deliberately mixing with immigrants who hitherto had been the most isolated from the Israeli experience.

He emerged with one firm conclusion: he would not artificially mix immigrants from different backgrounds. Making nieghbors of Moroccans, Indians, and Rumanians was not the best solution to their eventual integration. It had to be achieved more gradually. The Lachish region was developed with Yemenite, Kurdish, and Moroccan moshavim. This system enabled the large extended families to remain together in the same village. Mixing occurred naturally in the various rural centers and the main town of Kiryat Gat.

Although in Lachish the human needs of the immigrants were considered more than before, Eliav has admitted that there was still not enough understanding of their cultural patterns. The extended family may have been in the same village, but it was divided up into several farms. In a book written recently, Eliav describes this as a mistake. What happened was that the patriarch lost his status because his sons were better able to adapt to new farming techniques and the Israeli way of life generally. The breakdown of the patriarchal system was inevitable, but an attempt was deliberately made to accelerate it. There was the feeling that the Israeli veterans were doing the immigrants a favor by modernizing them. There was scant respect for the rich traditions of the communities. Because tractors and fertilizers were superior to primitive agriculture, the young immigrants grew up feeling that their entire way of life was inferior to the Israeli one. They were expected to feel ashamed of their "Levantinism." Indeed, "Levantine" is still one of the most pejorative words in Israel today.

This was the big human mistake of the period of mass immigration. In purely practical terms, it deprived Israel of thousands of Arabic-speakers, a vital asset in what we hope will be the new era of peace with Egypt. Even during the past decade of occupation of the West Bank and Gaza, the lack of Arabic-speakers has been sorely felt.

Not long ago, there was an extremely sensitive television documentary on Lachish. In it, some of the young immigrants (older now) complained about the policy of breaking up the extended family. One man was sure that it was a main cause of juvenile delinquency to this day, because of the breakdown of authority and the loss of values.

Another interviewee described his experiences in Africa, where he had been sent as an agricultural instructor. He explained that his own experiences in Lachish had taught him to respect the habits and customs of the Africans with whom he worked.

"As a result," he said, "I not only got on very well with the Africans, but I learned from them as well. It was a two-way traffic, and they were far more prepared to accept my suggestions because of the relationship of mutual respect that we had achieved."

With the best will in the world, he concluded, the Israeli veterans of the 1950s had not realized what they were doing. Had they possessed greater humility, the absorption of the oriental Jews into Israeli society would have been far more successful

Sad to say, when I discussed the program with an otherwise intelligent Israeli of European origin, I found that she had entirely missed the point. She agreed that the film had been interesting, and concluded, "Yes, they were so primitive, weren't they? We had to show them what modern life was all about."

I am glad to say that this sort of pig-headedness is not universal. Both on television and in the schools a real attempt is now being made to right the wrong and to give the culture of oriental Jewry the status it deserves.

* * *

But to return to Lachish. Whatever the human shortcomings, the scheme was a resounding success on the technical level. The presence of the design team on the spot from the outset guaranteed that the plans would be relevant to the topography and also ensured a proportion of veteran Israelis in the local population from the earliest days. This is important, not because of the country of origin, but because of the basic attitude of the settler to his region. An immigrant dumped in the middle of nowhere within hours of his arrival in Israel will not be, in the first instance, as positive toward his town as the Israeli citizen who came there voluntarily.

Lachish was not the first attempt at regional development in this country. As long ago as the 1920s, when the Emek was settled, there was an effort to coordinate services around the town of Afula, but it was largely unsuccessful. In Lachish, a coordinated development plan was launched, envisaging the integration of new villages with veteran kibbutzim, the grouping of moshavim around rural service centers, with the region as a whole receiving services and administration from the central town of Kiryat Gat (named after the Philistine town Gath). The farms would produce raw materials for the town's industries.

Not all the rural service centers have been successful, and Ashkelon is still the seat of the subdistrict administration, but the whole conception was realized. I have already described the physical change in the landscape. As for Kiryat Gat, it quickly passed its planned size and there has been full employment.

Before leaving Lachish, I would like to tell the story of the cotton gins. In 1955, two gins were on their way to Israel by boat. One was scheduled for Bet Shean in the Jordan Valley, where high-grade cotton had been grown; the second was supposed to be set up in Beersheba. Although Kiryat Gat was still really at the drawing-board stage, Eliav managed to bluff the ministers of commerce and agriculture into sending the Beersheba cotton gin to his town. Concrete foundations were poured just in time to receive the machinery. There was no building, it is true, but electricity and water supplies were somehow improvised. The region's first cotton crop was processed on time.

Today the area does not produce enough cotton for the gin, nor does it grow enough sugar for the sugar refinery, but Lachish is still the outstanding example of regional development in Israel.

The flatness of the land was deceptive. The hills rolled gently, and in some places deep wadis had been cut by the rain. I came suddenly on the town of Sderot, with its white houses and gray apartment blocks, which appeared with startling abruptness behind a wheat field. Instead of entering the town, I continued at a smart pace along the road. The weather was distinctly colder than it had been before the rains, although I was moving farther south all the time. In central and northern Israel, winter had obviously arrived. I hoped that in the Negev, autumn would linger a few more weeks. A slight pain developed in my right calf, which I tried to walk off. As I went on, it became worse. Why the right calf? Why now? I guess its turn had come round. My calves had been good up to now.

In midafternoon, the stream of black Mercedeses began. They were transporting Gaza Arabs back home after their day's work. I decided that it would not be a good idea to walk through this area in the dark, and started to consider where to spend the night. A look at the map made Netivot seem a reasonable target. As far as I could see, it appeared to be a small town. I had been observing a water tower for some time, and I concluded that it belonged to Netivot. I had lost my invaluable *Israel Tour Guide* in Ashkelon, so I consulted another well-known guidebook instead, to discover that Netivot was "a moshav in the Negev on the Gaza-Beersheba highway." This was awkward. I could find somewhere to sleep in the smallest town; but in a moshav where I knew no one, I wasn't sure.

I quickened my pace, despite the increasingly painful right calf. Like Sderot before it, Netivot took me by surprise, its tall apartment blocks emerging from behind a copse of eucalyptus. The guidebook should have known better: it certainly was not a moshav.*

---

* Even the latest edition of this well-known and highly regarded guide describes Netivot as "a moshav," although it has been a development town since 1955!

22

Because I knew no one at all in Netivot, I decided that my best bet was to find the local youth center. I was soon directed to the Center of Youth, Culture, and Sport, which turned out to be a handsome new building, with a large hall, library, meeting rooms, and offices. What was most impressive about it was that it was thronged with people.

I got talking to a stocky young man with a handsome, good-natured face, his hair receding rather fast for his twenty-five years. He was dressed snappily in green: olive-green trousers, green shirt, and a part-suede cardigan of the same color. Like every other male in sight, he wore a traditional skullcap. His name, I learned, was Rafi Abukassiss and he worked as a youth leader in the center, but the main job was teaching art in high school. He told me that he wanted to be an artist and was living (as he put it) "with one foot outside Netivot."

He had started drawing when he was fourteen, but his traditionalist Moroccan parents had torn up the pictures because they were images, prohibited by the Jewish religion. He had studied in technical high school to be an electrician; but, after completing his army service, he had returned to art and had graduated from the Art Teachers' Training College in Beersheba. He had an army friend who lived in Netanya and he hoped to open a gallery there. He knew that he couldn't make a living as an artist right away, but once he learned the market, he said, he would produce directly for it. There was no point in swimming against the stream, he remarked cynically.

How did his parents feel about his art now? He smiled. "They have a half-nude statuette of mine in their living room." If he made money, they would be delighted. He did not regard this as progress, though. On the contrary, he felt that his parents had lost their religious convictions, only to replace them with shallow materialism.

"Another sofa, a new washing machine, a color television set — is that what it's all about?" he demanded.

His feelings about the town were clearly ambivalent. On the one hand, he wanted to leave Netivot because he found it suffocating; many of his best friends had already gone. At the same time, he was part of a group of young citizens who wanted to reform the town. In the recent elections they had won three council seats — not enough to gain control, but a notable first step. He told me he was sure the youngsters would change the face of Netivot, but he added sadly that he didn't expect to be around to see it.

"The development towns have failed," he said. "We're raising a generation of children as deprived as their parents were. We need a revolution!"

"What sort of revolution?"

"I don't know," he confessed. "Clever people should sit down and work it out. A lot of money is being spent on education and youth activities, but we're not getting results."

What about him and his friends? That was because they had grown up outside the town. All of them had been to boarding schools of one sort or another, followed by the army. He invited me to come upstairs to the committee room where they were having a seminar for youth leaders. Rafi and his colleagues were very disappointed by the turnout. I thought it wasn't bad: seven girls and three young men to hear a talk by the southern region youth supervisor, a skinny ex-policeman, his black mustache prominent on his pale face.

We listened to a lengthy dissertation on the theory of education, tracing the classroom structure from a frontal approach, with the teacher lecturing, to one that allowed more give-and-take between teachers and pupils.

When it was time for questions, two of the girls brought up a practical problem. They had in their group a powerful, heavily built youngster who was terrorizing the other children. They had tried winning him over by giving him responsibility, but this had only made him worse. He was now trying to decide the program of each meeting, testing his authority against theirs. They admitted that they were almost totally unable to control him.

The supervisor looked around interrogatively to see if anyone else had any suggestions. A fellow youth leader suggested a system of rewards and punishments. For example, why not organize a group outing to Tel Aviv and exclude the boy if he did not improve his behavior? Another related how he had managed to start a photography group. This had proved very popular, so he made participation conditional on good behavior.

We now all turned expectantly to the lecturer, who told us a long, rambling story about a group of children who were compulsive smokers. He had tried to make them stop smoking, at least for a few hours. The scheme was to take them to the cinema at his expense, on condition that they didn't smoke during the performance. Prior to the show, he told them half a dozen times that they would not be able to hold out. Graphically, he pictured himself leading them into the cinema three times, only to lead them out again with the remark that he knew he wouldn't be able to count on them. Finally, they had gone to the film and the kids had not smoked, he concluded in triumph. I hoped that the other listeners found something relevant in his tale; I'm afraid that I did not.

"I'm a champion wrestler for my weight," he confided to me afterward (he must have been in the 100-pounds-and-under). "That's the reason for my great success. The kids know who I am and they respect me."

Half a dozen teen-agers came over to Rafi and started kidding around. Some of them towered above him, but he gave as good as he got, punching them playfully in the stomach or slapping their backs. The relationship seemed very friendly. Some of them had brought posters to decorate their neighborhood club, so Rafi took them off to do the work.

A young soldier-volunteer (I'll call her Vered) invited me back to her apartment for supper. Diminutive, with outsize glasses covering much of her face, she told me that she had volunteered to work with delinquent youth. A religious girl, she had asked a dozen rabbis whether she should serve in the army.* It was clear that Vered had simply continued asking until she found two rabbis who agreed with her. She had been determined to serve. Four other girl soldiers were doing youth work in the town, sharing the apartment with her, but she was the only one working with delinquents. She said she often put in a twelve- or thirteen-hour day, and from what I saw, she was not exaggerating. When she first started, she had quite literally gone out into the streets to talk to the children; now they tended to seek her out with their problems.

"I don't want you to get the wrong idea," she said anxiously. "Netivot is a law-abiding community — not like Ashkelon, for example." (I winced.) "Most of the kids are

* Religious girls are able to avoid army service by a simple declaration that they are religious or that they come from traditional families. This has caused much bitterness, the more so as many nonreligious girls make this declaration only to evade national service.

okay; only about thirty have contact with me." One of the main problems, she explained, was army service. Among the delinquent children, the attitude was strongly against going in the army. Those who served were looked on as suckers. It was a two-way struggle: first she had to persuade the kids to join up; then she had to persuade the army to take them.

We were walking through town to her apartment as she talked. A good-looking teen-ager walked by and then stopped to greet Vered. He had a pleasant smile and black, wavy hair.

"When I persuaded the army to call him up, he threatened to throw acid in my face," she told me when he had gone. "You see, he has a criminal record. Now he says he wants to join the paratroops. Of course he won't get in there, but funnily enough, he could do quite well if he did. He's strong and athletic."

Netivot was an entirely North African town, explained Vered. The whole population came from Morocco and Tunisia. It was a warm, open community and she loved it. The people were friendly, hospitable, and generous. The town's main problem, in her view, was the fundamentalist religion of the inhabitants.

"I suppose it surprises you to hear me say that when I myself am religious." She smiled. "They're not religious as I understand religion; they're superstitious. We need a revolution in Netivot!" (Again that declaration.)

"What sort of revolution?"

"Mental, physical, psychological, religious!" The skullcap, she said, had become an empty symbol. All the males in the town wore skullcaps to keep in with the authorities. The local council was dominated by the National Religious Party, but many of the best young people had become fiercely antireligious. She feared there would have to be a revolution against religion before a genuine religious life could be established.

At present, religion meant, on the one hand, the religious dominance of the party; on the other, a superstitious belief in Rabbi Abuhatzira, the local miracle-worker. To this elderly sage (a cousin of the present Israeli minister for religious affairs) were attributed divine powers of healing the sick and the lame. All the Moroccans, even those who no longer followed religious practices, believed in him. It was irrational, she declared.

Although Netivot had a population of some 8000, a large proportion were children. The families were very large; eight or nine children was not unusual.

"You ought to see them." She laughed. "The father has a long, gray beard and there's a three-month-old baby in the cot."

There was a knock on the door, and Yehiel came in with his girl friend, Fanny. He was the first male I had seen in Netivot without a skullcap. With long hair and a sallow but strong-featured face, Yehiel clearly enjoyed his role as a rebel. He was planning to start a coffee house, independently of the council, so that it could be open on the Sabbath. Vered was (unofficially, of course) encouraging him. She thought it might help keep youngsters in town, even if it did involve desecration of the Sabbath.

Yehiel told me that he wanted to stay in Netivot. He liked the small-town intimacy and was not attracted to a larger center, such as Beersheba. Most of his friends had left town, but he was going to stay and fight the establishment. He was one of the Likud activists, who had put three men onto the council in the recent election.

"I'm not really a Likud man," he said with a laugh. "In the national elections, I voted Sheli."*

The Likud list was purely a local matter, he explained. It didn't necessarily mean that he and his friends supported the Likud; the aim was to replace the dominance of the

---

* The Likud is the right-wing alliance that leads the present Israeli government coalition. Sheli is a small left-wing party.

National Religious Party with a young, efficient team. Organized religion was enemy number one. He narrated with pleasure how he had got together a group of children to light a fire outside the local yeshiva one Friday night.

"That is just a stupid provocation!" exploded Vered.

"I don't care," retorted Yehiel. "We need a revolution here." (The third time I had heard that phrase.) "I've nothing against religion, but I'm against religious coercion."

Yehiel told me that he worked in an army garage not far from Netivot. He had served his time in the army and was resentful of young men in the town who had not. He said that they'd got a three-year lead on those who had served. If it were up to him, he wouldn't even grant driving licenses to those who hadn't done their army service. As it was, the local council was prepared to give them permits for anything they wanted.

"Every little shit gets hold of a couple of Gaza Arab employees," he complained, "and then he's a contractor."

"That's one of the problems of Netivot," put in Vered. "Gaza!"

"It isn't Gaza that's the problem," countered Yehiel.

Vered claimed that the delinquent children with whom she was working received their drugs from Gaza. Yehiel discounted this. He said that there were plenty of other places to buy drugs. If Gaza was closed to them, they would still get hashish. He thought the social mixing between Arab and Jewish towns was positive. Vered demurred strongly. Entirely negative, she maintained.

Throughout these exchanges, Fanny had sat silent. A pretty girl, dressed in trousers (daring for Netivot), she seemed completely apathetic about everything. Maybe she would go in the army, or she might study; she was not sure. Netivot was all right — not bad; not particularly good. She might stay in Netivot, or she might go and live somewhere else. She was not religious anymore, but she was not against religion. It was okay, she supposed. She had no convictions about anything, and it was baffling to find her associated with Yehiel and his daring coffee-house scheme.

It was after eleven o'clock when a young boy, who couldn't have been more than eleven years old, burst in and announced, "There's a policeman looking for Vered." He turned to her. "About H——, eh?"

Shortly afterward, the policeman, Ammar, and his assistant came in. Vered made them coffee and told them about the boy.

"He knew that you were here about H——."

"You want to keep a secret in a town this size?" The policeman shrugged. He wore sunglasses, even indoors, and his hair was carefully combed in a quiff that came down over his forehead. All through the conversation, he sat with his pistol laid on the chair under his thigh.

Vered explained her case. H—— was one of the boys whom she had persuaded to sign on for the army. She had talked the army into accepting him, but not without difficulty. Now, three months before his call-up, he had been arrested on suspicion of stealing gold from his own father. Ammar was the policeman investigating the case. She told the policeman that she agreed the boy ought to be punished, even imprisoned; but she pleaded for a short sentence that would bring him out in time for the army.

Ammar pointed out that it didn't depend on him. The magistrate might release him altogether or give him a long sentence. Vered said come, come, they all knew how these things worked and that Ammar's report would influence the magistrate. She said that H—— was basically a good boy, but he hated his father. The theft, if indeed he was guilty, had been an act of revenge. Both policemen rejected this suggestion. There was no doubt in their minds as to his guilt. The gold had been taken from its secret hiding-place under a tile in the floor, without anything else in the apartment having been touched. That pointed to the boy. Furthermore, if he had stolen the gold only as an act against his father, why had he failed to identify the receiver in Gaza? The policemen were understandably fed up; the boy had led them a dance all over Gaza.

"If he goes to prison for a long term, he'll be a crook all his life," argued Vered. "The army will make a new man out of him."

Not necessarily, said Ammar. Quite often the reverse happened: the army provided good openings for the would-be criminal. Once a soldier had worked his way into a responsible position, he could easily steal a military vehicle, for example. This had happened before. Ammar went on to point out that there was a real chance that H—— might not be sentenced. Then what? Vered suggested that he might be persuaded to go and live with his brother in Rehovot. Ammar and Yehiel both knew the brother, and a discussion ensued, in which all three of them agreed that the brother was a good guy and an excellent influence on H——. Ammar also noted that a change of location did quite often have a positive effect.

In the discussion that followed, Vered was highly critical of the army review boards and the way they operated. Too many kids slipped through the net, she believed. The candidate just had to pretend to be an idiot, and he got away with it.

"I've seen it," she said. "The doctor asks, 'Where is Metulla?' and the boy replies, 'In the Negev.' 'Where is Netivot?' 'In Metulla.' 'How much are eight and eight?' 'Fourteen!' You can see the kid is shamming." She pointed out that quite a number of the boys who won exemption in this way changed their minds later on. Some of them came to her and pleaded to be allowed to serve; but once they had been rejected, it wasn't easy.

It was midnight before the guests left. Meanwhile, one of Vered's flat-mates had come in, an attractive girl whom I'll call Nira. She had just started working as a youth leader in Netivot. Like Vered, she was a soldier-volunteer, but her work was with ordinary children in the youth center. Although she also came from a development town, Kiryat Malachi, southeast of Ashdod, she was astounded by Netivot, with its single-sex schools and community consciousness. Kiryat Malachi was also mainly North African, but it had Russians, Poles, Rumanians, Persians, Indians, and a few sabras. She claimed that she had grown up quite unconscious of her Moroccan background. In Netivot, on the other hand, the Moroccans hated the Tunisians, the Tunisians despised the Moroccans, and both communities detested the yeshiva, which was mostly East European. There was nothing like that in Kiryat Malachi, she assured me.

*   *   *

The following morning I went to the youth center with the girls and was introduced to Meir Cohen, the small, slim Iranian-born Jerusalemite who ran it. He was busy on the phone, calming down a local resident who was complaining about the noise made by one of the neighborhood clubs. Though he was far too busy for a real talk, we exchanged a few words.

"Come back here after your walk, Danny," was his parting shot. "Come and work here as a volunteer; it's grade-A Zionism."

I also met Vered's boss, Yossi, a burly, bearded, affable man of Algerian origin. His relaxed manner contrasted with Vered's rather intense style. I experienced a feeling of relief when I saw him talking things over with the girl. Vered is intelligent and sincere, but she was at the limit of her emotional and physical strength.

They discussed one of their problem families, where all

three daughters worked as prostitutes in Gaza (they had got out of the army on *religious* grounds). The girls were up in arms against Vered for sending their younger brother to a boarding school. The fourteen-year-old boy had, in fact, been working as their procurer, but they complained that Vered had broken their mother's heart by sending him away. Yossi said that he would deal with the matter. If necessary, he would obtain a court order to prevent the sisters from interfering with the boy.

Before leaving Netivot, I decided to visit the famous Rabbi Abuhatzira, who received suppliants every morning. My calf was still aching as I walked through Netivot, seeing it by daylight for the first time. It was a strange mixture. Some parts were very shabby; but in other areas the apartment blocks were nicely maintained, trees lined the streets, iron railings were freshly painted. Washing and bedding, of course, hung out of the windows, even those of the occasional smart villa. Here and there I discovered enchanting corners, with green lawns and bougainvillaea.

Rabbi Abuhatzira occupied two apartments in an ordinary block. Apart from a slightly superior front door, there was nothing special about his home, except for the visiting times posted outside and the crowd of people waiting to see him. About a dozen people were there, mostly Moroccans from Netivot and the surrounding towns; but there were also two elderly Americans, who had driven down specially from Jerusalem, and a London-born religious kibbutznik.

A middle-aged man from Netivot — unshaven, with working boots and knitted cap — told me that he came regularly to see the rabbi. He was holding a bottle, which he would fill with water for the rabbi to bless. At this point I noticed that everyone had bottles and I cursed myself for leaving my water bottle back at the youth center. The man told me that one drank the blessed water, diluting it down so as to keep it going longer, and it cured your illness or trouble. He told me of a cripple who had arrived on crutches, only to throw them away after receiving the rabbi's blessing; of a woman, barren for eleven years, who had borne four children after his intervention; and of many others who had been helped. The rabbi would not see the waiting women, I was told. They would merely have their water blessed.

The door of the apartment opened and a plump young woman emerged with a shopping bag. This was the younger of the rabbi's two wives, it was said — whether truly or not, I don't know. Half an hour after the advertised time, the first bunch of suppliants was allowed in. I got in with the third group, which included the two Americans and the London-born kibbutznik.

"Why did you come?" I asked the latter in English.

"We have an incurable illness in the family," he said gravely. He was serious, wearing glasses, with a smart black skullcap.

"Do you really believe that this can help?" I pointed to his bottles of water. He shrugged.

"It doesn't do any harm to visit a *tzaddik*" (righteous man).

We waited in the modest apartment for our turn. The furniture was plain, the wallpaper old and shabby. The two Americans entered the rabbi's inner sanctum and I heard an aide shout, "A hundred dollars!"

This apparently bought them refreshments and extra time, because another aide went in with a plate of cakes, and they stayed inside for half an hour. Finally, it was my turn.

A gaunt old man sat on a mattress, reading psalms. He was dressed in a black robe, with a dark brown cloth wrapped turbanlike around his head. His bare feet rested on the floor beside a pair of long, black, pointed slippers. He had a long white beard, and his glasses were three quarters of the way down his nose. I had the impression that he couldn't see well and that he was almost deaf. The room, like the rest of the apartment, was furnished simply. The only sign of opulence was a glass cupboard crammed with silver candlesticks of various designs. On the table was a soup plate overflowing with Israeli and foreign banknotes, to which I added twenty pounds (one dollar).

As I waited, the aide, stern of expression, tall, black-suited, black-bearded, brought in some bottles of water from the women for the rabbi's blessing. He shouted into the rabbi's ear the names of the suppliants and the blessing requested — usually, "complete recovery." The sage mumbled inaudibly into his psalms. The aide then turned to me, and I told him that I wanted the old man's blessing for my project. I didn't specify and he didn't ask.

"Kiss the rabbi's hand," he ordered.

"What, now?" I asked. The old boy was immersed in his psalms, both hands gripping the book firmly.

"Now."

I grabbed a hand and kissed it. It was dry and rather cold. I then supplied my name and the names of my parents, which information was relayed into the rabbi's ear. The old man mumbled again, quite loudly this time.

"Kiss his hand again." I did as I was bade.

Two incidents must be recorded, the significance of which I will leave for the reader to judge. The first was that just after I left Netivot, I saw an owl, not the least blinded, as owls usually are when they venture out in the daytime, but flying happily from tree to tree in the sunlight. The second was that immediately afterward, the pain in my calf ceased, never to return.

Whistling happily, I swung along the road toward Beersheba.

Part III
The Negev

Mediterranean Sea

Beersheba Tel Sheva Tel Arad Arad DEAD SEA

Abu Rubiya Neve Zohar
Zohar Fortress

Tzin plant Neot Hakikar
Scorpions Pass

Sde Boker Ir Ovot

Avdat Tzin Valley

Mitzpe Ramon

Ramon Crater

Paran Valley

Walk Ends Arava Valley

SINAI

NEGEV

- - - - - - - WALK

· · · · · · · · BUS

▦▦▦▦▦▦▦▦ INTERNATIONAL BORDER

JORDAN

Elat

(Journey Ends) Taba

Gulf of Elat

23

I HAD BEEN walking through citrus country ever since Atlit, and the land had provided me with sustenance and refreshment all the way. In obedience to the Biblical injunction,* I had not loaded fruit into my rucksack, taking only what I could eat on the spot.

The last orchard that I saw was near the town of Ofakim. It contained only grapefruit, which I had resolved not to eat, but this last time I broke my rule and enjoyed a juicy specimen.

My visit to Rabbi Abuhatzira had made me late in starting, so I walked the last five miles into Beersheba in the dark. But not before I had caught sight of the real Negev, the endless red-brown plain with the pink hills beyond, fading into mauve and gray as the sun set. It was the desert I knew and loved: the sun, the space, the sharp, dry air. Once the desert started south of Rehovot, but the water pipeline — first from the Yarkon River and then from Lake Kinneret — has pushed it back to the very gates of the "capital of the Negev."

* "When thou comest into thy neighbor's vineyard, then thou mayest eat grapes thy fill at thine own pleasure; but thou shalt not put any in thy vessel." Deuteronomy 23:24. Rabbi Louis Rabinovich of Jerusalem, who was kind enough to furnish me with the reference, informed me that in the Talmud this was interpreted as applying only to people working in the vineyard. As a result of my sketchy knowledge of Jewish tradition, though, I filled my stomach with a clear conscience.

Not that cultivation ends here; but from now on it will be the turn of industry to dominate. The farms will appear as occasional patches of green in the dusty brown wasteland. I could have ended my walk here in line with one Biblical description of the extent of the Land of Israel, and I did feel a certain sense of accomplishment as I entered town; but I would not have missed the next stage of the trip for anything.

I came into the bright lights of the "old city" of Beer-sheba, which, despite the efforts of the planners, remains the real center of town. The strange, rectangular formation of its streets was the work of a German engineer who served with the Turkish army in the years before the First World War. For many years a Bedouin town of only a few thousand, it was deserted when Israeli troops entered in October 1948.

It is indicative of the change in the Israeli way of life that I had not yet on this walk enjoyed a *fellafel,* fried balls of ground chickpeas placed inside a hollow pitta together with a variety of salad and pickles and covered with tehina. When I spent a year in Israel in 1954, we had almost lived on fellafel, and even in the sixties it was the standard street snack, the equivalent of the American hot dog. Today it is losing the battle against pizza, hamburgers, and a host of Western-style sandwiches.*

However, in this as in many other things, Beersheba has a pleasing archaic quality. On the corner, as you enter town from the northwest, is the second-best fellafel stand in the country. (The best is farther down the main street, but it's open only from nine to eleven in the morning.) I enjoyed the remembered hot spiciness and wondered what I had ever seen in pizza.

Although it is far more civilized than it used to be, Beersheba still possesses something of its old frontier atmo-

---

* Since the above was written, the economic situation has worsened, and consequently fellafel is making something of a comeback.

sphere. Big semitrailer trucks park in the side streets; open
jeeps drive through the center; sunburned men with scuffed
boots and dust in their hair drink beer in the cafés, blinking
in the neon glare; young soldiers sip Coke, hitchhike, and
phone from the public booths. Beersheba no longer has an
open-air cinema or a night club called The Last Chance; it
now has a university and a music conservatory. Cassit, the
modest snack bar with its glass-fronted refrigerator display-
ing salads, where old Beersheba hands drank their morning
coffee and you could get a plate of chicken soup with *kre-
plach* (dough-wrapped meat patties) for five pounds, has
turned into a smart, air-conditioned restaurant. The railway station is still rather like something out of the Wild
West; but the bus terminal, where the Bedouin once squat-
ted in the dust, with their goats and chickens, has been
moved to modern premises, with paved sidewalks and
proper bus bays. Yet it is still Beersheba, capital of the
Negev: brash, bustling, bursting with energy. You don't see
too many ties or suits there, and most of the year, short
trousers are still acceptable wear.

I stayed the night with Joe and Eunice, friends from my
kibbutz days. Since leaving Amiad, Joe has worked in a variety of jobs, including warehouseman in Sdom on the
Dead Sea and purchasing agent for the town's only luxury
hotel. Today he is an insurance agent, and, since he happens to be my agent, I tackled him about compensation for
my theft in Ashkelon. No chance: Ashkelon beach is not the
"closed place" specified in my policy.

Eunice, a solid, sensible Scotswoman, had recently resigned from her job in the public relations department of
the university. I had founded the department a decade earlier, so I was interested in her account of the intrigues and
disputes there. Sadly, I concluded that things had not
changed very much.

It has been suggested that Israel has too many univer-
sities, and I think that seven may be a bit excessive for a

country our size facing the sort of economic problems that it does face. But were I dictator of Israel, the Ben-Gurion University of the Negev is the last one that I would close down. Founded in 1965 as a higher education institute, it has expanded into a full-scale university, serving the people of the Negev region as well as students attracted from farther north. The largely immigrant, mostly oriental population of Beersheba, Dimonah, Netivot, and other Negev towns now have a far better chance of getting higher education. Although the student body in Beersheba is still only one-quarter oriental, this is far more than in other colleges. Special training courses for soldiers from oriental families who did not manage to get a school-leaving certificate have been inaugurated with some success. The fact that students come from the north is also positive, in that many elect to remain in the Negev after their graduation. Moreover, the existence of the students and faculty members has transformed the cultural atmosphere of Beersheba. Schools are of a higher standard, visits by theater groups are more frequent than before, and the town supports its own orchestra. In Hatzor we saw the vicious circle of fewer people meaning fewer facilities, leading to a still smaller population; in Beersheba we can see the reverse process: a multiplier effect, where more jobs attract more people, who demand more facilities, leading to a growth in population.

I have pleasant memories of my work at the public relations department of the university. I got on well with the brash young students, who often conned me into providing funds for their activities from my departmental budget on the grounds that it was "good for publicity." In the case of a dance or party, this claim was largely spurious, but I was as liberal as I was allowed to be. I reckoned that the students, many of them married, all of them in the army reserve, most of them working their way through college, deserved any help that I could give them. Unfortunately, along with the pleasant memories are many unpleasant ones.

My relationship with the staff and administration was uneven. Some of the lecturers had come to Beersheba with a genuine desire to do something creative — but for all too many it was merely a step on the academic ladder. Professor X would be insulted because he did not appear on the platform at the graduation ceremony. On another occasion, when the professor was on the platform, he would demand to know why he was sitting three places away from the main speaker, when Dr. Y, a less senior member of the faculty, was sitting next to the main speaker. How, moreover, could I possibly presume to exclude Professor Z, who had contributed so much to the development of the university? And why did I allow those two incompetent clowns, Professor A and Dr. B, to play such a prominent role in the ceremony? The more degrees a professor had, the pettier he seemed to be.

It wasn't only the professors; I had no less trouble from the chairman of the board, a greatly respected veteran of Beersheba. On one occasion I managed to persuade the Israeli television to produce a feature on the university. It was the first time the institution had appeared on the small screen, and it necessitated a good deal of persuasion and diplomacy. Quite rightly, the producer of the program wanted to concentrate on the variegated student body; but after some special pleading, I managed to get the rector and the head of administration onto the show. I couldn't swing the participation of the chairman as well. On the day after the screening, I was invited to the chairman's office. He wished to tell me that the show had been a dismal failure, not (God forbid) because he wasn't in it, but because of the appalling quality. Strangely, the head of administration thought it had been an excellent program.

On another occasion, the editor of a now-defunct newspaper came down to Beersheba to get us to pay for an article in an advertising supplement. The meeting took place in the chairman's office. I was opposed to the idea. I explained (as tactfully as I could) that no one read those supplements anyway; that this particular newspaper had the lowest circulation of any in the country; that the requested fee was almost 20 percent of my entire departmental budget.

The editor was a shrewd man. He didn't say a word about the supplement. He began to talk to the chairman in a reminiscent tone about his contribution to development of Beersheba and the Negev. The old boy's contribution had indeed been considerable, but to hear the editor speak, Herzl, Weizmann, and Ben-Gurion would be mere footnotes when the real history of Israel came to be written, as compared with the chairman.

"Let's face it," he proclaimed, "only history will be able to judge you adequately. We, your contemporaries, are not equal to the task!"

I was deeply embarrassed and sure that he had oversold his pitch; but, sneaking a sidelong glance at the chairman, I saw that the old boy was positively basking in it. His craggy pioneer's face, with its halo of white hair, was lit up in sublime enjoyment. The editor piled hyperbole on hyperbole. I was too uncomfortable to listen, though I do have a vague memory of his linking the chairman's name with that of Moses. Of course we had to buy his article, but it was never published. The paper folded the following month.

As long as he lived, the old chairman dominated that university. His rival, the head of administration, a young, dynamic, ex-army colonel, was completely outwitted by him. He would try to force through his various schemes and to block the chairman's. Often he thought that he had succeeded — but the old man always managed to come back one more time, reconvening some committee, canvassing quietly but determinedly, and even going over the younger man's head to a high contact in the government or civil service. The head of administration would shout and bluster and say that he wasn't going to let the old dodderer put one over him, but the old dodderer invariably did.

I think that this story illustrates graphically the lasting dominance of the veteran generation in Israeli society. In national politics, examples abound. Ben-Gurion, when he was prime minister, ruled his younger colleagues with an iron hand. Golda Meir became prime minister at the age of seventy-one, despite the claims of two ambitious younger men, the late Yigal Allon and Moshe Dayan, generals who had played prominent parts in winning Israel's wars. Israel's present leader, Menahem Begin, is dominant in his cabinet (as President Sadat discovered to his disgust). The members of the second and third aliyot had iron in their souls that their successors cannot match.

To get back to Eunice. She told me that she was running an institute for the teaching of English in Beersheba and Ashkelon, in partnership with an American immigrant. It was hard work, involving a lot of traveling, but she was enjoying herself enormously because she was her own boss. I reflected that it was unusual for an English teacher to set up a private business rather than simply to get a job, and suggested that it was symptomatic of a malaise in Israeli society. Many people I knew had decided to work for themselves, out of a disenchantment with their boss. Eunice said that this was certainly true; even her partner had become disgusted after three years of working for the Ministry of Education. My friend Ben, from Raanana, had set up his own business, after his dissatisfaction with a series of jobs. My moshav friends, Tooli in Almagor, Vic in Ilaniya, had also fled from bosses. Joe returned, and I recalled that he too had held a series of good jobs until he had determined to work for himself.

Discussing the matter, we agreed that there is an individualistic streak in the Jewish character, but that the root of the problem lies in Israeli management. Americans are famous for their rugged individualism; but, as I reminded Joe, he and I had worked for an American company, where employees had been proud of their record of decades of employment.

With a few rare exceptions, the Israeli boss has not learned how to secure the loyalty of his employees. He does not know how to express appreciation of a job well done. He never encourages talented employees for fear of undermining his own position. Where there is office intrigue, he all too often fosters it, on the principle of "divide and rule," rather than stamping on it.

24

WALKING THROUGH Beersheba the next morning, I was (as I had been many times in the past) struck by its untidy sprawl. I was out of the old center, walking east through the new neighborhoods. In the study *New Towns in Israel,* written in 1966, Erika Spiegel observed:

> Beersheba is considered today, even by Israeli architects, the classical example of a planning blunder, the fundamental and well-nigh irrevocable mistakes of which leave the town's administration with almost insoluble problems.

She goes on to point out that the concept of designing Beersheba like "an English garden-city" was completely inappropriate to desert conditions. Since she wrote her book, Beersheba's parks have been extended, numerous trees, shrubs, and lawns have been planted; but her basic point remains: in the desert, greenery is a luxury. Shade is best provided by walls and buildings.

The town is too exposed and too spread out. The Histadrut's Egged bus cooperative has successfully maintained its monopoly all over Israel, but in Beersheba it wanted no part of providing the service. The municipality had to set up its own bus company, at considerable expense.

Beersheba is a monument to the great improvisation

phase of Israeli development. The town could not have been built any other way. The founders had no time to wait for plans to be drawn up, and their drive and initiative has paid off in some ways. With about a 100,000 population, Beersheba is the fourth largest city in the country, after Tel Aviv, Jerusalem, and Haifa. In addition to its cultural facilities, already mentioned, it has developed an industrial and commercial infrastructure, and the days are long past when businesses would be started there only if the entrepreneurs were offered bribes in the form of government grants and long-term loans. It is genuinely the capital of the Negev, providing a whole range of services for the entire region. So if Beersheba is a mess, it is a triumphant mess.

For some reason Israelis are at their best when they improvise. From the War of Independence to the rescue operation at Entebbe, from the invention of drip irrigation to the staging of the Eurovision song contest, this country has performed with brilliance. On the main Tel Aviv by-pass road, it took years to complete a bridge; but during the Yom Kippur War, a bridge was thrown over the Suez Canal in a matter of hours. Somehow this flair has not been felt in day-to-day life. Israel seems to need the stimulus of a campaign or the challenge of a countdown to show what it can do.

One of the most important of the services provided by Beersheba is the Central Negev Hospital. Patients come there from the Bedouin encampments as well as the villages and development towns of the region. It had been expanded considerably since I saw it last and now included an institute of life sciences, associated with the university. I had to ask my way to the urology department, where I found my friend Yunis Abu-Rubiya, the first Israeli Bedouin to graduate as a doctor.

With his gaunt, dark, sensitive face and deep liquid eyes,

Yunis is very much a Bedouin; but with his stethoscope and smart white coat, he is also very much a doctor. He told me that he would shortly be completing his internship at the hospital and starting full-time work at the Bedouin clinics in the region. At the time we talked, he was spending two days a week in the desert. He was keen to increase his work among his own people, noting that they had not had a full-time doctor since the retirement of the late Benjamin Ben-Assa.

A squat, bald, forceful Dutchman, Ben-Assa came to Israel after years of experience in the Far East. He was an iconoclast: he once gave a prize, which he had received from a Dutch organization in recognition of his work among the Bedouin, to a Jordanian refugee organization. He said he did it as a good-will gesture, but I am sure he did it just as much to annoy the Beersheba reactionaries. He loved his Bedouin patients, though he was far from being starry-eyed about them.

"The rascals are claiming an area about four times the size of the State of Israel!" he once told me when we were discussing Bedouin land claims. In point of fact, his exaggeration was far in excess of the Bedouin's, who are indeed claiming wide areas, but only a small percentage of the total area of the Negev. The latest Bedouin claims amount to a quarter of a million acres. The government offer is a fifth of this area plus $75 million. Not a bad offer, considering that legally the Bedouin don't have a leg to stand on. Negev land has never been registered. The Bedouin, however, are holding out for more land; they don't mind if they receive less money. My own feeling — not shared by many experts — is that the problem will sort itself out within a generation, as the young Bedouin abandon farming and herding for jobs in town. In Galilee, successful Bedouin villages have been constructed; to date, the permanent Bedouin settlements in the Negev have been failures.

The present government has been far stricter about moving Bedouin out of areas where they are not supposed to be (but have been for years), dismantling illegal camps and buildings, and causing great bitterness. The tribesmen feel particularly badly used because they have proved to be loyal citizens. Many Bedouin serve in the army, where they make excellent scouts and trackers. The imminent withdrawal of large parts of Israel's army from the Sinai has made the land problem more pressing, but the official harassment preceded the peace treaty with Egypt.

Yunis gave me news of his two brothers, who were also friends of mine. Hallil had just got married. He had graduated in law at the Hebrew University and was now specializing in Islamic law as practiced by the Bedouin. Aref was teaching and continuing with his studies. I asked Yunis whether it would be possible to stay with one of his family overnight. What a question to ask! I would be more than welcome.

He suggested that I stay with his uncle, Sheikh Hammad Abu-Rubiya, who was a member of the Knesset. Yunis told me that he would phone his uncle later and tell him to expect me. As a member of parliament, Hammad had been given a private telephone (which in his case meant a private telephone *line*) at government expense. At the time there had been a minor furor about the (then) exorbitant cost of $10,000.

From the hospital I cut straight across the open desert to the east. Over to my right was Nahal Beersheba, the dried-up riverbed where a Chalcolithic settlement had existed in the fourth millennium B.C. The inhabitants had dug subterranean dwellings in the soil. After initial attempts with the rectangular form, they had evolved egg-shaped rooms as the most suitable for the soil. Remains of decorated pottery, ornaments of ivory and bone, testify to the high cultural level of these people, who tilled the soil with stone and bone implements, growing wheat, barley, and lentils.

Their civilization passed out of history, and by the time of the Biblical Patriarchs, Beersheba was merely a collection of wells in the desert. Of course, to a nomadic people, such as that of Abraham, the wells were vitally important. We find Abraham making a deal with Abimelech, the King of Gerar. The king kept his shepherds away from Abraham's well and in return received a present of ewe lambs. The name Beersheba means the "well of the swearing," because the covenant was sworn there between the two men; but *sheva* is also the Hebrew for seven, and the new immigrants thought it meant seven wells. The Moroccans used to joke that the town should be called Beer-*shesh* (six wells) "because the Rumanians stole the seventh."

Beersheba has a very mixed community for a development town, containing Europeans and South Americans as well as the usual quota of orientals. Most of the Europeans hailed from Rumania and tended to look down on the orientals as "primitive." The orientals countered with the accusation that all Rumanians were "thieves."

Isaac built an altar in Beersheba, and Jacob later pitched his tent there. Many years later it was important enough as a Canaanite center to be mentioned during the conquest of Joshua. Later still, the prophet Samuel sent his sons to be judges there, and Elijah fled to Beersheba from the wrath of Queen Jezebel.

Farther over to the east, the ancient tel is clearly visible. The archaeologists found a well there 130 feet deep, which they identified as the well of Abraham. In more recent layers, they uncovered a tenth-century fortress of the time of Solomon, with channels, fed from the roofs of the houses, leading to a well outside the gate. Later layers indicate settlement during the Persian, Greek, and Roman periods.

After about an hour's walk, I arrived at the memorial to the Negev Brigade of the Palmach, created by Dani Karavan, one of Israel's leading sculptors. He designed this monument as a sort of "happening," with trenches, bunkers, and pillboxes. Children (and adults, for that matter) can clamber up, over, around, and through it, getting the claustrophobic feel of the defense of Yad Mordechai, Negba, and other kibbutzim against the numerically superior forces of Egypt in 1948.

Sitting on the monument, I felt that I was really in the Negev at last: the beige loess soil, slashed by deep gulleys, the rolling pink and mauve hills, stretching to the horizon, the bright sun burning out of a perpetually blue sky. Once east of Beersheba, I always find myself breathing more deeply; I sense a new snap in my movements; the dry air sets the adrenalin racing. What is so special about the desert? Those who have never lived there find it hard to understand; those who have, don't need an explanation. I lived there for a decade, and never a day goes by without my thinking about it. When I lived there, I thought that I would never leave, and in a way I don't think that I did. For my friend Geoff, nothing can beat Galilee. He says that there is nothing on earth to equal that moment when you come over the hills and Lake Kinneret is there beneath you, blue and sparkling in the sun. Angela, like most Jerusalemites, has a special place in her heart for Israel's capital, with its variegated population, clear light, and sandstone buildings. My special love is for the spaces of the south.

*   *   *

My next stop was at the animal hospital, some two miles east of town, where I met the head veterinarian, appropriately named Dr. Bark. Connected to the department of life sciences of the university, the hospital has facilities for the treatment of cattle, horses, dogs, and cats, with a camel clinic once a week.

Bark took me to watch an operation in the beautiful, green-tiled operating theater. Two surgeons, robed and masked, were operating on a mongrel bitch; an anaesthetist was in attendance.

"The original intention was a simple ovary removal," explained Bark. "But then we found some other problems, so we decided on a complete hysterectomy."

I was particularly interested in the camel clinic, run by Dr. Shemtov Bali, whom, unfortunately, I was not able to meet. He was in the Sinai, inoculating Bedouin sheep flocks to prevent a possible outbreak of Nile Valley fever. Dr. Bali, an Iraqi Jew who learned his veterinary medicine with the British army in India, was the expert on camels, explained Bark. He had been treating the local Bedouins' sheep and camels (the donkeys apparently are not worth troubling with) for twenty years. The camel clinic had been opened some months before in the presence of the local sheikhs, but so far it had not been a great success. Bark thought they had chosen the wrong day. The Beersheba Bedouin market takes place on Thursday, so they had designated Tuesday as camel clinic day, but the Bedouin had not been bringing in the animals. Now they were going to try Thursday as clinic day so that the Bedouin could call in on their way to and from market.

What did the camels suffer from? I wanted to know. Mainly skin diseases and digestive complaints, replied Dr. Bark. He went on to tell me about a new scheme for breeding Arab horses that would be controlled by the hospital. Some American partners had been mobilized by the hospital's director, Dan Cohen (presently on Sabbatical in the United States), and the hope was that the breeding would provide useful income for the hospital, as well as a new export industry for the country. He showed me the plans for an ambitious equine surgery.

"We'll be able to use the facilities for camels also," Dr. Bark assured me.

Walking south and then east, along tracks through the plowed loess soil, I soon arrived at Tel Sheva, a Bedouin village, close to the ancient site of Beersheba, designed and built in the 1960s. Unfortunately, the village is a failure, with few Bedouin electing to live there. The place had a forlorn look, the streets full of rubble, many of the houses clearly empty, and only an occasional tree or shrub. The failure is emphasized by the fact that Tel Sheva is clearly a Bedouin center. Many tents and unauthorized buildings have been erected in the surrounding area.

The school, at least, was in use, and a group of teachers stood in the sunshine during a break in classes. I asked them why they thought Tel Sheva had failed.

"Look at the houses: matchboxes!" exploded one of them. "Would you like to live in a concentration camp?"

He was not being fair. Tel Sheva was designed by an Arab architect, who had made efforts to work out a plan suitable for the Bedouin character. A modern village cannot be built on the pattern of a Bedouin camp, with a house every hundred yards. The cost of sewage lines, water pipes, and electric wires would be prohibitive, not to mention that of roads and pavements. The village had been laid out in groups of houses joined together, each with its own high-walled yard to ensure privacy. As to the size of the houses: well, that just shows the difference in expectations between the 1960s and the 1970s. The three-room houses compared favorably with what was being built for Jews at the time. Today, both Jews and Arabs want more.

Turning to the subject of the school, I learned that all the teachers were now Bedouin. When I had lived in the area, ten years ago, most of the teachers (including all the headmasters) were from Galilee or the Arab villages in the central part of the country.

"I learned under Kassem Abdul-Kader," said one of the teachers with a smile. "We were absolutely terrified of him!" This amused me, because I remembered how my friend Kassem used to say how easy it was to keep discipline in a Bedouin school.

"The Galilee Arabs have learned *hutzpa* (cheek) from the Jews," he had told me. "The Bedouin are naturally well behaved." His children always used to rise whenever I visited a classroom, seeming to bear him out. Now I heard the other side of the story. All the teachers confirmed that the situation had improved since the Bedouin teachers had taken over. I was also informed that, unlike in my day, all the girls now went to school. (Not all of them; I observed a number of young ones tending sheep as my walk continued.)

One of the teachers told me that, although he was a Bedouin, he came from Galilee. I wouldn't know his village, which was only a small one. Curious, I asked him for the name of his village. Zarzir, he told me.

My mind went back some weeks to the dirt road opposite Moshav Nahalal, where I had walked northward for a stretch, with only the jet planes overhead for company, until I had come to some hovels. Later there had been the school, the jostling children, the boy with startling red hair, and the ornate houses with television, not marked on the map.

"Of course I know Zarzir," I told him. "But I'm still puzzled by it. On my map, there's a village of Zarzir, but there were only a few hovels there. Later on, I found some fine houses; but they're not marked at all."

He laughed. "Don't worry; we'll be on the next maps. The old village has been almost abandoned. You saw the new village. What did you think of it?"

"Fantastic," I told him. "Really elegant houses!"

"You see?" He turned to his companions. "You see what he says about our village?" He explained to me that his southern Bedouin colleagues refused to believe that Zarzir was a modern village and often teased him about his primitive hamlet.

I assured the group (amid some laughter) that Zarzir was "better than Omer!"*

The desert was crisscrossed with tracks east of Tel Sheva. After consulting with the teachers, I settled on a route due east, which, I hoped, would bring me to Aksayfe, where I was to spend the night. Except where there were paths or steep-sided wadis, the vast plain was all plowed up for the winter crop. The air was crisp and the sun shone. For once, my legs and feet seemed in good order.

The path took me past a number of Bedouin encampments, where the buildings and huts now outnumbered the tents. The tents there were still long, low, and black, without the plastic sheeting that had disgusted me in Galilee; but most Bedouin now prefer to live in simple structures of blocks and corrugated iron. Whenever I neared a camp, I was pursued by packs of snarling dogs. At first I drove them off with clods of earth (there were no stones), but I quickly learned that ignoring them was the best policy. They only chase you if you keep looking at them. Turn your back, proceed on your way, and they content themselves with frantic barking until you've left their territory.

*   *   *

Arriving at an impoverished camp, consisting of some half-dozen huts, I asked an aged, toothless Bedouin the way to Aksayfe. Pointing out the path, he told me (if I understood his Arabic correctly) that I still had twelve miles to go. I knew now that I had spent too much time with Yunis, Bark, and the teachers. Night would fall in about two hours, and I didn't want to get caught in the middle of the desert. I pressed on as fast as I could for another hour, and then turned northward to the Beersheba-Arad road, walking with the sun behind me, casting my shadow straight ahead.

* Omer is a former moshav, some three miles north of Tel Sheva. It has become Beersheba's smart suburb, where many of the university staff live.

I increased the pace, walking up and down the steep hills that I found farther north, until I saw the black ribbon of the road.

For the next two hours I continued along the road toward Arad. Just before dark, a car screeched to a stop: it was Dinah, one of our best friends in Arad, with whom I would be staying the following night. We greeted each other warmly before continuing on our ways. I was now in a bit of a dilemma as to what to do. There was no problem about walking in the dark as long as I stuck to the road, but it would be foolhardy to walk across the desert by night, particularly on such a dark night. The moon was a mere sliver, which just about enabled me to see the road. Arriving in the vicinity of Aksayfe school, I saw a light. There were two men there with a van full of water drums, drawing water from the well. I was pleased to see them, for my water had run out — the first time this happened to me on the walk. I drank my fill of the fresh sweet water after receiving an assurance that it was okay. Members of the Abu-Rubiya tribe, they confirmed what Yunis had told me: Hammad's house was some three miles south of the road. The problem was how to find it in the dark. Suddenly I remembered Hammad's private telephone line and blessed the Knesset's decision to give it to him. It was only a few yards off the road — it came eastward from Arad — and I soon found it. It was worth all of $10,000 to me that night, as I followed it through the desert, panting up the hills and down into the wadis for more than an hour.

Hammad had not spoken Hebrew when I knew him. He still would not make speeches or give interviews in that language, though he now spoke it fluently. A tall, handsome man, with a thin-line mustache, dressed in traditional Bedouin galabiya and keffiya, he received me with what I can only describe by using the cliché "typical Bedouin hospitality." I enjoyed the simple meal of scrambled eggs, tehina, two huge pitta loaves, and hot, sweet tea. After the meal, one of his young sons brought me water, holding the bowl while I rinsed my hands.

Hammad then took me to the new house that he had built next door. His two houses illustrated perfectly the change in living standards between the 1960s and the 1970s. The original house, where he still lived, was a pleasant, squat, four-room villa, similar to many that had been built in Arad when we lived there. His new home was a two-story mansion, with fancy pillars and arches. It contained a huge reception room, with an open hearth in which a fire had been lit. I sat in front of the fire with Hammad, several sons, and an elderly uncle. Of all those who heard about my walk through the country, none were so amazed as this uncle.

"What, all that way on *foot?*" demanded the old fellow, who must surely have walked thousands of miles in his lifetime. "Weren't you tired? How did you eat?" He had that thin, piping voice possessed by many Bedouin.

"My uncle is very worried about you," said one of the teen-age Abu-Rubiya children, laughing. In contrast to the traditional clothes of their elders, the boys wore jeans and sweaters, though their feet were bare, even on this cold winter night. I saw nothing of any of the female members of the family, not surprising in this Bedouin household.

I asked Hammad about the land issue, but he wouldn't be drawn. A member of parliament for four years and a Bedouin who had always cooperated with the Israeli government, he was, I sensed, almost baffled by what had been happening.

"They say there is going to be order now," he said grimly. "Well, we shall see." He was more expansive on the question of housing, coming out strongly in favor of permanent Bedouin villages — but not like Tel Sheva. The Bedouin must be allowed to build their own houses. He believed that they could learn to accept a high density of construction. They wanted all the modern facilities. His own hope was for Aksayfe to become a large, modern village, with a proper school, "just like the rest of Israel."

In Galilee I had traveled some of the way on horseback; now, in the Negev, I was keen to try to go part of the way by camel. I put the idea to Hammad, but he replied, a trifle brusquely, that he didn't have camels anymore.

I turned to the boys, who spoke Hebrew naturally and well. The younger ones told me that they were still at school. The others had jobs in the area: one was a driver, another was a trade-union official in Beersheba, a third worked at a food-processing plant in Arad. I did not get the impression that farming and herding interested them. This only confirmed my impression that the land issue is transient, which makes the present government policy of harassment all the more incomprehensible.

Some time after the completion of my walk, the problem of building three new airfields in the Negev came to the fore. The new facilities are to replace those which Israel is leaving behind in the Sinai, for, under the terms of the peace treaty with Egypt, this country will withdraw from the entire Sinai peninsula by 1982. Two of the airfields are being built in areas where no Bedouin are presently living. The third one will be in the region through which I walked, and several thousand Bedouin will have to move.

Great controversy has been caused in Israel by the first draft of the Negev Lands Bill, legislation introduced in the Knesset to facilitate the evacuation. Bedouin families who leave of their own accord have been offered quarter-acre plots for building their own homes and some $6000 in various grants and loans. Under the proposal, the right of appeal was severely limited, but, after a storm of criticism, the possibility of appeal will be written in. However, because of the urgency of building the airfield, appeals can relate only to the amount of compensation; a family cannot appeal against expulsion per se.

In a recent interview Yunis Abu-Rubiya was quoted as saying that the Bedouin, loyal citizens of Israel, realize that they will have to leave the area; but each family should get two and a half acres to enable them to preserve something of an agricultural life. Challenged with statistics indicating that less than 7 percent of Bedouin are engaged in agriculture today, Yunis retorted that all Bedouin had some connection with farming, even if they worked at something else. He added that they must also have enough grazing land for their 150,000 head of sheep and goats.

In the same interview, Yunis mentioned two other things that had upset him: the attitude of government officials (which has changed for the worse in recent years), and the size of the compensation offered. The Bedouin have been told that they are the "casualties of peace." Fine, said Yunis, but what about those other "casualties of peace," the Jewish settlers of the Sinai? They are being offered more than ten times as much per family as the Bedouin. (At the time of writing they have rejected this offer as insufficient.) The official answer to this query was that a farm on a Sinai moshav or a flat in the town of Yammit is worth more than a dusty stretch of desert. This argument does not stand up: the settlers obtained their flats and farms on ridiculously easy terms and did very well out of their years living in the Sinai. Some of the moshav farmers literally became millionaires (in Israeli terms, of course).

One ought, in fairness, to make the observation that the clash between the needs of a modern state and of its nomadic community is not confined to Israel. The solution is not simple, but the Bedouin are not just being stubborn; they are prepared to talk. At a conference on the problem, attended by Bedouin and Jews, Yunis said, "We have been loyal citizens of Israel. We have fought for the country in its wars and served it in times of peace. Do not turn your friends into enemies."

Not long ago, he was appalled at hearing, at a demonstration outside parliament, the chant "We are all Palestinians!" This was no part of the Bedouin struggle, declared Yunis. They wanted their rights; that was all. The chant, however, indicates all too vividly the dangers inherent in the mishandling of the Bedouin land problem. Hammad Abu-Rubiya met recently with the prime minister, and one hopes that, following their chat, wiser counsels will prevail. The solution, as has been said, is not simple; but it is much less complex than a lot of the other problems surrounding the Israel-Arab question, and it can be resolved.

* * *

After a couple of hours, Hammad and the elderly uncle covered their faces with their headdresses, rose abruptly, and left. The boys brought me a mattress, cushions, and heavy eiderdowns, wished me good night, and retired. Snug and warm, I fell asleep to the sound of dogs barking.

On the following morning, one of the young sons wakened me with a bowl of warm water, soap, and a towel. Afterward, breakfast: hard-boiled eggs, olives, pitta, and tea. The uncle called in to say good-by. He was dressed in his Thursday-best for Beersheba market day: gleaming white keffiya, clean galabiya, shiny leather belt, and polished shoes.

I went outside, seeing Hammad's camp for the first time in daylight. There were dozens of houses, huts, and tents clustered around his two homes. Since there is no problem about cutting across the desert by day, I made a beeline for the tel that is the ancient site of Arad, about four miles northeast of Hammad's home.

* * *

As at Hatzor in Galilee, the Arad tel has layers of settlement going back more than 5000 years. By far the largest settlements were those of the earliest period, dating to the third millennium B.C. The Canaanite town of that period covered some twenty-five acres, and among the most interesting remains turned up were pottery vessels from the Egypt of the First Dynasty. These finds not only confirm the dating of the Arad settlement; they indicate the existence of trade between ancient Canaan and Egypt (now, we hope, about to be resumed!).

How could such a large community have existed in the middle of the desert? Part of the answer, undoubtedly, lies in the reliance on intelligent storage policies. There are rainy years in this region, when successful crops can be grown, and ancient silos uncovered in the excavations indicate that grains were stored in considerable bulk. Archaeologist Ruth Amiran, who headed the dig in the Canaanite part of Tel Arad, believes that the climate has changed in the last 5000 years and that there was more rainfall in the third millennium. Another theory is that the ancient Canaanites knew about run-off agriculture, which was later practiced by the Nabateans and the Byzantines. Later on my walk I visited one of their cities farther south, and will describe the run-off technique in due course.

The Canaanite King of Arad prevented Joshua and his Israelites from entering the Promised Land via a southern route, but signs of this period have not been found at Tel Arad. The Arad of Joshua's time was apparently at Tel el-Milkh, to the south, not far from where I had spent the night.

However, by the time of King Solomon, the main Arad region settlement was back on our present site, although it was far less extensive than its Canaanite predecessor. In the royal fortress of Solomon, a sensational discovery was made: a sanctuary modeled on the Temple of Jerusalem, complete with courtyard, outer chamber, and Holy of Holies. In the outer chamber was a large altar, two and a half yards square. This corresponds to the measurements specified in the Book of Exodus: ". . . five cubits long and five cubits broad, the altar shall be four-square and the height thereof shall be three cubits."

It was built of undressed stone, although the fortress itself was built of dressed stone. This is in line with the injunction in the Book of Deuteronomy: "And there shalt thou build an altar unto the Lord thy God, an altar of stones: thou shalt not lift up any iron tool upon them."

All this obedience to the ancient traditions would be a fine tribute to Solomon and the later kings — but for the fact that the sanctuary had no business being there at all. After the building of the Temple, sacrifice was supposed to be offered only in Jerusalem, but in the two small altars of the Holy of Holies at Arad, the burned remains of organic matter were found and analyzed as animal fat.

It is no secret that the Israelites did continue to offer sacrifices on the "high places" even after the Temple was built, to the vocal displeasure of the prophets; but it is also recorded that Hezekiah, the righteous King of Judah, who reigned from 720 to 692, "removed the high places and brake the images."

Sure enough, in the third season of excavations, it was found that a wall, dating from the end of the eighth century, was built slap through the sanctuary.

The Arad fortress was in existence right through to the end of the Judean period. Later still, the Persians, Greeks, and Romans built outposts there to guard the approaches to Edom and Elat.

The site used to look like any hillock from a distance, but since I had last seen it, there had been some reconstruction work carried out. The Judean fortress now looked like a backdrop for a filming of *Beau Geste*.

Suleiman, the Bedouin guard, told me that the restoration had only just been completed. Unfortunately, Yohanan Aharoni, the archaeologist who had excavated the Judean and later fortresses, had not lived to see it.

When we used to live in Arad, our summers were enlivened by the expeditions led by the silver-haired scholar. Angela and the other women from the town would help sort out the ancient pottery fragments; I was always able to file some stories for the *Jerusalem Post*. There would be evening lectures on ancient Arad, and members of the team would return from the site, burned by the sun, dusty and excited, to report on the discovery of some ancient inscription.

I left my pack with Suleiman and climbed the steep slope to the Judean fort. I could see that a section of the Canaanite town had also been restored; it was too large for a complete reconstruction. The entrance to the fort was around the other side, but a sudden attack of juvenility prompted me to force my way in through a narrow water channel and to climb into the fort from a cistern. I only just managed it.

The outer chamber was much as it had been when it was discovered, with its large, square altar; but the two small altars from the Holy of Holies had been taken to the Israel Museum in Jerusalem. I inspected the solid walls of the Judean kings, but (despite past explanations) found myself unable to distinguish between the different periods.

The view was splendid in all directions. Over to the east, the towers of new Arad were clearly visible. I could see the copse of trees, about a mile from the town, where we had sometimes gone for picnics, but there were also patches of brighter green in the beige desert I hadn't known before. I later learned that they were agricultural experiments with Arad's sewage water that were being carried out by Kibbutz En Gedi.

A final chat with Suleiman answered a question that had been nagging me for some time: How did the Bedouin television sets work? There were aerials everywhere, but I knew that only the larger camps had generators. Suleiman explained that he ran his set off the battery of his truck. Others, he said, made use of their tractor batteries.

Walking eastward, I came to the first of the green patches. Great spouts of water shot up, spraying the area. The smell was terrible, and I pressed on past the fenced-in reservoir with all possible speed. I was walking well within myself and felt as fit that day as at any time on the walk.

I had almost arrived in Arad when a Bedouin youth hailed me from a rock, where he was sitting reading. Homework, he explained. Like all children of his age, he was out of school because of the teachers' strike. Would I like a cup of tea? he asked. I would.

We sat on a hand-woven rug in a low, black tent. There were no huts in this camp, which was modest in the extreme. The boy told me his name was Abdullah. His father no longer worked and, as the oldest child, he would have to get a job. For the time being, he was still in high school, but he hoped to start taking driving lessons in Arad soon. He wasn't too sure about his future plans. His brother and sister, two barefoot scamps, joined us and looked at me with their big, dark eyes. The girl, as often with Bedouin, was blond. Much to my surprise, an unveiled old lady also came and sat with us. His grandmother, Abdullah told me. Through him, she asked me what I was doing. She was just as appalled as the elderly Abu-Rubiya uncle had been.

I thanked them for the tea and walked the last few miles to Arad. The ground was uneven and covered with the brown flint that I remembered. The last Bedouin camp was pitched right up against the line of poles marking city limits. I went through it, ignoring the barking dogs, climbed up the bank of a steep wadi, and found myself walking between tall apartment blocks.

25

From Metulla to Elat, there is no town quite like Arad. It is the antithesis of improvised Beersheba; it was meticulously planned from the outset. This is not to criticize Beersheba. When Arad was conceived, in 1960, Israel had the resources to plan and implement projects. I am not objective about Arad, of course, having lived there for almost a decade; but my walk through the length of the country convinced me that Arad is the cleanest, neatest, best-designed, and best-looked-after municipality in the land. No wonder that the mayor, Avraham Shohat ("Baiga" to me and his other friends), had just been re-elected with the largest majority of any town in Israel.

As I walked through the streets between the neat apartment blocks, some of them seven stories high, each with its communal television aerial, I thought back to the way it had looked when I first saw it. It was in July 1962 that I and my friend Vic (the same who now lives in Moshav Ilaniya) found ourselves in a battered, old-fashioned bus, with broken windows, bumping across the reddish plain to Arad. There were about a hundred Bedouin on the bus, which kept stopping to let them off. It wasn't that it stopped at the camps; often it pulled up in the middle of nowhere, and the bearded, berobed passengers alighted. At that time we were not familiar with the terrain and didn't realize that many of the camps were concealed in valleys and wadis invisible from the dirt road along which the bus traveled. Dirt road is perhaps a hyperbole; on one occasion my head hit the luggage rack from a bump, and the brown dust swirled in at the windows, covering us and making us choke. The bus raced and bucked over the uneven ground until it finally stopped and we were told that we had arrived. Where the apartment blocks now stand, there was nothing at all. Up a hill to the side was a complex of low buildings forming the advance camp, where the planning team already lived. We staggered up to it and propped ourselves against a wall, gulping black coffee from Vic's thermos flask as we surveyed the emptiness.

"This is it, Vic," I said. "I'm for it: we must be stark, staring, raving mad!" It was love at first sight. Six months later, we moved in with some fifty other new families. Some of the families were sabras; others had lived in the country a number of years. We were the only new immigrants.

We didn't suffer the normal hardships of the early pioneers. True, we had to manage without hot water for two months and we were compelled to clamber over rocks and ditches to get to the shops; but our asbestos, prefabricated huts were airy and well designed, with brightly painted walls and doors, and we weren't short of anything.

Every morning, Vic and I would cram into one of the four wheel–drive station wagons that took us and a dozen others down to work at the Dead Sea dike construction project. We had signed on to learn crane-operating, but the American foremen soon found out that we knew English, so we were taken on as clerks. I didn't last long there because my wife developed a slipped disc that caused her endless pain. I quit work so that I could be around the house. I was worried and wanted her to go to a hospital, but Angela had faith in the town's temporary doctor, Menahem Frank, of Tel Aviv's Beilinson Hospital, who was carrying out some research in Arad. His first suggestion was conventional enough: a hard bed. Boards belonging to the construction company were lying around all over the place. A naïve request to purchase a few pieces was heartlessly refused. After a futile outburst at the foreman, I got wise and returned in the evening, when I was able to steal some half-dozen. It was Dr. Frank's second suggestion that frightened me: he insisted that she walk (yes, *walk*) to his surgery each day for heat treatment. The Bedouin workers were quite open in their sympathy as we struggled together over the stones. I was afraid that I was making my wife into a cripple for life, but Dr. Frank, a stern man, with a penetrating gaze behind steel-rimmed spectacles, completely dominated us. On the eighth day, Angela suddenly cried out; "I'm walking, I'm walking!" And she was. It was like a scene out of the New Testament. Dr. Frank was jubilant. The heat treatment, he now informed us, had been almost irrelevant; it was the walking that did the trick.

Dr. Frank's research concerned the entirely unrelated fields of asthma and kidney diseases. With its dry, desert climate, Arad was found to be ideal for people suffering from respiratory diseases. Not everyone was cured, but many asthmatics who came to live there found their lives transformed. Children in particular, who had been semi-invalids, would be playing soccer after a couple of weeks with us. Dr. Frank was concerned about controlling planting in the new town. Certain types of pollen aggravate asthma. Dr. Frank saw to it that plants producing those types of pollen were not grown in Arad.

If the region was ideal for asthmatics, it was disastrous for sufferers from kidney complaints, and this was Dr. Frank's other project. It had been noticed that Israelis in general suffered more from kidney stones than the rest of the world's population. What was more, Negev Israelis suffered to an even greater degree. The explanation for this was believed to be quite simple. Israel was a country of immigration, where people came from temperate zones to a hot climate. They were simply not drinking enough to compensate for the additional loss of water through sweating. Interestingly, the body did not look after itself naturally. Even children did not automatically drink enough fluid; they had to be made to drink.

This was the object of Dr. Frank's campaign. We must drink more, he ordered, and we must prove that we were doing so by urinating more. Every citizen of Arad became the proud possessor of a plastic bottle, into which he was commanded to urinate. What about those of us working down by the Dead Sea? Dr. Frank became even more serious. Down there it was hotter; we were in even greater danger; the bottle had to go down to work with us in the morning. On the Dead Sea project, we were the butt of jokes from our Dimonah and Beersheba colleagues. Before I left the work, I used to travel around with the others to deposit my check in the Beersheba bank (we didn't yet have a bank in Arad), and on one occasion Vic left his bottle at the bank. Had it been an American or British bank, the bottle would simply have been thrown away. But Israelis are notoriously curious and intrusive. The mind boggles!

Once we were sitting in our hut on a winter's night. The rain lashed down and the wind howled around us. Suddenly, a knock sounded on the door. Who the devil would be out on a night like this? Angela looked at me rather nervously as I got up and went to the door. It was Dr. Frank, those formidable spectacles dripping water. He was dragging a huge sack filled with plastic bottles. He extracted two, handed them to us, and ordered "a complete twenty-four-hour portion" from each of us.

The climax to his campaign came one summer evening, in the house of the Arad project director. We did not know why we had been invited, and some forty of us sat around expectantly. Dr. Frank entered dramatically. He stood up to speak, glaring at us angrily.

"You are my failures!" he thundered. "All of you have

averaged less than six hundred and fifty cubic centimers of urine per day! I am prepared to accept eight hundred — though by rights it should be a liter — but all of you are in grave danger of kidney stones. Have you any conception of how painful that is?" He then read out a list of our names, starting with the worst case (the grocer's wife with barely 300 cc), and working upward to the slightly better performers. As each person's name and capacity was presented to the public, he or she blushed and looked modestly downward. And when, in order to show the contrast, he read out the names and figures for the town champions (who had attained an average production of nearly two liters per day), all those present broke out into prolonged applause.

Dr. Frank was visibly unamused. He harangued us for fully ten minutes: we must do better; we must make greater efforts; for our own sakes and the sakes of our children we had to take ourselves in hand. It was the first and last Zionist speech that I ever heard in Arad.

Angela and I improved. We never made a liter, but Dr. Frank was satisfied with our progress.

"You English," he told us with unconcealed admiration, "you have discipline!"

With Angela's recovery from her slipped disc, it became imperative for me to find work. My neighbor, Zvi, a failed contractor from somewhere near Tel Aviv, offered me a job. He owned a plant that made sun-dried building blocks, using a rather primitive diesel-powered pressing machine. We had to mix up the concrete, shovel it into the molds for pressing, put the blocks out in the sun to dry, and finally stack them. There were four of us: Zvi (whom I quickly dubbed the "Managing Director"), myself, and two Druze called Ali and Masud, who camped out in an old bus, which doubled as our equipment store. My job was collecting the bricks from their molds and stacking them, for which I was paid one agora and two mills per brick. (The mill, one tenth of an agora, was even then obsolete, but Zvi revived it for my benefit.) To translate the whole deal into comprehensible terms: I got one pound twenty — at that time forty cents — for stacking a hundred bricks. Not a princely sum.* I had just started writing, and the rough blocks tore my hands, making it difficult for me to type in the evenings. But it was neither the tough work nor the low wage that made me give up. The trouble was that Zvi was too temperamental. He would turn up one morning in a smart business suit, with a tale about having to go to Tel Aviv; but suddenly he would lay down his briefcase, tuck his trousers into his socks, and pitch in with a shovel. On other occasions, he left early "on business." As often as not, we would sit in the sun all day, chatting and drinking coffee. Take away from this the rainy days, when we couldn't work anyway, and we were left with a derisory production record. If my family was to eat, I had to find other work. For a time I was driver for the town's only grocery store, but I found myself nodding off to sleep on the hypnotic black ribbon of road, which (by now) connected us with Beersheba. I resigned.

So it was that I went to work with the Bedouin, clearing the ground around our huts for laying footpaths, and digging foundations for the neat flint walls, which gave Arad an orderly appearance from the outset. My seven-man gang was entirely Bedouin except for me. Mahmud, dignified, with beard, mustache, and keffiya, was our foreman. It was unskilled work, done with picks, shovels, and a heavy short-handled hoe called a *turia*.

* In February 1980, the pound itself became worth so little that it, too, was abandoned. Its place has been taken by the shekel, worth ten pounds. The shekel, a unit of currency in Biblical times, was a silver coin and undoubtedly had greater value than the new shekel. The pound-to-dollar comparisons that I give throughout this book were true for the time of my walk, before inflation became even worse.

The turia is something of a symbol in Israel. The early pioneers of the second aliya used it to level roads, drain swamps, and dig irrigation channels in the citrus groves. Having worked with a turia was equivalent to a public school education in Britain, or an Ivy League university degree in the United States. As a loyal graduate of the Habonim youth movement, I had the feeling that I had "made it." To my lasting disillusionment, my fellow citizens did not share my reverence for the turia. They looked on my work with a mixture of pity and contempt. I found myself the object of sympathy for "having to work like a Bedouin."

I was appalled at this attitude for two reasons. First, I was disappointed at the materialism and the lack of respect for pioneering and physical labor. Most of my fellows seemed far more concerned with acquiring consumer goods than with building the town. Second — and more important — I was shocked by the attitude toward the Bedouin. The tribesmen played a large part in building Arad, but, for the most part, they were not welcome there. There was no discrimination, but there was no friendship and little common courtesy. Possibly there were complex reasons for this: one lady, who refused to sit next to Bedouin on the bus ("I can't stand the smell!"), was firm friends with a modern Bedouin who lived in the town, and was even rumored to be having an affair with him.

I cannot say that I enjoyed working in the Bedouin gang. I got on well with my fellow workers, but our relationship was entirely superficial. More enduring friendships were formed years later with educated Bedouin like Dr. Yunis Abu-Rubiya and his brothers, but I had little in common with my workmates. We really had nothing to talk about during tea breaks. Had my own friends been working alongside, it may have been different. As it was, I found the work soul-destroying. When the job of local tourist officer came up six months later, I swiftly abandoned physical labor, never to return to it.

*   *   *

But to return to my present trip. I walked through the town center and climbed the hill to the advance camp. With its interlocking courtyards and low buildings, it hadn't changed much since those first days. The local council offices were still located there, and Baruch Neuberg still ran the hotel and restaurant. The restaurant was smarter than I had remembered it, with red curtains and linen tablecloths. It was being laid out for some celebration, but Baruch insisted on standing me to a late lunch.

Stocky, red-faced, jovial, Baruch had been a driver for the gas-prospecting company that drilled the wells in the region in the early 1950s. At some point, he had taken over the job of supplying meals to the gas men. When the planning and design team moved to Arad a year before the rest of us arrived, Baruch was asked to run the restaurant and hotel for them. He has been doing it ever since.

"Arad has changed," he told me. "I don't even know the family that's having a celebration here this afternoon." The town had developed well, he noted, if not so fast as planned. As far as he was concerned, there was no hurry. The town now possessed all the services that it was going to get: shops, swimming pools, a community center, music conservatory, schools, clinics, hotels.

"What will more people bring us?" he demanded. "Apart from *tsuris* (problems)? A hospital we won't have, nor a university!"

I thanked Baruch for the lunch and walked down toward the original neighborhood of asbestos huts. The soccer field on the left was now a green lawn, instead of the dusty brown expanse of former years; the pine trees on the right, which had been waist-high, now grew well above my head.

The asbestos houses were supposed to be temporary, to be demolished after the founding citizens moved to permanent homes; but there is a modern Israeli proverb that says: "There is nothing as permanent as a temporary building." And they are still there. Why were they built at all? Why didn't a properly planned town, as Arad undoubtedly was, have permanent apartments and houses from day one?

Arad's first project director was Lova Eliav, the man who planned the Lachish scheme. Eliav felt he had succeeded in Lachish in regard to regional planning; but he was disappointed with Kiryat Gat from an urban point of view. He was determined that Arad would be Israel's first properly planned town, but he is also a very Israeli pragmatist. I have mentioned how he conned the government into giving Kiryat Gat a cotton gin before it was really ready for it. Now he reasoned that if he could move 100 families into Arad, the project would be given a push forward. With 100 families shouting, thumping official tables, and demanding services, the plans would be less likely to remain on the drawing board and more likely to be implemented. Unfortunately, he left the project before the first citizens arrived in Arad, so he wasn't around to see how right he had been.

In my day, the huts were gray on the outside; now they had been painted a pale pink. They still served as a sort of transit camp for ex-kibbutzniks and others who could not afford to purchase homes straight off. As I walked through, I wondered how the present inhabitants regarded the thin asbestos walls between the duplex huts. On the day I moved in, I sneezed in bed and my neighbor cried, "Bless you!" from his bed. Did they, I wondered, still tell the "Arad joke"?

An Arad citizen was repeatedly awakened by his wife with the news that their neighbor was making love. The man kept telling her to be quiet and ignore it. Finally, he asked in exasperation, "What has it got to do with you if he's making love?"

"But he's making love to *me!*" was the tearful reply.
Yes, those walls were very thin.

*   *   *

From the huts, I crossed the wadi and climbed the hill to the private-housing neighborhood. Arad stretched below me, looking just like the sketches of the town plan. Two of the apartment neighborhoods were finished; two more were under construction. A large part of the town center had been built, and three suburbs of private houses and duplex apartments were in various stages of completion. Over the hill, on a promontory overlooking the Dead Sea, four hotels already stood.

As at Lachish, Eliav had insisted on bringing his young design team to live in the desert. He wanted them to get the feel of the region and to design a town suitable for the climate and topography. He liked to tell the story of how a Tel Aviv architect involved in his Lachish scheme had placed an immigrant village bang in the middle of a wadi that flooded every winter. That sort of thing, he vowed, was not going to happen in Arad.

The team responded to the challenge, developing the idea of a high-density town that would be a sort of fortress against the desert. Buildings would be grouped around squares; the paved walkways would be shaded by the tall blocks. There would be greenery, planted in small, concentrated areas that would be possible to maintain and would not need too much water.

Gerald Zeffert, a young architect on the team who had emigrated from South Africa, took the idea a stage further and designed a special apartment block for the town. His conception was of a multistory "casbah," with high walls, each apartment having its own patio. The upper patios shaded the lower ones, and the lower ones shaded the footpaths. Unfortunately, only half a dozen blocks of patio apartments were ever built. A new form, it naturally contained a number of errors: four stories was too high for this design; too many apartments led off the central stairwell; it was noisy and difficult to keep clean. All these faults could have been ironed out had the project been allowed to develop, but special interests were to prove too powerful, so the brave experiment was buried. All that is left of it are the half-dozen rather shabby apartment blocks, regarded as a failure by those who live in them.

The general town design was carried out to the letter, but the concentrated areas have proved less popular than was expected. Anyone who could afford it elected to build his own house rather than live in the high-density neighborhoods that the planners thought most suitable for life in the desert.

It was through this first suburb of private houses — a strange mixture of vulgarity and good taste — that I now walked to the house of my friends Lix and Yul. Their low, cabin-style house, which Yul built with his own hands, is inhabited by the two of them, their three sons, a dog, and about a dozen cats. Yul, a balding, gray-haired sabra, used to look older than the rest of us, when we all came to Arad sixteen years ago. Today, we have all grown older, but he looks exactly the same, and I am sure his ruddy, wrinkled face isn't going to change in the next thirty years. Originally manager of a local cooperative, Yul has been for some years in charge of maintenance at the big chemical complex a dozen miles south of the town.

After our initial greetings, I asked him whether he could arrange for me to stay at the Tzin phosphate plant (thirty miles south of Arad), because this was an area without ordinary human habitation. Yul at once got on the phone to a colleague at the Tzin plant, and I heard him shouting, joking, and cajoling in his characteristic way.

"Well, I've fixed it for you," he said, returning from the phone. "But it's cost me a generator." They had run into some problem at the Tzin plant, he explained, that he thought could be solved if he lent them the generator. He told me a bit about the plant, which he said was not using the phosphates in the right way. According to him, the material was being dug out of the ground and sold more or less in its natural form. In his view, the world market was becoming more sophisticated, and Israel should be processing raw materials and selling far more complex chemicals. I knew that his own plant, the chemical complex, was trying to do just this, but the national press had reported heavy losses. Not true, retorted Yul. There had been technical problems and money had been lost, but now they were making a small profit. He would shortly be in charge of building a new plant that would manufacture even more complex products. Recently he had toured the United States, partly on holiday and partly to look at plants over there.

He was full of this, his first trip to America.

"When they say that the car will be ready at eleven on Monday morning, it's ready on Monday morning at eleven," he recounted in evident amazement. "Not Wednesday at four." He was clearly overwhelmed by the trip, singing the praises of the people, who were so friendly; quite the reverse of what he had been led to believe. He showed me photographs of his tour.

There is a bond between Yul and me — apart from the fact that we shared our first car without a single quarrel for two years — because we were both deeply involved in the early political struggles in Arad. We bowed out when the national political parties became involved in the town's affairs.

The main dispute in those early months had centered on the personality of the Arad project director, Yitzhak Pundak, a gray-haired ex-army colonel, who thought a director's job was to direct. A number of us who had grown up

in the youth movements and the kibbutzim had other
ideas. We were for democracy and participation, and we
demanded a citizens' committee, which would function as
an embryo town council. I have vivid memories of the first
time the question arose.

It was a cold, clear winter's night; the first hundred citizens of the new town were huddled in their overcoats in the
doorless and windowless hut, which served in daytime as
the school. It was our first meeting with Pundak, and initially he made a superb impression: forceful, dynamic, efficient, charming. He apologized for the school's having no
doors and windows, for the absence of paths and roads, for
the lack of hot water; but he noted that if he hadn't made
the decision that the families should move in, delays would
have been far longer. He carried us with him all the way.

Then somebody raised the idea of a committee. Yes, indeed, agreed Pundak. Not one committee, but several.
There should be committees for education, culture, security, neighborhood maintenance, and so on. Oh, no, said
the proposer. Mr. Pundak had misunderstood his intention.
Aside from the subcommittees the director had mentioned,
there should be a general committee, a full partner with
him in running the town. Pundak's mood changed
abruptly.

"What would it do?" he kept demanding. "What would
it *do?*" He wasn't looking for partners.

The town swiftly became polarized around two camps:
for Pundak and against him. Yul served on the first citizens' committee; I was chairman of the second one. It
would be tedious to relate the intrigues of those early years
(although those of us who lived through them never tire of
reminiscing about them). Suffice it to say that I became
convinced that no normal person can ever be a success in
public life. He is always likely to be outsmarted by the
twenty-four-hour-a-day political operator, for whom offer-

ing, persuading, and cajoling is a way of life. Our party, ex-kibbutzniks and mostly sabras, was naïve and principled; but we were (I must admit) a clique, a bunch of snobs. Pundak's supporters were, for the most part, older people, several of them survivors of the Holocaust. They had already had a taste of life. Where we had come to Arad to make a start, they had come for a *new* start.

Many attempts were made to bridge the gap between the two groups, both of which essentially wanted the same thing: the successful development of Arad. But somehow we always found ourselves outmaneuvered. I remember climbing into bed at four o'clock one morning, tired but satisfied, telling Angela that this time everything was settled.

"Don't be a fool," she muttered, half-asleep. "They'll change their minds in the morning." She was right.

The time has come to say something about the sabra, the native-born Israeli. We have met him several times in this book: my son Etan; Hezi, the moshavnik from Margaliot; Vodak and Dandy in Amiad (although they were not actually born here); Yaacov and Aliya Zarchi in Ginnegar; Solly and Yossi Snir in Zichron; Yehiel, Rafi, and Vered in Netivot; and the university students in Beersheba. I would even classify Abdul Rahim of Kafr Kassem and Yunis Abu-Rubiya as sabras, albeit of a distinct subgroup.

A sabra is really a cactus fruit, prickly and awkward on the outside, difficult to penetrate, but soft and sweet inside. These characteristics are supposed to be true of the native-born Israeli. It is as simplistic a characterization as the most famous portrayal of the sabra in literature, the vigorous, muscular, crude boor of Arthur Koestler's *Thieves in the Night*.

The first point to make about the sabra is that (of course) he does not exist. There is no prototype. There are as many types of sabra as there are of Englishman or American.

That being said, I am going to describe two types of sabra that, I hope, will give a true picture, if an incomplete one.

One must first understand the word *hevre*. *Hevra,* meaning "community," is the real Hebrew word, and stands for the membership of a group, kibbutz, or moshav. Hevre, which is slang, is a sort of development of this term and is used more loosely. It means the gang or the crowd. Most immigrants acknowledge that they have never penetrated the hevre because of a lack of similar background and experiences. I would not be so bold as to say that we made it, but I think we did gain a measure of acceptance during our decade in Arad.

Now to the two types. The first is the *shvitzer-sabra,* the brash hevreman (man of the gang), with a hail-fellow-well-met approach, noisy, sweaty, loudest of hand-clappers in the sing-song, which he usually initiates, interrupter of jokes (in order to tell his own — inferior — versions), great *talker* about sex, and bullshitter par excellence. His female counterpart is sharp, hard-voiced, self-confident, and rather obviously flirtatious.

The second has something of the former type in him (my friend Yul once said to me, "Show me a sabra who isn't a shvitzer!"); but he hates bullshit. Shy and retiring, he feels very deeply about things, but is scared of showing any emotion. Once you break through the barrier, you will find the second version, male and female, among the kindest, most loyal, and sensitive people you have ever met.

The hatred of pretension can lead to a frightening pragmatism and a ruthless rejection of sentimentality. Who but the sabra would have invented jokes about the Holocaust? Yes — unbelievably — there are such jokes, so tasteless that I am not going to repeat them here. Some argue that this indicates a lack of sensibility so crass as to cast doubt on the sabra's basic character. I reject this absolutely. The Holocaust joke is merely an extreme reaction to the brainwashing of the older generation. A less strident example is the equation of the word Tzionut (Zionism) with the bullshit that he or she hates so much. Zionism has become almost a swear word in certain sabra circles.

Little wonder that the middle-aged East Europeans found it so hard to comprehend the confident young sabras in Arad.

*   *   *

When there were elections for the town's first mayor, Pundak won decisively. Yul, the defeated candidate, dropped out of public life and I went with him. Two years later Pundak left Arad to become an ambassador, and one of our group (the present mayor) won the subsequent election. But by then the national political parties had taken over the various town factions, and our age of innocence was over. Did we really drop out, or did the professional politicians drop us? I think it was a bit of both. I always felt that Yul should have remained active in local affairs, but he insists that it is not his scene.

Yul's wife, Lix, came back from Beersheba and made us supper. Born in Berlin and brought up in Kenya, Lix is one of the most English people that I know. A part-time lecturer in psychology at the Ben-Gurion University, she is a fervent disciple of B. F. Skinner. For her, the highlight of the American trip was attending a lecture by the master. I always get into terrible arguments with her about Skinner, not because I disagree with all he says — I accept a good deal of it — but because I refuse to accept everything that he says. As far as Lix is concerned, this half-agreement is far worse than disagreement. It proves that I simply do not understand. For her it isn't a question of "if Skinner's ideas were applied . . ." It is "when Skinner's ideas are finally applied, the world will be livable-in." On this occasion I managed to avoid a dispute, but she was as scathing as usual about the way everything in the country and the world was being mismanaged.

I left their house and walked down the road to the house where we had lived. Two contractors and ourselves had gone bankrupt in building it, and we never could afford to furnish it properly or to make it really pleasant. It is nothing like as nice as the house I now inhabit — but it remains home in a way that nowhere else can ever be. I didn't go in, but continued down the road to the house of Dinah, where I was going to stay the night with my friend Ben from Raanana. Ben had suggested that he join me in my walk for a couple of days, and we had arranged to meet up in Arad. The two of us spent a pleasant evening at Dinah's home, watching television and reminiscing about the past.

Dinah is a widow of the Six Day War of 1967, and as we relaxed in her comfortable lounge, I couldn't help remembering the effort that her late husband, Reuven, had put into building their home.

Driven by a nervous energy that did not permit him to sit still, but with a marvelous sense of humor, Reuven looked every inch the typical sabra. In fact, he was the archetypal "wandering Jew." Born in Barcelona of Polish parentage, he had lived all over Europe and North Africa before coming to Israel in the first years of the state. He grew up in a moshav, without much formal education, and then served in a crack paratroop unit. He was the very first man in Arad, volunteering to come to the site even before the planning team in 1961. Although he was basically a farmer, he said he was prepared to turn his hand to anything. For several months he had worked as an unskilled laborer; then Lova Eliav found him a job with the planning team. When I first knew him, he was in charge of the archives and library, and also took on other administrative work that needed doing.

He became the foreman of one of the town's first factories, a plant producing marble chips for tiles. During this period, he built his own house, after work hours, much of it with his own hands. You could see that for him it symbolized the end of his wanderings; his two sons would grow up in it in security. Their childhood would not be like his.

The Six Day War came on all of us in Israel, including Arad, with devastating suddenness. On Independence Day of 1967, the whole town was out dancing the *hora* (traditional Israeli pioneers' circle-dance). War could not have been further from our minds as (parents and children together) we stamped and whirled about to the tunes of the accordion.

Then, in less than a month, Arad became a town almost without males. Nearly everyone was mobilized. In those days I was stationed in Arad itself, so I was not to see action. Reuven was one of the last to be called up. I so well remember him pacing impatiently, already dressed in his uniform, phoning his unit, demanding to know why he hadn't been mobilized. In Biblical times, he wouldn't have been.

"What man is there that hath built a new house, and hath not dedicated it? Let him go and return to his house, lest he die in the battle . . ." (Deuteronomy 20:5). But, alas, we live in an age of total war. Reuven was finally mobilized and fought in the battle for the Old City of Jerusalem. He was killed by shellfire just under the Lions' Gate in the Eastern Wall. I mourned him as I have mourned few others.

With heart-warming courage, Dinah, alone of the five Arad widows of that war, decided to remain. Of mixed Egyptian-Iraqi parentage, she has a large, loving family in Jerusalem, but she was determined to raise her sons in the house that Reuven had built for them with such grit and determination. Nir and Ran, today delightful teen-agers, vindicate her decision.

I said to Dinah that Reuven would have approved of my walk. It was he who taught me to love the desert, who took me on many an exciting trip to the ruins of an ancient fortress or a lookout point above some beautiful valley.

I miss him dreadfully; but it isn't only he whom I miss. It is the part of all our lives that we lived in Arad. The clock can't be turned back, but how I wish that it could be; that we could sit on the wall as we did in the past: Lix and Yul, Angela and I, Dinah and Reuven, and all the others, and gossip with the children playing nearby, as the sun sets blood-red over the desert.

26

I WAS WRONG about the weather all along the line. After my soaking in Galilee, I had told myself that once I got south of Rehovot I would be safe. In the event, the weather was perfect until Rehovot, when it started clouding over. Only the theft of my belongings in Ashkelon saved me from several rainy days. My next self-imposed deadline was Arad. From there, or so I reasoned, I was descending into the desert of the rift valley and would return to the high ground only at Sde Boker, much farther south. Because of my proven incompetence as a weather forecaster, then, it should surprise no one that Ben and I set off from Arad on a gray, gloomy day that robbed us of the normally superb view to the east down to the Dead Sea and across to the mountains of Edom in Jordan.

I can never have enough of the sun, and in the normal way the weather would have depressed me, but for one thing: I now had company. After more than three weeks alone on the road, it was delightful to converse with one of my best and oldest friends. Ben wasn't put off by the weather. He enjoyed the rocky desert scenery, suggesting, as many had before him, that the moon must look something like this. His reflections on the landscape led him to speculate on other worlds, and he put forward the idea that we humans were laboratory animals of some superior civilization who had been planted on the earth as an experiment.

He said that he often felt we were being watched by superior beings, who probably derived considerable amusement from our stupidity. I believe I have mentioned that my friend is an economist; he never tires of pointing out the irrationality of people, particularly in his own field of specialization.

The road from Arad to the Dead Sea descends some 3000 feet in fifteen miles. For a time we walked along desert tracks more or less parallel to the road, but we found that the road had utilized most of the best routes down. Though there was a path eastward away from the road, it would have added unduly to our mileage. We did go down into the Bokek Valley for a bit, but the going was too rough, so we returned to the road. Even without the benefit of a clear day, the view was very fine. The brown rocks were splashed here and there with pink and mauve, where there were marble deposits, and the steep-sided gulleys and canyons led off in all directions.

On my walk so far I had been spoiled with regard to nourishment. Apart from the oranges, there was always somewhere to buy food and drink. Now it was different. I carried two water bottles instead of one. Ben had a thermos flask, which Dinah had insisted on filling for us. He had also brought some biscuits. My pack was weighted down with a bit of dried fruit and some cans of corned beef, but I was keeping them for an emergency.

After some twelve miles, we arrived at a promontory from which we looked down on the Zohar Fortress at the junction of the Zohar and Yizrah valleys. Down in the valley, the flint gives way to limestone, and the fortress is built on top of a hillock that the rushing floodwaters have carved out over the centuries. From this point, the En Gedi Field School has obligingly marked out a steep track, which leads down to the fortress. Off the road at last, we followed the green blazes painted on the rocks, down over the crags and through the gulleys to the bottom. The Zohar Fortress was part of the Roman *limes* system of border fortifications, which guarded the empire. Earlier forts have been found at the top of the hill above the road at Rosh Zohar. No one but the Romans would have built right down on the valley floor, but Roman power was based on the Roman road. Of course, in terrain such as that around the Dead Sea, nothing like a classical Roman road is feasible, but negotiable tracks approach the Zohar Fortress from three directions.

We inspected the large water cisterns, plastered on the insides, and Ben wondered aloud how a garrison could have been forced to remain in such a godforsaken place. I pointed out that the soldiers most probably would have been local auxiliaries rather than Romans. I speculated that Rome would not have been too scrupulous about exerting pressure on them and that quite likely their families would have been held hostage for their good behavior.

As we walked down the Zohar Valley to the Dead Sea, it started to rain, a light English-style drizzle. The wet rocks gleamed rust and gold, adding to the beauty of the scene. Ben was fascinated by the desert trees and shrubs that clung tenaciously to the sides of the canyon, sending their roots into cracks in the rock face.

Another mile and we arrived at the Neve Zohar complex, which includes a museum, a youth hostel, and a modest hotel. The museum, which was open but unstaffed, is partly archaeological, but also deals with the more recent history of the Dead Sea. The development of the potash industry is illustrated with models, charts, and photographs. In the museum yard, we inspected the wooden hulk of a boat, which was used by the Irish explorer Christopher Costigan when he surveyed the Dead Sea in 1836. He was found on the shore by Bedouin, but he died later from exhaustion and dehydration. The boat was subsequently discovered in an English country garden by the Israeli geographer Zeev Vilnay, who arranged for it to be brought back to Israel and erected outside the museum. Inscribed on the side of the hull is the legend: "This boat was built 1836, visited Acre, Cana of Galilee, Lake of Tiberias, Jordan, Dead Sea, Jerusalem, Joppa — 1847."

There were a number of boat expeditions in the nineteenth century that started, like Costigan's, in Lake Kinneret and sailed down the Jordan to the Dead Sea. Most of them ended in disaster. Then, in 1848, Captain W. F. Lynch of the United States Navy made a successful survey of the sea, the results of which led to the development of the modern potash industry.

There was nobody at the youth hostel, so we made our way to the hotel, where the elderly proprietor gave us coffee. He told us there was nothing to eat until supper, at seven o'clock. Then, changing his mind, he extracted some congealed, fried potato cakes from his refrigerator. We nibbled at them for politeness' sake, and he charged us twenty pounds (one dollar) for them. Supper was not much better, but our beds in a rather shabby hut were comfortable enough, and we appreciated the hot showers.

Ben was very stiff from the walk, and so (to my utter disgust) was I. I had been certain that my days of stiffness were past. Since leaving Netivot, I had been covering twenty miles per day and feeling fine, but the steep descent from Arad had made me hobble once more. After my walk was over, all my friends told me how well I looked and suggested that I must be fearfully fit. I did feel well (and my belt went in five notches), but I do not believe all this nonsense about being fit. Fit for what? If you swim a lot, you are fit for swimming. If you run, you are good at running. Ditto jogging, cycling, weight-lifting, skipping. I was apparently very fit for walking *on the level* — I had been doing this since Galilee — but it did not help me when I had to walk downhill to the Dead Sea.

*   *   *

The next day was also overcast, as we set out without breakfast along the shore of the Dead Sea. Our route took us southward, so we would be missing the ancient fortress of Masada, some dozen miles to the north. Masada has a very special place in Jewish history — and in Israeli mythology — so we shall let the walk take care of itself for a bit and consider the story of this desert fastness.

Mention has been made more than once in this account of the great Jewish war against Rome in A.D. 66–73. After Jerusalem fell in the year 70, three desert outposts continued to hold out undefeated. It was three years before Masada, the last of them, was sacked.

The Sicarii, an extreme Zealot sect (named for the *sica* — dagger — with which they assassinated their opponents), seized Masada in the early stages of the war. The rock of Masada is a section of the cliff top that overlooks the Dead Sea a thousand feet below. It is cut off by steep wadis on all sides, which makes it almost inaccessible. On this bare hunk of flint, in the searing wastes of the Judean desert, the paranoiac King Herod had built an impregnable fortress as a retreat from his potentially rebellious subjects. Securing their base there, the Sicarii proceeded to Jerusalem, where they took over the leadership of the anti-Roman uprising. In the bitter infighting that occurred between the Jewish groups, Menahem, the Sicarii leader, was murdered, and his followers returned to Masada to regroup. (Menahem was the grandson of Hezekiah, the rebel leader hunted by Herod a century earlier in the cliffs of Arbel in Galilee. It was he who killed himself and his family rather than fall into Herod's hands.)

The new Sicarii leader, Elazar Ben-Jair, the nephew of Menahem, waited out the war at Masada. He and his followers were joined by other groups, particularly after the fall of Jerusalem. When the Roman Tenth Legion arrived at the foot of the rock with its auxiliary forces, early in

A.D. 73, there were just under a thousand men, women, and children living in the fortress.

Silva, the Roman commander, set about the seige in methodical Roman fashion. First he built small forts at every possible point of egress from the rock. Then he linked the forts with a wall circumventing the rock, blocking even the impossible escape routes.

Capturing Masada was rather more difficult, for the rebels had more than adequate supplies of food and water. The largest wadi had been dammed and from it an aqueduct fed a line of cisterns cut in the side of the rock but accessible from the summit. Silva destroyed the aqueduct, but there was plenty of water in the cisterns from previous years. Herod's storehouses were crammed with grain, oil, other food, and wine.

The Romans constructed an enormous ramp of earth and wood, which filled the wadi to the west. A gigantic engineering feat for those days, the ramp is still there, pointing like a sword at the fortress. On top of the ramp, the attackers constructed a siege tower, under cover of which they battered the walls of Masada. They broke through the outer stone walls, only to discover that the defenders had constructed an inner wall of wood packed with earth, which was impervious to a battering ram.

In due course, the Romans set this inner wall alight. The soldiers were surprised at the speed with which the fire spread to the whole of the fortress. The following morning, they discovered why: when they entered the charred remains of Masada, they found the bodies of the defenders laid out in rows. The men first had killed their own families and then drawn lots for a final ten to kill the men, upon which one man killed the others and then himself. This epic tale, recounted by Flavius Josephus in his book, *The Jewish War,* has become one of the most significant legends for modern Israel.

Masada was first identified by the American explorers

Edward Robinson and Eli Smith in 1838. Ten years later, Captain Lynch, the Dead Sea explorer, sent a party to climb Masada, and fired off a salute "in honor of the illustrious dead." French, Dutch, and British explorers followed, but the first thorough study of the site was made in 1932 by the German scholar Adolf Schulten.

In the following years, youngsters from the kibbutzim and the youth movements began to make expeditions to climb Masada, which became a place of pilgrimage. The man who did most to turn Masada into a national shrine was Shmariyahu Guttman, a kibbutz archaeologist, who restored one of the Roman siege forts and the snake path, which winds up to the summit from the Dead Sea shore. A tiny, leathery man, with wings of white hair, Guttman has a genius for making the past come alive. He has no university degree, but he is undoubtedly one of the finest archaeologists in Israel and has a delightful style of exposition, based on anecdotes. Shmariyahu also participated in the exploratory dig of the mid-1950s.

In 1963, Yigael Yadin, the former Israeli chief of staff, who excavated Tel Hatzor, led two seasons of spectacular excavations at Masada. It was a major event for those of us living in Arad. With the help of the army engineering corps and assisted by hundreds of volunteers from all over Israel and all over the world, a host of archaeological treasures was uncovered. Fragments of some of the earliest Biblical scrolls and documents of the Dead Sea sect were found, as well as numerous inscriptions, jars with the remains of food (preserved in the dry climate for almost two millennia), mosaics, and wall paintings. Herod's magnificent palaces, with their ornate frescoes and a complete Roman-style bathhouse, were uncovered. The biggest collection of coins ever found at one site was dug up.

It was the scrolls that most excited the experts; but the discovery that moved the whole nation was of the Sicarii living quarters, mostly in the casemate perimeter wall, their

ritual baths, their synagogue, the traces of the fire they ig-
nited, and, in some cases, the very remains of their final
meal. The skeletons of a man (still wearing his suit of
armor), woman, and child were found under the rubble of
Herod's northern palace, and weapons, including the
stones the defenders had prepared to roll down on the be-
siegers, were located.

The country caught its collective breath when Professor
Yadin announced the discovery of a collection of inscribed
pottery fragments, which could have been the very lots
drawn by the defenders to decide which of them would kill
the others. One of them was inscribed "Ben-Jair."

Flavius Josephus had originally been called Joseph Ben-
Mattitiahu and had been one of the leaders of the Jewish
revolt in Galilee. When his town was captured, he (by his
own account) opted out of a suicide pact, similar to that at
Masada, and went over to the Romans, adopting the name
Flavius Josephus. For this reason, many scholars had
doubted his account of the siege of Masada. The speech he
wrote for Elazar Ben-Jair, with references to Indian phi-
losophers, among others, was eloquent but unconvincing.
Moreover, the very act of suicide is totally alien to Jewish
doctrine.

Although the excavations did not provide irrefutable
proof of the mass suicide — the bodies were not found, except for the three mentioned and thirty more in a cave —
there are strong indications that the Josephus account is a
true one. His description of the rock, the fortress, and the
Roman siege-works is entirely accurate.

Josephus' version can be accepted if we consider the es-
chatological beliefs of the time, which we have touched on
when passing by Lake Kinneret and Yavne. Many of the
Jewish sects of the first century, as shown in their literature,
including documents found at Masada, believed that they
were living through the Messianic age foretold by the

prophets. I have already quoted from the Book of Daniel and I would like to add to it a sentence from the War Rule of the Dead Sea Scrolls: "And with the seventh lot, the mighty hand of God shall bring down (the army of Satan and all) the angels of his kingdom and all the members (of his company in everlasting destruction)." Masada, it should be noted, fell in the seventh year of the war.

The excavating and reconstructing of Masada, the restoring of the paths to the summit — and even the erection of a cable car — have made it far more accessible; but they have done nothing to reduce its mystique. It is still a national symbol of heroism and a place of pilgrimage for Israeli youth. Young soldiers being inducted into the armored corps swear their oath of allegiance atop the bleak mountain with the vow "Masada shall not fall again!"

This, then, is Israel's Masada complex, or Holocaust complex, or whatever you will: a determination that this country will survive and (if necessary) defeat its enemies. The notion that Israel would, Samson-like, bring down the world in an atomic holocaust exists only in the minds of "serious" journalists and authors of potboilers.

*　　　*　　　*

Let us return now to our walk, as Ben and I struggled across the sand and rocks of the Zohar Valley, southward. I was reminded of the many times that I had seen this valley in full flood: a raging, frothing, brown torrent, sweeping large boulders (and sometimes even cars) in its wake. We had, on occasion, been turned back when we were on our way to work on the Dead Sea construction project. I don't remember deep regret about getting the day off.

Ben wondered aloud whether there was not a danger of our being caught by a flash flood, but I discounted this. Not that it was out of the question, but the Zohar Valley was wide. The real danger was being caught in one of the narrow-walled canyons that one can find in these cliffs. When the floods did burst forth suddenly, the result of rains far away, there was usually time to reach the high ground. Most of the accidents that do occur are caused when people try to cross one of the raging torrents, thinking it is shallow. If the water does come frothing down the valley, the answer is to climb as high as possible and wait until it subsides.

Of course, you may have to wait for several hours — or even several days. In the first years of Arad, the town was sometimes cut off on all sides, and food had to be flown in by army helicopter. When the first twins were born in the town, this was the situation, and the mother had to be flown to the Beersheba hospital. The proud father announced that the twins would be named Arad and Storm, a proposal promptly vetoed by the mother when she came home.

In descending the 3000 feet from Arad, we had returned to the Syrian-African rift, which I had climbed out of at a point above Tiberias; but the Dead Sea is even farther below sea level. At minus 1290 feet, it is, in point of fact, the lowest place on the earth's surface. As we walked along, I smelled the bitter, acrid smell that I remembered so well, for the Dead Sea is an exceptionally rich mineral deposit. Ten times as salty as the Mediterranean, it is estimated to contain 42 billion tons of salts. Today, potash for fertilizer is the main product; but bromine, salt, and magnesium chloride are also extracted from the sea. Those in the know say that magnesium is the product of the future.

I could see that the southern end of the sea had almost entirely dried up. This is largely because of Israel's use of the water of Lake Kinneret and Jordan's use of the Yarmuck River. Both the Kinneret and the Yarmuk feed the Jordan River, which is the Dead Sea's main source of water. In summertime, the temperature can reach 120° Fahrenheit, so the evaporation rate is formidable.

The drying up of the southern portion of the sea was anticipated when the Dead Sea Works built its network of twenty miles of dikes in the early 1960s. This giant construction project was what I had worked on when I first came to Arad. The road that Ben and I had descended the previous day wasn't completed then, and the equipment — including a dredging vessel, the largest types of cranes and excavators, and giant barges — had to be cut into sections and transported down the narrow winding road that leads to the Dead Sea farther south. Some sections had to be carried by four semitrailer trucks.

As we passed the entrance to the yard, I noted that one forlorn hut was all that remained of the project. I had felt very young and inexperienced the first time I walked into the yard. Vast cranes rumbled out to the dikes; a mile-long conveyor belt transported rocks to the shore; bulldozers and excavators were tearing up the soil, their steel tracks screeching on the rock; great trucks started up with sudden shrill coughs.

It was my first experience of American-style dynamism. "Don't go easy. If the tractor breaks, we'll bring a new one. Drive it all out, fella. I've got a deadline to meet!"

In fact, the three-year contract went into five years and a dispute broke out between the contractors and the Israeli company. In the end, it was the Dead Sea Works that completed the placing of the clay core in the dike walls. I worked for both companies and would give the Americans higher marks, despite the bullshit. The Israelis had twice the administrative staff for half the labor force and kept far less comprehensive records.

In the early months of the project, there had been a strike over wages, and the yard (so quiet as we walked past it today) had been filled with angry, shouting men. An atmosphere of violence had been in the air. The Israeli personnel manager had fled to Beersheba, but Gino, the stocky, American project manager, had outfaced the strikers.

"Tell them if they're hot-blooded Israelis, I'm an Eyetal-
ian and I'm hot-blooded too!" he shouted through an inter-
preter. "I have one principle: a good day's work for a good
day's pay." He had won the men's hearts.

"He's a *gever* (a man)!" the translator informed his
friends, the finest compliment an Israeli male can pay.

*   *   *

The dikes have turned the Israeli half of the southern end
of the sea (the border with Jordan runs down the center)
into a network of artificial lakes. The lakes contain water,
pumped back from the deeper, northern end. Not only industry benefits from this: farther north there are a number
of hotels with the highest occupancy rate in Israel, summer
and winter alike. They are full of Europeans who have been
sent there by their doctors, for the water of the Dead Sea,
the mud of the shores, and the local springs that flow into
the sea from along the coast, are supposed to cure a wide
variety of skin diseases, as well as rheumatism, arthritis,
and other ailments. Scandinavians, sent by their health
services, are among the most numerous visitors.

Now that the sea has retreated, the vacationers bathe in
the largest of the artificial lakes. I write "bathe" because
you cannot swim in the Dead Sea; you bob like a cork in ordinary water because of the density of the salt fluid. It is a
strange feeling. You can stand in the water, your feet not
touching bottom, with your head and shoulders out. You
can lie either way — but be careful to keep your eyes clear
of the water. The best position is reclining, as if in an armchair. You can read a paper or book without its getting wet.
Not only the eyes, but even the smallest cuts (to say nothing
of the natural bodily openings), smart fiercely after contact
with the water; but if you're careful, a dip in the Dead Sea
can be a most amusing experience. When you come out, the
salt feels oily on your body. At most beaches — certainly by

the hotels — there are showers to wash it off, but there are some who prefer to drive back as far as Arad or Beersheba before showering.

The Emperor Vespasian is said to have thrown manacled slaves into the Dead Sea in order to test the stories he had heard about it. They did not drown, according to Josephus.

*   *   *

The air was warm and heavy, despite the gray skies; Ben and I sweated under our rucksacks. My friend was singing as he walked, but I did not recognize the tune. When I asked him about it, he laughed and said that was not surprising; his brother had composed it to a poem by John Masefield. Unfortunately, he could remember only the beginning, but he taught that to me and we sang it as we swung along.

> *One road leads to London,*
> *One road leads to Wa-aa-aa-ales,*
> *My road leads to the far and distant da-aa-aa-ales.*

A little farther south, we crawled into a cave in the cliffs, thinking it was the famous "Lot's Wife" cave. The story is told in the Bible that when Abraham and his family fled from the wicked cities of Sodom and Gomorrah, minutes before God's vengeance rained down fire and brimstone on them, Lot's wife had looked back, in defiance of God's explicit command, and had been turned into a pillar of salt. We had mistaken a pillar too far north for the real thing, but the cave was much the same as that of the traditionally accepted site: a narrow entrance between limestone walls, and then a large cave with a tall chimney, coated with salt, open to the sky thirty feet above. Lick your finger, rub it on the wall, and lick it again. You'll taste the salt.

We had conned some rather dry cheese sandwiches out of

the hotelier along with our supper the previous night, and we now sat down under the cliff to eat them. Ben said the scene reminded him of his honeymoon in England. He and his wife had been cut off by the tide while holidaying in Cornwall. They had been forced to climb the steep cliffs, but they had managed to get only about halfway up. Fortunately, after an hour or so of frantic waving, they had attracted attention. The locals were evidently used to such incidents, said Ben, because a rescue operation was speedily mounted. A chair attached to a rope had been lowered from the cliff top and it was explained that they should sit in the chair and walk up the cliff face, holding on to the rope. His wife, Denise, had gone first. When it was Ben's turn, he had been pleasantly surprised at how easy it was to scale the cliff. He told me that he thought he must be pretty fit, but when he arrived at the top, he found seven strong Cornishmen hauling on the rope.

We walked past the Dead Sea Works, with their enormous piles of white potash. The piles are always there, but this time they were bigger because of a prolonged strike at the plant. When the plant is open, special barges move over the artificial lakes contained by the dikes, and the potash is dredged out and pumped to the drying plants. The Dead Sea Works lost money for nineteen years until a change in the world demand for potash fertilizer made it into one of Israel's most profitable industries.

We were still stiff from yesterday's walk and limped along painfully. Ben was in particularly bad shape because the walk had reactivated a skiing injury in his knee from his Geneva days. To add to our troubles, it started raining hard. I rationalized once more: Neot Hakikar, our next port of call, was off the main route south. If we were to hitchhike there and back to the main road, it wouldn't be breaking my walk.

My plan had been to spend the night on the lawn outside the house of an army friend, Ehud Tzeiri, but the weather had made this impossible. It rains in this area only a few days a year, but we had hit on one of those days. To be honest, I didn't know Ehud that well — but I need not have worried. We were received with the sort of hospitality that I was fast coming to accept as a sort of natural right. Ehud's wife, Sarah, an attractive sabra, dispensed tea, our first hot drink for seventeen hours. We had just finished drinking it when Ehud arrived. A dark, bespectacled Yemenite, a graduate of the Hebrew University in Arabic and Islamic history, Ehud has been at the moshav for eight years. In the army, I always used to kid him about how much money the moshavniks were making, and now again I asked him what he was doing with his "third million."

Neot Hakikar was originally a private farm run by a company of seven individuals, who employed a variegated work force of people from Israel and abroad. It was assumed that the more conventional forms of settlement were impossible in the unbearable climatic conditions in the salt marshes to the south of the Dead Sea. The Neot Hakikar community had a reputation as a wild lot. They sometimes turned up at our parties in Arad: sheepskin jackets, long, unruly hair and beards, and, despite the cold winter weather, bare feet. In addition to winter vegetables and an experiment with Rhodesian beef cattle — my friend Mike Leaf brought the first batch from Africa in the early sixties — the company ran a desert-tours business, touring the Judean desert, the Negev, and later the Sinai in command cars. The company still operates, based in Elat, but it has abandoned this site. Later, the location was resettled as a normal moshav. Like many of the villages in the Arava (that part of the Syrian-African rift between the Dead Sea and the Red Sea), it has become very prosperous. The villagers grow tomatoes and cucumbers, eggplant and melons, which ripen earlier than elsewhere in Israel. They fetch good prices on both the domestic and export markets.

Ehud smilingly admitted that he was doing well and told

us he planned to spend a whole year abroad in a few years' time, when his children would be older. The settlements of the region are a good illustration of the Gino principle of "a good day's work for a good day's pay." The Arava farmers work very hard indeed, but they also earn a good bit of money. They usually knock off completely for two or three months in the summer, when temperatures reach well over 110° in the shade, and, as often as not, they can afford to go abroad.

We all went out to help Ehud sort and load his day's crop of cucumbers. A remarkably high proportion of them were grade A. We traveled down to the moshav warehouse on the back of Ehud's tractor. The produce is marketed cooperatively, but recently the farmers had reason to suspect the probity of the large marketing cooperative that handled their vegetables. Millions of Israeli pounds were involved, and legislation was pending. I asked Ehud about hired labor and he pointed to a Bedouin working in the warehouse. He was from the Abu-Rubiya tribe. They took on a few hired workers for the harvest, but Neot's prosperity was not based on hired labor, he insisted.

We admired the attractive air-conditioned houses, painted a pale blue or green wash. Ehud told us that they had been built by an American process not yet in general use in this country. Made of cast concrete, the walls were poured into aluminum molds instead of the traditional wooden ones. The molds could be used time and time again. Each house took one day to build, he said with enthusiasm. We expressed amazement. Then another three years to finish them off, he added, deadpan. They had gone mad waiting for their homes to be completed. Until three years ago, the families had led a forced communal life in army-style barracks, which were all they had at the time.

At supper, Ben remarked on the delicious taste of the tomatoes and cucumbers. Ehud said it was the result of the salty water with which they were irrigated. Neot Hakikar, he told us, was self-sufficient in water. The spring of the oasis supplied their drinking and domestic needs; the field crops were irrigated with brackish water from local drillings. When he heard that my friend was due to return home the following day, Ehud insisted on loading him up with the vegetables.

"Tell everyone they're from Neot Hakikar," he ordered.

Ehud had been at a family wedding in Tel Aviv until the early hours of the morning, after which he had put in a full day's work in the fields. In consequence, he kept nodding off to sleep in front of the television screen. We were glad of the excuse for an early night.

It was still overcast the following morning, when we hitched a ride back to the main road. Ben was limping, but said he felt much better. He walked with me for a couple of miles, until we came to the turning of the main road northward via Dimonah. I left him by the bus stop. His last words to me were: "Now that I'm leaving you, the weather will clear up."

He was right. As I pounded south down the Arava, setting a sharp pace, the clouds disappeared and my beautiful blue Negev sky returned. The visibility was magnificent, as it always is in the desert after the rain has washed the dust from the air. To the right, the flint and limestone cliffs of the Negev rose to their heights; to the left, twelve miles away, were the towering, rugged red mountains of Moab. I felt that I had entered the last lap.

27

AFTER an attempted short cut — stimulating in its way, but one which finally convinced me that in the Negev the road takes the shortest route, even when it doesn't seem to — I forced the pace south along the road. I was still stiff, and the road shoulders were hard and rocky; but with the sun shining, nothing could damp my cheerfulness. I stopped for lunch at a picnic site that somebody had thoughtfully provided: wooden tables and benches under a thorn tree. I munched a cheese sandwich that Sarah Tzeiri had given me, with some delicious Neot cucumbers.

The Arava road is not made for walkers. Notices warning of the danger of flooding alternate with commands, posted by the army, to "stay on the road because the surrounding area might be mined." If you mustn't stay on the road and are forbidden to stray off it, what are you supposed to do? Fly?

I arrived at Ir Ovot at sunset, a flaming Negev sunset of the type I remembered so well. The village and its trees stood out dark against the orange sky, the puffy clouds tinged with pink and gold. Behind me, to the east, the mountains of Moab were changing color from pink, to mauve, to deep purple, the wadis etched dark gray. I felt almost groggy from the beauty of it all.

The dining hall of Ir Ovot is a rudimentary, white-washed hut, with a stone-flagged floor. When I entered, a group of people was engaged in a lively discussion around a long table. Simha Perlmutter looked up, and I reminded him that we had met previously, when I had done army service nearby. I asked whether he could provide me with "somewhere to put my sleeping bag."

"Of course you can have a bed," he replied, adding sternly, "you'll have some supper with us too." The atmosphere was akin to that of a kibbutz back in the 1920s, and that is not inappropriate, for Ir Ovot had just decided to turn itself into a kibbutz.

Simha (Sandy) Perlmutter has been living in the Arava with his two wives, Judy and Jan, his elderly parents, his eight children, and about a dozen disciples and hangers-on for thirteen years. At first shunned by the Jewish Agency (which is responsible for agricultural settlement) and the government, he was forced to go to the supreme court in 1971 to obtain water for his village. Recently, his unique group won recognition from the authorities. They want to organize themselves along kibbutz lines, but for various reasons they will be associated with one of the moshav movements.

Simha is a good-looking man, his thick brown hair only slightly flecked with gray. His movements suggest the youthful vigor of a far younger man. His face bears the signs of thirteen tough years, but it lights up quickly with a smile. He wears a skullcap and observes the Jewish religious rules, but he and his followers believe that Jesus of Nazareth was the Messiah. For some time it was thought that Simha was a missionary.

"We came to the Arava because there was no one here," he told me. "We could prove that we were not missionaries and at the same time take on a pioneering challenge."

They settled in tents in this region, where the summertime temperatures reach 110° in the shade, and dug for water by hand. Life was incredibly tough, but they stuck it out. Originally, they had encamped farther south; but the army had agreed they should move into their present site, an abandoned village, when it wanted their original camp area for manoeuvers. The army, Simha told me, had been the first official body to treat them decently. The head of southern command had apparently been impressed with their tenacity.

They had repaired a number of the houses, but, with recognition, they had now received a number of attractive, air-conditioned caravans, and plans were at last underway for a permanent village. They were, in fact, discussing that very subject when I arrived. Three young Negev architects were talking about the design and layout with Simha's wives.

"You see, we don't have a normal desert climate here," Judy was saying. "Deserts are usually cold at night; we don't have that contrast between day and night."

Michael Kaplan, a young American architect from Dimonah was skeptical about the prospects. Planning in Israel was far too centralized, he maintained. Where had I heard that one before? I asked him what he thought of the Arad plan. He said the principles were correct, but they hadn't been carried far enough. The density should have been even higher; the public areas even smaller. The two other architects were from the Negev College at Sde Boker, where I was due in two days' time. They were reassuring about the route, saying they had once driven from Sde Boker to the Arava in a Volkswagen.

Two soldiers arrived from a nearby camp, one of them complaining about a cough. Simha examined his chest and back with a stethoscope and recommended aspirin. There was no congestion as far as he could hear, he told the soldier, but he should see the army doctor tomorrow. He expressed concern about my stiffness, saying that there was no reason for it after nearly four weeks on the road. He dismissed my theory that it was a result of the steep descent from Arad. Calcium deficiency, he pronounced, giving me some very expensive-looking pills, for which he refused payment. Following his instructions, I put one in a glass of water, where it fizzed furiously. It had a pleasant orange flavor. As with the blessing of Rabbi Abuhatzira, I don't know whether it was the treatment or the course of time, but the stiffness wore off gradually until it disappeared.

On an earlier visit, while I was serving in the army, I thought that I had sensed a slight tension between the two wives. They seemed to be rather severe with each other's children (at least, I guessed it was always the other wife's child that was being shouted at). Fairness compels me to record that on this longer visit I saw no evidence at all of strain; the three adults were clearly living in harmony. Judy smiled, showing fine teeth, when she told me about a journalist who had visited them without knowing about their ménage.

"You should have seen the poor guy when I told him; he nearly flipped!" I had read somewhere that Simha believed monogamy was introduced into Judaism because the Jews were living in a Christian culture. Judy, asked by the journalist how she had been able to accept a second wife in her household, had replied cryptically, "There have been more difficult things in my life."

Simha told me that they already had four generations at Ir Ovot. His eldest daughters had children of their own, making his parents now great-grandparents. His father and mother had recently moved into a caravan. They showed me around it proudly; it was comfortable, spacious and well appointed. Paneled in wood, it was air conditioned, with a well-equipped kitchen and bathroom.

I drove with Simha and Jan to make a phone call from the Hatzeva Field School nearby, and Simha told me about a book he had written, "reclaiming Jesus for the Jewish people," as he put it. There was only one role for a Gentile, he said, that of the Biblical Ruth. A Gentile who wished to carry out God's purpose should attach himself to a Jew. He asked me whether I thought he could get it published. I replied that his views would not be too popular with either Christians or Jews; it seemed nicely balanced to arouse the ire of both.

Coming back to the dining hut, I was accosted by a bearded American, who claimed he had met me before. He flicked his fingers, trying to remember.

"I've got it," he said. "Mike's house in Safed."

"Tom," I replied, proud of my memory. "You were with Aryeh Porat."

Tom had found Safed too cold in the winter, so he had closed his house and come south. He had tried a couple of villages on the Sinai coast, but he rather thought he would like to stay at Ir Ovot. He took me down to the sorting house, where the members of Ir Ovot were packing the day's bumper crop of eggplant. I stood beside him, pushing the purple-black vegetables into crates. There were some twenty youngsters in the brightly lit shed, all in high spirits. Someone brought a case of cold beer, and we drank as we worked. One of Simha's sons was organizing a sweepstake, in which we all had to guess how many crates had been picked. I was optimistic and guessed 310; the actual number was 254.

*   *   *

From Ir Ovot I walked westward along the brand-new road built especially for the Tzin phosphate plant. The black road was bordered by fresh yellow lines and had a clean white broken line down the middle; but there were no electricity wires, telephone lines, or other signs of civilization. Early in the morning I saw a gray van and three vast semitrailer trucks, obviously loaded with phosphates, traveling in the direction of Elat. They were the only signs of humanity I saw all day.

The road sloped gently up and then down into the Sif Valley. The landscape was deep Negev, the beige limestone hills sprinkled with rust and gray flints. The heights of the central Negev plateau rose some miles ahead, mauve marked with cream wadis and fissures. In the valley there were still signs of the recent rains, the mud drying fast around the low trees and scrub.

After four hours of steady walking, my stiffness disappeared, and I reached the turn-off for Scorpions' Pass, the steep descent from the plateau to the Tzin Valley, where the old road to Elat used to go. Leaving my rucksack behind a rock, I walked northward for a mile until I reached the hairpin bends of the old road, climbing until I was a third of the way up.

It is still the most spectacular road in Israel, plunging down a series of dizzying loops that follow each other with frightening suddenness. I had first seen it twenty-four years ago. We were traveling in a truck with a machine gun bolted to the back, and even Herskovitz, the mad driver, whose speeding across the desert had earlier terrified us, made us get out of the vehicle while he drove gingerly down the corkscrew. I sat drinking in the scene: to the right, the Negev heights, great slabs of primeval rock, slammed together in a giant's sandwich. Below, the purple-gray lunar formations of the valley, the smoke of the Tzin phosphate plant curling up from behind flat-topped Mount Tzin, also known as Hor Hahar. In the distance over to the left, the mauve mountains of Moab. But this beauty, a natural beauty that comes from the absence of what is usually regarded as nature, is haunted. The rusty metal drums that line the road have not been able to prevent numerous accidents. Only one month ago, a tour truck slipped into the abyss when its brakes failed. The death toll was fourteen. It was only one of the many fatal accidents there. The most famous tragedy was caused by a terrorist attack. In 1954 a busload of travelers coming from Elat was shot up by an armed gang that had come from Jordan. Thirteen lost their lives on that occasion.

The remainder of the walk through the Tzin Valley that afternoon was beautiful enough, if something of an anticlimax. I arrived at the plant quite early in the afternoon. It looked to me like all the Negev chemical factories. Huge yellow beasts clawed up the soil; giant scoops loaded it onto trucks that tipped it onto conveyors. From these, it was poured into the plant, a vast edifice of funnels, pipes, and scaffolding. After processing, the soil was loaded onto railway trucks, which carried it north to Ashdod, or onto motor trucks, which carried it south to Elat.

Rafi, the corpulent, gray-haired plant foreman, was expecting me.

"You're the guy walking from Elat."

I gently corrected him, explaining that I was on my way to Elat. He told me that he had been asked to help me in any way he could, and handed me a plastic bag containing a snack which was so substantial that I saved half of it for my walk the following day. He showed me to my room, which, with shower, was equal to that of an A-class hotel.

Rafi, who had emigrated from Morocco more than a quarter of a century ago, told me that he lived in Dimonah. He had worked as a laborer at the Oron phosphate plant farther north. In 1975, he had been part of the team that set up the Tzin plant, working his way up to shift foreman and then to his present post. He pointed proudly to the neat paving and the small, tidy garden around the offices.

"The plant prospered and I prospered with it," he said, not without satisfaction. He was now on a twenty-four-hour shift, something he had every ten days. He had been on duty on the night of the recent Scorpions' Pass tragedy. A fourteen-year-old girl had managed to walk to the plant from the scene of the accident, and Rafi had launched the rescue operation.

After supper, which was excellent, Yossi, the night-duty nurse, showed me around. The scaffolding gleamed with a hundred lights against the night sky. We had coffee with the technicians in the laboratory, and then donned hard hats to climb up the structure via a series of staircases, girders, and walkways. I looked through the grid to the ground far below — but not for long; I have no head for heights. At the top were giant vats in which the excavated material was washed. They contained an enormous mud soup, topped with white froth, that dripped onto us as we descended. From the vats, the mud is piped down to the drying ovens.

We entered the plant control room, which to my untutored eye looked like the command post of a galactic space ship. Three young geniuses were somehow in control, watching what seemed like a thousand flashing lights. A red light flashed, and the young, bearded foreman shouted something through an intercom. A green light came on, which caused him to go to the wall and throw a few switches.

"It's not really difficult," he insisted. "Not much can go wrong: a funnel or pipe blocked, a pump malfunctioning, the oven overheating. We either solve the problems on the spot, or send directions to the appropriate foreman."

My friend Yul had complained in Arad about the primitiveness of this plant, arguing that it should be manufacturing more sophisticated products. It looked complex enough to me.

*   *   *

The full moon was bright and low in a royal blue sky, when I set out the following morning. I had more than twenty miles before me, all of it over open desert, and I wanted to make an early start. My path led almost due west along the Tzin Valley, and as I progressed it became muddier. The recent rains had washed away the track in several places; I doubted whether anyone would have been able to make it in a Volkswagen today. Passing the flat-topped Hor Hahar, I saw that it was not, as it had seemed to be, a tabletop, but rather a double saddle. Actually, it looked something like the mountain in the movie *Close Encounters of the Third Kind*, and in that landscape I was prepared to believe anything. The mud stuck to my boots, making the going difficult. I saw a train, loaded with phosphates, slowly climbing into the hills. Other than a couple of camels and an airplane high in the sky, that was the only sign of life. The few morning clouds had long disappeared. The sky was as blue as ever. The walk through the empty desert was at once inspiring and a little frightening. Yesterday I had been alone, but on a metaled road; now there was only the track. Another half-hour and I saw, not without relief, the high span of the railway bridge, under which my path led. A mile farther and I was encouraged by a triple signpost: Scorpions' Pass, back the way I'd come; En Yahav, to the left; Sde Boker, straight on. Hooray! It was getting muddier all the time, and I realized that two days before, the route would have been barely passable.

I came to a fork with no signpost. Consulting my map, I guessed left. Wrong again. I emerged at least two miles farther south than I should have been, but I could see Sde Boker, or at least some of it. Perched high up on the red cliffs was something that looked like a white doll's house.

There are, in fact, two Sde Bokers, the kibbutz where David Gen-Gurion spent his last years, and the Negev College, whither I was bound. Now there were several signs pointing toward Sde Boker. However, there was no indication as to whether they pointed to the kibbutz or the college, which are almost two miles apart. I struggled through the muddy valleys below the cliffs, cursing the young architects and their Volkswagen. There was no clearly defined path anymore. After almost two hours of slipping and swearing, I found myself at the bottom of a winding track.

It was already four o'clock and the air was growing cool, so I didn't rest but walked quickly up the track. As I approached the buildings, which were half-hidden by the slope, I heard the shouting and laughing of children playing. It was the first human sound I had heard all day. The view almost surpassed that from Scorpions' Pass: the beige and mustard limestone hills, shaded black; the flint hills beyond, brown washed with ocher, shading into a delicate mauve; and the purple-gray of Edom in the hazy distance.

I walked along the shady paths of the Negev College, between well-tended gardens and lawns, to the house of Miriam and Levi. Miriam is the sister of Dinah from Arad. There was no reply to my knock, so I let myself in and made some coffee in the kitchen. A sleepy Miriam came in just as I was drinking it.

"*Kol hakavod* (Well done)!" she exclaimed.

I have to confess that it rather conveyed my own feelings.

28

WHEN HE RETIRED from politics, the pugnacious David Ben-Gurion went to live at Kibbutz Sde Boker, at the time a tiny, isolated outpost in the heart of the southern desert wastes. I had been with a party that visited him there during an earlier retirement in 1955, between his terms as prime minister. We drove for miles and miles through rocks and dust to the small collection of huts, dwarfed by the vast countryside around it. BG, short, plump, pink face framed by white wings of hair, looked like one of the seven dwarfs — or really like two of them: Grumpy, when telling the (mostly American) group that they should come to live in Israel; Happy, when rhapsodizing about the wonderful Israeli youths who were living at Sde Boker.

The "old man" did not exactly live the life of a normal kibbutznik there. His security men were always present, and he spent much time with his books and writings; but it was still a formidable display of guts for a man in his eighties to live in the central Negev. It symbolized the way he felt about the southern desert area.

Ben-Gurion led the fight to include the Negev within Israel's borders and continued to call for its settlement and development. If Israel's first president, Chaim Weizmann, believed that science was the key to this country's future, and the Weizmann Institute is the living symbol of his personality, one could say that the Negev College fulfills the same function for Ben-Gurion, for he was sure that the Negev was the key to Israel's future.

In a way, BG's obsession with the Negev is strange. I have noted that Zionism is based on the link with the past and, although the Negev does have a Jewish past, it is not central to Jewish history in the way that Jerusalem, Judea, and Galilee are. I think it was the practical man in BG that attracted him to the Negev. He was the supreme pragmatist, always estimating the best that the Jews could get and then settling for it. More than any other Zionist leader (except Weizmann), he favored partition as the best deal available. He knew that things would not get better for Israel internationally. For example, could one conceive of getting a two-thirds majority in today's United Nations for partition and the establishment of a Jewish state? Ben-Gurion recognized that the Negev was quite simply the largest area in which the world would allow the Jewish people to grow and develop. It seems that he was right. Israel will be out of the Sinai in another two years, and whatever happens in Judea and Samaria, the West Bank of the Jordan, Jewish settlement there will be, at the very least, severely curtailed. In practical terms, Israel will be left with the area that I walked through: Galilee, the coastal plain, and the Negev.

The Negev College, created at BG's behest, is situated a couple of miles south of the kibbutz where he spent his last years. It is divided into three main sections. The Arid Zone Research Institute coordinates all aspects of desert biology, agriculture, and architecture. It is directly linked to the university in Beersheba. Then there is the Ben-Gurion Institute, for the study of his papers and records. In view of the central role BG played in the pre-state period and the early years of the state, this is a major center for the study of modern Israeli history. Third, there is the Center for the Environment. Dinah's older son, Nir, is a student at the environmental high school, and her brother-in-law, Levi, is in charge of retraining courses at the environment center.

I had first known Levi when he was principal of the En Gedi Field School north of Masada by the Dead Sea. There he had led interesting hikes into the Judean desert and illustrated his lectures on wildlife with live scorpions and poisonous snakes, which he handled with nonchalant aplomb. Later on, Levi studied at the university in Beersheba, but the former kibbutznik is very much a do-it-yourself sort of expert. He noticed that many desert animals were black, despite the fact that this made them prominent against the light beige background of the hills and afforded no protection from the sun's heat. His reaction was to dress entirely in black — like a Bedouin woman — and walk around in the desert for several days. He came to the conclusion (also suggested by more orthodox scientists) that, though white and light colors reflect the glare of the sun, black provides better protection from radiation.

Levi's hair and trim mustache had acquired flecks of gray in the last few years, and the lines around his eyes were more pronounced; but, as usual, he looked fit and well, burned a brick-red color by hours in the sun. He and Miriam took me to eat in the fine modern dining hall, overlooking the Tzin Valley. This was the "doll's house" I had seen from below. At the present time there are 80 families at the Negev College; but the eventual plan calls for 200. Each family lives separately, but lunch every day and supper on Friday night are eaten in the dining hall. Although wages are paid in the normal way, the ambience is that of a sort of academic kibbutz. As in the case of the earliest kibbutzim, it was the reality of the physical environment rather than ideology that was molding the society. The Friday night communal meal was distinctly kibbutzlike.

Afterward, we sat in Levi and Miriam's lounge and talked about trips they had made in recent years to East Africa. Levi remarked that he was now a certified African safari guide for Israelis. Unfortunately, he noted, the number of African countries to which Israelis could travel had shrunk.

At about ten o'clock there was a knock on the door: it was Mike Leaf. Although we had arranged to meet at Sde Boker, I had almost despaired of his turning up. But I should have known better than to doubt him. He looked pale and a bit drawn, but was in his usual boisterous humor. He had a friend with him, he said apologetically, who wanted to walk to Elat with us. If I objected, the friend would go right back home, he promised. I told him that of course I was delighted to have the friend along, but I hoped it would not be too much trouble for Miriam. Certainly not, said Miriam indignantly. There was plenty of room — even a double bed, if they wanted.

"But what would your husband do?" demanded Mike, quick as a flash. Miriam laughed. She whipped up a quick supper of omelettes and salad, but Mike's friend said he wanted only a glass of hot water.

Tall, broad, and bearded, Mully had become a naturist-vegetarian six months earlier. He had taken this step for medical reasons, after developing an ulcer. He ate only uncooked fruit and vegetables and drank only water — hot water, when he could get it. Mike told us that he had brought along about a ton of nuts and raisins for the trip. I was tired after my day's trek and went to bed; but I heard Mike and Mully yarning away with our hosts, Mike and Levi swapping African anecdotes.

*   *   *

The following morning, Levi recommended that we walk through the valley to the spring of Avdat. He even provided us with a guide, his eight-year-old son, Sahar. He was a real child of the desert, stopping every now and then to identify the various bird cries. We followed him down the steep slope south of the college and into the canyon where the springs were situated.

Sahar led us a hell of a dance in the cleft, clambering nimbly up and down the cliff face, where we, loaded down with our packs, were hard put to it to follow him. It was a beautiful spot with the freshwater pools, the greenery clinging to the limestone cliffs, the birds chirping. There was a grove of hazel trees by the upper spring, their leaves copper and gold. Fortunately, Levi and his minions had constructed safe paths up the cliff; otherwise, we would never have made it. To Sahar's patent disgust, we refused to visit the caves, preferring to climb straight to the cliff top. The ascent had to be made by means of iron rings in the cliff face, and the negotiating of narrow ledges provided us with more than enough thrills. Mully, something of a photography buff, was busy all the time with his camera.

From the top of the cliff, we looked down into the giant crack, with its splashes of green color. Sahar pointed out some wild goats, which he had spotted with his keen, desert-trained eyes. We could not see them at first, but then something startled them, and they poured up the almost perpendicular cliff face like quicksilver. I have seen these wild goats many times in the desert, particularly at En Gedi, and I never cease to be amazed at their agility over the rocks.

After a short rest, we continued southward until the ruins of the ancient city of Avdat came into sight.

This land is remarkable for civilizations that sprang up suddenly and vanished just as abruptly. The Philistines were one such people; the dwellers in the egg-shaped caves at Beersheba were another. But by far the most illustrious example is the Nabateans, who dominated Edom and the

Negev in the first centuries B.C. and A.D. An Arab tribe, they first appeared in the region in the third century B.C., and at one time their influence reached as far as Damascus. Allies of the Hasmoneans, they were finally defeated by the Romans at the start of the second century A.D.

Their capital was at Petra, in what is now Jordan, where they carved a complete city out of the red granite cliffs. Avdat, with a population of some 10,000, guarded their trading routes from Elat and Edom to the Mediterranean. After the defeat of the Nabateans by the Romans, Avdat went into a decline, until it was rebuilt in the third century.

The Nabateans are remembered, not for their power and influence, but because of their amazing success in farming the desert, a success that we are only beginning to match. The Byzantines, who succeeded the Romans, reconstructed the ancient agriculture, and around the sixth century, Avdat had surpassed even its Nabatean period.

The town of Avdat, excavated and reconstructed by archaeologists in the early 1950s, is one of the most impressive sites in Israel; but what makes Avdat really fascinating is the reconstruction of the ancient Nabatean and Byzantine agriculture, which has again turned the area into a desert garden. It was during a siesta on a hot summer's day in 1956 that botanist Michael Evenari and two colleagues conceived the idea of reconstructing the ancient farming. Today, there are eight acres under cultivation at Avdat, growing a variety of fodder, wheat, onions, carrots, asparagus, artichokes, apricots, grapes, peaches, almonds, peanuts, and pistachios. All these crops are grown by the runoff system; no water is brought in from the outside. There are now three run-off farms in the Negev that use water from the winter rains. What had started as an attempt to discover the secrets of Byzantine and Nabatean agriculture has become an important research project for farming the desert. Professor Evenari notes, moreover, that by using only what is present in the desert, his system does not upset the delicate ecological balance of the area.

The principle of the run-off system is the catching and storing of winter rainfall. I have written about the winter floods in the desert and of the steep-sided gulleys they cut in the soil. The local soil of the Negev is of the loess variety. It is nonabsorbent and forms a hard crust when the rain falls. The water runs from the high ground to the low ground, cutting channels, wadis, valleys, and canyons, until it reaches the Mediterranean, the Red Sea, the Dead Sea, or (in some cases) simply evaporates. The run-off system collects the water in a network of fields and terraces, which are fed by dams, channels, and slopes. Variations of the system include gently sloped catchment fields, where each fruit tree has its own catchment area.

The summer before last, my son Etan was casting around for a subject for his high school matriculation thesis. He had always loved the desert, having grown up in Arad, and he asked Professor Evenari if he could spend a month at Avdat. I was sure he would get bored stiff long before the month was up. I knew he was not afraid of the work or the heat, but there were only four overseas students for company in Evenari's isolated, reconstructed Nabatean house in the desert. In fact, he remained for two and a half months and left only because he had to return to school. He said it had been the most interesting period of his life.

We had visited Etan while he was staying at the farm, and he had showed us round the project. It was startling to see the bright green fields and orchards in the middle of the desert and to know that not one drop of water had been piped in. Etan showed us that the quality of the crops was good and explained that the yields were impressive.

A disadvantage of the system is that it tends to be labor-intensive, but this could be overcome in certain underdeveloped countries, where labor is not a problem. In addition, modern equipment can easily carry out the earth work involved. Of course, large areas are needed, and much of the Negev is mountainous. Industry (and now the army) is claiming large tracts, but there should be room for run-off farming as well. One of Evenari's forthcoming projects is a recreation and picnic site near Avdat, with lawns, trees, and shrubs grown by the run-off system. The system is not widely used yet, but Kibbutz Sde Boker grows fodder for its sheep, using run-off irrigation, and one hopes this method will spread.

*   *   *

Another hour's walk across the flint rocks brought us to the reconstructed town and citadel. We wandered through the city, marveling at the skill of the ancient peoples. In the city, as in the fields below, every drop of water was saved. Channels on the roofs and in the streets led to a central plastered cistern of impressive proportions. The view from the hill is a fine one, though in this season many of the fields below were without crops. Led by the impatient Sahar, we descended the numerous steps to the valley.

We had arranged to meet Miriam and Levi at Avdat in order to give Sahar back. When we found them, it was to discover that the splendid Miriam had brought us a superb hot lunch from Sde Boker. Even Mully stretched his naturist diet slightly.

While we were eating, Mike tried to buy a donkey from the Bedouin guard, but he wouldn't hear of it. No matter, said Levi; there was a plague of them in the Negev.

I expressed surprise at this, because I knew that all the Bedouin had been moved out of the area south of Sde Boker. Levi contradicted me.

"They will never get rid of *all* the Bedouin," he said. "Maybe they think they have, but there are always some left." He went on to give us instructions about dealing with a donkey.

"The first thing, after you've caught him, is to sit on him — that's the Bedouin way. Then he knows he belongs to you."

The animal becomes tired after about thirty miles. At this point he recommended, we should release the donkey and look for another one.

"I'll eat the bugger!" proclaimed Mike.

Finally we said good-by to the hospitable couple and their son and started walking fast down the road to Mitzpe Ramon. Mike walked on the right-hand side of the road; I walked on the left, with Mully behind me. I remarked that I had now been on the road for four weeks. Although I had enjoyed it, I confessed that I was rather looking forward to returning to the fleshpots.

"Hot showers in the morning, reading the paper over breakfast in my dressing gown, a comfortable bed every night — know what I mean?"

"I know what you mean," muttered Mully. "I already feel like that!"

And, indeed, a mile later, Mully left us. He wasn't really supposed to be exerting himself so soon after beginning his new diet, and he was not feeling well. He also remarked that, with his car waiting at Sde Boker, ready to speed him to wherever he wanted to go, he didn't really see the point of it all.

After the walk was over, Mike wrote to me and offered the following account of Mully's feelings when he left us:

According to him, when we hit the road to Mitzpe Ramon, we started stepping out at a mad pace, tearing up the roadway like a couple of men possessed. He also felt that the hike was something between the two of us that had a meaning which did not include himself. This not in a bad sense, but in a way he sensed and accepted. So he quit without making any effort to tag along.

We reached Mitzpe Ramon in the dark — and I have never seen a deader town. There was hardly any street-lighting and nothing was open. The town center was entirely blacked out, the solitary café closed. The only activity we discovered was a youth club for very young teen-agers. Eventually, we found the local youth hostel, which was just as dark and empty as every place else; but the door to the dining hall was unlocked, so we went in and turned on the light.

We opened our packs and began to feast off Mully's store of dried fruit and nuts, along with a loaf of sweet Sabbath bread that Miriam had given me. Mike lit a cigarette, and we had just resigned ourselves to sleeping on the tables, when a young, bearded man, with French-accented Hebrew, looked in and asked us what we thought we were doing.

When we told him that we had walked from Sde Boker, he was impressed. He introduced himself as the hostel warden and gave us beds for the night. A pleasant surprise was the availability of hot showers. We took full advantage of them and were asleep by eight o'clock.

29

Up to now, my route had been carefully planned. I had always known more or less where I would spend the night, even if sometimes it had not turned out as I expected. From now on, we would be walking blind. We had one aim: to reach Elat in three or four days. Once we reached the Arava Valley, there would be settlements, gas stations, and roadside restaurants; but between us and the Arava were more than seventy miles of very empty desert. There were a number of points where we hoped to acquire water; for food we had my tins of corned beef, Mully's dried fruit, and some bread and biscuits. We would sleep wherever we fancied and whenever we felt inclined.

In the early morning mist, Mitzpe Ramon was almost as dead as it had been the night before. The only people we saw were some huge blacks, working in the municipal part. They loomed out of the mist in their knitted skullcaps and wished us *shalom* in American-accented Hebrew. I realized that they were members of the Black Hebrew sect, who believe that they are the true descendants of the Israelites of the Bible.

The Messianic movement was formed in Chicago in the early 1960s. Its members first immigrated to Liberia, where they made an unsuccessful attempt to settle near Monrovia. Today, they say that the Liberian venture was their "desert" period, equivalent to the forty years spent in the desert by the Children of Israel under Moses.

The first member of the sect to arrive in Israel came unnoticed in 1967. After the Six Day War, thousands of volunteers came to work on kibbutzim. There was nothing suspicious about a black volunteer called Charles Blackwell, nothing to indicate that he had come to spy out the land for his "nation."

The first group arrived in Israel two years later. Five families, passing themselves off as Falashas (black Jews from Ethiopia) who had lived in the United States, were settled in Arad. I was living in Arad when they arrived, and I met some of them down in Sdom, where I had a temporary job helping with the liquidation of the equipment left over from the construction project of the Dead Sea dikes. The men were very friendly, soft-spoken, and hardworking. When our secretary had to leave, they offered one of their women for the job. Apart from being a stately beauty, she was a person of great dignity — tall, turbaned, and clothed in flowing garments. I was amused at the effect she had on our American supervisor, a blatant womanizer. He treated her with awe. "She's a real lady," he told me reverently.

There my personal knowledge of the sect terminated, although for the next decade, their doings periodically hit the headlines. In 1970 the leaders of the sect arrived in Dimonah, where most of the families had by now settled. Both in Arad and Dimonah, the blacks had settled down well, sent their children to the local schools, and gained a reputation as quiet, hard-working citizens. There was some problem about their professed Judaism, but there had been a suggestion that this could be easily solved by their going through a formal process of conversion to Judaism. Now this was all changed. Ben-Ami Carter, the sect's leader, introduced a strict, sectarian regime and started carving out a sort of autonomy for his "nation." The children were taken out of school; the sect practiced a regimen of vegetarianism and were not permitted to smoke or drink alcohol. Carter emerged as the "Chosen Prophet" and the "Prince of Peace."

The Israeli authorities were at a loss. Immigrants to Israel who wish to become citizens have to go through a process of naturalization, as in all countries, unless they are Jews. Jews may claim immediate citizenship under the Law of Return. In the case of communities where Jewish customs had lapsed, such as the Bene Israel from India and the Falashas from Ethiopia, they won this right only after a struggle with the rabbis. But the Black Hebrews presented a special problem. Not only did they refuse to convert to normative Judaism; they insisted that theirs was the true religion. Carter said that his was the true nation of Israel; other Israelis could join them if they wished.

Meanwhile, large numbers of Black Hebrews were making their way into the country. The first group came to Mitzpe Ramon in 1972 and another group found its way to Elat, but the majority found their way to Dimonah, where the overcrowding became chronic. They had tried, unsuccessfully, to squat in extra flats, but they were successful in expropriating a number of bomb shelters for school classes. Their band, the Soul Messengers, became popular in Tel Aviv and Jerusalem, but its late-night practice sessions were far from popular with their Dimonah neighbors.

There was a murder within the sect. Those involved were tried and deported. The Israeli supreme court ruled that the Ministry of the Interior had the right to deport all the sect's members because they had arrived under false pretenses; but a rider was added to the judgment, suggesting that only newcomers should be expelled. Those already living in Israel should be allowed to stay.

The sect intensified its rhetoric. Carter said he was laying claim to the entire Land of Israel to the "fullest extent of its Biblical borders." The other Israelis, he said, were usurpers. At the same time, he directed a campaign in the United

States, complaining that the Israelis were racists, discriminating against his people because they were black. They were being confined to a ghetto in Dimonah, he said, and their children were not being allowed to go to school. The climax of their hostility was expressed when they entered the local supermarket, took $1000 worth of goods, and refused to pay.

The whole affair was causing considerable concern among American Jews and blacks, traditionally allied in the civil rights movement. It more or less coincided with the weakening of that alliance for other reasons; but some American blacks, notably Bayard Rustin, intervened with the Israeli government on the sect's behalf. Rustin has a long record of loyal support for Israel, and his efforts bore fruit.

The Israeli government set up a special committee, headed by David Glass, one of the country's most humane legislators. He has disclosed that he thinks the sect's members already here should be allowed to remain and should be given their own village in the Negev. Carter has accepted this idea and has undertaken, for his part, to tone down his rhetoric and not to smuggle new members into Israel. The expansion of the "nation" will come from natural increase and conversion. They genuinely believe that other Israelis will join them in the "way of righteousness."

*   *   *

We were soon descending the tremendous Ramon crater, which gives the town its name. The pink-brown earth was marked with splashes of ocher, purple, red, blue, and even bright green, indicating the presence of numerous minerals in the soil. The experts are divided about the origin of the Negev's three craters, of which the Ramon Basin is by far the largest. One theory is that they were caused by meteorites; another sees their origin in volcanic activity. Be that as it may, the craters add yet another element to the region's amazing scenery. The Ramon crater is a geologist's paradise, and some academic institution has marked out a geological tour continuing about a dozen miles south from Mitzpe Ramon.

On the floor of the crater, surrounded by the steep flint cliffs, we discovered that it was not as deserted as we had thought. A signpost pointed to a marble quarry and grinding plant, and a little farther on we discovered the plant's offices, nestling unexpectedly in the shade of half a dozen thorn trees. We had our breakfast there, by the camp of the Bedouin guards, and again negotiated for a donkey. We were as unsuccessful as we had been at Avdat. They would not sell us their donkey or lend us one of their camels.

As before, Mike walked on the right shoulder of the road and I was on the left. My friend was smoking like a chimney, but it didn't slow him up. He was looking much better today. He had caught the sun, and the greenish hue had left his gaunt cheeks. He admitted to me that on his way down he had tried something rather strong. I told him off as severely as I knew how, but it is no good telling Mike anything. Careless about his physical health, he is the supreme experimenter and has to try anything at least once. He fiercely resents any attempts to curb his often pigheaded independence.

"Bullshit, man!" was his reply to my remonstrances.

Some three hours later, we caught sight of three unattended camels. Although they were hobbled, and therefore privately owned, we decided that, under the circumstances, it was permissible to "borrow" one for a few days. Mike pulled some rope from his pack, and, rather gingerly, we began to stalk them. Somehow they always managed to keep just a few yards away. After about a quarter of an hour's fooling around, we gave up.

"Frankly, Mike, I'm scared of the bastards," I told him. "They look bloody enormous to me."

"Just what I was thinking, mate," he agreed. "They've got a nasty bite, you know." He went on to tell me about his journey through Africa, when he had gone to see his parents before coming to Israel. He had crossed the Sahara from Morocco with an Arab camel caravan; but that had been a long time ago, and anyway the Arabs had dealt with the camels. He didn't think he remembered enough about camel-riding to lead even our minor expedition.

Although he had hitchhiked some of the way, he had made it to southern Africa mostly on foot. Beat-up trucks, vans, and once a light aircraft, had taken him only about a third of the way. Once, in the Belgian Congo (now Zaire), he had hitched a ride in a hollowed-out canoe. He claimed that an African chief had offered him one of his wives for a night. He had declined: "I was afraid of getting the pox!" If true, it was surely the first and last time that Mike had shown such self-restraint. He admitted that he had been less careful about what he ate and drank. As a consequence, although he did not contract venereal disease, he got just about everything else.

He had arrived at his parents' house in Bulawayo in a completely unrecognizable state. His beard, dirty and matted, covered his chest; his hair hung down his back; he was lousy and delirious with fever. He had walked up the suburban path, singing Al Jolson's "Mammy." He said he had just reached the line "I'd walk a million miles for one of your smiles," when he collapsed in a dead faint.

*   *   *

In the afternoon, we left the road, hoping to take a short cut across the desert. For a time it seemed as if we were succeeding, but then my earlier experiences repeated themselves and we were forced to clamber up and down the steep sides of wadis. We had lunch in one of the valleys, and Mike slept in the shade of a thorn bush.

We gained the road and climbed up out of the crater, the

road now totally deserted. We continued to keep a lookout for donkeys, but all we ever saw were their droppings. What happened to Levi's "plague" of the creatures, I don't know. Mike continued to talk about his African experiences and told me he didn't think he would be admitted to either South Africa or Rhodesia today. He had been actively involved with various African freedom movements, and he expressed himself forcefully on the subject of apartheid. From there, the talk drifted to racial discrimination and the color bar, and I mentioned my great admiration for the American black leader Martin Luther King, Jr. Mike heartily concurred. Here, let me quote again from the letter that Mike sent me after the walk.

> We were almost jogging down a fairly steep hill — late afternoon — a fantastic backdrop of jagged red mountains, the quiet desolation of the Negev, when, raising your hands, you cried out in an authentic dreamer's voice: "I have a dream!" and delivered practically the whole fucking speech, including the "Yeah man" interjections.
>
> I don't know whether you are familiar with the phrase "head trip." But it was then that I realized you were tripping. "Head trips" are one of my specialities. From the moment I realized the trip aspect, I went over the whole journey in my mind again with a far greater understanding of the undercurrents, of the hitherto unimportant minutiae that had, by some process of selection, stuck in my mind. The surface story of three guys setting out for a walk and where and how they finished was merely (although an intriguing episode in itself) a symbolic and meaty extension of the real factors and forces that caused three guys to set out together on a much more elusive "trip."
>
> If only I could write; what a story! And I realize that I am the only one who could write it, because I am the only one who knows what the hell I am talking about!

Not quite true. I have an inkling of what Mike is talking about. There is something about the Negev — its bleakness, space, and light. It is the planet Earth stripped to its barest elements. I understand why Moses, Jesus, and Muhammad experienced their visions in the desert. Surely God (if He exists) lives here in the searing wastes, rather than in the gaudy shrines of established religion. Ever since Beersheba — certainly since Ir Ovot — I had felt that my journey was something more than a mere walk.

By the side of the road, we discovered an installation consisting of a number of pipes and dials and (providentially) a water tap. We drank greedily and filled our water bottles. The sun was low in the sky, so we started looking around for somewhere to sleep. We were only slightly discomfited by the presence of three (!) memorials within less than a mile, commemorating soldiers and road workers "murdered by enemies." The killings, by Arab infiltrators from Jordan and Egypt, had, after all, taken place a long time ago.

We found a sheltered spot that had once been a camp for someone, and set about collecting wood. We scavenged a remarkably substantial pile and made a campfire. It was time to eat the first of the cans of corned beef. The meat was awful but sustaining. We got rid of the taste with some of Mully's delectable fare, but, to tell the truth, we were both getting a little tired of dried fruit and nuts. We hankered after a hot drink. Mike told me that in Galilee he had caches of food, water, and saucepans hidden in favorite spots. This enabled him to walk without a pack.

It was a beautiful sunset, the jagged mountains black against a muddy, golden sky. We rolled up in our sleeping bags and went to sleep by the fire. I woke some hours later, cold and stiff, to see Mike sitting cross-legged in the moonlight. There was a full moon and I fell in with his suggestion that we should try a night walk. In its own way, the scenery was even more beautiful at night, although of course the colors were missing. The moon bathed the scene in its silvery light, and the saw-toothed mountains stood out against the stars to the west. It was cold, but once we got going the walking was good, and I felt fit to continue until morning.

Not so Mike; his wounded left leg was giving him trouble. I have mentioned how he was shot almost to death in the Sinai Campaign. I knew he had received a burst of bullets in the stomach. What I didn't know was that two of the bullets had lodged in his leg, one of them hitting a vital nerve. Mike kept fit by doing a lot of walking, but from time to time the nerve caused him problems. Counting the night walk, we had covered almost fifty miles in two days. We found another spot, made another fire, and shivered in our sleeping bags until dawn.

The following morning, Mike, his long, stubbly face burned pink by two days of sun, made such a charming picture among our scattered belongings that I was prompted to take a photograph. As luck would have it, an army van passed along the road just then. We didn't know it, but we were in an area where taking pictures was forbidden. The van screeched to a halt and an aggressive-looking man in a blue tracksuit jogged over to us, trailing half a dozen soldiers.

"No photographs allowed," he snapped.

"Don't drive us crazy!" growled Mike. (Only in Hebrew the phrase is far cruder.)

"We didn't know!" I shouted, trying to drown out Mike's words. "Here, you see. No pictures. I'm putting the camera away."

"What are you doing here anyway?" demanded the man.

"We are free Jews, walking in their land," intoned Mike. The rhetoric was that of the ultra-nationalist, which, coming from the radical Mike, was a laugh; but it seemed to satisfy our interlocutor.

"No photos, mind," he repeated, turning on his heel. "You shouldn't be sleeping here anyway; it's dangerous."

For several minutes, Mike fulminated against the petty-minded of this world. He told me that he frequently went walking in Galilee at night. Whenever he ran into soldiers, they always warned him how dangerous it was.

"If we can't go for a bloody walk in the hills, man, day or night," he proclaimed, "then it isn't our country!"

I should explain that, by walking through the Negev unarmed, Mike and I were breaking an Israeli taboo. Even on the shortest hikes, the average Israeli goes armed. I am prepared to accept the validity of this for organized trips — particularly where there are children — but I fail to see what good a pistol could do in the middle of the desert, and I was damned if I was going to lug a rifle. Mike agreed and told me that he had walked through Africa armed with nothing more lethal than a kitchen knife.

I have run out of words to describe the Negev. Let me say simply that our descent into the desolate valley of Paran, which the Israelites under Moses passed through on their way to Canaan, matched all that had gone before. We felt utterly insignificant in that endless, craggy waste.

And then Mike's left leg finally went.

I had been egotistical and selfish, thinking only of getting to Elat. From time to time, I had asked Mike whether he was sure he could continue, but I had been all too ready to accept his cheerful assurances. Now I saw that he was pale, sweating, and in pain. I gave him a couple of aspirins from my pack, and we had a long rest. We struggled on for another mile or so until we arrived at a large wire enclosure, with a huge loudspeaker over the barred gate. Some distance away, within the fenced area, was a building. There was a notice outside the fence in English, reading CUP OF WATER — but of the water there was no sign. I pressed a button on the gate, and a disembodied voice demanded, "Who's there?"

"Two hikers who need water," I replied.

"What do you mean, 'Two hikers?' Who are you?"

I went as near as I could to the loudspeaker and enunciated, "Get fucked!"

Then I turned to Mike and said, "That's it, boyo; journey's end."

There was an old road through to the Arava at this point. Mike had brought me far enough, and I could have made it alone from there; but when I thought about it, there didn't seem much point. The walk had come to a natural end. An "act of God," the insurance companies call it.

I made him rest in the shade of a thorn bush and started hitchhiking. There weren't too many vehicles, and those which did pass sped by at high speed. I tore a couple of sheets from Mike's sketchpad and wrote "Injured," in Hebrew and English. Mike suggested that there was something wrong with one of the Hebrew letters, but it looked all right to me. (Later, it afforded my children endless amusement. It was as if I had written "Insured" instead of "Injured.")

Whatever the deficiencies of my Hebrew script, it did the trick. A bus filled with schoolchildren took us the last seventy miles in two hours. We descended through the beautiful pass into the Arava and stopped at the giant milk bar of Kibbutz Yotvata for refreshments. Mike, who claimed to be feeling better, got on a bus heading north. He was full of apologies, but I told him that I was the one who ought to apologize for being so selfish.

The teacher in charge of the bus told me that the children had been rather relieved to see the back of Mike, who, I must admit, did look a fearsome sight. They had been certain that he was a terrorist. One of the kids had even claimed to have seen the word *Palestine,* imprinted on the sole of his boot.

30

In the late afternoon, we sped southward down the Arava Valley after leaving Kibbutz Yotvata, today a flourishing enterprise that supplies Elat and the surrounding area with all its milk and much of its fruit and vegetables. When I first saw it in 1955, it had been a collection of wooden huts. Fifteen years later, when I had done a stint of army service there, we had been able to wander down the leafy paths, sit on the green lawns, swim in the spacious pool. On guard at night, we would partake of a snack of Ogen melons (a winter luxury at the tables of exclusive European restaurants) or enjoy the various milk products of the dairy, finishing up with coffee topped with the whipped cream that they produced in aerosol cans.

A bit farther on, the bus turned west to King Solomon's Mines — an added bonus, for I could not, at this stage of the game, have summoned up the energy to walk there. Solomon built a port in Elat in the ninth century, receiving assistance from his Phoenician ally, Hiram, King of Tyre, who provided him with ships and sailors. He is also reputed to have met the Queen of Sheba there when she came to admire his wisdom. Apparently it was not only his wisdom she admired; the Falashas are thought to be the result of their dalliance.

The ancient copper-smelting plants look simple enough: ovens for roasting the ore, with stone channels to collection vessels below, for the copper. But the wonder of the installations lies in the ventilation system. The air channels were deliberately angled to catch the prevailing north wind down the Arava. American archaeologist Nelson Glueck, who discovered the mines and smelting works, notes that the usual bellows would have been unnecessary in view of this ancient automation.

The massive Pillars of Solomon, sheer outcroppings of Nubian sandstone, are a natural formation, as is the Mushroom, a flint rock shaped like a giant specimen of the tasty fungus. Strangely, mushrooms are now grown at the Timna copper mines a little farther south. The mines have been closed down by the government because of the slump in world copper prices; but members of the maintenance team, which still works there, have discovered that the cool caverns are ideal for the cultivation of mushrooms, which they find a profitable sideline.*

The mountains around Elat are even more beautiful than those farther north, with great chunks of ocher granite and spectacular formations of the copper-colored Nubian sandstone complementing the honey limestone, cream chalk, and purple-brown flint. In the setting sun, they were changing color by the minute.

Elat had been in my mind since that day in Metulla when I started walking south. The 500 miles covered was not a great distance, but I felt that it was quite an achievement. In my imagination, I had often conjured up my triumphant entry into Elat, the trumpets sounding (in my head if nowhere else). But it was not to be. I sped smoothly past the airstrip in the bus, as I had so many times before.

I have mentioned Ben-Gurion's devotion to the Negev.

---

* I have just learned that the Timna company ordered the closing down of this enterprising endeavor, which supplied the citizens of Elat with the delicacy at reasonable prices. No one seems to understand the reason for the company's arbitrary decision.

As early as the First World War, BG had foreseen the importance of the Gulf of Akaba as an outlet to the Indian Ocean and Asia. It was Chaim Weizmann, the elder statesman, already blind and infirm, who won diplomatic battle at Lake Success to have Elat and the Negev included in the United Nations partition plan. Of course, as on other fronts, what had been approved in New York had to be confirmed by force of arms. It was not until March 1949 that the Israeli army reached the Red Sea and hoisted an improvised, ink-marked Israeli flag above the police station at Umm Rushrush, opposite the Jordanian port of Akaba. A decade later, the population was still only around 3000. Israel's leaders had fought hard for Elat, but its citizens must often have wondered why they bothered.

Elat citizens are characterized by a fierce local patriotism; the people who live there fall in love with the place. But the central government has never paid more than lip service to its development. New immigrants were not directed there, and the town's only industry, the Timna copper mines, were abruptly closed down, one of the first victims of the government's sudden preoccupation with profitability.*

By Israeli standards, Elat is far away from the center of the country. Elatis half-jokingly talk about "going to Israel" when they travel north. The climate is harsh, although the locals would not change it. Today, air conditioning is widespread. In the earliest days, Elatis used to spread damp sheets over their windows. Following this, the famous *dezercooler* (Hebrew for desert-cooler) was in use. Based on the principle of the damp sheet, it blew air through a wet screen. There is no doubt that the climate discouraged many from settling here.

---

* In February 1980, the present government decided to reopen the mines owing to the rise in copper prices on the world market.

Things improved slightly after the Sinai Campaign opened up the Red Sea to Israeli shipping, and the population tripled; but even then government policy was somewhat ambivalent. After the Six Day War, eleven years later, the Sinai coast, with its marvelous underwater life, was opened up to tourism. This was a boost for the town: hotels were built, charter flights started bringing European tourists — notably Scandinavian sun-worshipers — directly to Elat. Yet much of the development took place farther south.

A complete town was build at Ophira, at the southern tip of the Sinai, soon to be returned to Egypt. The same investment in Elat would have revolutionized the city. The Jordanians built a railway to Akaba, across the water (admittedly, it is their only port), but Israel is still only talking about extending the railway to Elat.

Until quite recently, Elat rested on an economic tripod: the mines, the port and oil pipeline, and tourism. The mines have been closed. The port still functions, but the pipeline, which used to carry Iranian oil from Elat to the Mediterranean, had greatly reduced its functioning with the opening of the Suez Canal. Today, after the revolution in Iran, it serves no purpose. The Suez Canal has also greatly reduced traffic at the port of Elat: the price of peace.

The withdrawal of the army from the Sinai and the building of new airfields in the Negev should improve matters; but even here, the other Negev towns seem to be booming rather than Elat. Apartment prices have skyrocketed in Beersheba, Dimonah, and Arad. In Mitzpe Ramon, the government has had to freeze sales to keep homes available for Sinai personnel. In Elat, no one is freezing anything, and dozens of apartments remain empty.

There remains the third pillar of the tripod: tourism, for which this sunshine city, with its clear, fish-filled sea, its coral reefs, and its splendid backdrop of multicolored mountains, is eminently suitable. For there is nowhere in Israel quite as fascinating as Elat, that strange collection of odds and ends, its pioneer population leavened with beats and beachcombers. Many of the latter migrated southward to the oases of the Sinai coast, but I would guess they will be back, once the Egyptians take over again. A stroll through the downtown mess in the warm night, or a meander through the untidy commercial center, with its tatty bars and night clubs, is still an exciting experience. It is at once cosmopolitan and Israeli; Zionist yet un-Jewish. Like Kiryat Shmona, it does have dozens of little synagogues for different communities; but the buses run on Sabbath by special dispensation, and there is no religious problem in the town.

In more than the geographical sense, Elat is Israel carried to an extreme. Set apart from the rest of the country, it guards its border. Half the young people wear army uniforms; the other half, beads and sandals. I have never been here without being sorry to leave; never left without vowing to come back more often.

*   *   *

I spent that last night of my walk with Ilana and Mel Goldberg and four of their delightful children (the fifth was in America on an exchange program). Mel arrived late from his job as deputy manager of one of the town's hotels, work he clearly takes very seriously, staying up until all hours of the night if a group of tourists comes in late.

He worked for many years at the Timna copper mines, supervising the maintenance of the mining machinery. He told me a hair-raising story of how his jeep was crushed by an excavator that went out of control. He had lost consciousness, and the man who pulled him out of the jeep was sure he was dead, even calling on Ilana later to offer condolences. Mel said that he didn't know how he had survived: the last thing he could remember was the excavator bearing down on him. Then he had woken up in the hospital. The jeep had been a write-off, but he had been able to walk home.

Mel was compulsorily retired with the rest of the Timna work force when the government decided to close down the mines. I have always regarded the closure as a stupid mistake. The Dead Sea Works (as I have noted) lost money for nineteen years before becoming profitable, and, anyway, development towns inevitably cost money. Mel and Ilana disagreed. Despite the blow to Elat caused by the shutdown, they were not in favor of keeping an unprofitable concern open, but they were concerned about the future of the town.

Speaking in the same angry tone I remembered so well from youth movement meetings more than two decades ago, Ilana said that Elat was going to have to pull its socks up. Not enough was being done to develop tourism: people were too content to rely on the sun, the sea, and the superb scenery. Maybe that was enough for one visit, but it wouldn't bring visitors back a second time, particularly not if they had been scalped. She indignantly showed me a recent copy of the town journal, in which the local hotel-owners' association complained about overcharging in some of the restaurants. A case was quoted in which 500 pounds ($25) had been charged for four fellafels and four Cokes. The association warned that if this sort of behavior was allowed to continue, tourists would stop coming to Elat.

Ilana recalled that initially she had refused to come and live here. She had told Mel that he could get a job in Timna if he wished, but on no account would she live in Elat. Now she wouldn't live anywhere else. Aside from the beauty of the town, she loved the atmosphere, the individuality of the people.

"We can go away without locking our doors," she told me, "provided we tell the neighbors to keep a lookout for us. No one would get away with a pin. On the other hand, if we didn't tell them to watch things, someone could come and load up the whole house onto a truck, and no one would interfere."

*   *   *

The following morning, I took a taxi to Rafi Nelson's holiday village at Taba, some four miles south of town, which some say will return to Egypt when the Israeli withdrawal is completed. Rafi Nelson, black eyepatch, sombrero, boots, swimming trunks, and shark's-teeth necklace, was not worried. He based his optimism on the Turkish map of 1906, on which the border with Egypt ran from a point about 300 yards south of his village.

Rafi is a sort of professional Elat playboy-beachcomber, acting his role with a self-mocking macho. His holiday village, with its thatched roofs, lunch bar, disco music, and bohemian ambience, in the shadow of a magnificent chunk of granite, is fashionable. Even on this winter's day, three couples of "beautiful people" from Tel Aviv were relaxing on the sunny patio.

He lent me a snorkel and mask, and (one week before Christmas) I went for a swim in the clear water. In all that I had seen, nothing could match the beauty of this underwater scene: a world of pink, gold, and rust corals, the fishes gliding silently, russet, emerald, black, deep purple, striped and dappled or clouds of brilliant orange flames.

When I was leaving Rafi Nelson's village, I saw three donkeys.

"Where were you when we needed you?" I screamed at them.

On the way back into Elat, I visited the maritime museum. The underwater observation dome enables you to stand for hours, without worrying about your supply of fresh air, and observe the fish and corals. Upstairs, the tanks contained all that I had ever seen in the water and more: seahorses, a baby shark, box fish, and puffer fish, as well as the deadly stone fish. The museum is one of the seven wonders of the modern world — but nothing equals the experience of swimming through the azure Eden that is the Red Sea, the glide through the clear water, the colors, the silence, the luminous space. It is another dimension of existence.

*　　*　　*

I flew back. It had taken me thirty-one walking days from the Good Fence to the Paran Valley. Back halfway by air, to Jerusalem, was some thirty-one minutes. I looked at the pink-brown desert stretched out below me. It still looked vast. Had I really walked across it? My perception of the mountains of Moab and Edom changed. On foot, they had seemed formidable barriers to some forbidden kingdom. Now they were merely the sides of a plateau, with towns and villages dotted on it.

*　　*　　*

I had not walked to Elat; not quite. Three more days would have done it — two going all-out — yet I had no regrets. The past days had been a splendid interlude, but it was time to return to real life.

I had journeyed through Israel from the rolling hills of the north to the dusty spaces of the southern desert; from the limpid Sea of Galilee to the oily crater of the Dead Sea; from the choppy, blue Mediterranean to the aquamarine mirror of the Gulf of Elat. I had climbed oak-covered Mount Carmel and scaled the bleak, stunning heights of the Negev. I had stayed in communes and cooperatives, villages and towns. I had slept at inns, hostels, and private homes, and out under the stars. I had argued with nationalist Arabs and prayed with religious Jews. I had formed new friendships and renewed old ones. I had been through the sun and wind and rain. I had felt the land through my feet and had borne witness to its wonderful variety.

Ever since I was a small boy, I had yearned to wander, to dally, to take that turning, climb that hill, stroll down that beckoning lane. For weeks I had done just that.

It had been a good walk. It hadn't turned out quite as I had planned it; but, after all, what ever does?

Afterword

THIRTY-ONE DAYS. Walking in a straight line, I could have made it in a little over two weeks. A small country. And that, basically, is my conclusion. Not as obvious as it may seem, for we are small neither in our aspirations nor our pretensions. The time has come to cut these down to an appropriate size.

Our smallness is a fact of life and we should, at very least, make a virtue out of necessity; but I would go further and say that Israel's finest qualities are its intimacy, its friendliness, its involvement and sense of community, all of which are a result of its size.

Many Israelis would argue that the state has to grow larger for stark reasons of survival, situated as it is in the midst of a hostile Arab world. Without considering whether or not this situation is changing, it may be noted that even if the entire Jewish people of some 12.5 million settled here, the Arabs would still outnumber the Israelis by more than ten to one.

Israel has proved large enough to defend itself. Imagination, daring, ingenuity — these are the guarantees of Israel's survival, not the might which it can never possess. Gideon understood this at En Harod, when, faced with an enemy larger than he was, he reduced his force still further and led his small, mobile unit into the enemy camp. David understood this when he went to meet Goliath. Seeing the immense spear, sword, and shield of the giant, he made no attempt to acquire weapons of equivalent power; he changed the rules of the game. Jonathan the Hasmonean understood this. After his brother Judah, with his blind faith, had led the people to near-disaster, Jonathan learned to control his courage with caution, and he, too, won through against the odds. The modern Israeli army has understood this. From 1948, right through to 1973, mobility, speed, improvisation were the order of the day. Only in the Litani operation was massive force used, and with unfortunate results.

What we Israelis have to get into our heads is not only the fact of Israel's smallness, but the truth that *it does not matter.* The country was built by immigrants, but for the time being it seems that almost all those who wanted to come here have arrived. Big enough to defend itself, Israel has also been big enough to be a haven for the refugees: no Jew has ever been turned away.* Today we should not be too concerned at the low rate of immigration, nor should we panic at the phenomenon of emigration. Israel cannot compete with the opportunities offered in Western Europe and the United States. Emigration — including the "brain drain" of some of the best and brightest — is a fact of life for any small country. We should accept it with the same equanimity as our Mediterranean neighbors, Greece, Turkey, and Italy. Instead of devising schemes to encourage immigration, or beating our breasts over emigration, we should concentrate our efforts on making the best of what remains.

Of course, a small Israel cannot hope to absorb the West Bank and Gaza, even though many Israelis would like to try. This is all to the good. There is no future for us in try-

* One exception was Meyer Lansky, the American crime figure. In 1972 he sued for permission to remain in Israel as a citizen under the Law of Return. The Supreme Court of Israel turned him down on the grounds of his criminal past.

ing to dominate 1.5 million Arabs. We are better off without them, and they are better off without us. Withdrawing from much of the West Bank (with proper security guarantees) will be in the tradition of modern Zionism, where the idealistic vision was always tempered with a healthy dose of pragmatism. It was that arch-pragmatist, Chaim Weizmann, who told the Anglo-American Committee of Inquiry on Palestine in 1946:

> There is no counsel of perfection in this world and there is no absolute justice in this world. What you are trying to perform, and what we are all trying in our small way to do, is just rough human justice.

In 1946, tragically, Weizmann was premature. Today, after the signing of a peace treaty between Israel and Egypt (the most powerful Arab country), his modest vision is attainable. Any reasonable solution will be unsatisfactory to both sides. The Israelis must give up most of Judea and Samaria (the West Bank); the Arabs will have to abandon the idea of wiping Israel off the map.

The Arabs living in Israel will also have to forgo something. They must give up the idea of living in a sovereign Arab state. Abdul Rahim can surely expect to attain his aim of a life for the Arabs of Kafr Kassem, as good in every way as that of the Jews of Petah-Tikva. Hammad Abu-Rubiya can realistically demand that the Aksayfe encampment should become a modern Israeli village, with all that it entails. But Mansur Kardosh's suggestion of "a little autonomy" for Nazareth will surely have to be limited to such fields as culture and education. Conversely, Jews who wish to live in Judea and Samaria will have to acknowledge Arab sovereignty.

The Jews would be giving up much of their historical heritage in relinquishing most of the West Bank and Gaza;

but, as we have seen, there is no "historical" Israel, clearly defined. At different times, the Jewish state had different shapes and sizes, reflecting the current realities. In the time of Saul and David, the Philistines and the Phoenicians held the coastal plain; later the kingdom split in two; and later still, after the return from Babylon, Judah was confined to a tiny area around Jerusalem. Today, we will have our work cut out to consolidate our hold in Galilee, the coastal plain, and the Negev. Let us see Jews in the Galilee countryside; let us walk through the Negev at night, unarmed and unafraid. Weizmann's "rough human justice" happens also to be practical good sense.

Once we stop overextending ourselves, we can mobilize the human and material resources to tackle the very grave problems that we face. I have mentioned Nazareth, Kafr Kassem, and Aksayfe. I could add Akraba, but the Arab problem is not the only one that Israel faces.

There is the economy, with its national debt of gargantuan proportions (in this at least we are not small!) and a yearly rate of inflation running at an incredible 111.5 percent. There is the horrifying emergence of organized crime, including protection rackets, dealing in hard drugs, and prostitution, on a scale hitherto unknown in Israel. There is the social and economic gap between Israelis of European and oriental origin, the problem of religious coercion, the inefficient service, inferior work ethics, the bad driving, and the lack of elementary courtesy and consideration in human relationships.

Instead of directing our energies outward, we should direct them inward. We have spread ourselves too thin, physically and morally. It is true that we did not seek the West Bank, the Sinai, and the Golan Heights. In 1967, it was the Arabs who made war on us. But afterward we did expend far too much effort in trying to settle these territories. I have suggested that Elat could have been transformed with the resources that were used to build Ophira in the southern Sinai. In the northern Sinai, the town of Yammit is soon to be evacuated. Imagine the human and material resources of Yammit in Netivot. Katserin is a new town on the Golan Heights. What a difference the people and buildings of Katserin could make to Kiryat Shmona, or those of Ariel in Samaria to Or Akiva.

I know little about economics and will not comment on the various types of shock treatment proposed for getting us out of the present impasse; but I am not demonstrating any special expertise when I say that the long-term answer must surely lie in increased production, particularly for export.

On my walk through the country, I did not scrutinize the bank accounts of the farmers, nor did I study the balance sheets of the industrial plants, but I did see the produce in the fields and the products in the factories. This country, much of it formerly rocky hillside, swamp, and desert, is producing. People are working. Kohner, the kibbutz inventor from Amiad, and Rafi, the shift foreman at Nahal Tzin, each in his own way indicates promise for the future.

If we can harness this energy and talent to produce more, we can surely put the economy in order and find the resources to tackle the social questions, the crime, and the violence. When I think of some of the volunteer work I saw in such places as Kiryat Shmona and Netivot, I am not discouraged by the prospects.

I have mentioned the shortcomings of the absorption of the mass immigration of the 1950s, the mistakes that were made, the residue of bitterness that poisons the country's social relations to this day — but then I think of the plight of today's Vietnamese boat people. Eighty thousand of them have found shelter on an Indonesian island, and the Indonesians (a nation of more than 100 million) stress that the refuge is temporary, that the refugees are putting an intolerable strain on their society.

In its first three years, Israel absorbed 700,000 Holocaust survivors and refugees from Arab lands into a Jewish population of only 600,000. Even if Israel was fulfilling its Zionist raison d'être, the scale of the enterprise is astounding.

On my walk I saw failures, like Hatzor in Galilee; I visited the unidentical twins of Or Akiva and Caesarea, Ashkelon and Afridar. I saw the retreat from egalitarianism, the cause of bitterness, frustration, and crime; but I also perceived the partial success of Kiryat Shmona, the successes of Ashdod and Beersheba, and the flourishing moshavim, where former immigrants have achieved manifest prosperity.

Only a small proportion of Israel's population lives on the kibbutzim, yet to much of the world they personify Israel. They do indeed represent much of what is most positive in our society. The kibbutz has not, it is true, created a new human being, nor has it really revolutionized human relationships; but a productive, equitable, and efficient framework for living has been developed. Its success, as we have seen, is a result of its ability to temper the white-hot, idealistic vision of the founders with the cold water of pragmatism. The blueprint was amended as the society grew.

The contribution of the kibbutzim and the moshavim to national life continues to be formidable. Apart from clearing the rocks, draining the swamps, planting the desert, developing advanced industries, and defending the borders, they have produced a disproportionate number of national, civic, and military leaders. The army's elite volunteer units are full of village children, and they form the backbone of the young officer corps.

Although the kibbutz exercises less influence than it did and does not set the tone of national life, as it did formerly, the egalitarian ethic has not disappeared entirely. We have seen that inequality exists, but the inequities are not extreme. Businessmen have made money, but wage differentials (particularly after income tax) are not large. The domestic may earn more per hour than the teacher or social worker whose house she cleans, and she buys her clothes in the same store.

*   *   *

I have said that our aspirations and pretensions are too large and that we have spread ourselves too thin, morally as well as physically. David Ben-Gurion used to say that Israel must be a "model society" and a "light unto the Gentiles." With all due deference, I would suggest that, in this, the old man failed to discipline his ardor with his usual pragmatism. This inflated version of ourselves has been responsible for much that is negative in our society. One of the most irritating characteristics of the Israeli is that he talks too much and does not carry out what he undertakes to do. Often he does not have the slightest intention of doing what he says. This is because there is such a thin line between vision and reality.

"I promised that," Levi Eshkol, Israel's third prime minister, is said to have remarked. "I did not promise that I would *do* it!" The story is no less significant if it is apocryphal. How can the Israeli not confuse theory and practice when his leaders tell him that his dirty, untidy, inefficient, dishonest, and inconsiderate society is supposed to be a "light unto the Gentiles"? We should stop prating about our Messianic mission and try to keep the streets cleaner, put the "model society" in cold storage and encourage good craftsmanship.

*   *   *

But there is also much good in our society. If we accept ourselves for what we are and forget about what we might be, we can foster that intimacy, friendliness, hospitality, sense of participation. These are our finest qualities.

Abie Nathan is an Israeli campaigner for good causes. Once he flew a small plane solo to Egypt, in an unsuccessful attempt to talk peace with President Nasser. Later he took food to the starving Biafrans. Now he is in the thick of efforts to save the Cambodian refugees. A recent drive for Cambodia elicited an amazing response in Israel, despite the difficult economic situation.

"I am proud to belong to a people that cares," declared Abie, in a television appearance.

"Israelis don't lack hutzpa," grumbled a letter to the *Jerusalem Post* the next morning, wondering what American Jews (constantly called upon to donate money for Israel) would make of this "generosity."

True, they do not lack hutzpa, but they really do care. It takes a war to bring out the very best in us; but even other incidents — a car overturned, a hiker looking for a bed for the night, starvation far away — can elicit a heart-warming response.

Again, for all its faults, Israel is an exciting, dynamic society. To illustrate this I would describe an afternoon when I drove out of Jerusalem. Coming down the hill was a Jaguar limousine (still unusual in Israel) and *it was being overtaken* by a local bus. In this image, you have crystallized much of what is good and bad in Israel. On the one hand, the arrogance and cockiness, the rejection of a sensible order of things, the lack of savoir faire. On the other hand, the initiative, the originality, the daring, and the refreshing refusal to accept things as they are.

*   *   *

When a boorish driver nearly murders me on the road, when I miss the last bus home because it suited the driver to leave early, when I try to make an inquiry at an empty government office during working hours, I am discouraged. When I hear that a group of Gush Emunim are refusing to leave Arab land in the West Bank, even when ordered to do

so by the supreme court; that Yammit citizens are demanding sky-high compensation for their apartments, to be
evacuated in the Sinai withdrawal; that witnesses are being
intimidated by criminals; or that another demonstration
has turned violent, I become depressed about the future.

But my walk through Israel did help, as I had hoped it
would, to restore a sense of balance. When I think of the
young Americans Marsha and Bob in Kiryat Shmona; of
Vered the soldier-volunteer and Yehiel the young rebel in
Netivot; of Yaacov Zarchi in Kibbutz Ginnegar and Ehud
Tzeiri at Neot Hakikar; of Dinah, who stayed on in Arad;
of Mike in Safed; of Abdul Rahim and Yunis Abu-Rubiya — then my faith is restored. These are the creative,
constructive, decent Israelis. They represent a minority;
but, together with the warm, involved, well-meaning,
noisy, untidy, brash, and sometimes boorish majority, they
will prevail over the strident extremists, and make Israel,
not a "model society" or a "light unto the Gentiles," but a
stimulating, variegated, friendly place to live.

*   *   *

That is the most that we can hope for at this time and in
this place. And that, I fervently believe, we shall have.

Motza, Jerusalem, December 1979.